ALSO AVAILABLE FROM TOKYOPOP®

MANGA

*INDICATES 100% AUTHENTIC MANGA (RIGHT-TO-LEFT FORMAT)

CINE-MANGA™

NOVELS

TOKYOPOP KIDS

ART BOOKS

ANIME GUIDES

VOLUME 1

BY
RA IN-SOO
&
KIM JAE-HWAN

LOS ANGELES • TOKYO • LONDON

Translator - Lauren Na
English Adaptation - R.A. Jones
Retouch and Lettering - Tom Misuraca
Cover Layout - Patrick Hook
Graphic Designer - Mark Paniccia

Editor - Mark Paniccia
Managing Editor - Jill Freshney
Production Coordinator - Antonio DePietro
Production Manager - Jennifer Miller
Art Director - Matthew Alford
Director of Editorial - Jeremy Ross
VP of Production & Manufacturing - Ron Klamert
President & C.O.O. - John Parker
Publisher & C.E.O. - Stuart Levy

Email: editor@TOKYOPOP.com
Come visit us online at www.TOKYOPOP.com

A  Manga
TOKYOPOP® is an imprint of Mixx Entertainment, Inc.
5900 Wilshire Blvd. Suite 2000, Los Angeles, CA 90036

ISBN: 1-59182-187-8

First TOKYOPOP® printing: June 2003

10 9 8 7 6 5 4 3 2 1
Printed in the USA

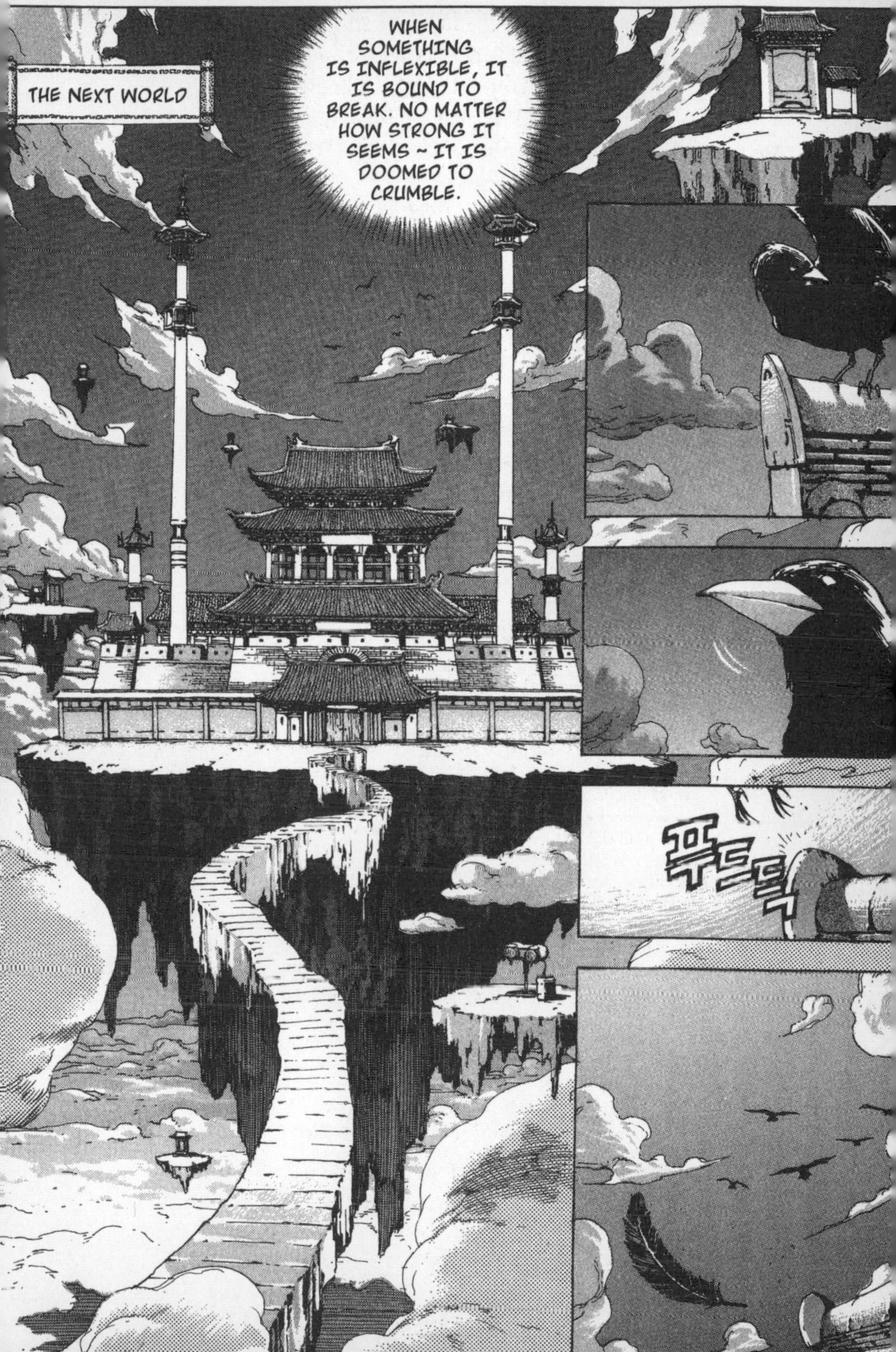
THE NEXT WORLD
WHEN SOMETHING IS INFLEXIBLE, IT IS BOUND TO BREAK. NO MATTER HOW STRONG IT SEEMS ~ IT IS DOOMED TO CRUMBLE.
푸드득

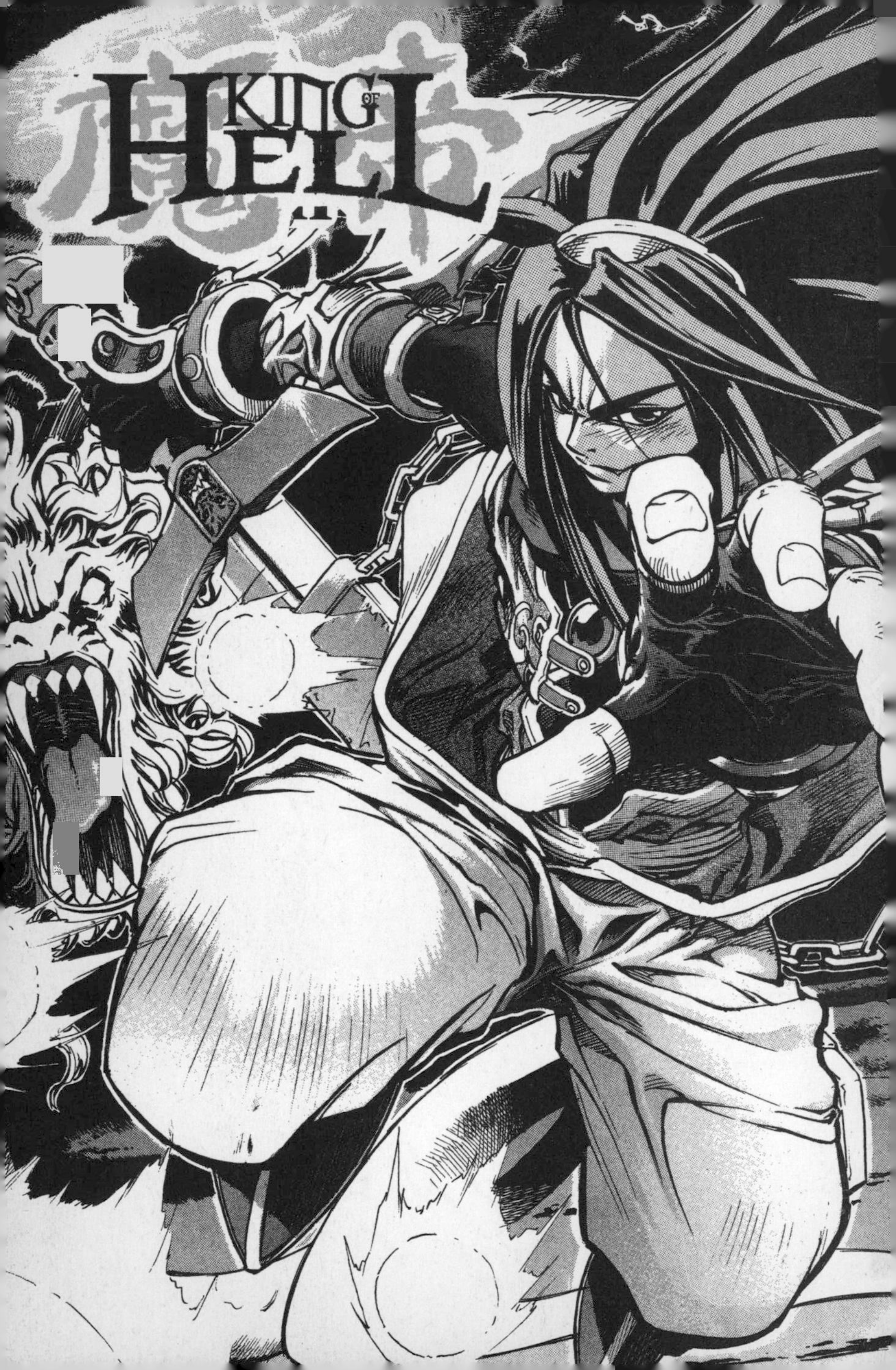
KING OF HELL

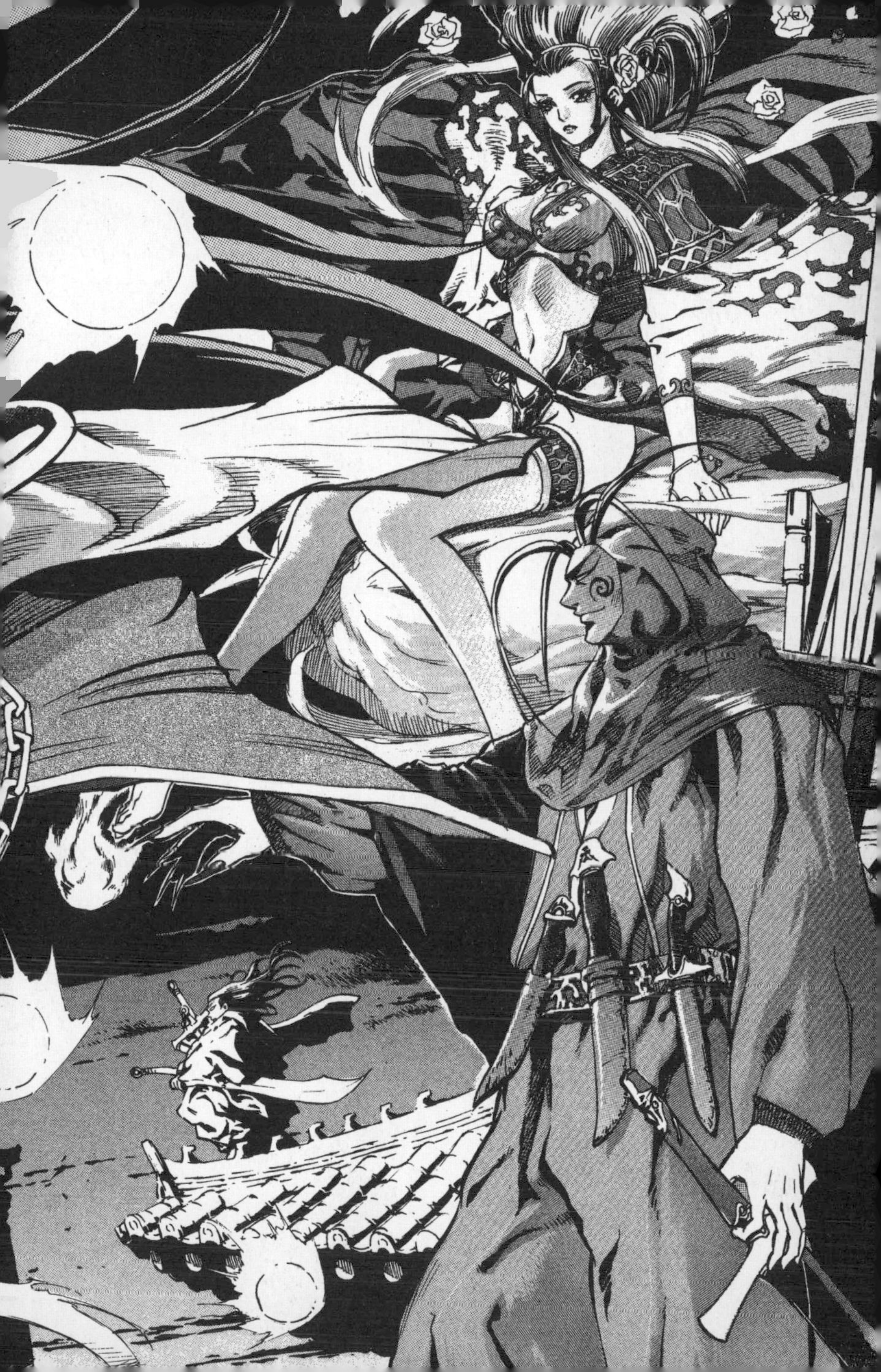

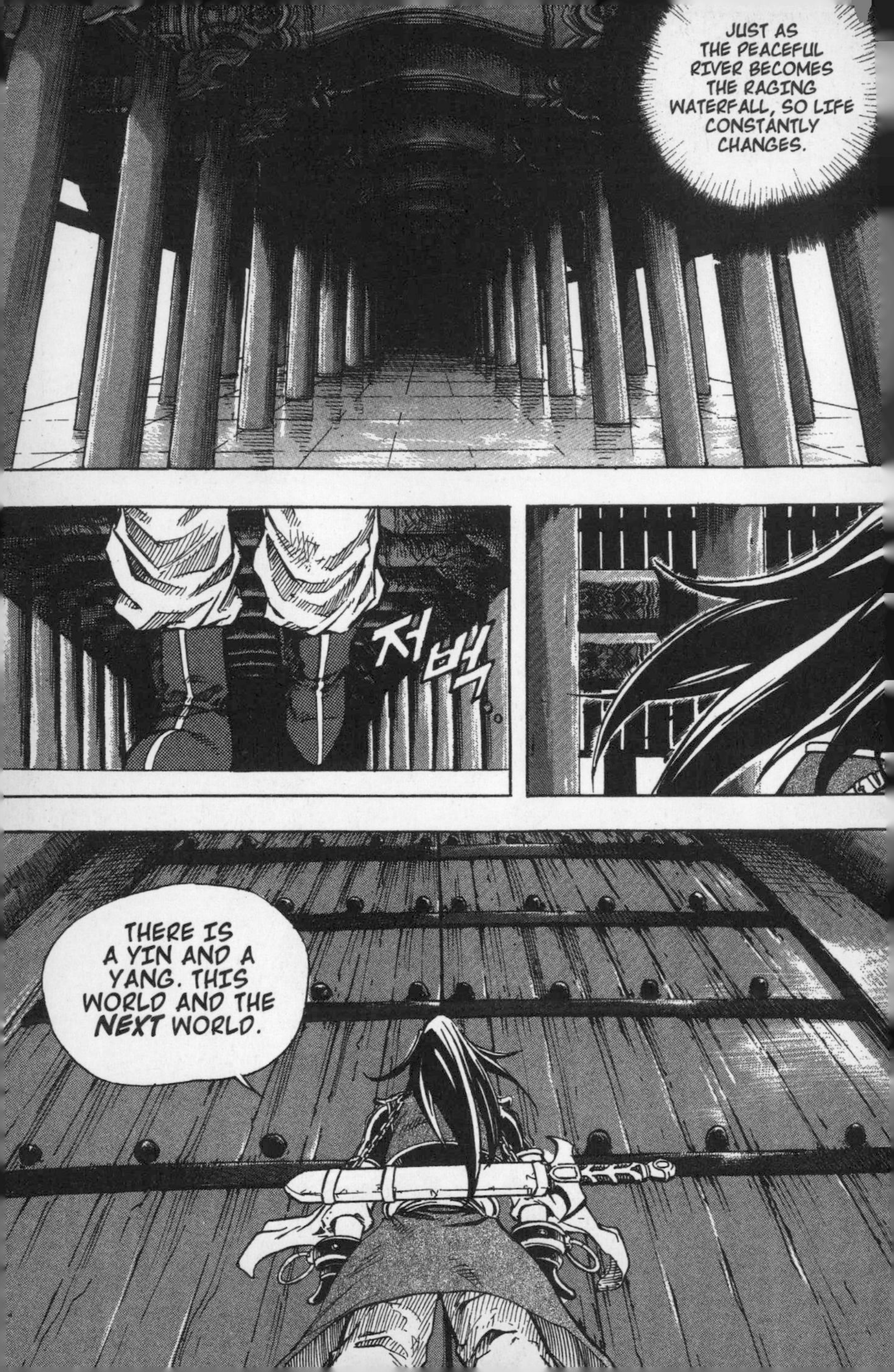
JUST AS THE PEACEFUL RIVER BECOMES THE RAGING WATERFALL, SO LIFE CONSTANTLY CHANGES.
저벅
THERE IS A YIN AND A YANG. THIS WORLD AND THE *NEXT* WORLD.

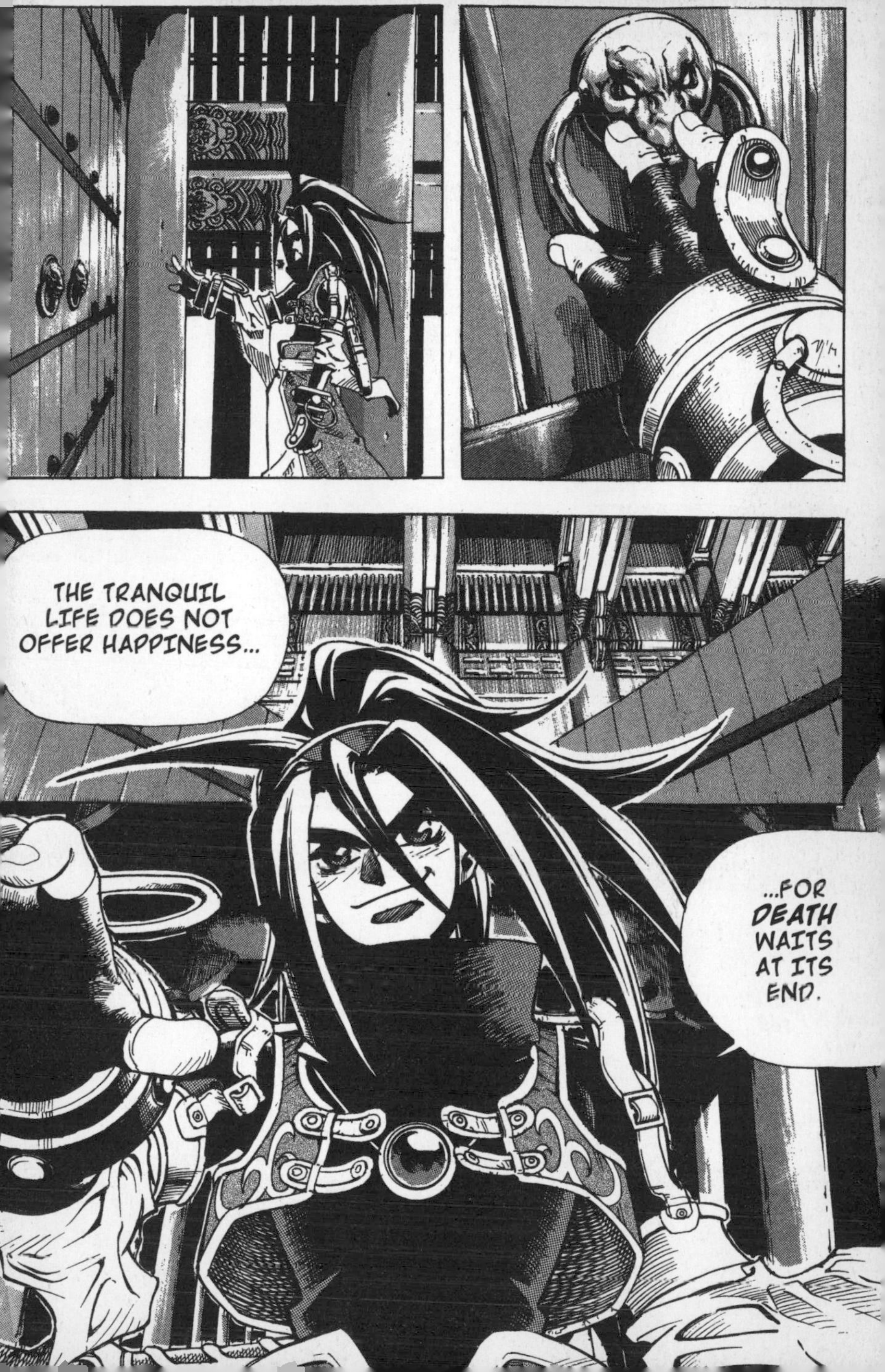
THE TRANQUIL LIFE DOES NOT OFFER HAPPINESS...
...FOR DEATH WAITS AT ITS END.

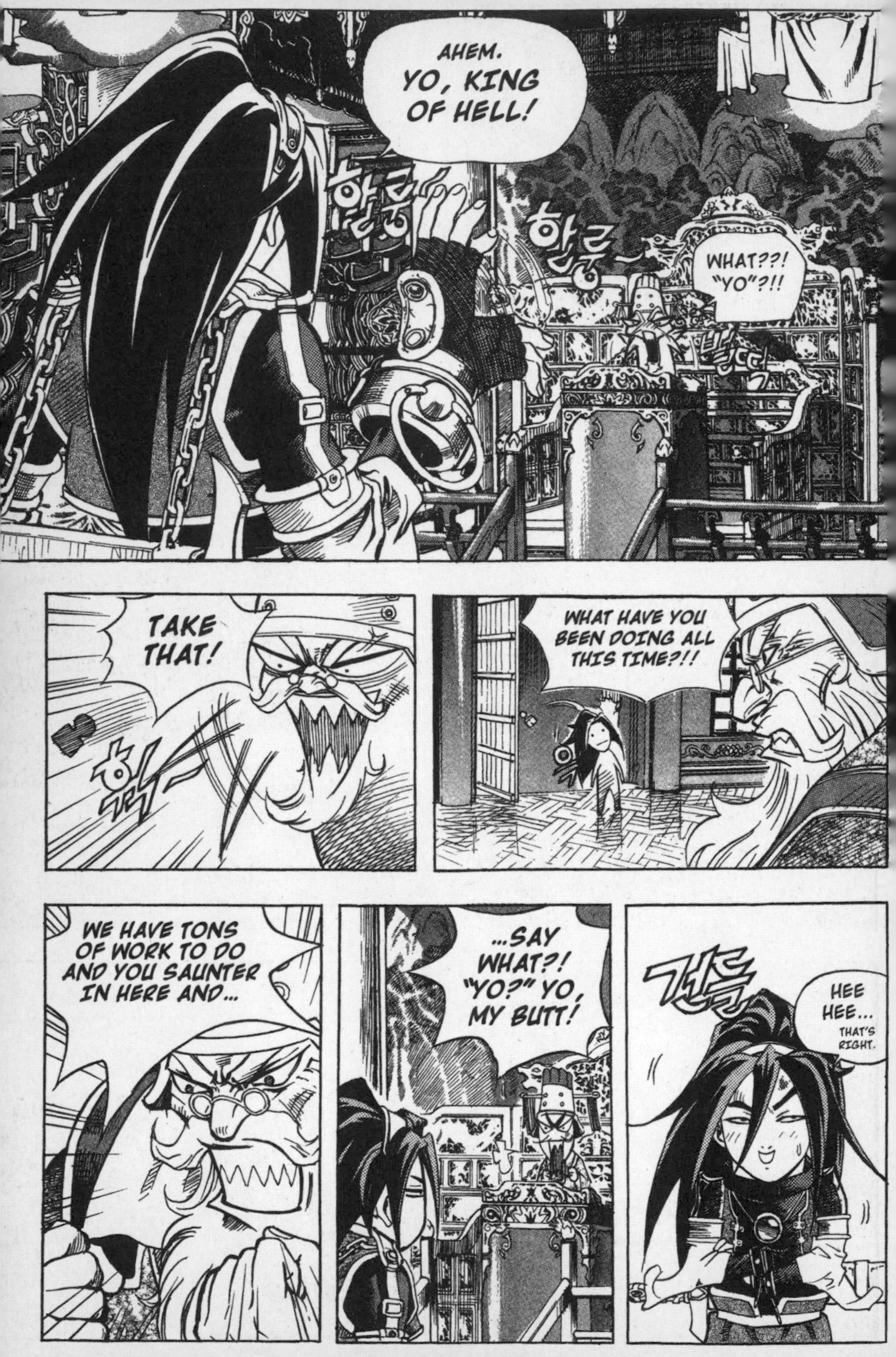
AHEM. YO, KING OF HELL!
WHAT??! "YO"?!!
TAKE THAT!
WHAT HAVE YOU BEEN DOING ALL THIS TIME?!!
WE HAVE TONS OF WORK TO DO AND YOU SAUNTER IN HERE AND...
...SAY WHAT?! "YO?" YO, MY BUTT!
HEE HEE...
THAT'S RIGHT.

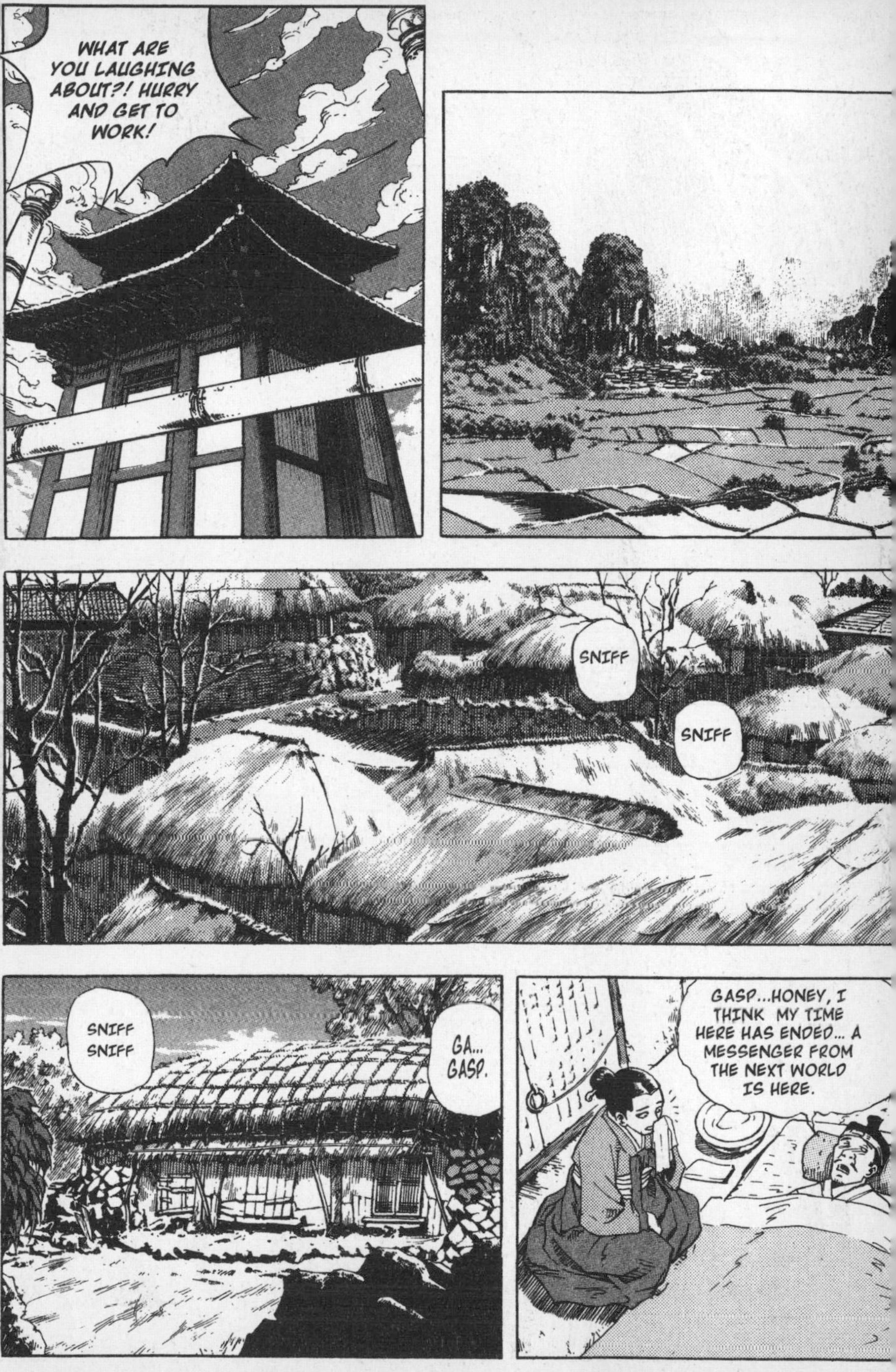
WHAT ARE YOU LAUGHING ABOUT?! HURRY AND GET TO WORK!
SNIFF
SNIFF
SNIFF SNIFF
GA... GASP.
GASP...HONEY, I THINK MY TIME HERE HAS ENDED... A MESSENGER FROM THE NEXT WORLD IS HERE.

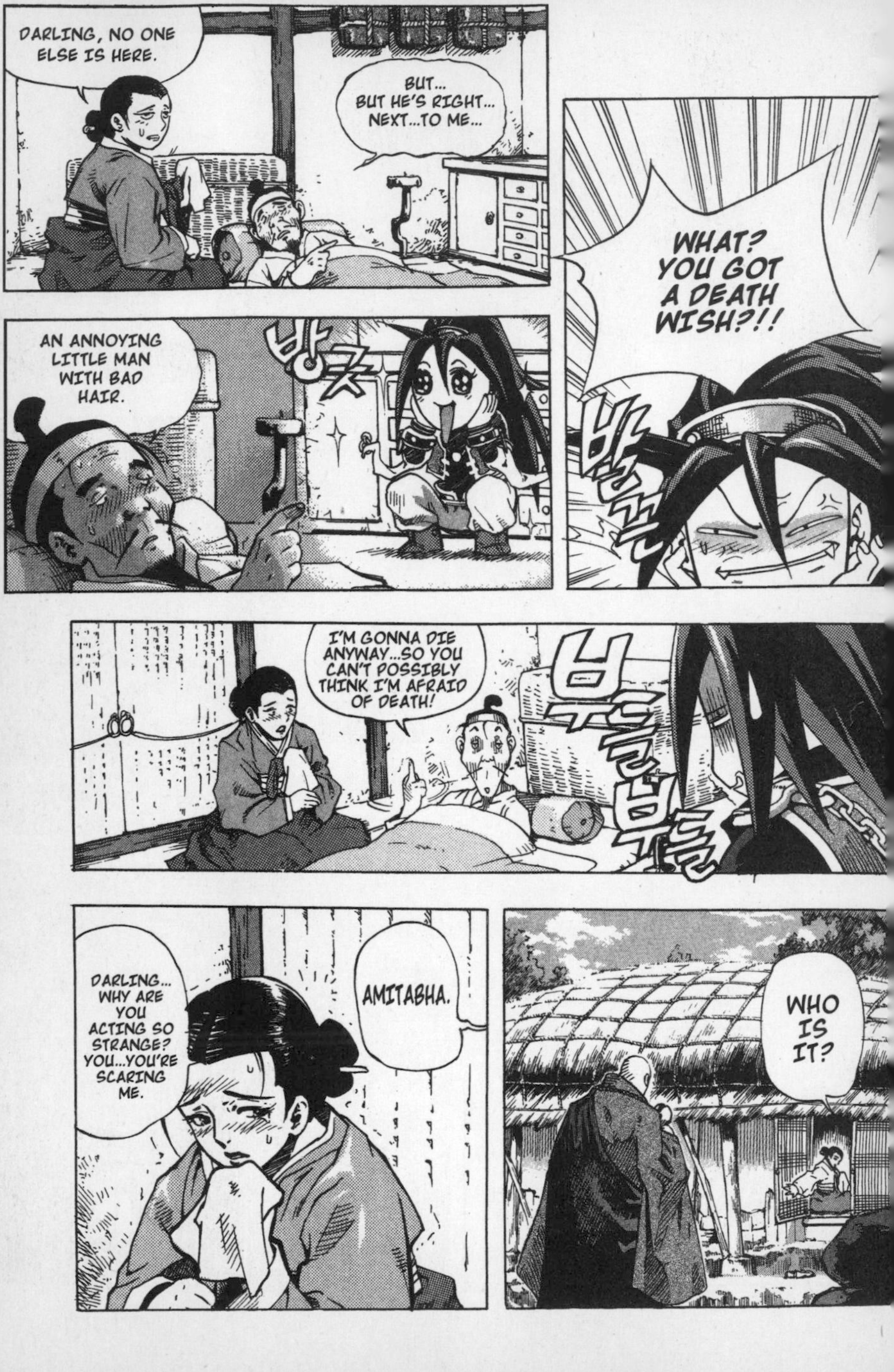
DARLING, NO ONE ELSE IS HERE.
BUT... BUT HE'S RIGHT... NEXT...TO ME...
AN ANNOYING LITTLE MAN WITH BAD HAIR.
방긋
WHAT? YOU GOT A DEATH WISH?!!
I'M GONNA DIE ANYWAY...SO YOU CAN'T POSSIBLY THINK I'M AFRAID OF DEATH!
부들부들
DARLING... WHY ARE YOU ACTING SO STRANGE? YOU...YOU'RE SCARING ME.
AMITABHA.
WHO IS IT?

WOULD YOU PLEASE GIVE AN OFFERING?

AMITABHA.

WHY DON'T YOU ASK THE MONK TO PRAY TO BUDDHA FOR YOU? YOU NEVER KNOW! YOU MIGHT BE ABLE TO GET INTO PARADISE.

ALTHOUGH JUDGING BY YOUR ATTITUDE, I'D SAY YOU'RE BOUND FOR HELL... HEH, HEH...!

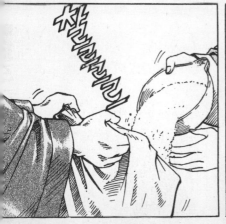

THANK YOU VERY MUCH.

13

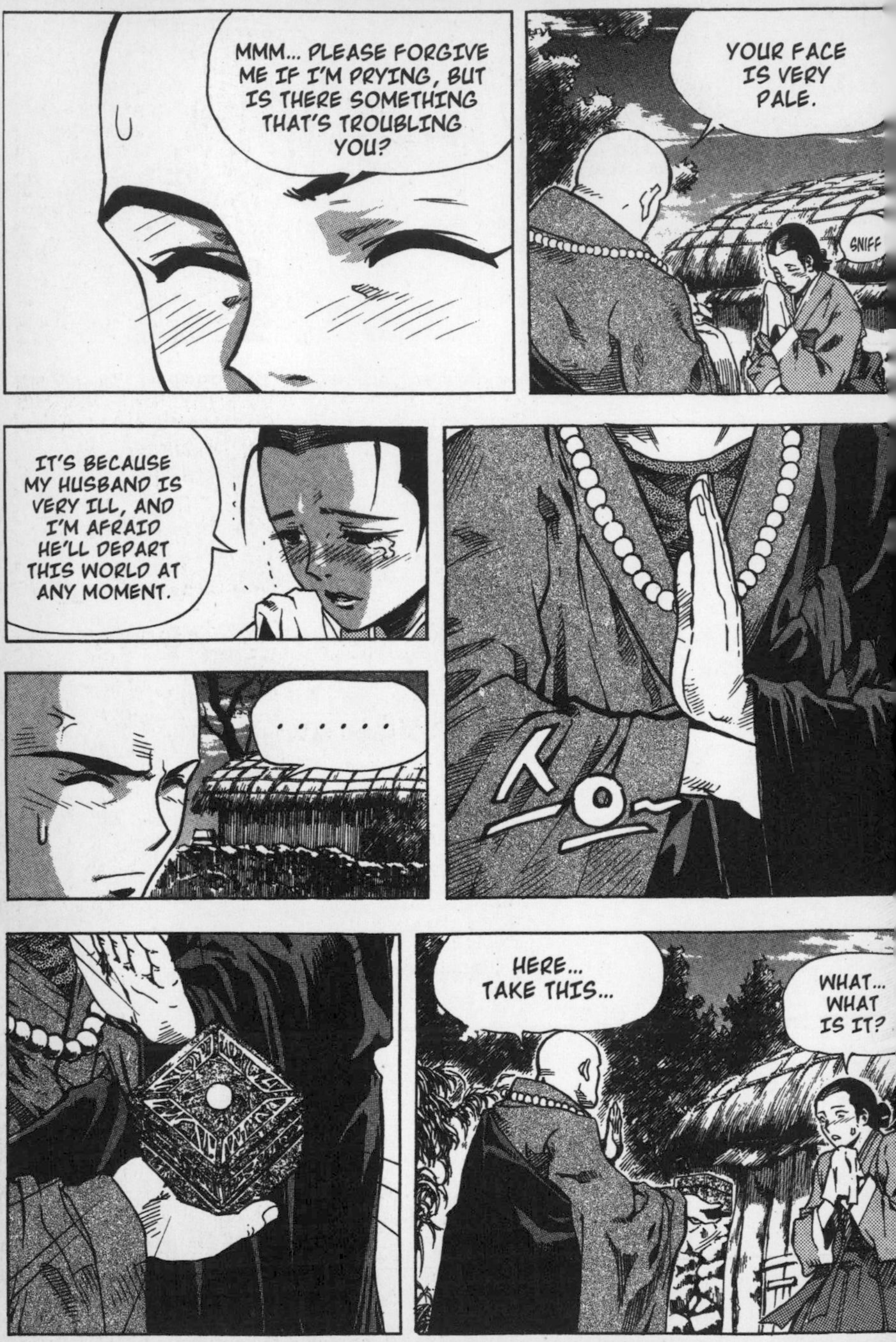
MMM... PLEASE FORGIVE ME IF I'M PRYING, BUT IS THERE SOMETHING THAT'S TROUBLING YOU?
YOUR FACE IS VERY PALE.
SNIFF
IT'S BECAUSE MY HUSBAND IS VERY ILL, AND I'M AFRAID HE'LL DEPART THIS WORLD AT ANY MOMENT.
......
HERE... TAKE THIS...
WHAT... WHAT IS IT?

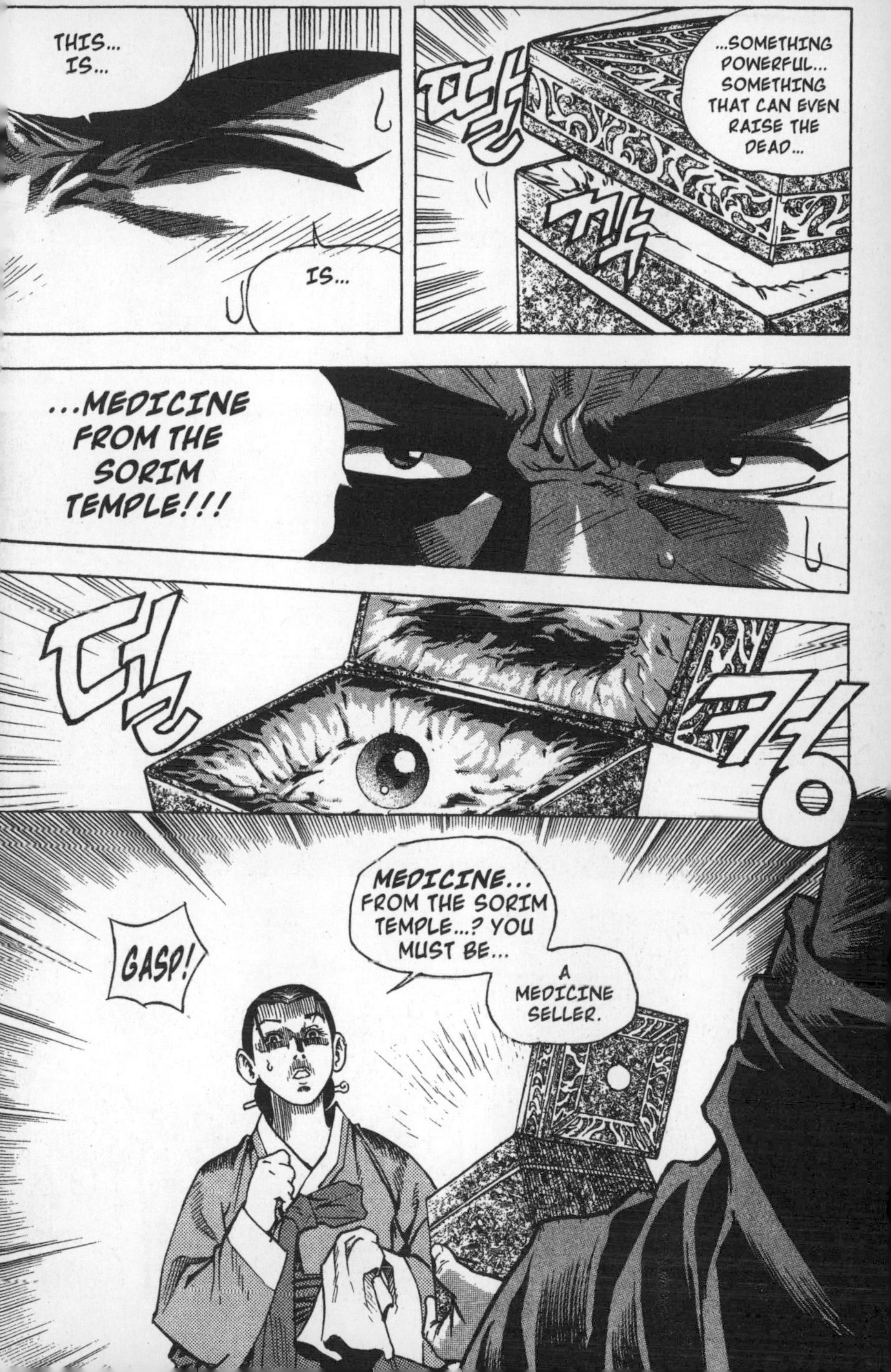
THIS... IS...
IS...
...SOMETHING POWERFUL... SOMETHING THAT CAN EVEN RAISE THE DEAD...
...MEDICINE FROM THE SORIM TEMPLE!!!
GASP!
MEDICINE... FROM THE SORIM TEMPLE...? YOU MUST BE...
A MEDICINE SELLER.

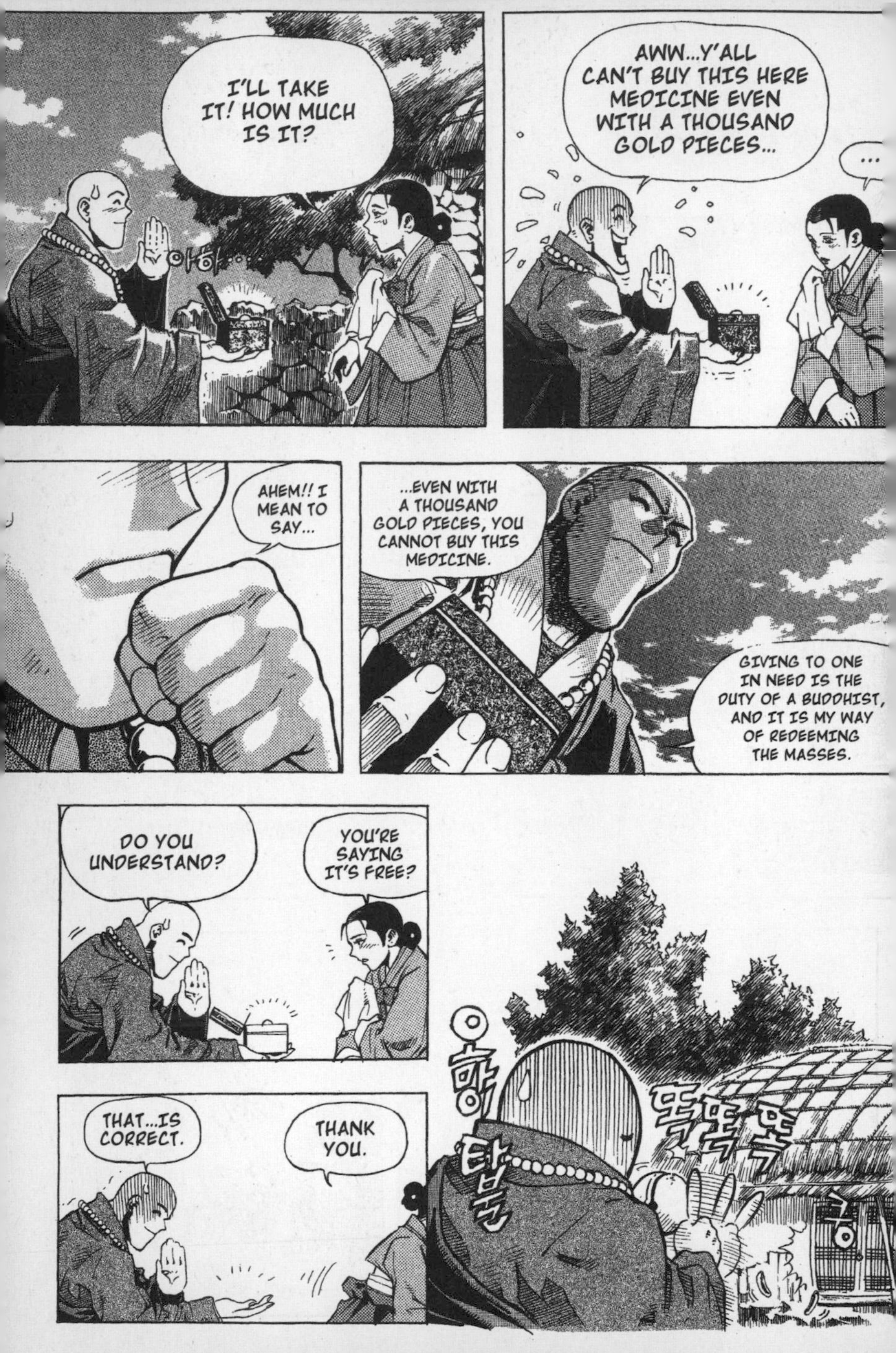
I'LL TAKE IT! HOW MUCH IS IT?
아하...
AWW...Y'ALL CAN'T BUY THIS HERE MEDICINE EVEN WITH A THOUSAND GOLD PIECES...
...
AHEM!! I MEAN TO SAY...
...EVEN WITH A THOUSAND GOLD PIECES, YOU CANNOT BUY THIS MEDICINE.
GIVING TO ONE IN NEED IS THE DUTY OF A BUDDHIST, AND IT IS MY WAY OF REDEEMING THE MASSES.
DO YOU UNDERSTAND?
YOU'RE SAYING IT'S FREE?
THAT...IS CORRECT.
THANK YOU.

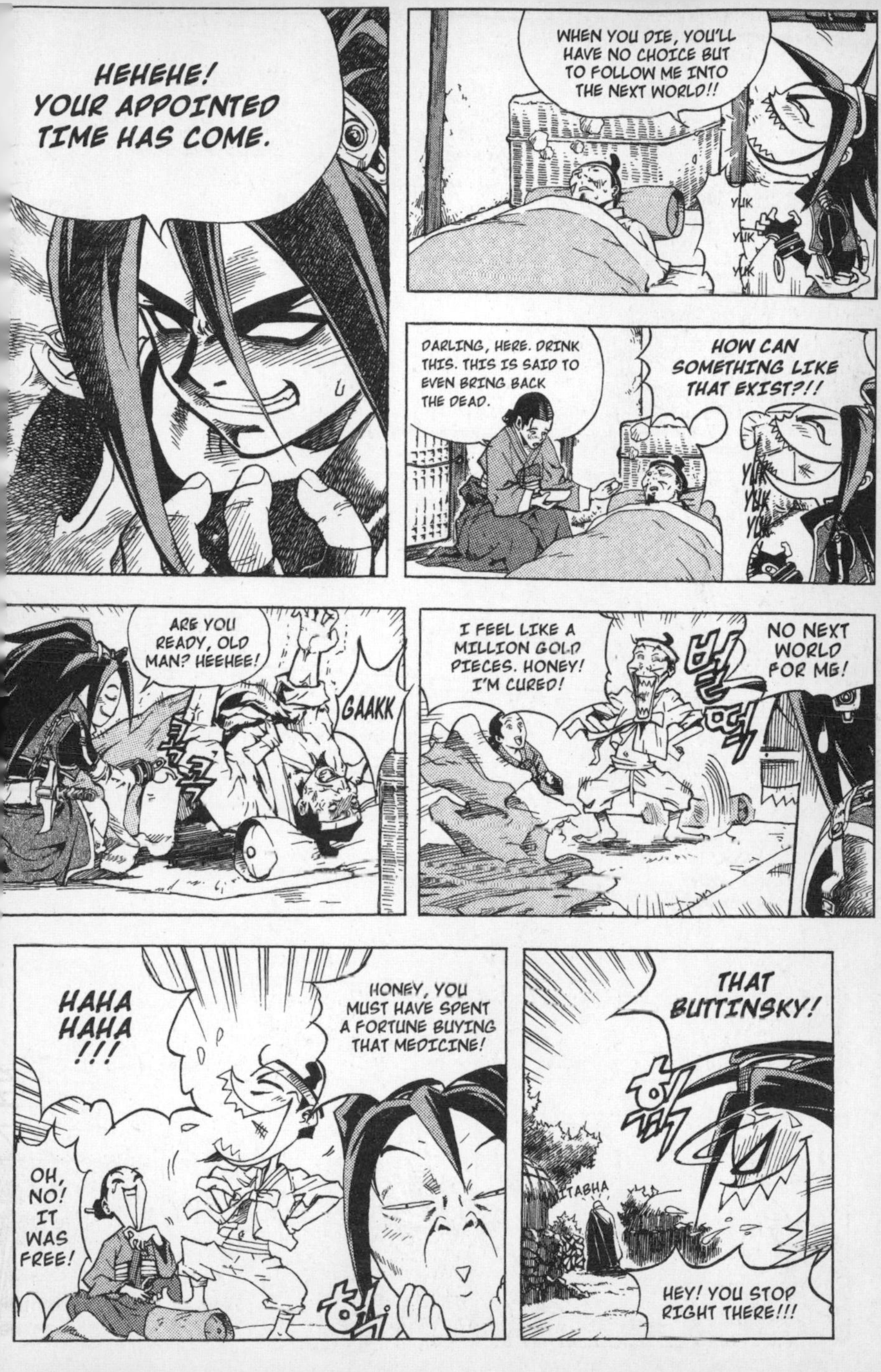
HEHEHE! YOUR APPOINTED TIME HAS COME.
WHEN YOU DIE, YOU'LL HAVE NO CHOICE BUT TO FOLLOW ME INTO THE NEXT WORLD!!
YUK
YUK
YUK
DARLING, HERE. DRINK THIS. THIS IS SAID TO EVEN BRING BACK THE DEAD.
HOW CAN SOMETHING LIKE THAT EXIST?!!
YUK
YUK
YUK
ARE YOU READY, OLD MAN? HEEHEE!
GAAKK
I FEEL LIKE A MILLION GOLD PIECES. HONEY! I'M CURED!
NO NEXT WORLD FOR ME!
HAHA HAHA !!!
HONEY, YOU MUST HAVE SPENT A FORTUNE BUYING THAT MEDICINE!
OH, NO! IT WAS FREE!
THAT BUTTINSKY!
HEY! YOU STOP RIGHT THERE!!!

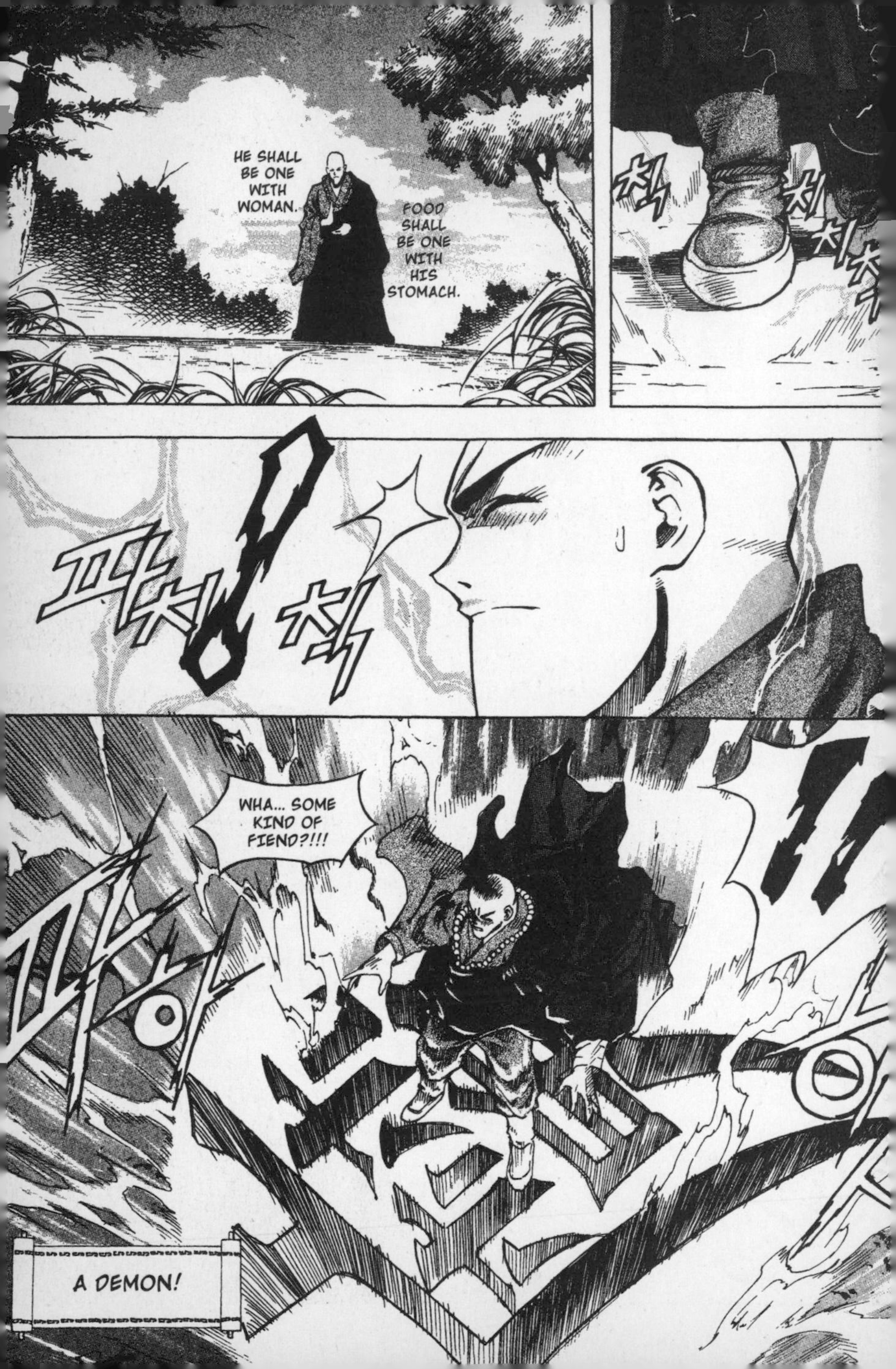
HE SHALL BE ONE WITH WOMAN.
FOOD SHALL BE ONE WITH HIS STOMACH.
WHA... SOME KIND OF FIEND?!!!
A DEMON!

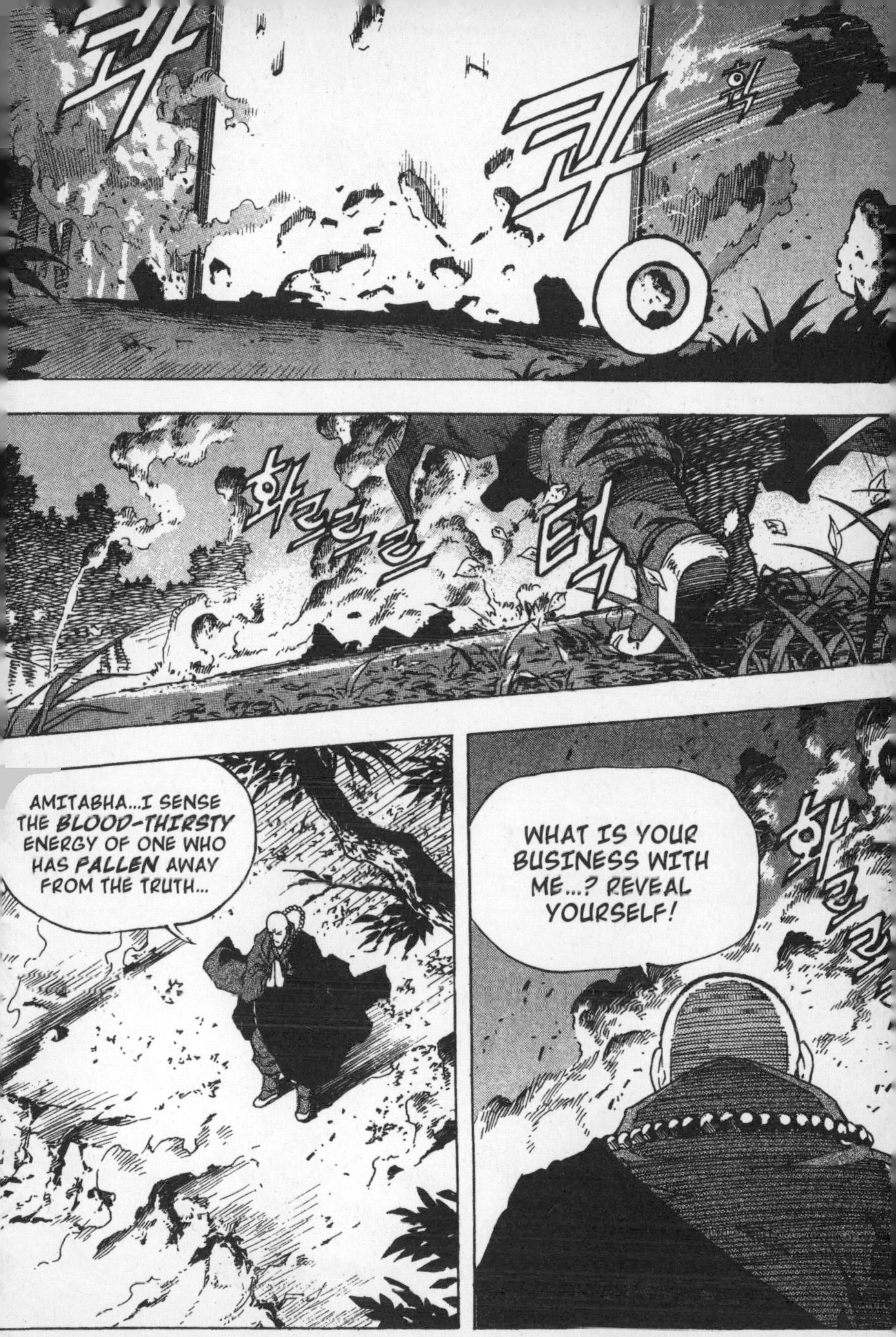
콰
콱
AMITABHA...I SENSE THE BLOOD-THIRSTY ENERGY OF ONE WHO HAS FALLEN AWAY FROM THE TRUTH...
WHAT IS YOUR BUSINESS WITH ME...? REVEAL YOURSELF!

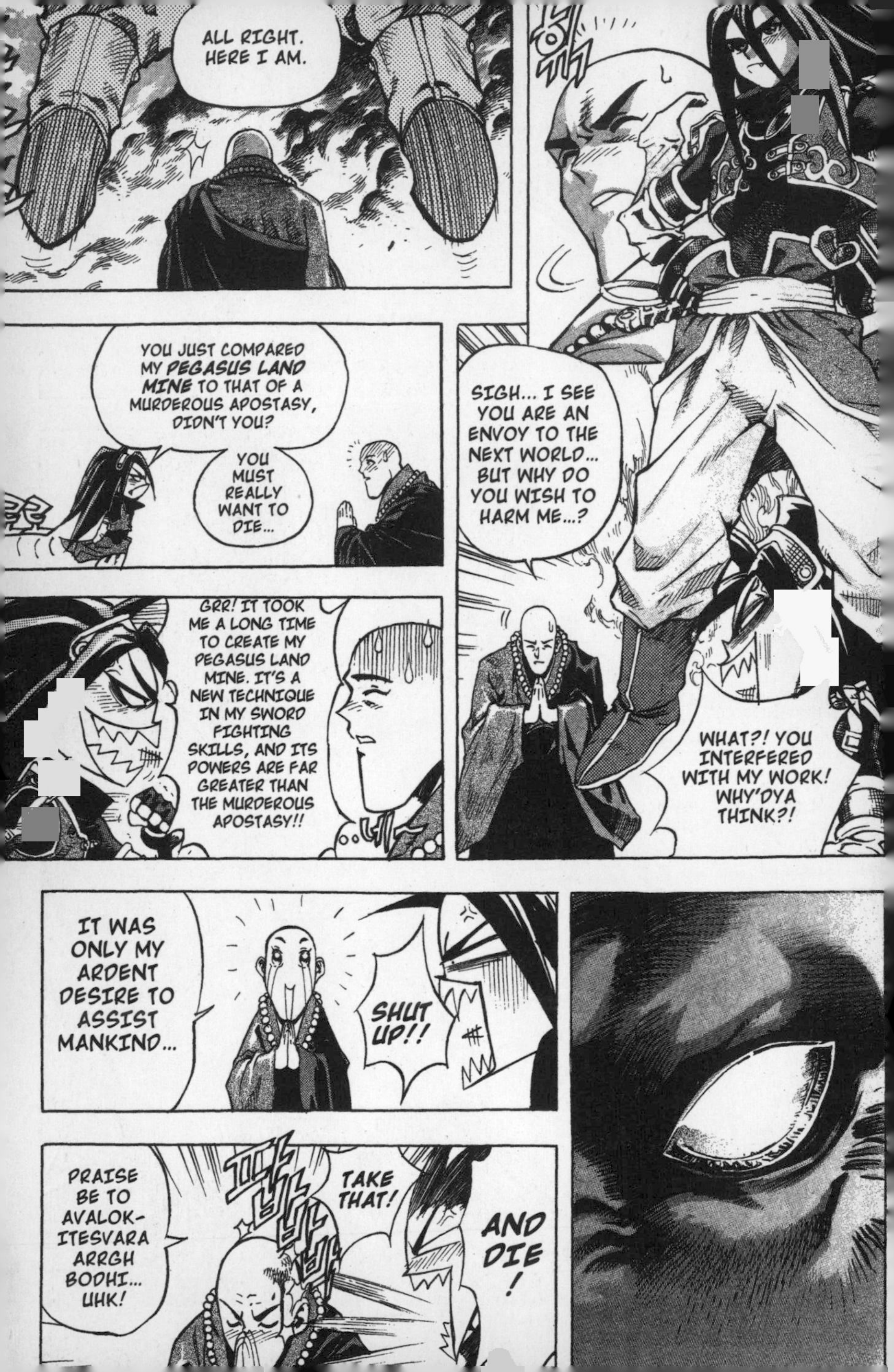

ALL RIGHT. HERE I AM.
YOU JUST COMPARED MY PEGASUS LAND MINE TO THAT OF A MURDEROUS APOSTASY, DIDN'T YOU?
YOU MUST REALLY WANT TO DIE...
GRR! IT TOOK ME A LONG TIME TO CREATE MY PEGASUS LAND MINE. IT'S A NEW TECHNIQUE IN MY SWORD FIGHTING SKILLS, AND ITS POWERS ARE FAR GREATER THAN THE MURDEROUS APOSTASY!!
SIGH... I SEE YOU ARE AN ENVOY TO THE NEXT WORLD... BUT WHY DO YOU WISH TO HARM ME...?
WHAT?! YOU INTERFERED WITH MY WORK! WHY'DYA THINK?!
IT WAS ONLY MY ARDENT DESIRE TO ASSIST MANKIND...
SHUT UP!!
PRAISE BE TO AVALOK-ITESVARA ARRGH BODHI... UHK!
TAKE THAT!
AND DIE!

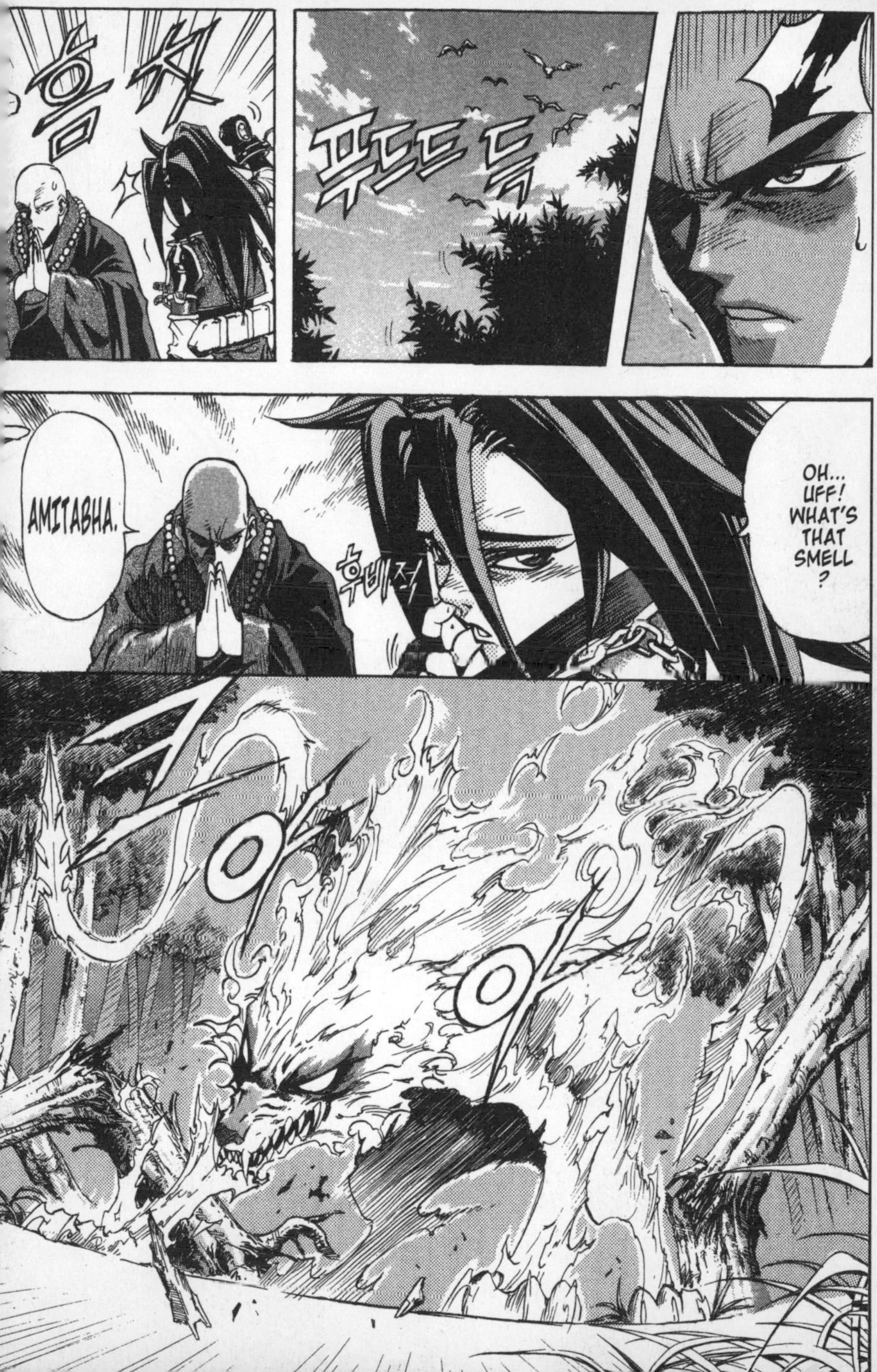
흠칫
푸드드득
AMITABHA.
후비적
OH... UFF! WHAT'S THAT SMELL?

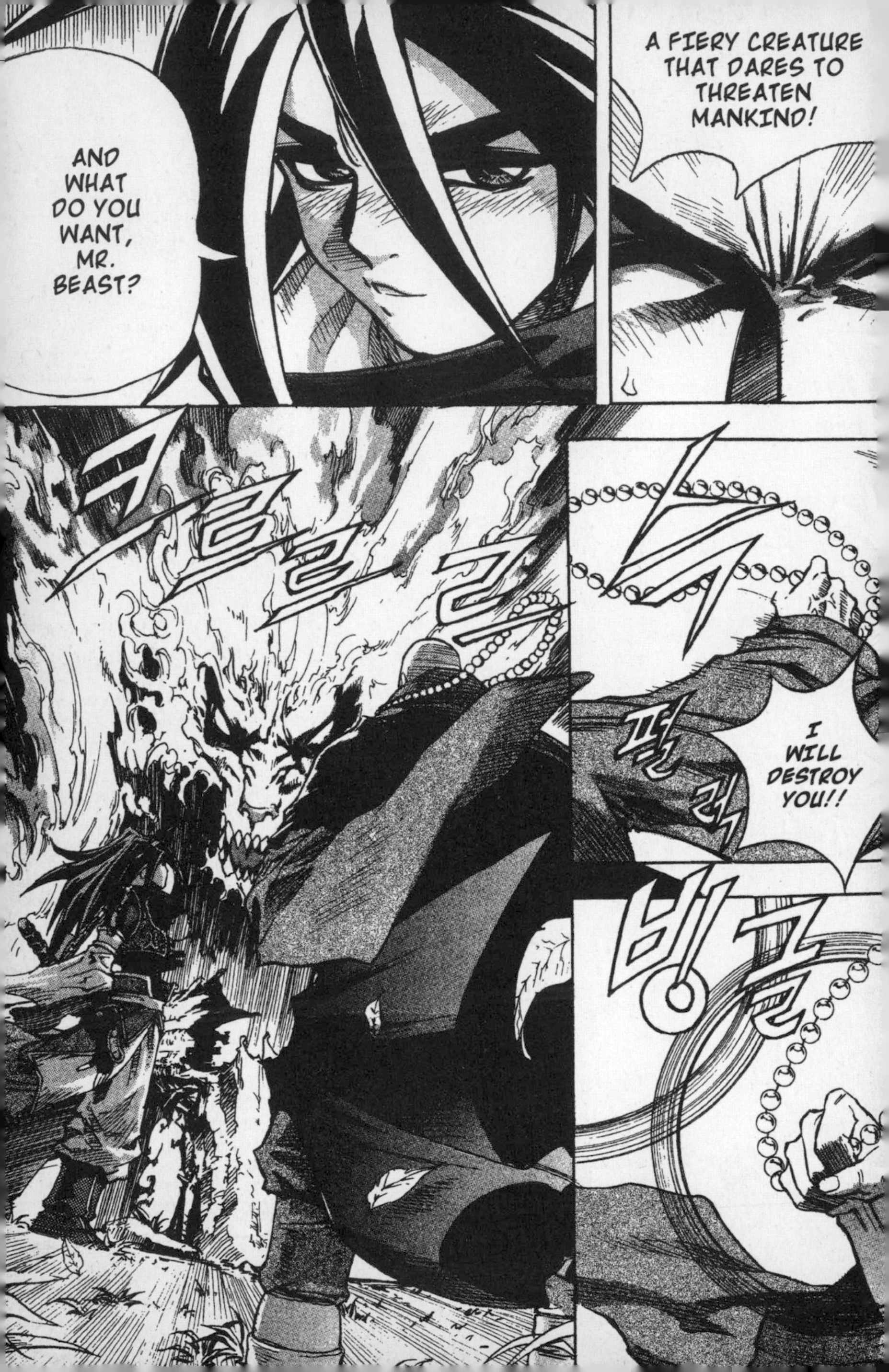
AND WHAT DO YOU WANT, MR. BEAST?
A FIERY CREATURE THAT DARES TO THREATEN MANKIND!
I WILL DESTROY YOU!!

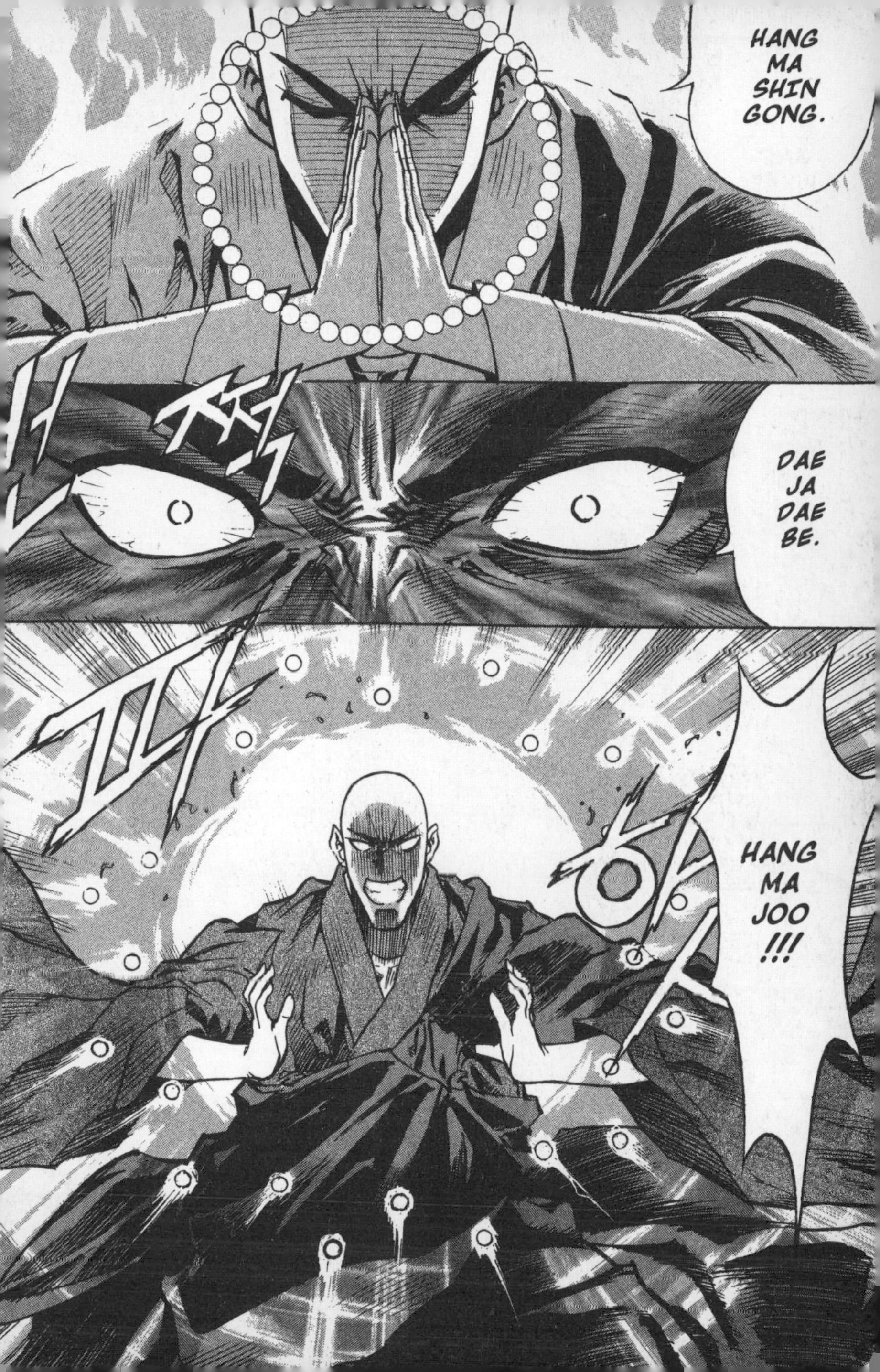
HANG MA SHIN GONG.
DAE JA DAE BE.
HANG MA JOO!!!

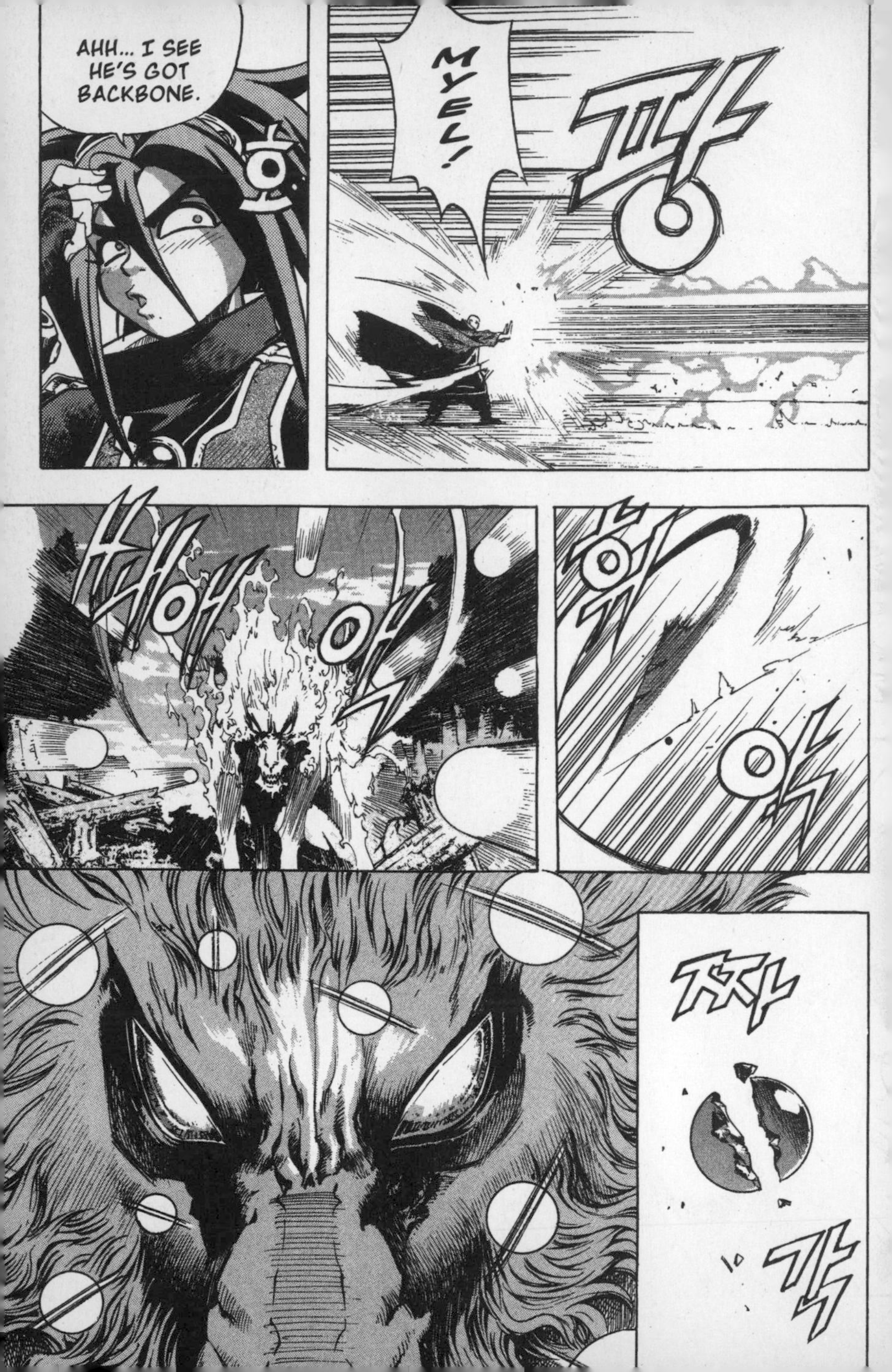
AHH... I SEE HE'S GOT BACKBONE.
MYEL!

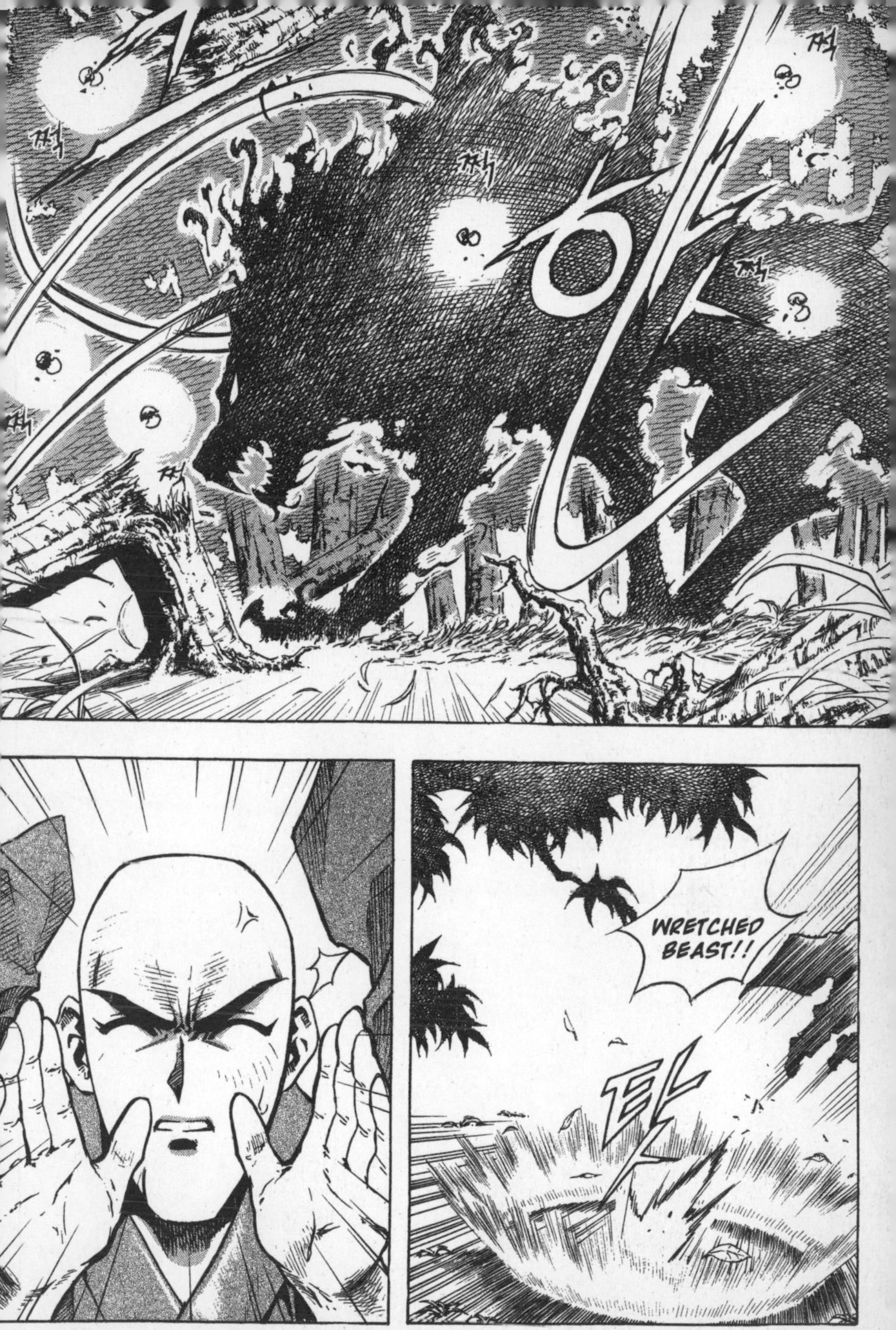
WRETCHED BEAST!!

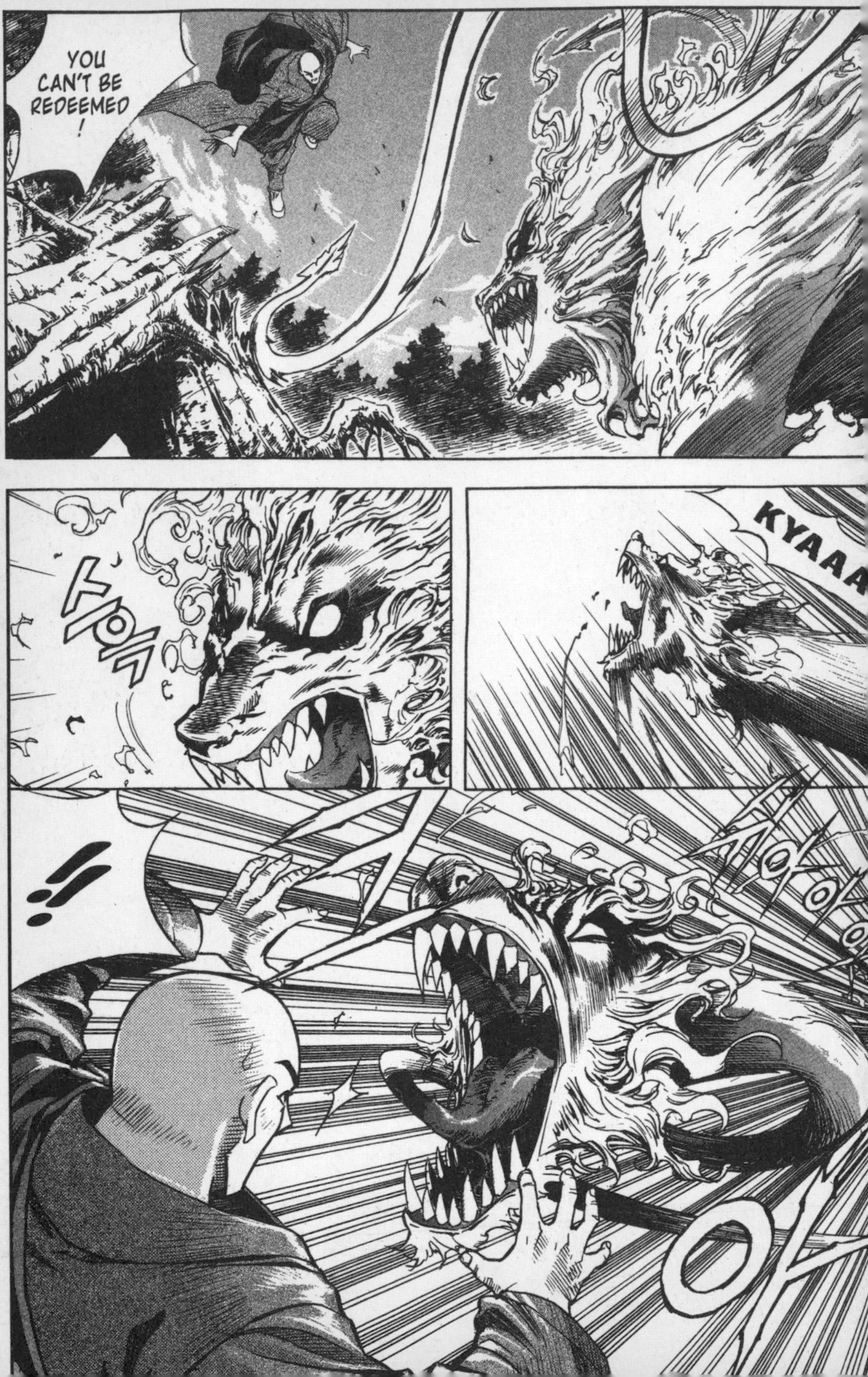
YOU CAN'T BE REDEEMED!
KYAAA
!!

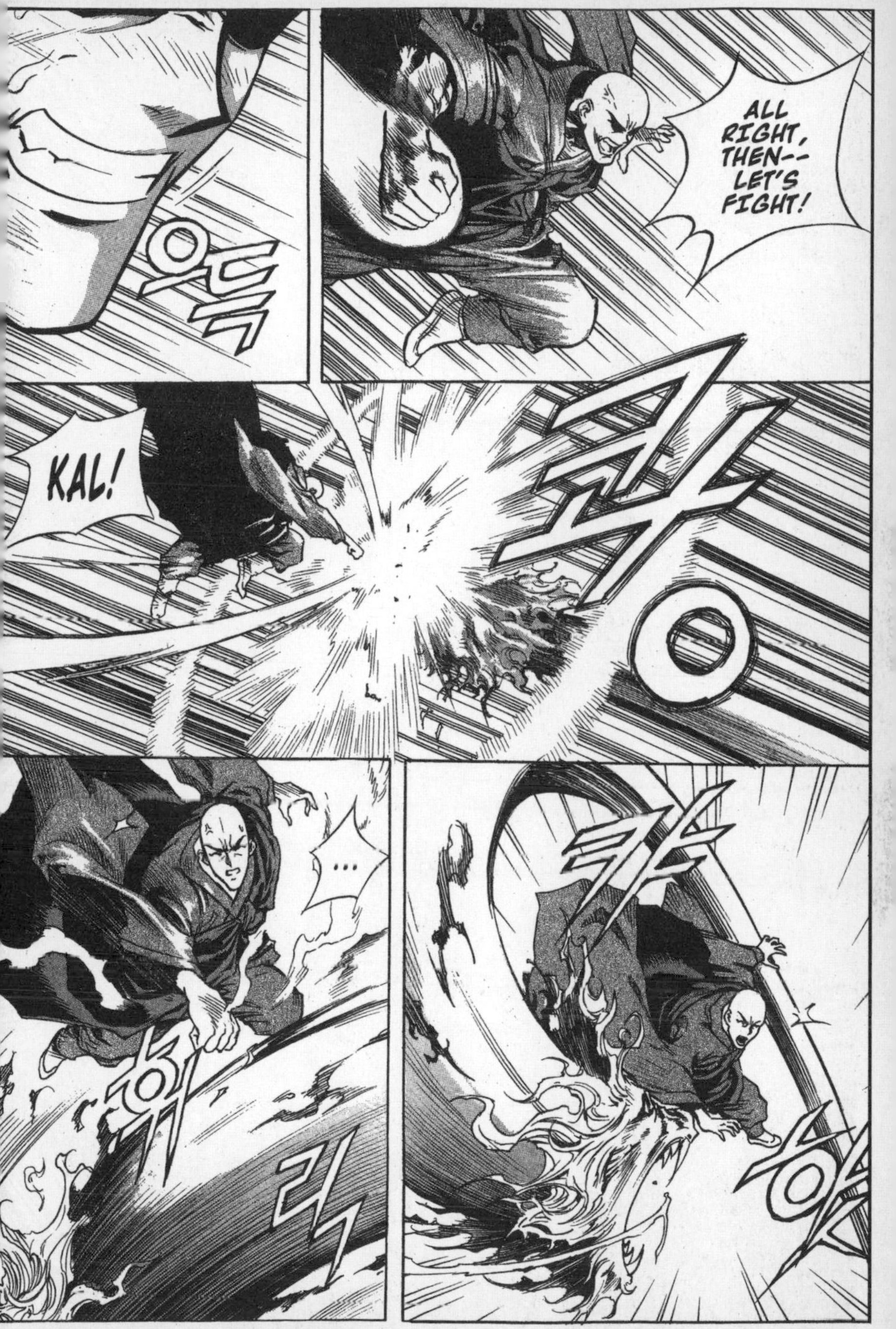
ALL RIGHT, THEN--LET'S FIGHT!
KAL!
...

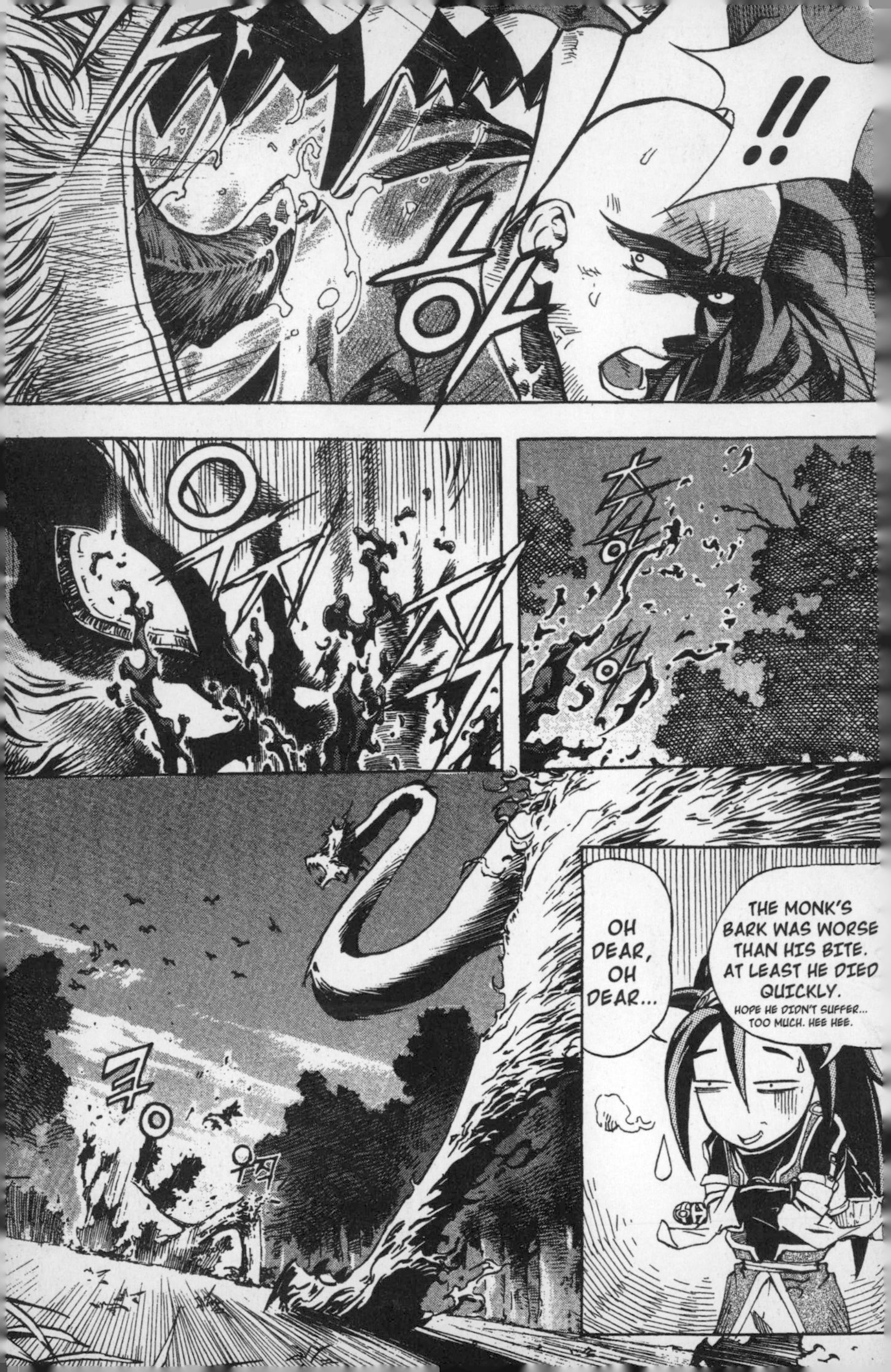
!!
OH DEAR, OH DEAR...
THE MONK'S BARK WAS WORSE THAN HIS BITE. AT LEAST HE DIED QUICKLY.
HOPE HE DIDN'T SUFFER... TOO MUCH. HEE HEE.

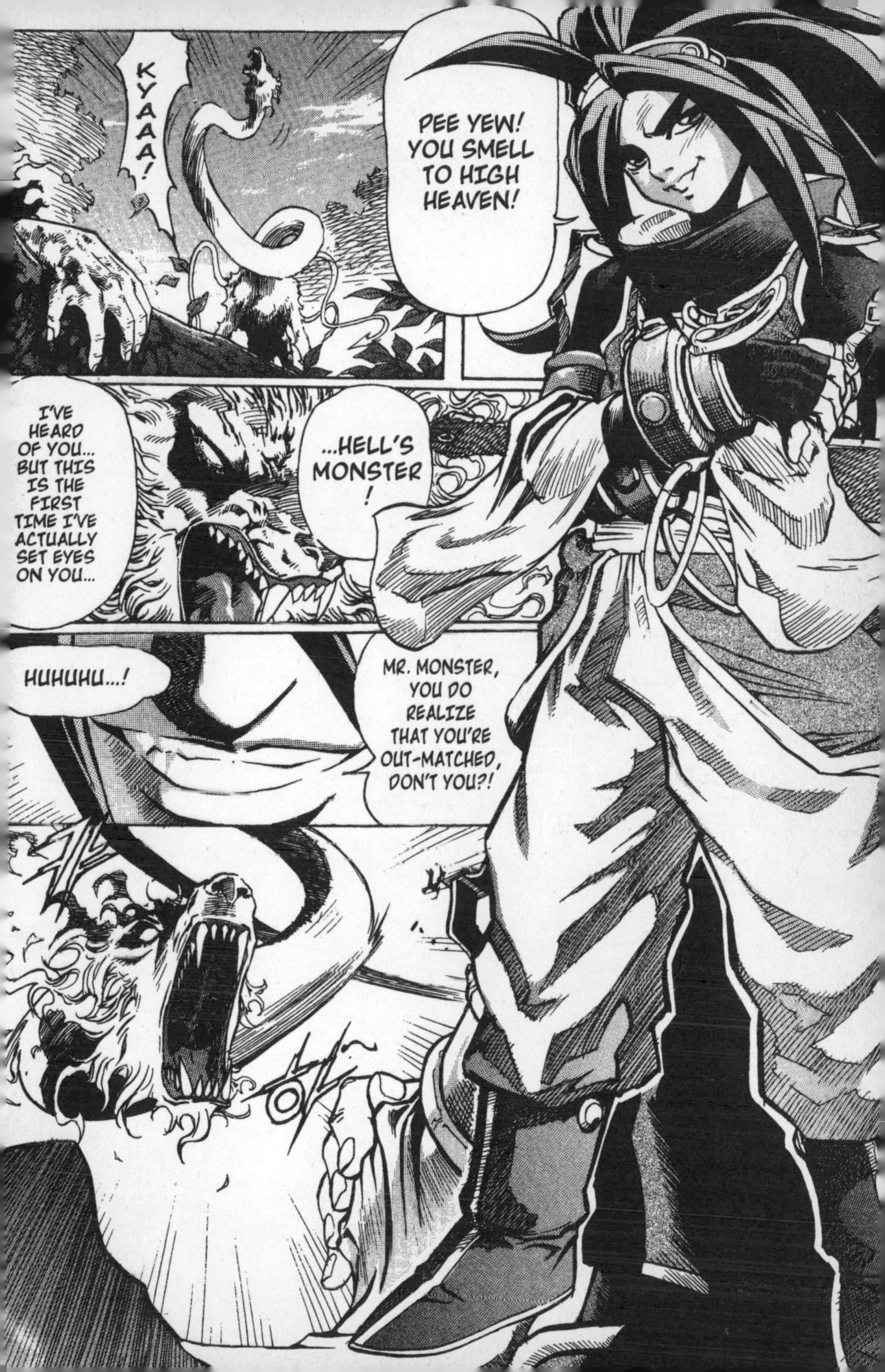
KYAAA!
I'VE HEARD OF YOU... BUT THIS IS THE FIRST TIME I'VE ACTUALLY SET EYES ON YOU...
...HELL'S MONSTER!
HUHUHU...!
MR. MONSTER, YOU DO REALIZE THAT YOU'RE OUT-MATCHED, DON'T YOU?!
PEE YEW! YOU SMELL TO HIGH HEAVEN!

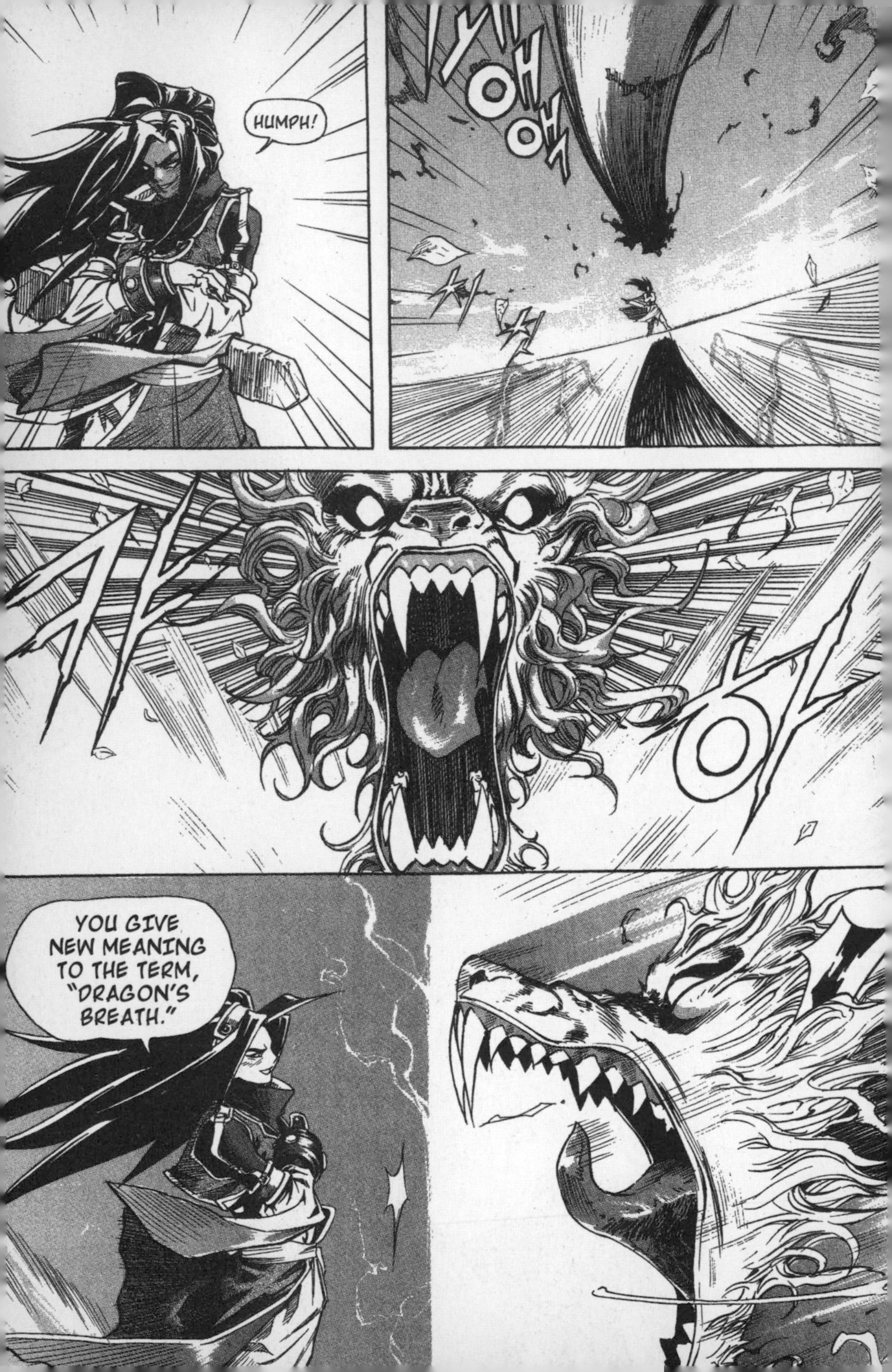
HUMPH!
YOU GIVE NEW MEANING TO THE TERM, "DRAGON'S BREATH."

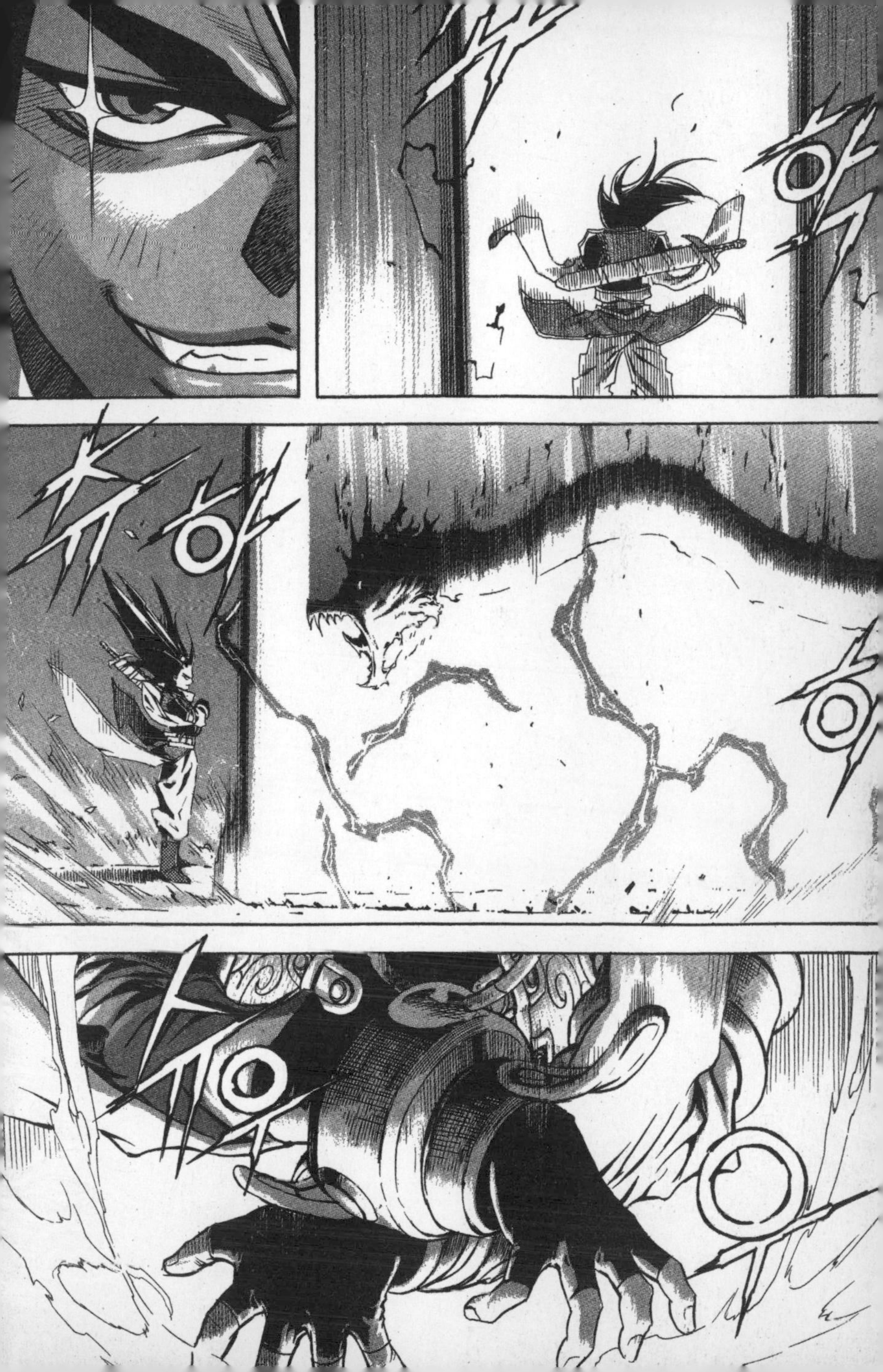

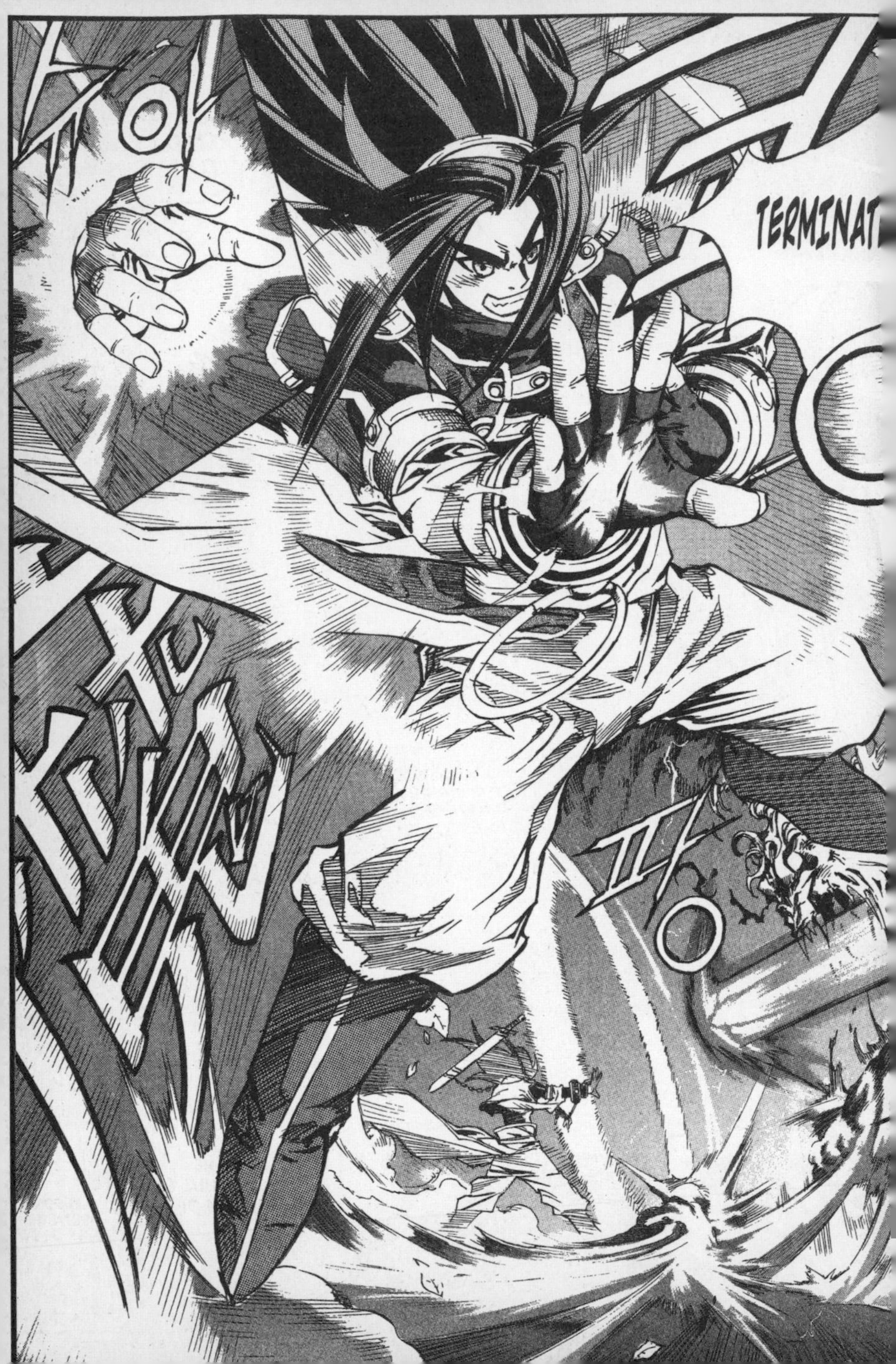
TERMINAT

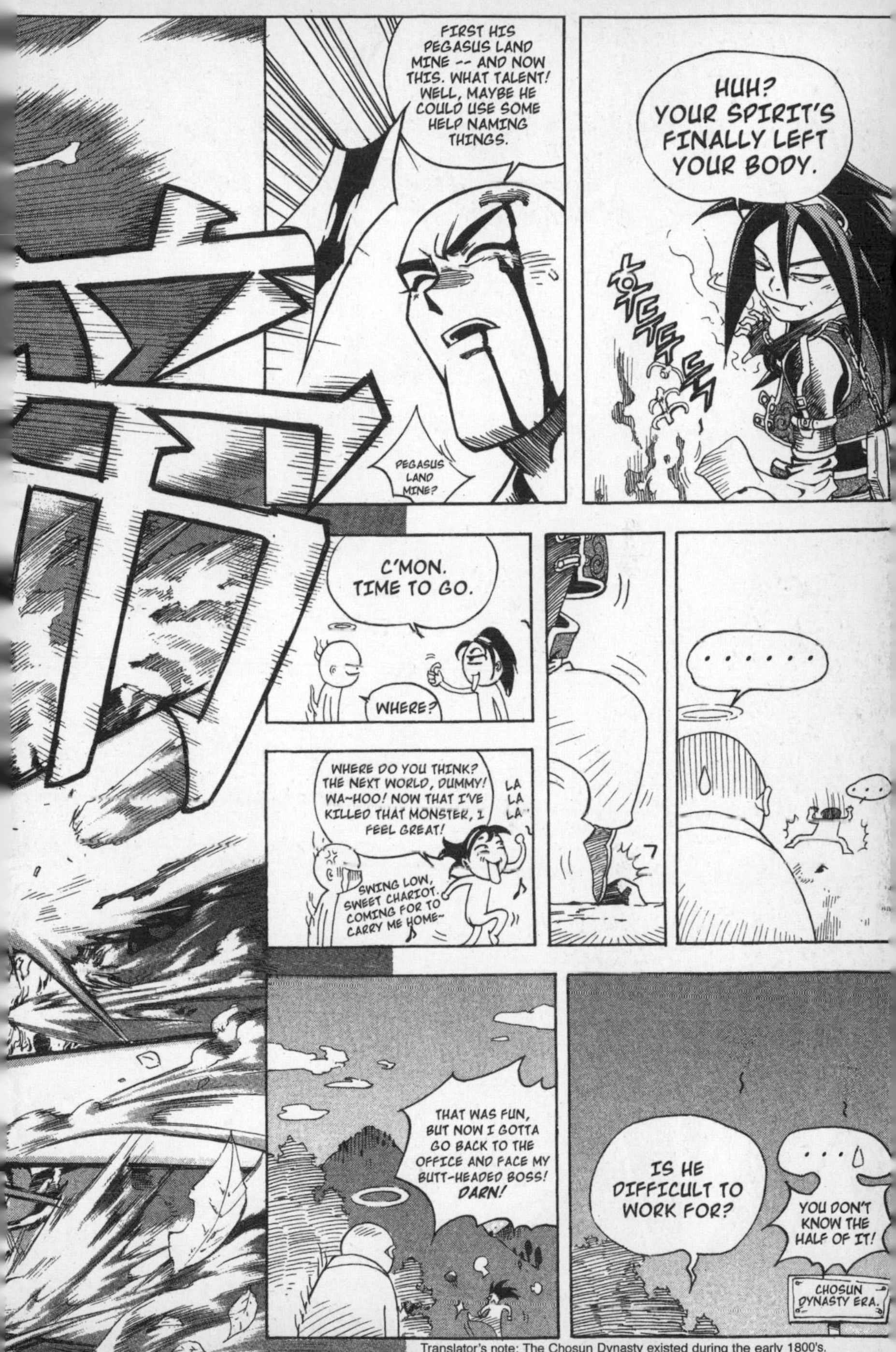
FIRST HIS PEGASUS LAND MINE -- AND NOW THIS. WHAT TALENT! WELL, MAYBE HE COULD USE SOME HELP NAMING THINGS.
PEGASUS LAND MINE?
HUH? YOUR SPIRIT'S FINALLY LEFT YOUR BODY.
C'MON. TIME TO GO.
WHERE?
WHERE DO YOU THINK? THE NEXT WORLD, DUMMY! WA~HOO! NOW THAT I'VE KILLED THAT MONSTER, I FEEL GREAT!
LA LA LA
SWING LOW, SWEET CHARIOT. COMING FOR TO CARRY ME HOME~
......
THAT WAS FUN, BUT NOW I GOTTA GO BACK TO THE OFFICE AND FACE MY BUTT-HEADED BOSS! DARN!
IS HE DIFFICULT TO WORK FOR?
...
YOU DON'T KNOW THE HALF OF IT!
CHOSUN DYNASTY ERA.

Translator's note: The Chosun Dynasty existed during the early 1800's.

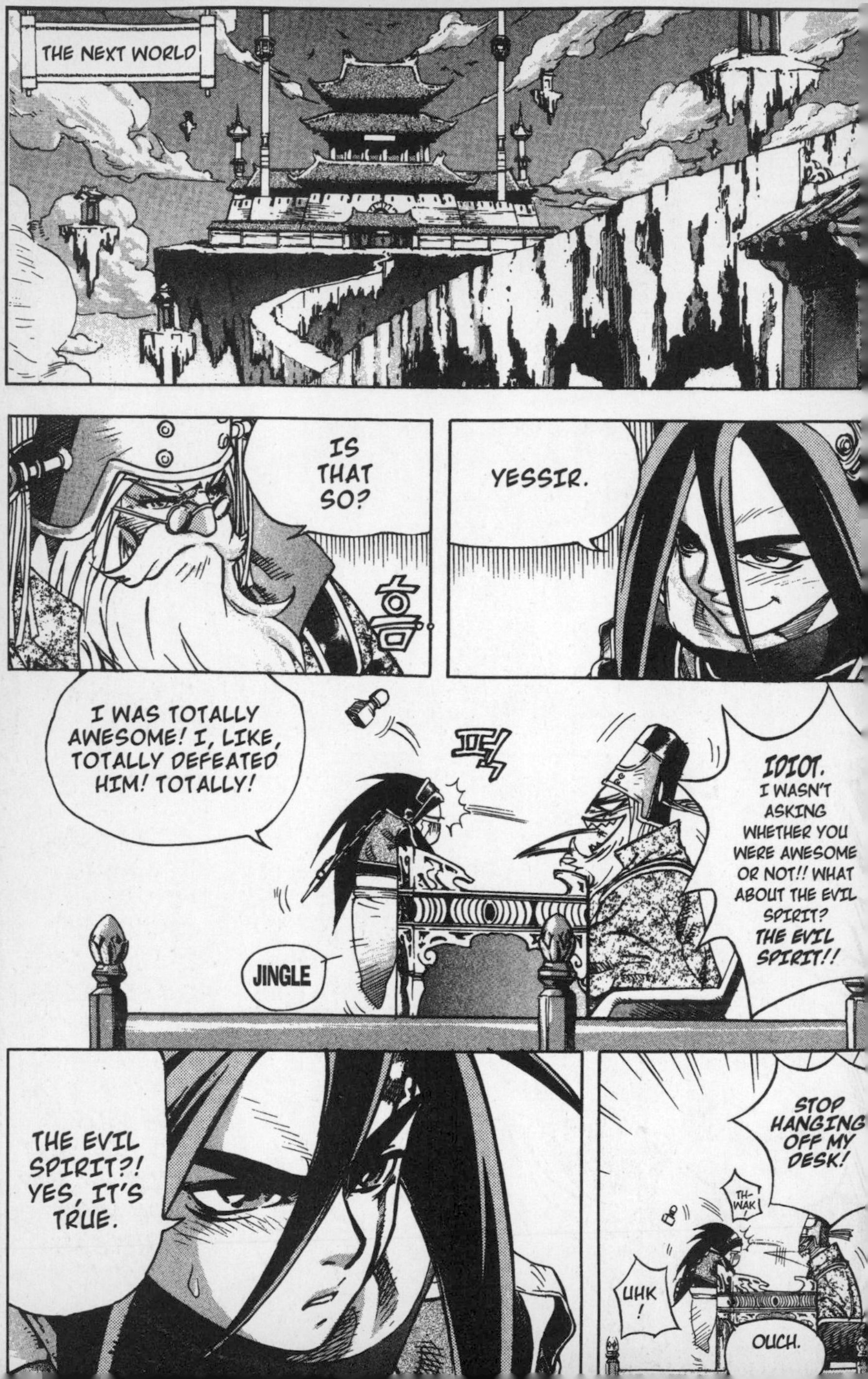
THE NEXT WORLD
IS THAT SO?
흠
YESSIR.
I WAS TOTALLY AWESOME! I, LIKE, TOTALLY DEFEATED HIM! TOTALLY!
JINGLE
IDIOT. I WASN'T ASKING WHETHER YOU WERE AWESOME OR NOT!! WHAT ABOUT THE EVIL SPIRIT? THE EVIL SPIRIT!!
THE EVIL SPIRIT?! YES, IT'S TRUE.
STOP HANGING OFF MY DESK!
TH-WAK!
UHK!
OUCH.

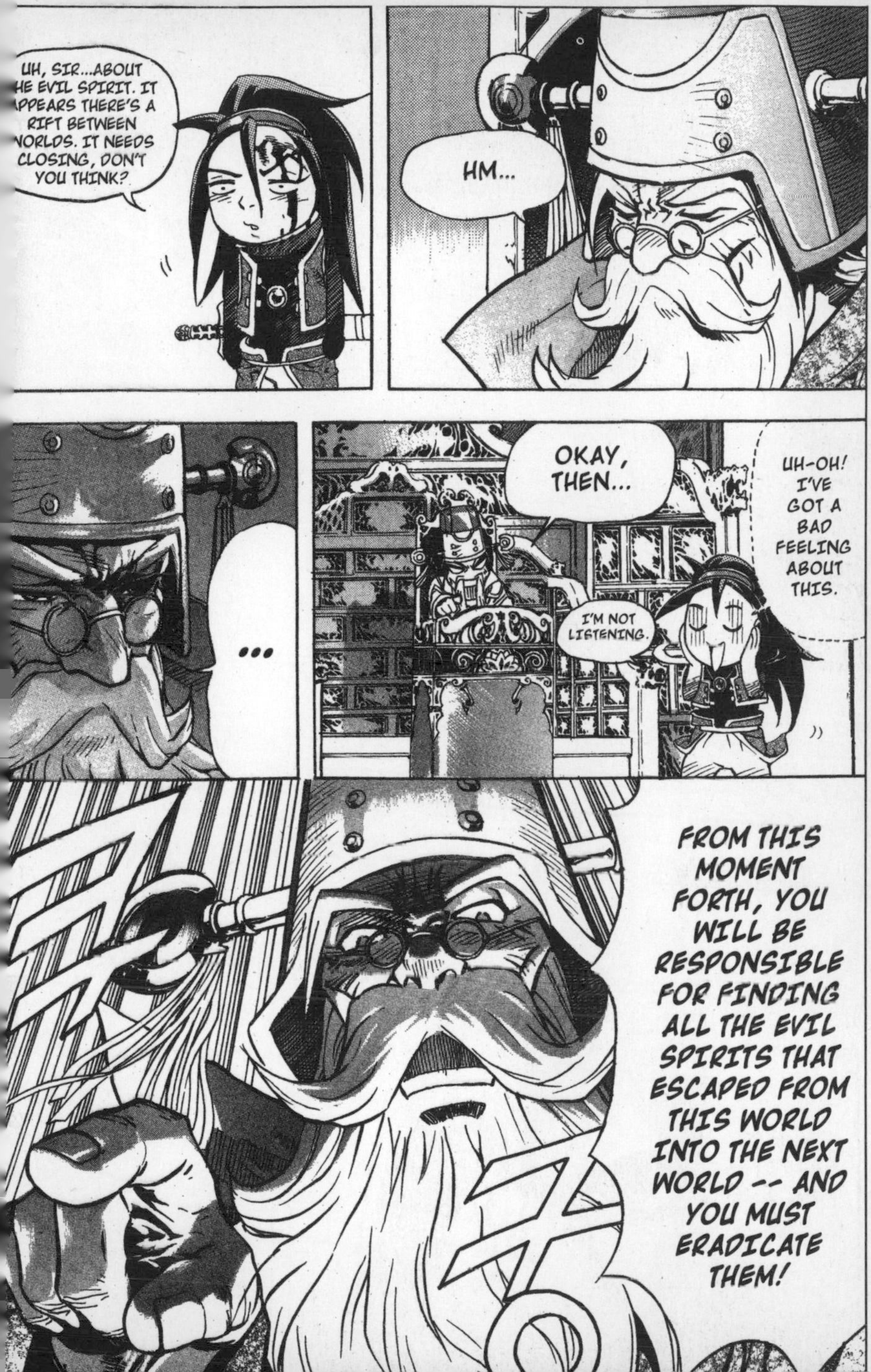
UH, SIR...ABOUT THE EVIL SPIRIT. IT APPEARS THERE'S A RIFT BETWEEN WORLDS. IT NEEDS CLOSING, DON'T YOU THINK?
HM...
...
OKAY, THEN...
I'M NOT LISTENING.
UH-OH! I'VE GOT A BAD FEELING ABOUT THIS.
FROM THIS MOMENT FORTH, YOU WILL BE RESPONSIBLE FOR FINDING ALL THE EVIL SPIRITS THAT ESCAPED FROM THIS WORLD INTO THE NEXT WORLD -- AND YOU MUST ERADICATE THEM!

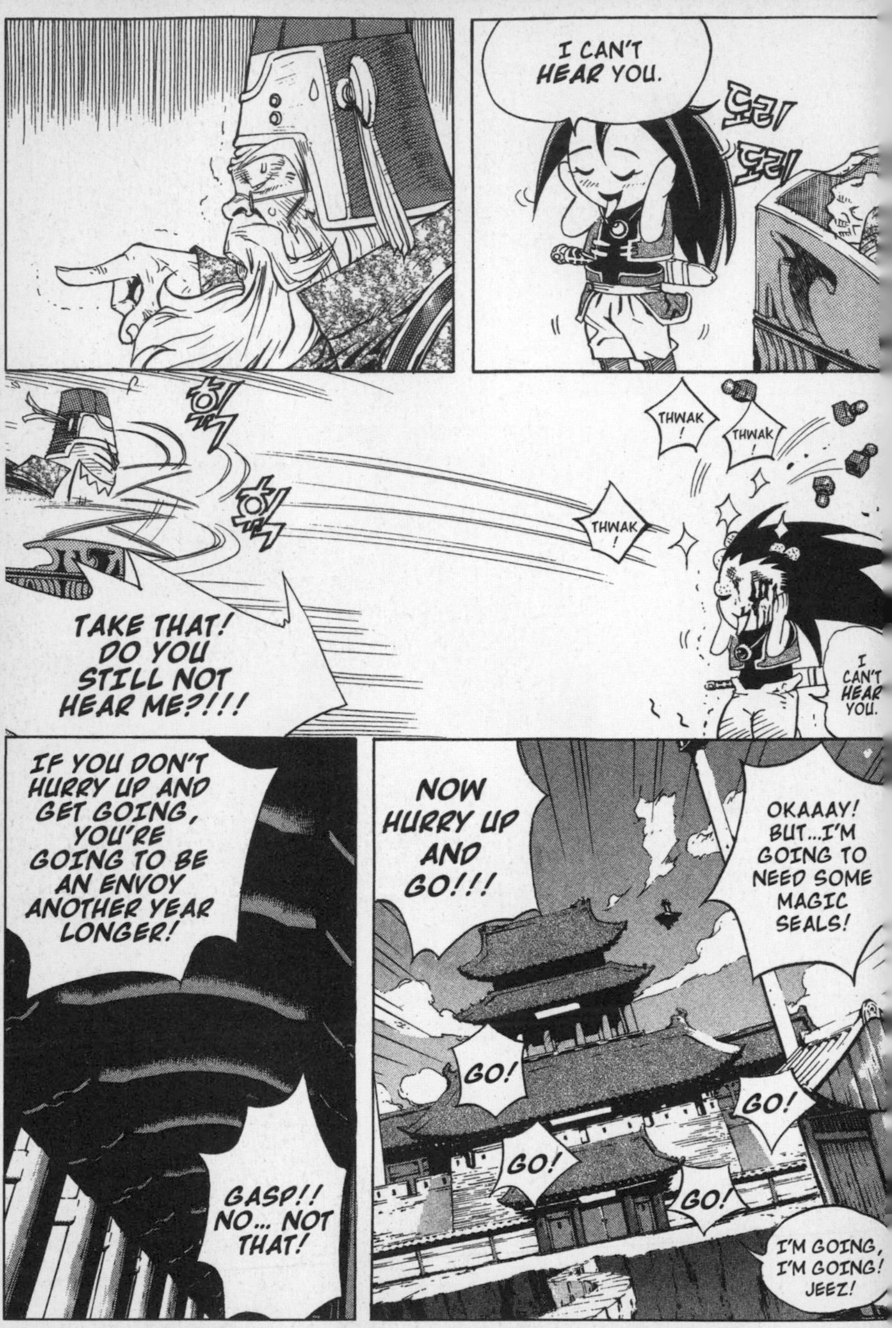
I CAN'T HEAR YOU.
THWAK!
THWAK!
THWAK!
TAKE THAT! DO YOU STILL NOT HEAR ME?!!!
I CAN'T HEAR YOU.
IF YOU DON'T HURRY UP AND GET GOING, YOU'RE GOING TO BE AN ENVOY ANOTHER YEAR LONGER!
GASP!! NO... NOT THAT!
NOW HURRY UP AND GO!!!
OKAAAY! BUT...I'M GOING TO NEED SOME MAGIC SEALS!
GO!
GO!
GO!
GO!
I'M GOING, I'M GOING! JEEZ!

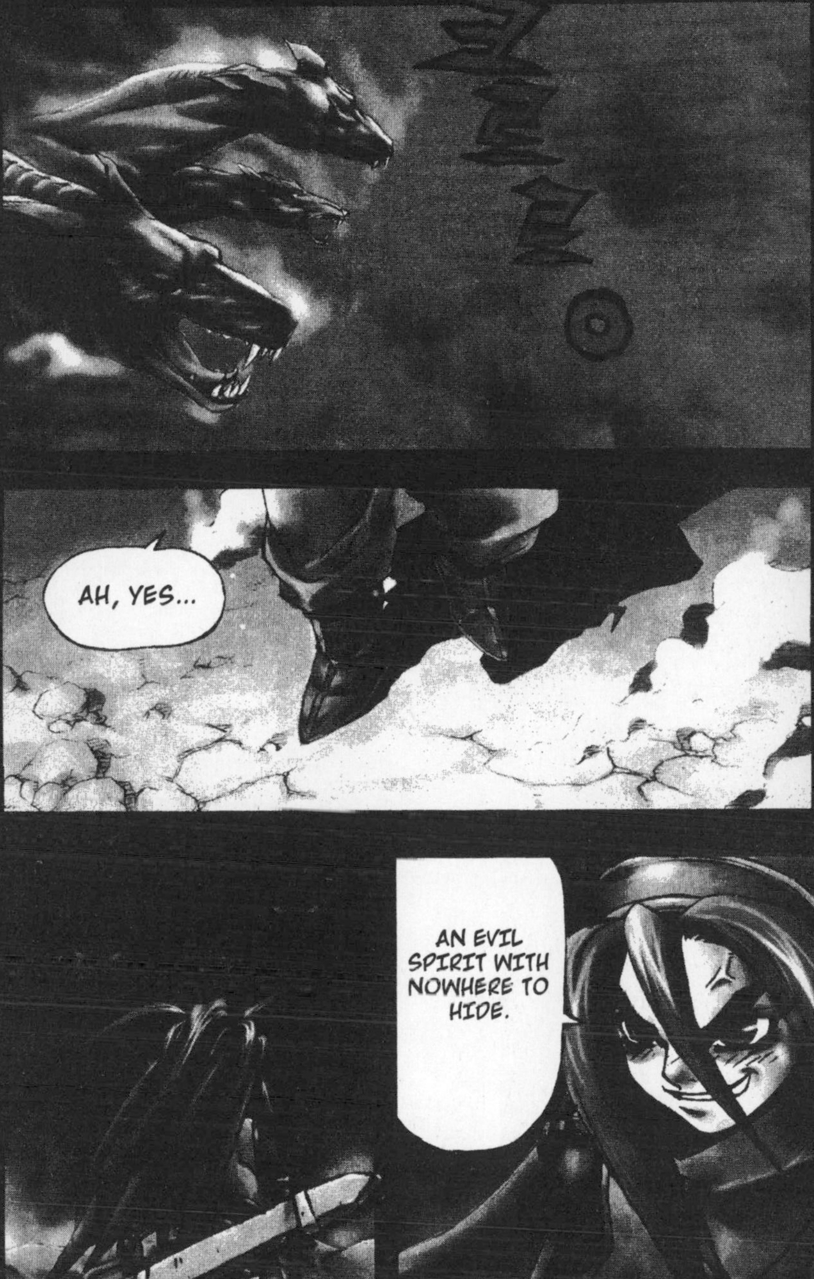
AH, YES...
AN EVIL SPIRIT WITH NOWHERE TO HIDE.

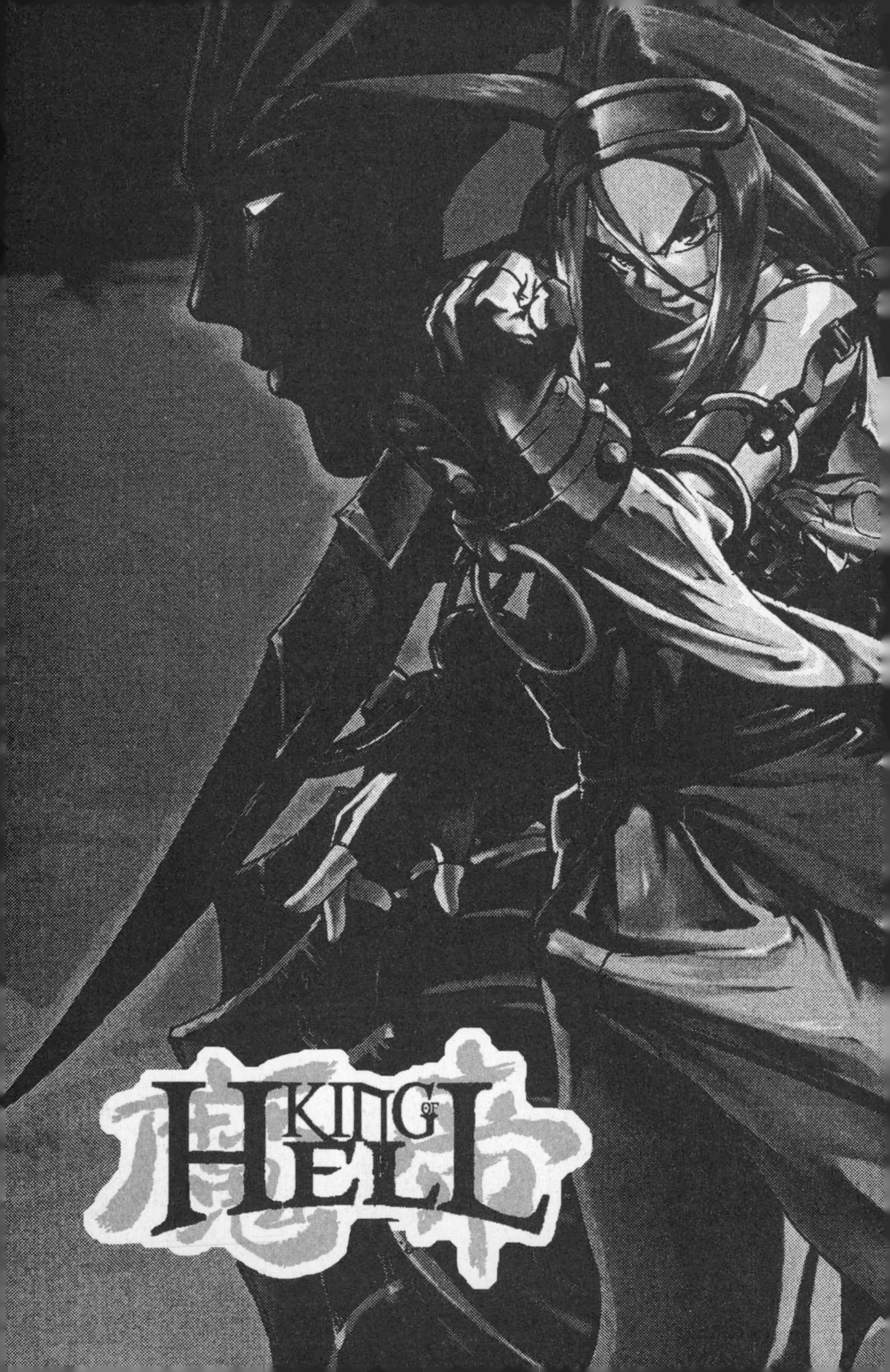
KING OF HELL

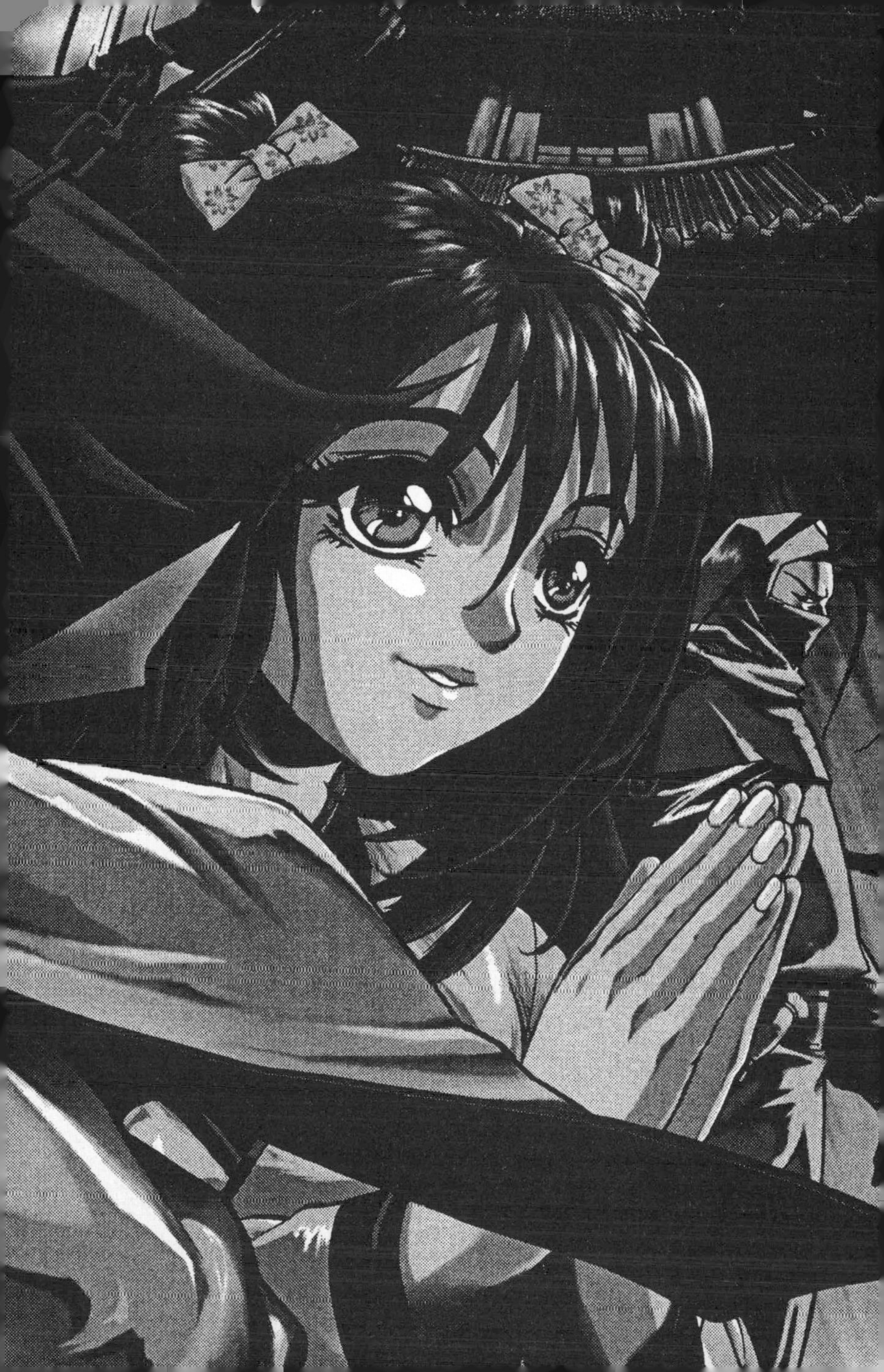

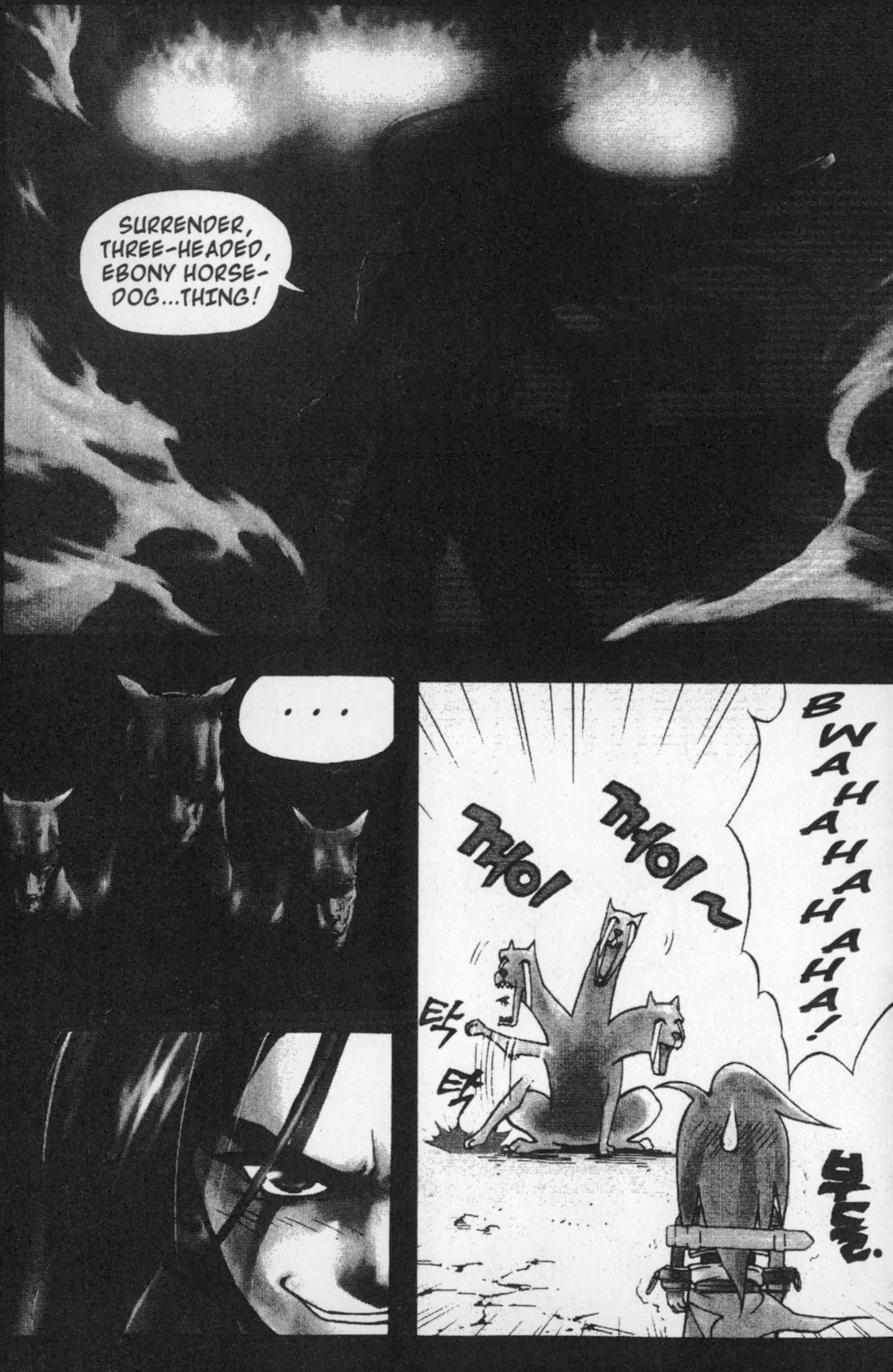
SURRENDER, THREE-HEADED, EBONY HORSE-DOG...THING!
...
THOI! THOI~
BWAHAHAHAHAHA!
탁
탁
부들.

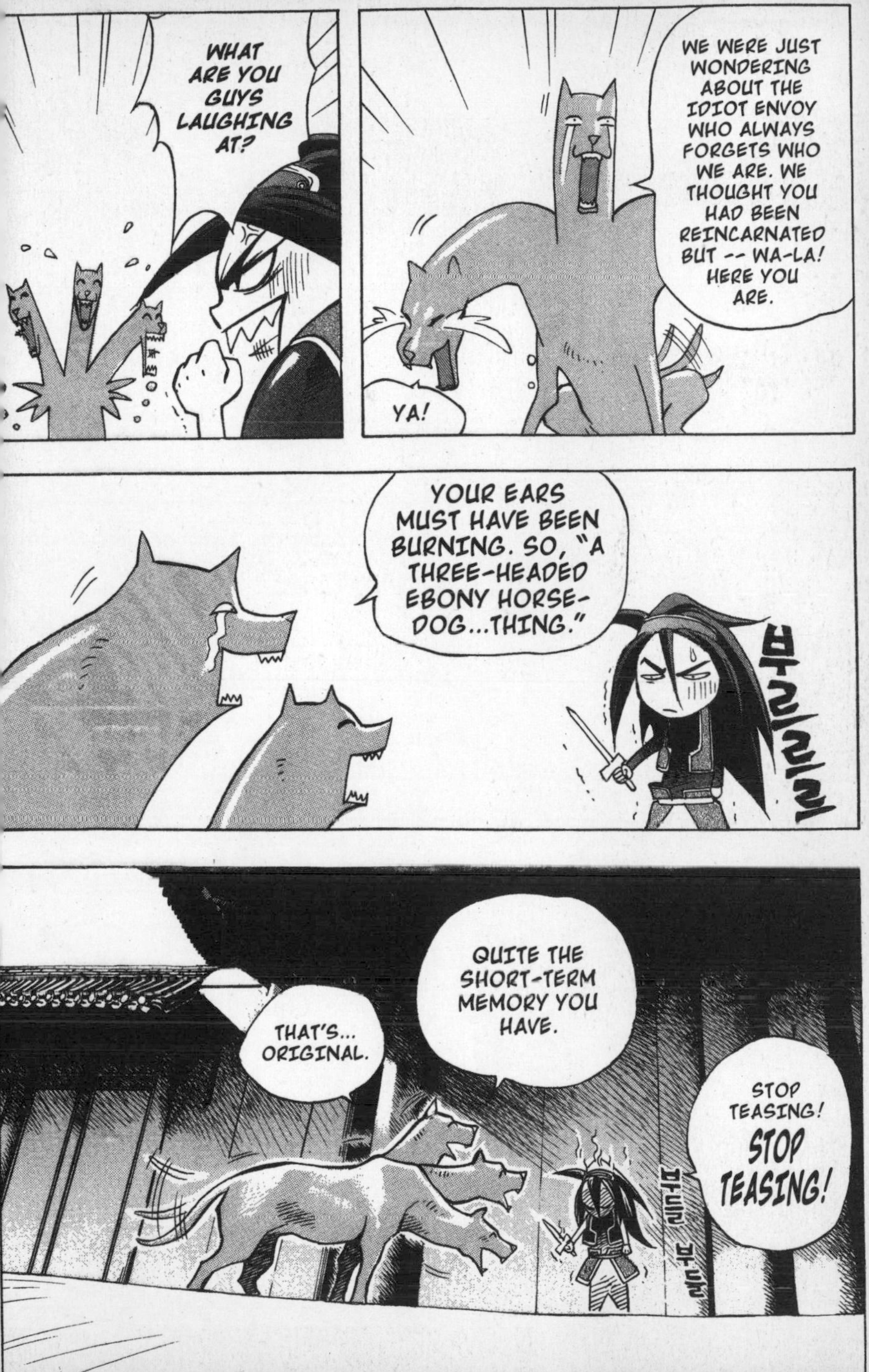
WHAT ARE YOU GUYS LAUGHING AT?
WE WERE JUST WONDERING ABOUT THE IDIOT ENVOY WHO ALWAYS FORGETS WHO WE ARE. WE THOUGHT YOU HAD BEEN REINCARNATED BUT -- WA-LA! HERE YOU ARE.
YA!
YOUR EARS MUST HAVE BEEN BURNING. SO, "A THREE-HEADED EBONY HORSE-DOG...THING."
THAT'S... ORIGINAL.
QUITE THE SHORT-TERM MEMORY YOU HAVE.
STOP TEASING! STOP TEASING!

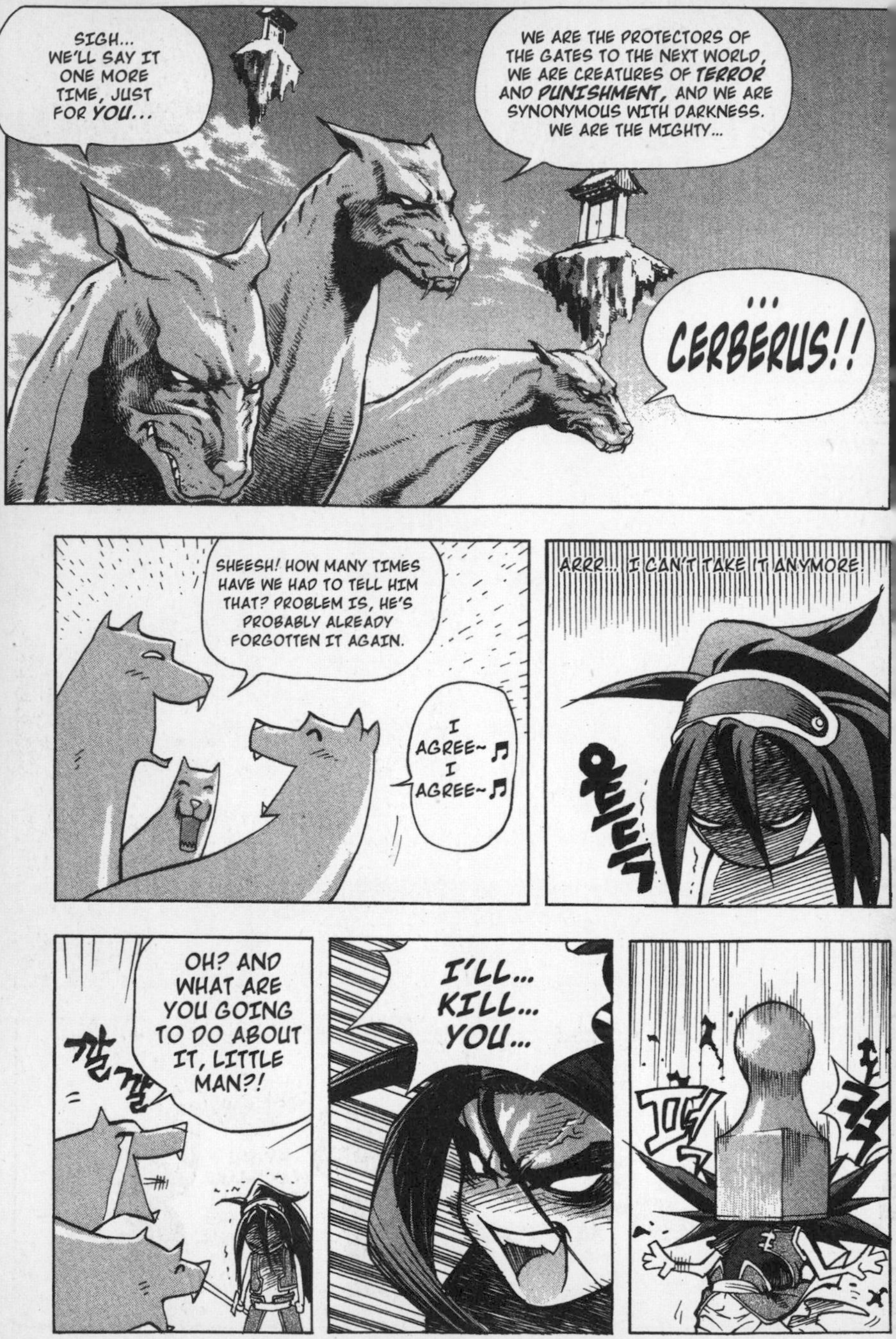
SIGH... WE'LL SAY IT ONE MORE TIME, JUST FOR YOU...
WE ARE THE PROTECTORS OF THE GATES TO THE NEXT WORLD, WE ARE CREATURES OF TERROR AND PUNISHMENT, AND WE ARE SYNONYMOUS WITH DARKNESS. WE ARE THE MIGHTY...
... CERBERUS!!
SHEESH! HOW MANY TIMES HAVE WE HAD TO TELL HIM THAT? PROBLEM IS, HE'S PROBABLY ALREADY FORGOTTEN IT AGAIN.
I AGREE~ ♫ I AGREE~ ♫
ARRR... I CAN'T TAKE IT ANYMORE.
OH? AND WHAT ARE YOU GOING TO DO ABOUT IT, LITTLE MAN?!
I'LL... KILL... YOU...

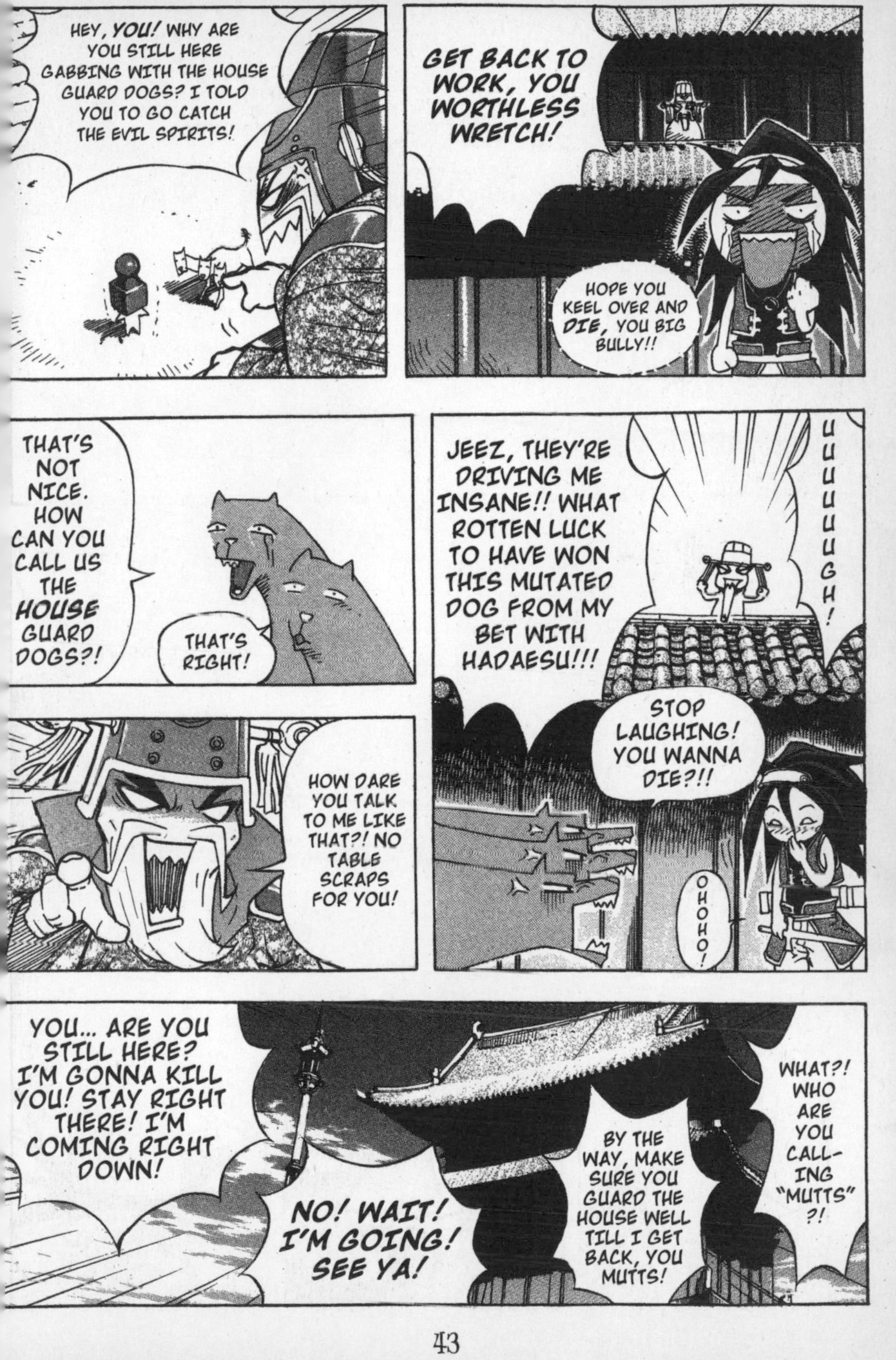
HEY, YOU! WHY ARE YOU STILL HERE GABBING WITH THE HOUSE GUARD DOGS? I TOLD YOU TO GO CATCH THE EVIL SPIRITS!
GET BACK TO WORK, YOU WORTHLESS WRETCH!
HOPE YOU KEEL OVER AND DIE, YOU BIG BULLY!!
THAT'S NOT NICE. HOW CAN YOU CALL US THE HOUSE GUARD DOGS?!
THAT'S RIGHT!
HOW DARE YOU TALK TO ME LIKE THAT?! NO TABLE SCRAPS FOR YOU!
JEEZ, THEY'RE DRIVING ME INSANE!! WHAT ROTTEN LUCK TO HAVE WON THIS MUTATED DOG FROM MY BET WITH HADAESU!!!
UUUUUUUUGH!
STOP LAUGHING! YOU WANNA DIE?!!
OHOHO!
YOU... ARE YOU STILL HERE? I'M GONNA KILL YOU! STAY RIGHT THERE! I'M COMING RIGHT DOWN!
NO! WAIT! I'M GOING! SEE YA!
BY THE WAY, MAKE SURE YOU GUARD THE HOUSE WELL TILL I GET BACK, YOU MUTTS!
WHAT?! WHO ARE YOU CALLING "MUTTS"?!

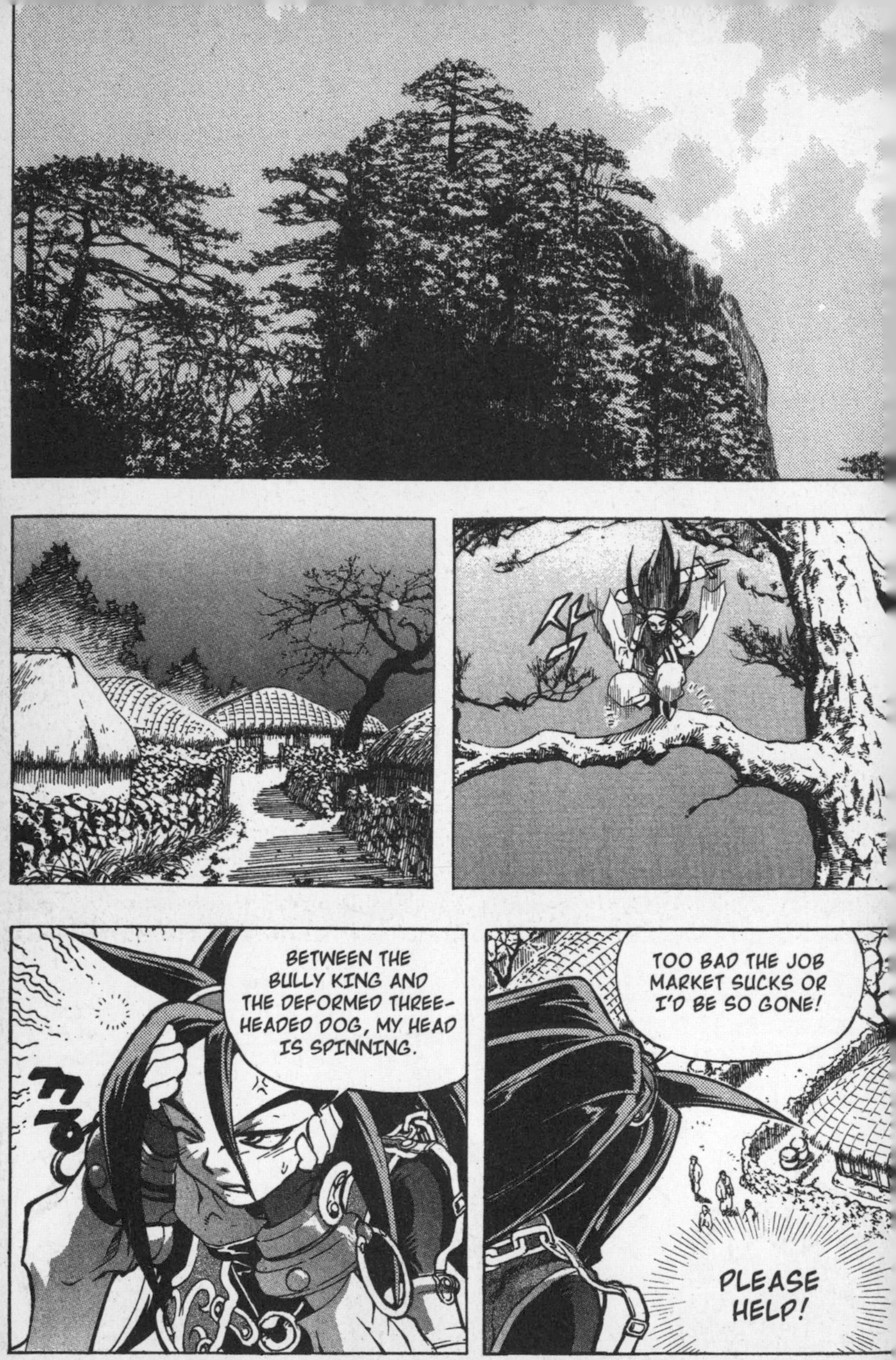
BETWEEN THE BULLY KING AND THE DEFORMED THREE-HEADED DOG, MY HEAD IS SPINNING.
TOO BAD THE JOB MARKET SUCKS OR I'D BE SO GONE!
PLEASE HELP!

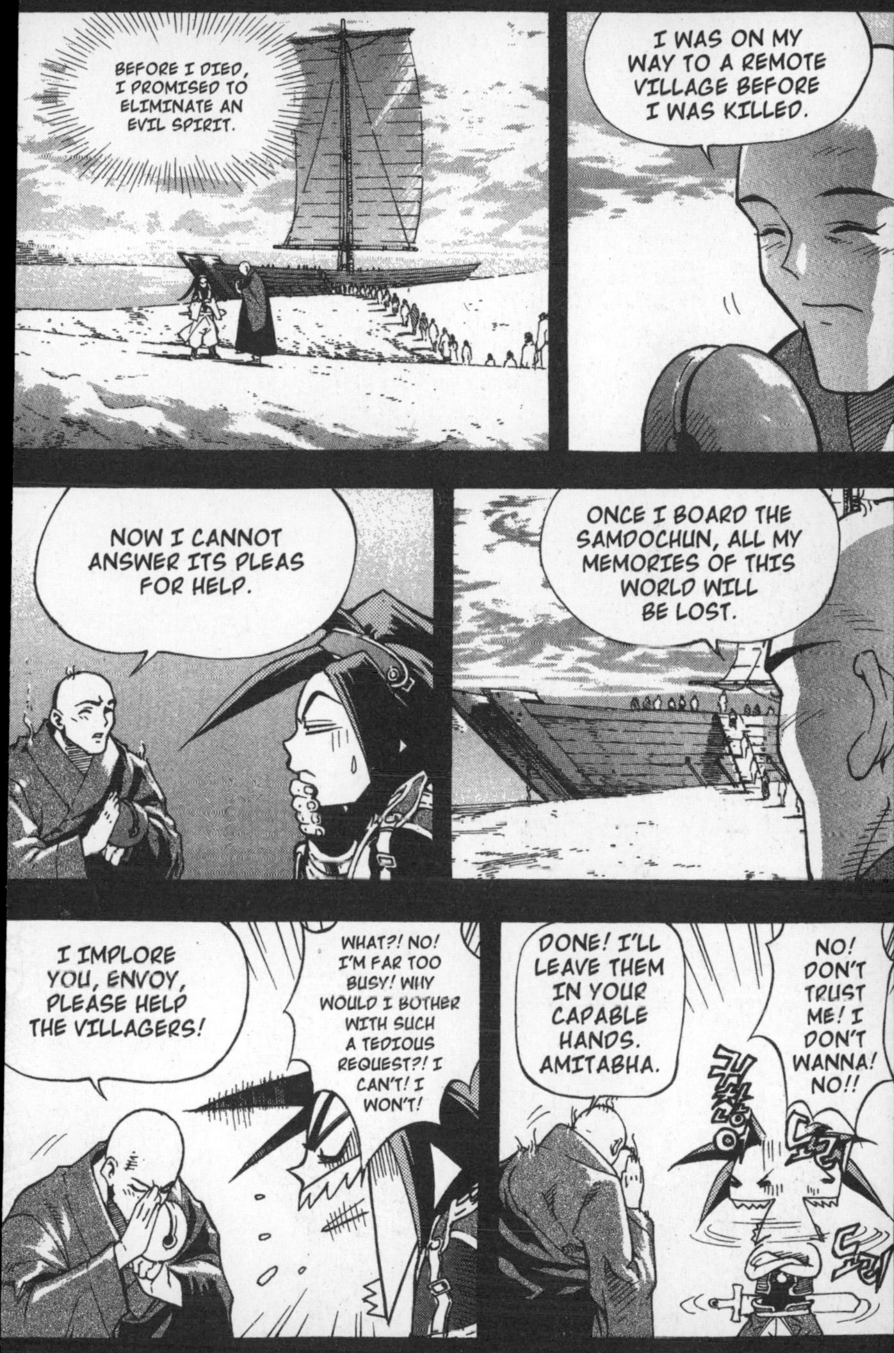
BEFORE I DIED, I PROMISED TO ELIMINATE AN EVIL SPIRIT.
I WAS ON MY WAY TO A REMOTE VILLAGE BEFORE I WAS KILLED.
NOW I CANNOT ANSWER ITS PLEAS FOR HELP.
ONCE I BOARD THE SAMDOCHUN, ALL MY MEMORIES OF THIS WORLD WILL BE LOST.
I IMPLORE YOU, ENVOY, PLEASE HELP THE VILLAGERS!
WHAT?! NO! I'M FAR TOO BUSY! WHY WOULD I BOTHER WITH SUCH A TEDIOUS REQUEST?! I CAN'T! I WON'T!
DONE! I'LL LEAVE THEM IN YOUR CAPABLE HANDS. AMITABHA.
NO! DON'T TRUST ME! I DON'T WANNA! NO!!

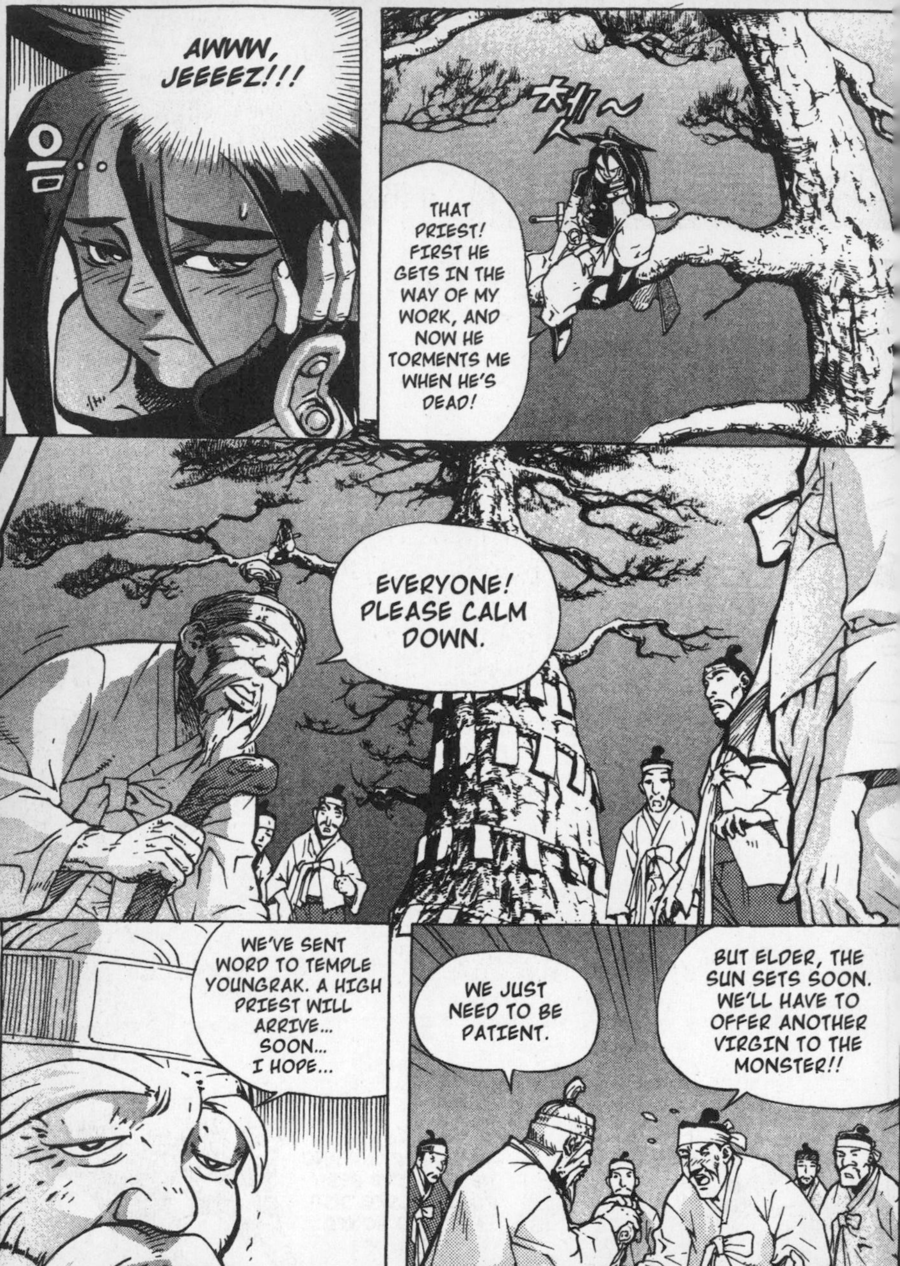
AWWW, JEEEEZ!!!
음
칫~
THAT PRIEST! FIRST HE GETS IN THE WAY OF MY WORK, AND NOW HE TORMENTS ME WHEN HE'S DEAD!
EVERYONE! PLEASE CALM DOWN.
WE'VE SENT WORD TO TEMPLE YOUNGRAK. A HIGH PRIEST WILL ARRIVE... SOON... I HOPE...
WE JUST NEED TO BE PATIENT.
BUT ELDER, THE SUN SETS SOON. WE'LL HAVE TO OFFER ANOTHER VIRGIN TO THE MONSTER!!

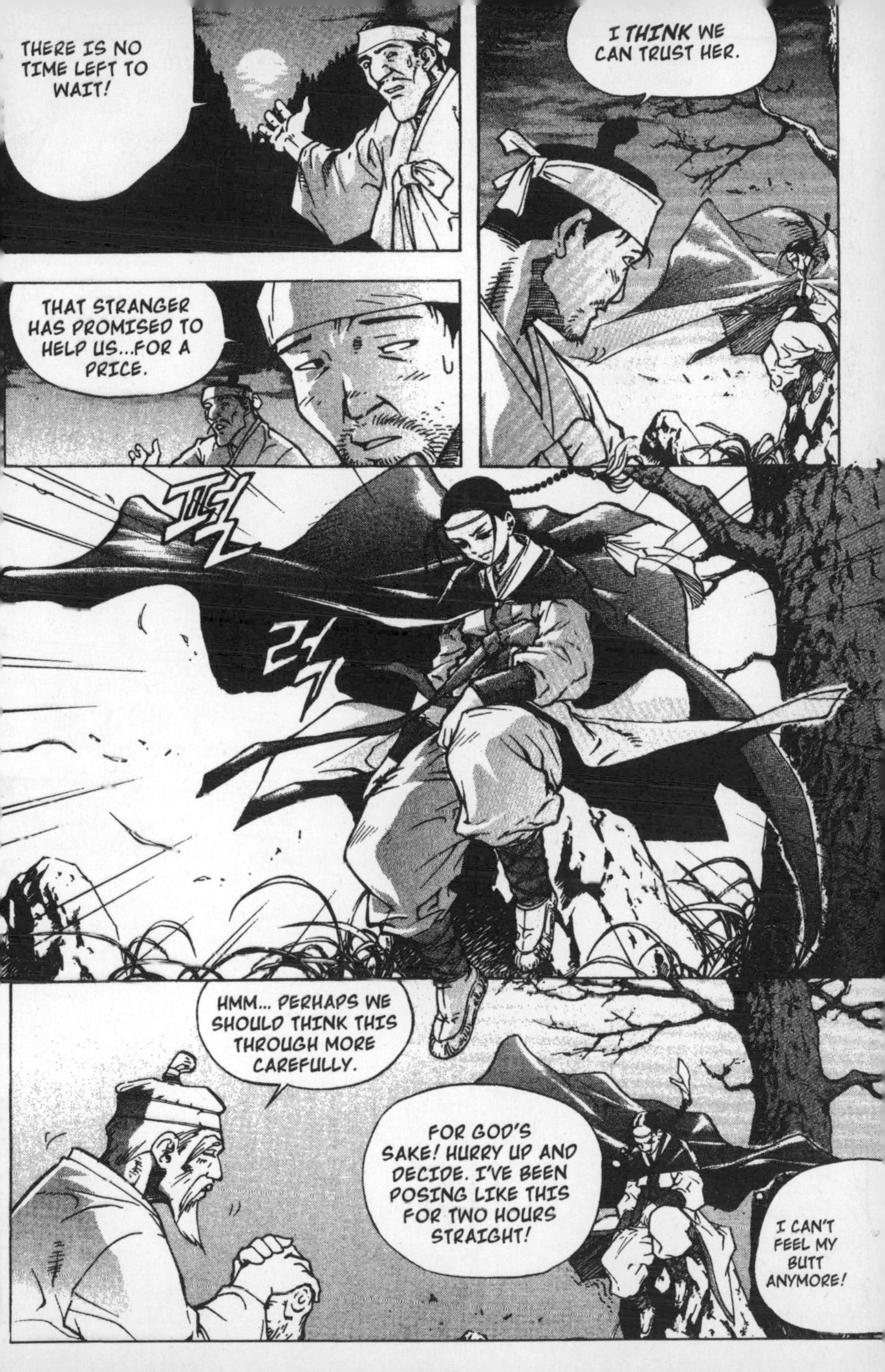
THERE IS NO TIME LEFT TO WAIT!
THAT STRANGER HAS PROMISED TO HELP US...FOR A PRICE.
I *THINK* WE CAN TRUST HER.
HMM... PERHAPS WE SHOULD THINK THIS THROUGH MORE CAREFULLY.
FOR GOD'S SAKE! HURRY UP AND DECIDE. I'VE BEEN POSING LIKE THIS FOR TWO HOURS STRAIGHT!
I CAN'T FEEL MY BUTT ANYMORE!

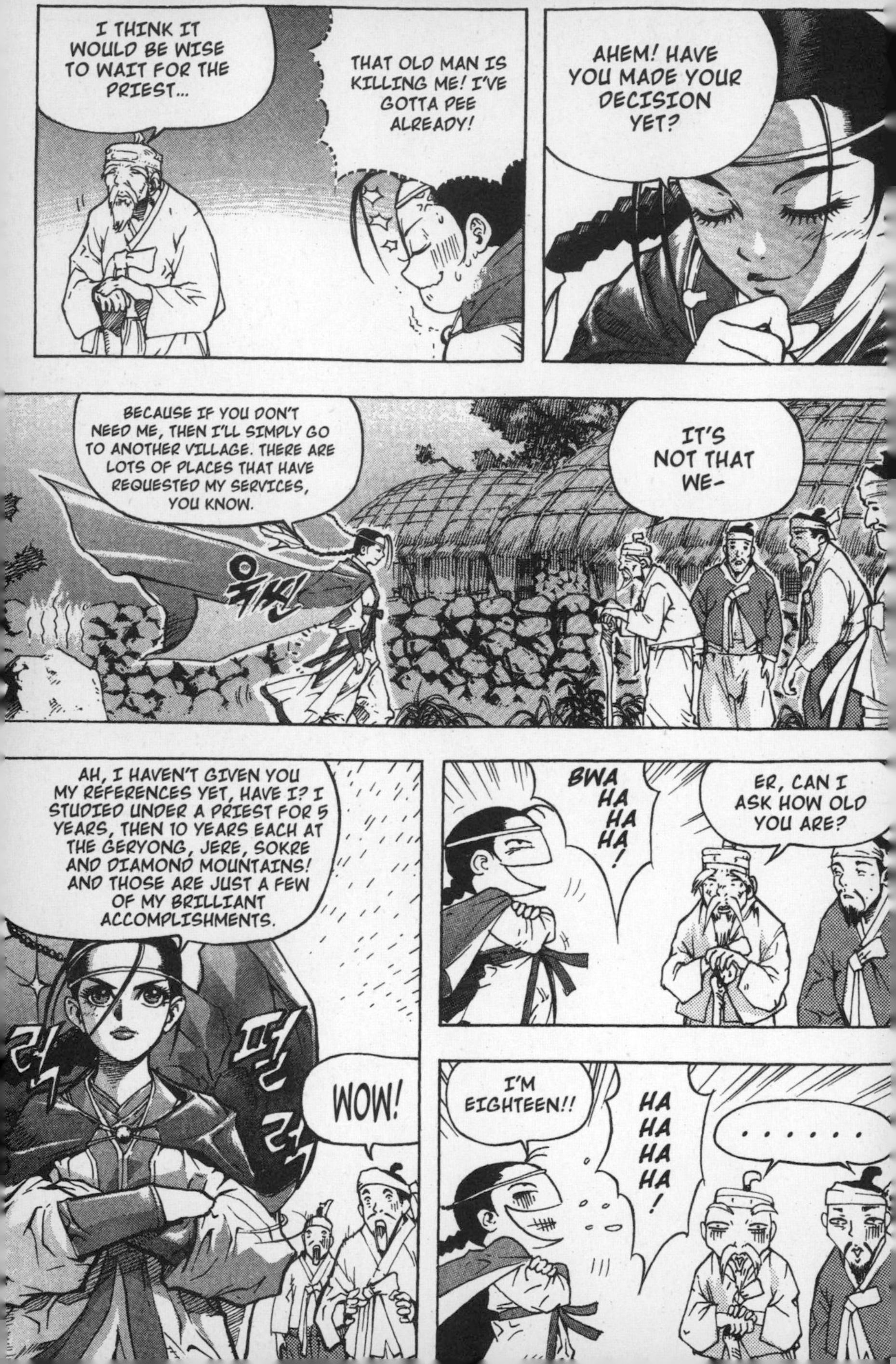
I THINK IT WOULD BE WISE TO WAIT FOR THE PRIEST...
THAT OLD MAN IS KILLING ME! I'VE GOTTA PEE ALREADY!
AHEM! HAVE YOU MADE YOUR DECISION YET?
BECAUSE IF YOU DON'T NEED ME, THEN I'LL SIMPLY GO TO ANOTHER VILLAGE. THERE ARE LOTS OF PLACES THAT HAVE REQUESTED MY SERVICES, YOU KNOW.
IT'S NOT THAT WE-
AH, I HAVEN'T GIVEN YOU MY REFERENCES YET, HAVE I? I STUDIED UNDER A PRIEST FOR 5 YEARS, THEN 10 YEARS EACH AT THE GERYONG, JERE, SOKRE AND DIAMOND MOUNTAINS! AND THOSE ARE JUST A FEW OF MY BRILLIANT ACCOMPLISHMENTS.
WOW!
BWA HA HA HA!
ER, CAN I ASK HOW OLD YOU ARE?
I'M EIGHTEEN!!
HA HA HA HA HA!
......

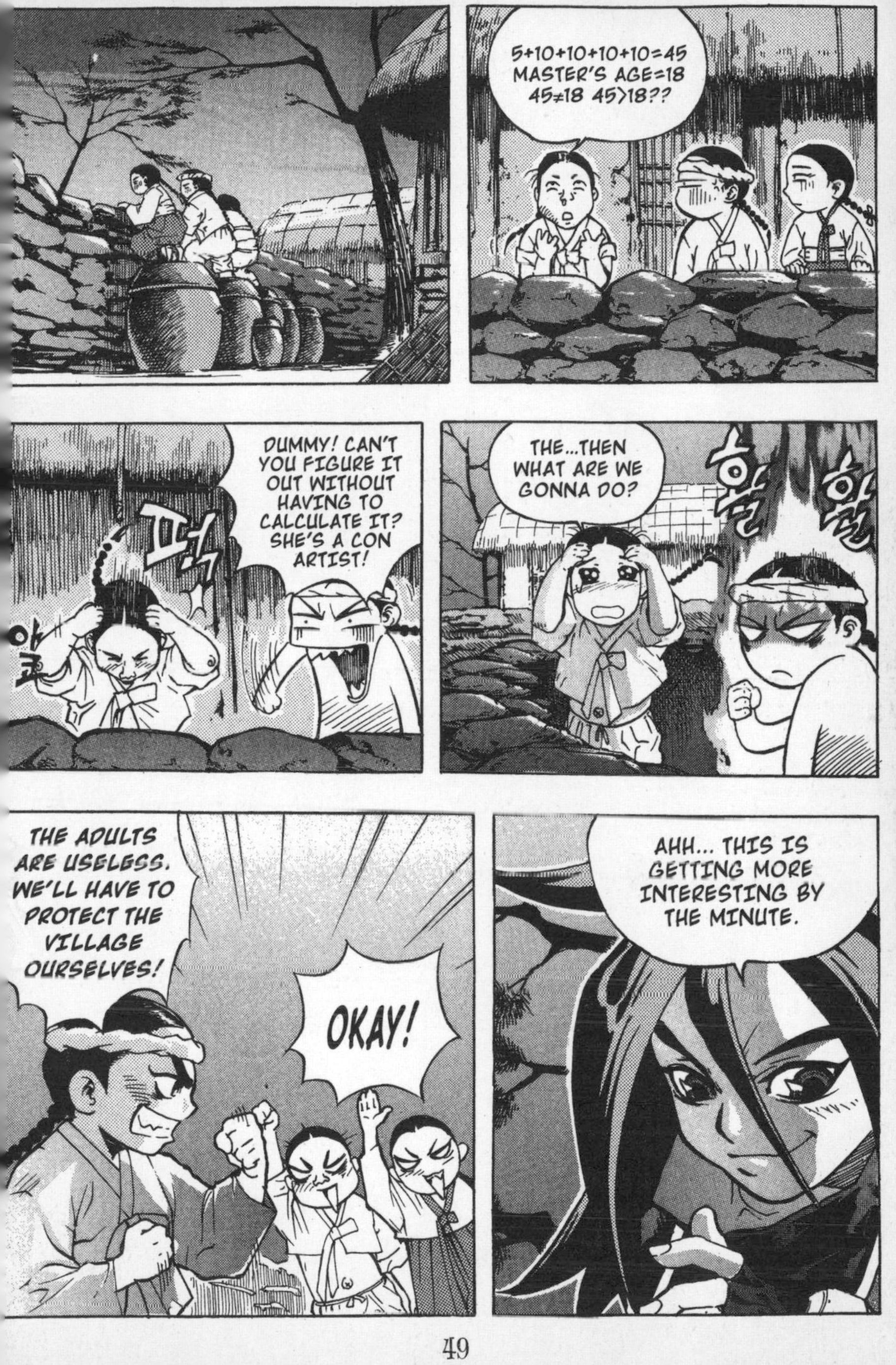
5+10+10+10+10=45
MASTER'S AGE=18
45≠18 45>18??
DUMMY! CAN'T YOU FIGURE IT OUT WITHOUT HAVING TO CALCULATE IT? SHE'S A CON ARTIST!
THE...THEN WHAT ARE WE GONNA DO?
THE ADULTS ARE USELESS. WE'LL HAVE TO PROTECT THE VILLAGE OURSELVES!
OKAY!
AHH... THIS IS GETTING MORE INTERESTING BY THE MINUTE.

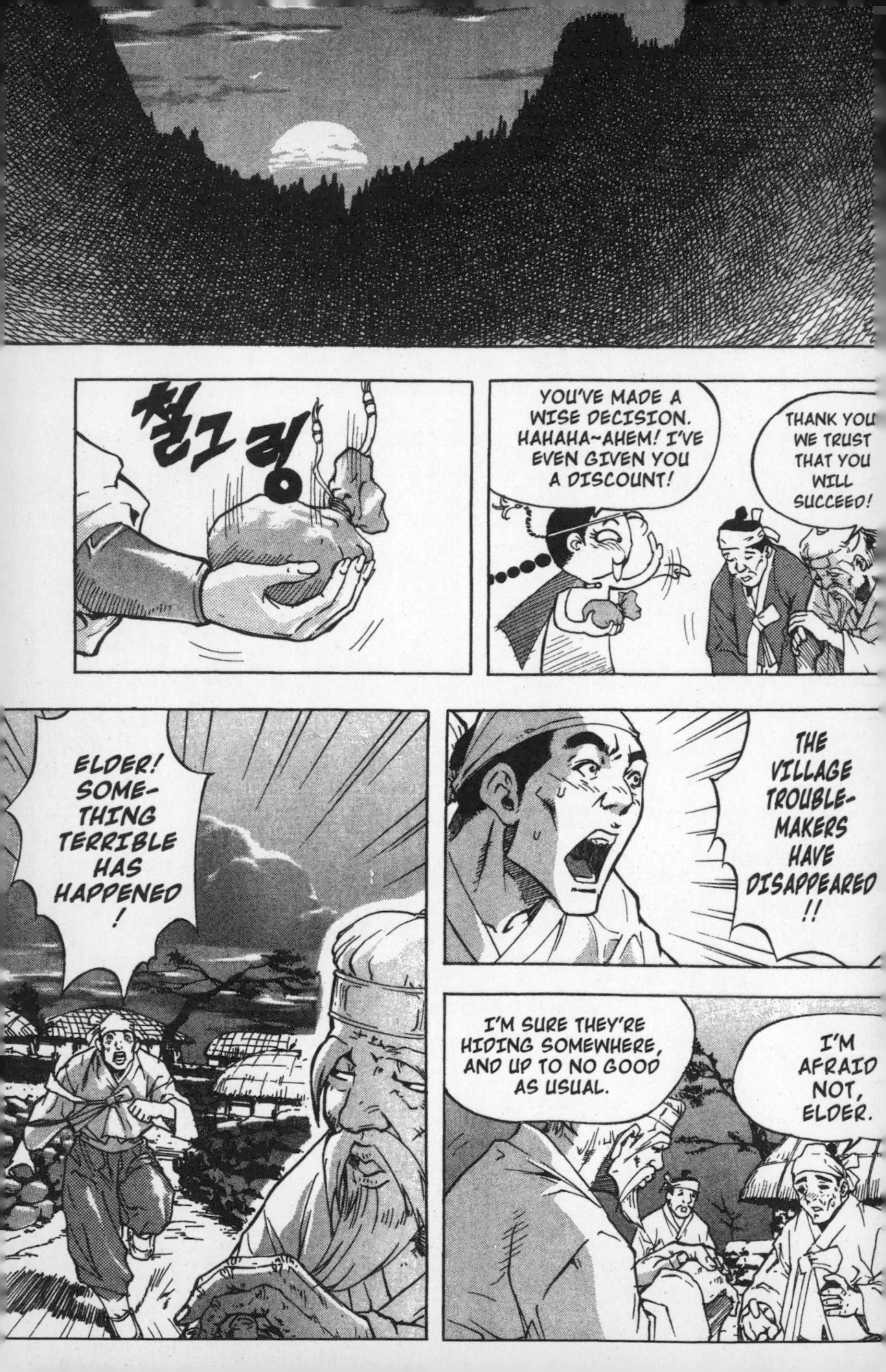
철그렁
YOU'VE MADE A WISE DECISION. HAHAHA~AHEM! I'VE EVEN GIVEN YOU A DISCOUNT!
THANK YOU WE TRUST THAT YOU WILL SUCCEED!
ELDER! SOME-THING TERRIBLE HAS HAPPENED!
THE VILLAGE TROUBLE-MAKERS HAVE DISAPPEARED!!
I'M SURE THEY'RE HIDING SOMEWHERE, AND UP TO NO GOOD AS USUAL.
I'M AFRAID NOT, ELDER.

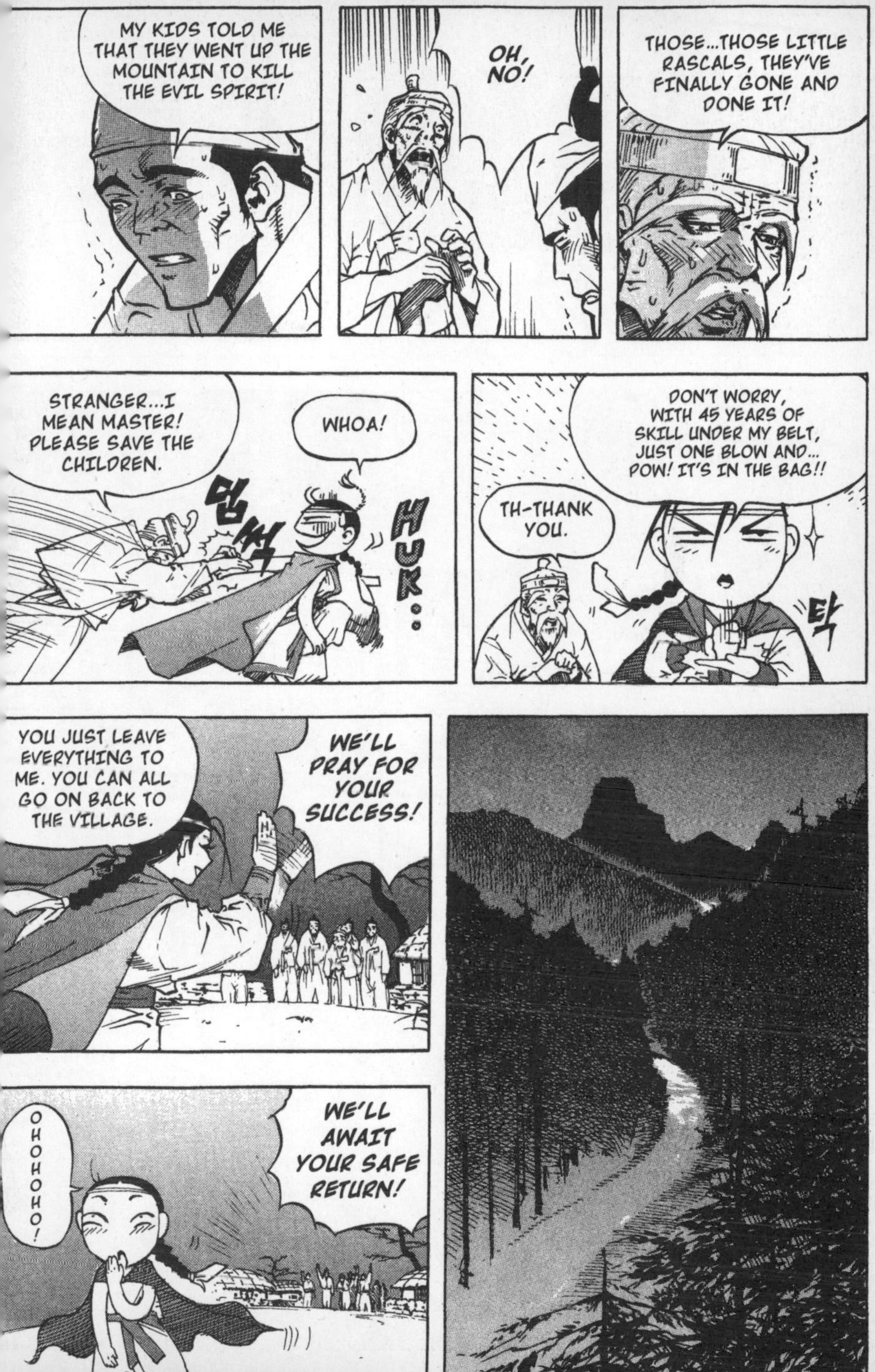
MY KIDS TOLD ME THAT THEY WENT UP THE MOUNTAIN TO KILL THE EVIL SPIRIT!
OH, NO!
THOSE...THOSE LITTLE RASCALS, THEY'VE FINALLY GONE AND DONE IT!
STRANGER...I MEAN MASTER! PLEASE SAVE THE CHILDREN.
WHOA!
HUK..
DON'T WORRY, WITH 45 YEARS OF SKILL UNDER MY BELT, JUST ONE BLOW AND... POW! IT'S IN THE BAG!!
TH-THANK YOU.
탁
YOU JUST LEAVE EVERYTHING TO ME. YOU CAN ALL GO ON BACK TO THE VILLAGE.
WE'LL PRAY FOR YOUR SUCCESS!
OHOHOHO!
WE'LL AWAIT YOUR SAFE RETURN!

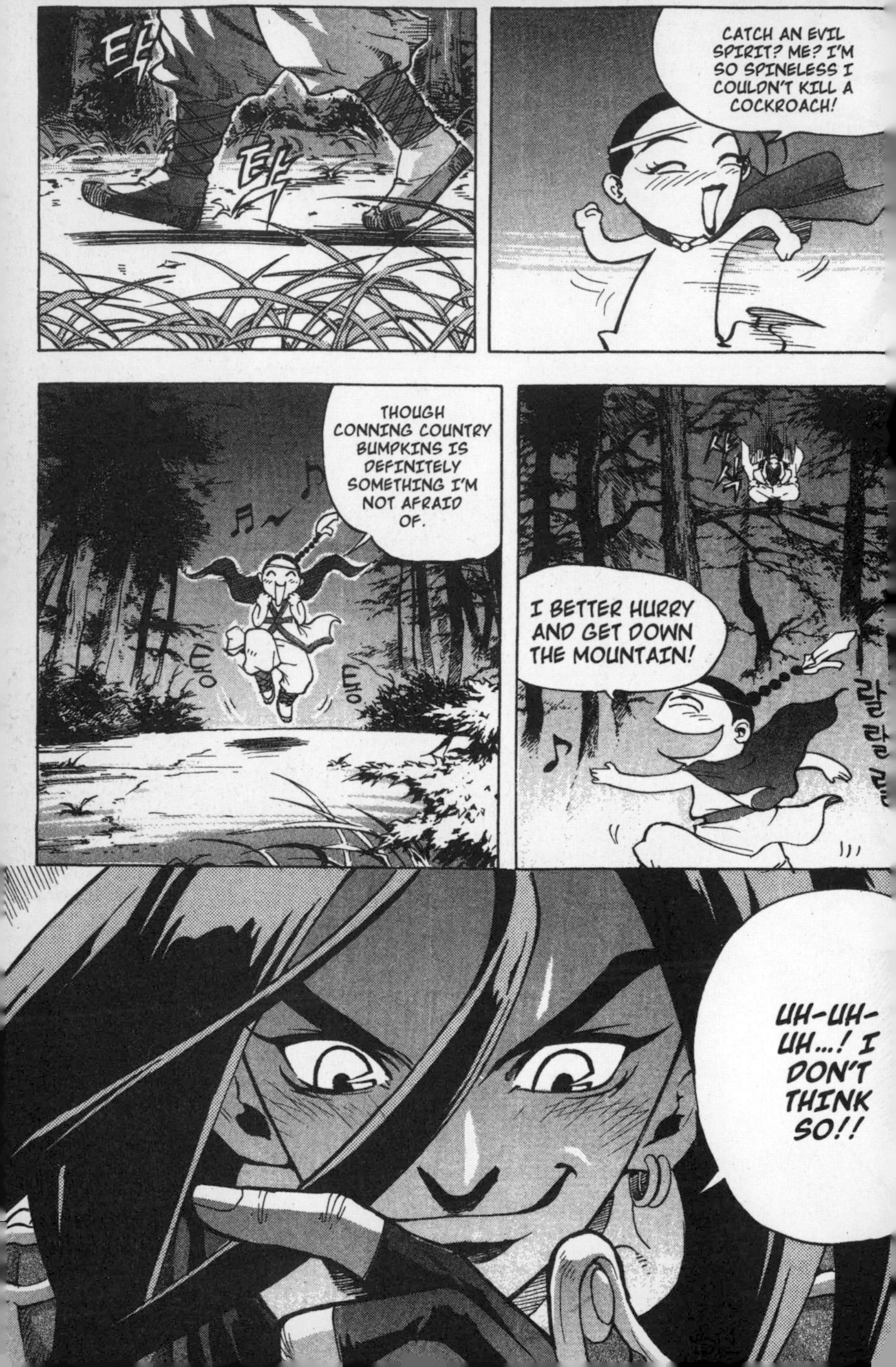
CATCH AN EVIL SPIRIT? ME? I'M SO SPINELESS I COULDN'T KILL A COCKROACH!
THOUGH CONNING COUNTRY BUMPKINS IS DEFINITELY SOMETHING I'M NOT AFRAID OF.
I BETTER HURRY AND GET DOWN THE MOUNTAIN!
UH-UH-UH...! I DON'T THINK SO!!

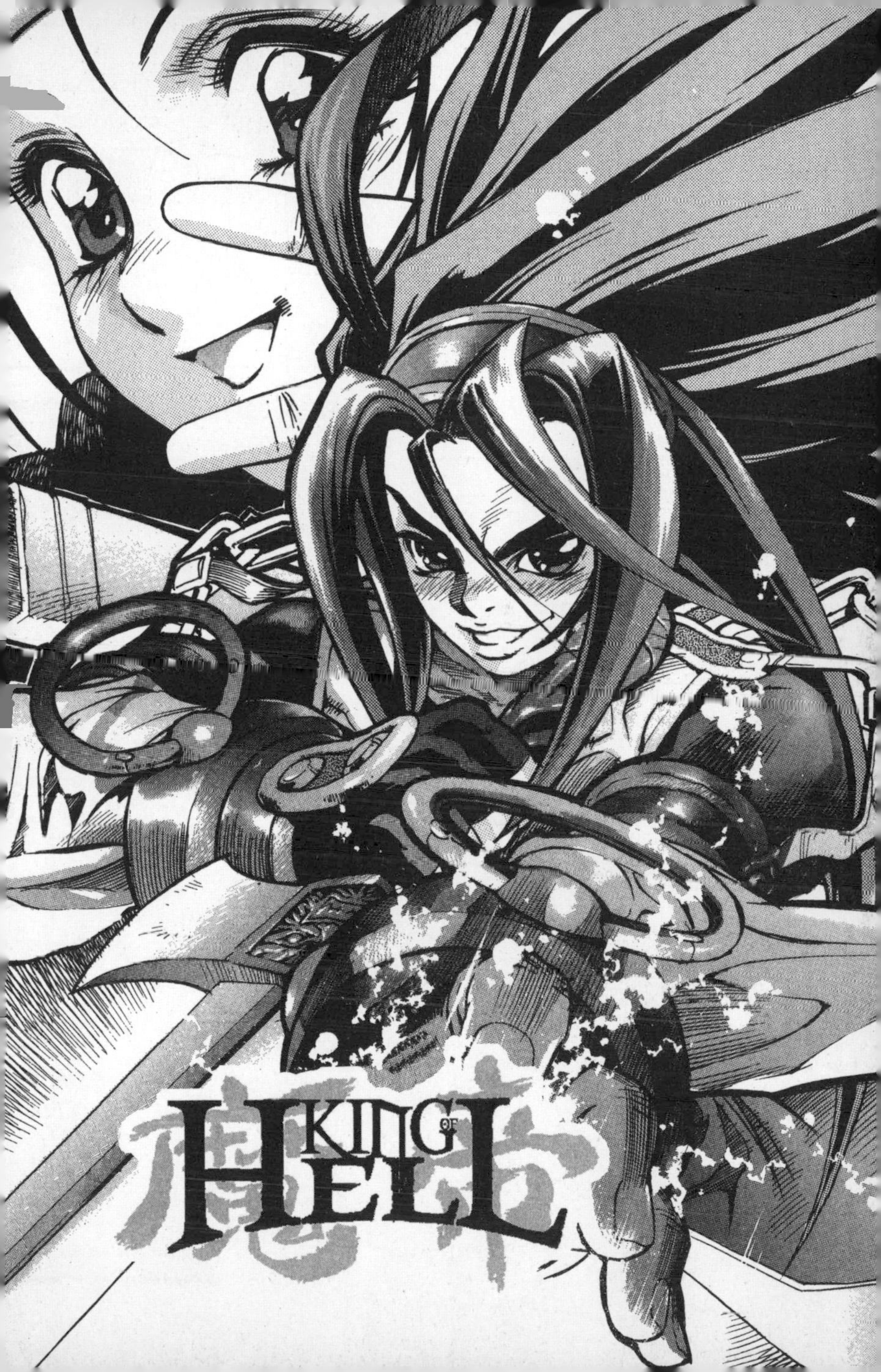
KING OF HELL

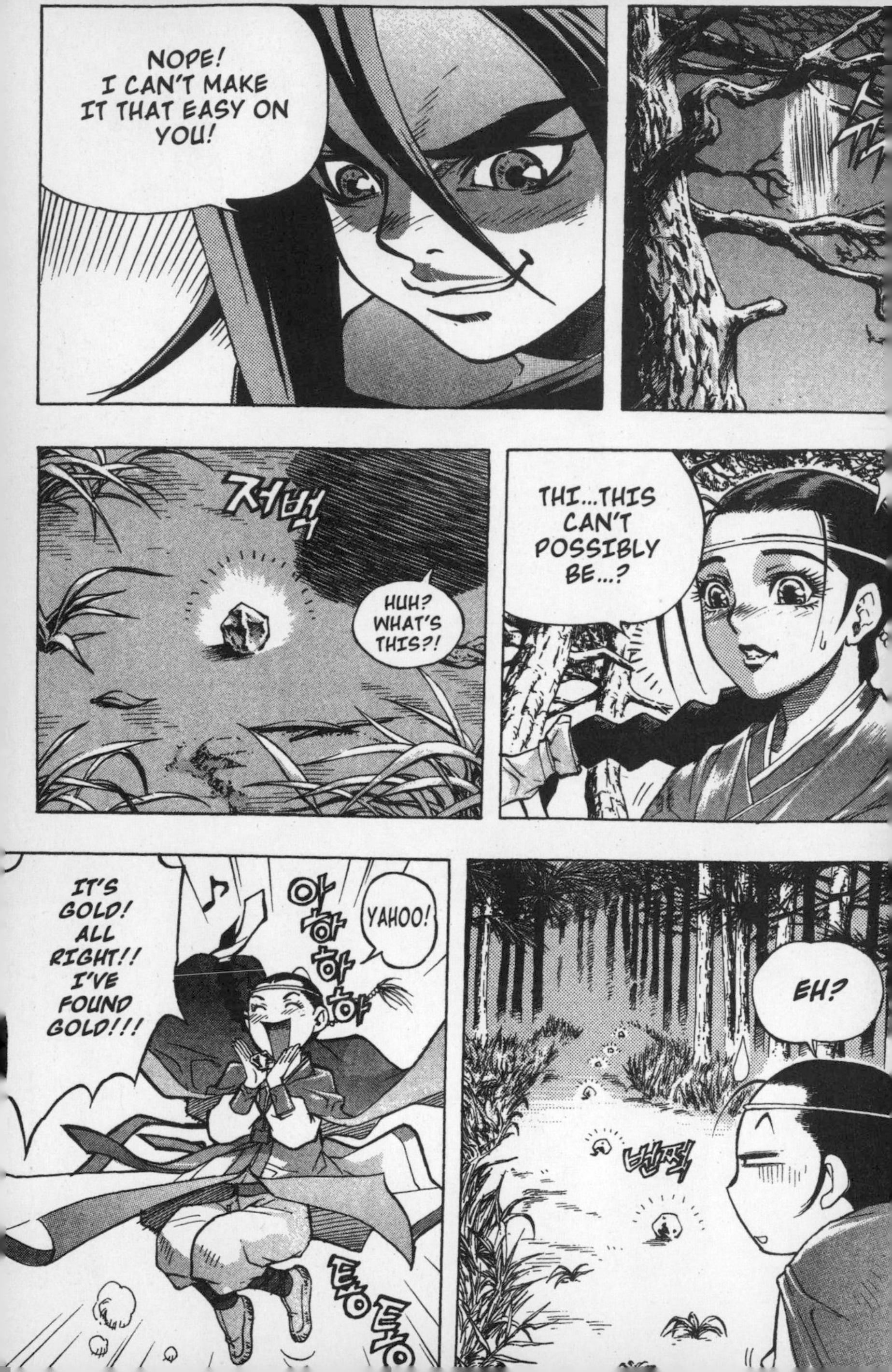
NOPE! I CAN'T MAKE IT THAT EASY ON YOU!
저벅
HUH? WHAT'S THIS?!
THI...THIS CAN'T POSSIBLY BE...?
IT'S GOLD! ALL RIGHT!! I'VE FOUND GOLD!!!
아하하하
YAHOO!
통통
EH?
반짝

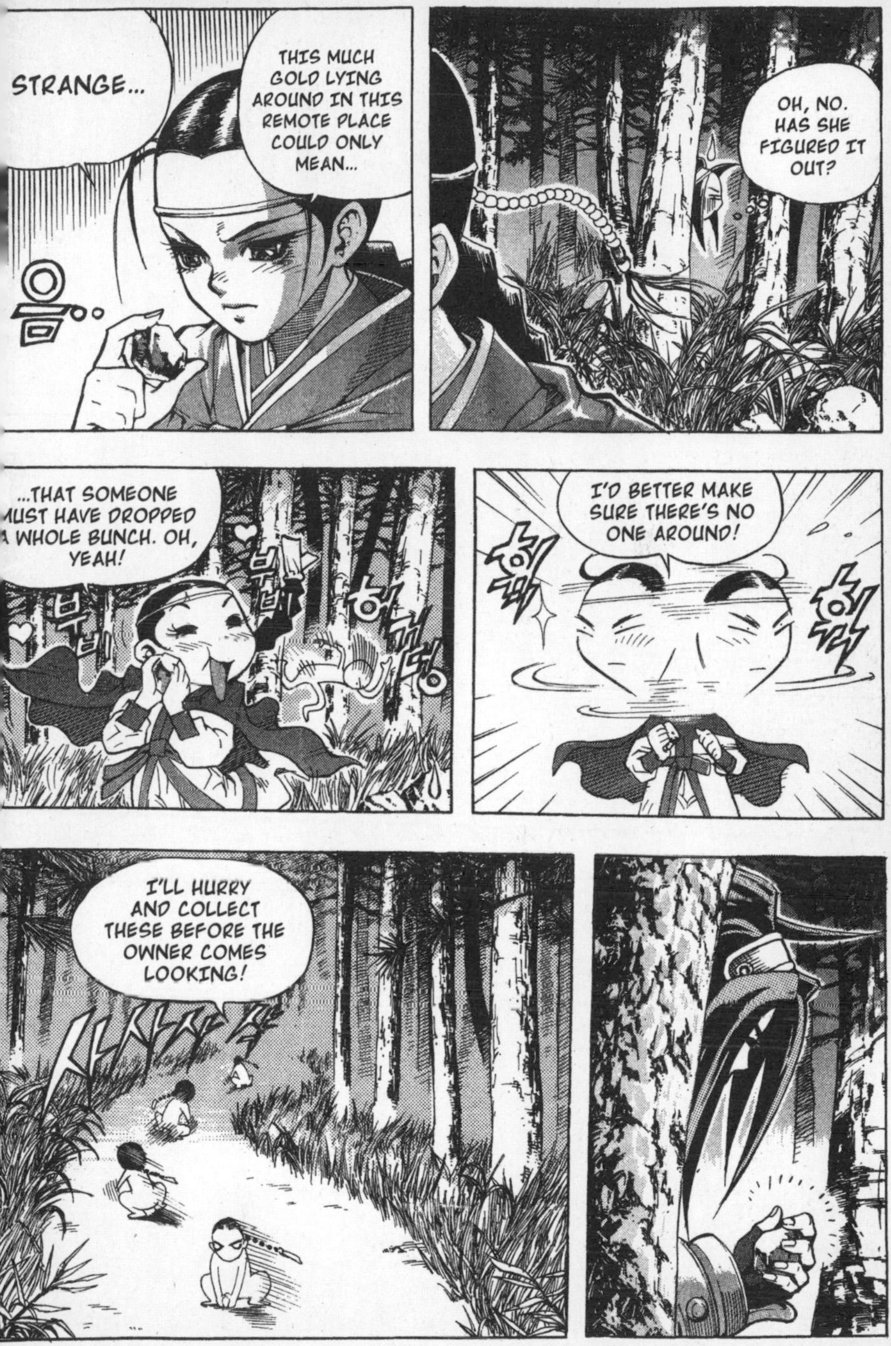
STRANGE...
THIS MUCH GOLD LYING AROUND IN THIS REMOTE PLACE COULD ONLY MEAN...
음
OH, NO. HAS SHE FIGURED IT OUT?
...THAT SOMEONE MUST HAVE DROPPED A WHOLE BUNCH. OH, YEAH!
I'D BETTER MAKE SURE THERE'S NO ONE AROUND!
I'LL HURRY AND COLLECT THESE BEFORE THE OWNER COMES LOOKING!

YOU CALL YOURSELF A MASTER...

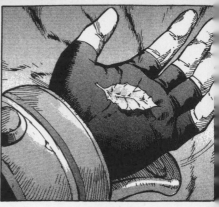

...AND THEN FALL FOR THIS OLD TRICK?

I CAN'T WAIT TO SEE YOUR FACE WHEN YOU REALIZE YOU'VE BEEN DUPED.

OOAAAAHH!!!

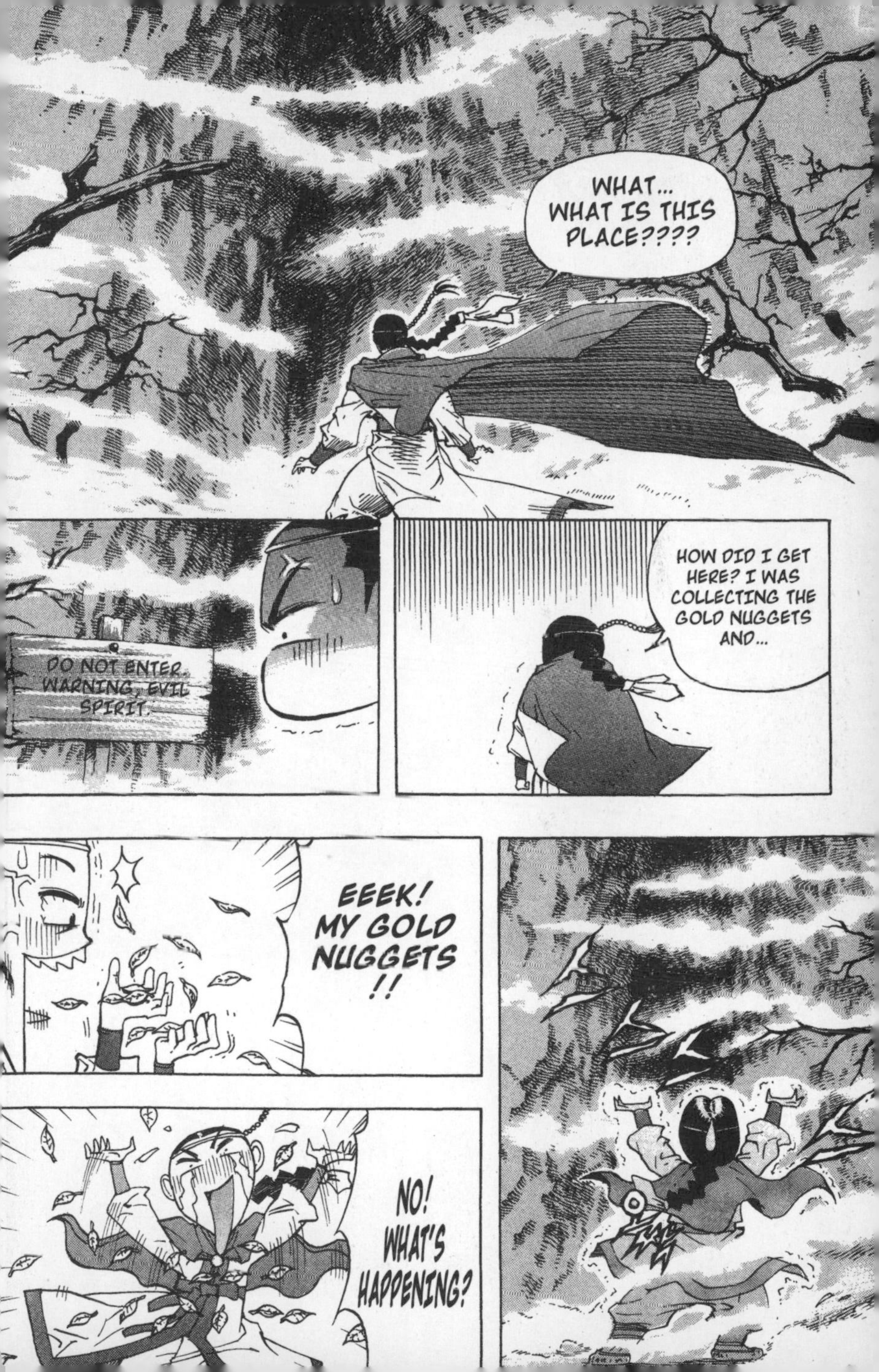
WHAT... WHAT IS THIS PLACE????
DO NOT ENTER. WARNING, EVIL SPIRIT.
HOW DID I GET HERE? I WAS COLLECTING THE GOLD NUGGETS AND...
EEEK! MY GOLD NUGGETS !!
NO! WHAT'S HAPPENING?

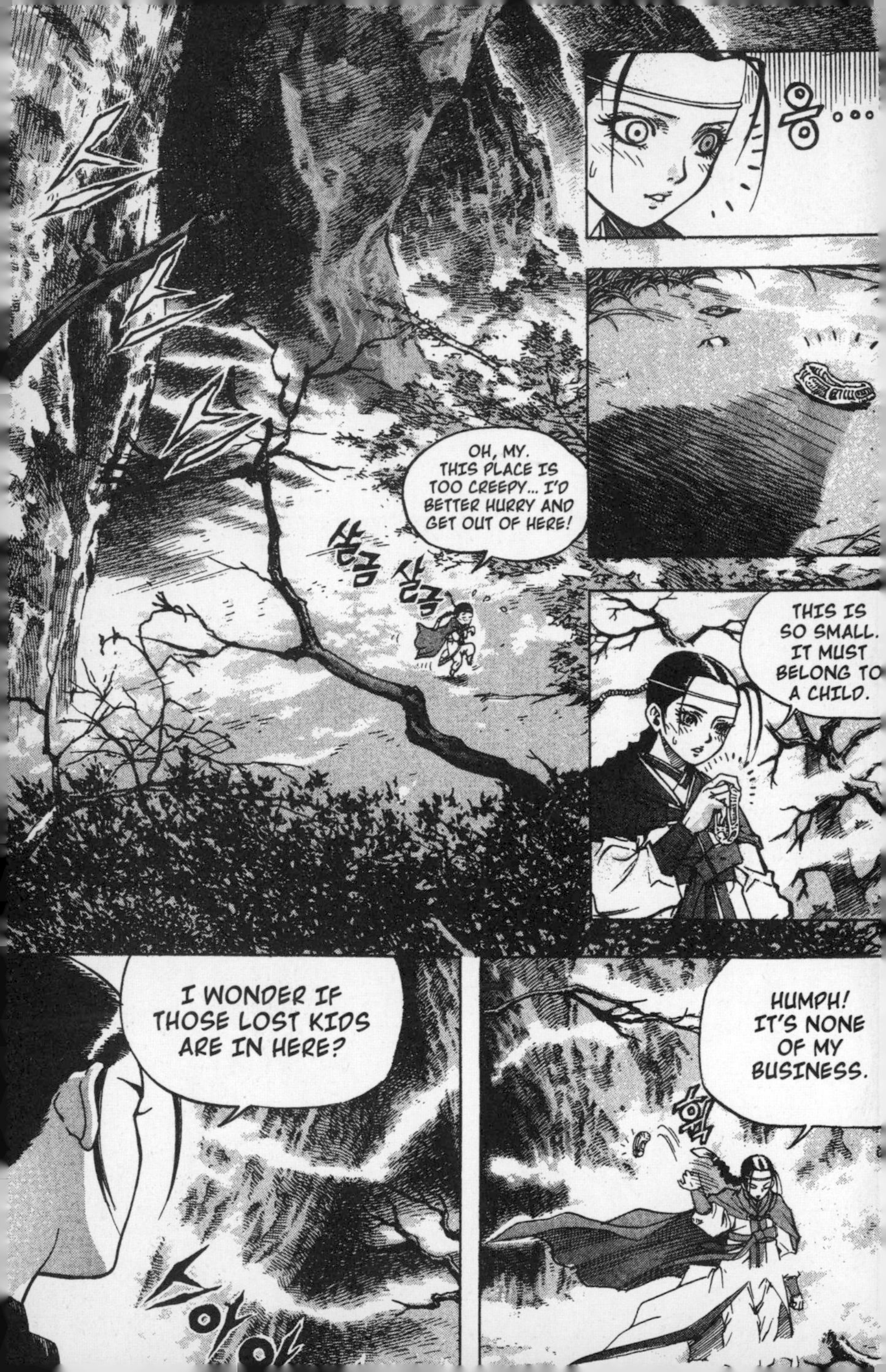
OH, MY. THIS PLACE IS TOO CREEPY... I'D BETTER HURRY AND GET OUT OF HERE!
살금 살금
응···
THIS IS SO SMALL. IT MUST BELONG TO A CHILD.
I WONDER IF THOSE LOST KIDS ARE IN HERE?
HUMPH! IT'S NONE OF MY BUSINESS.

PLEASE, I BEG YOU!

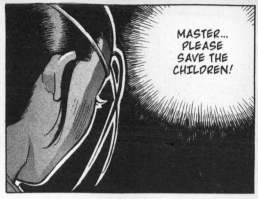

MASTER... PLEASE SAVE THE CHILDREN!

DAMN!

THE CHILDREN...

I'M NOTHING BUT A CON ARTIST!

I HAVE NO POWERS AND I'M SPINELESS TO BOOT!

SO, DON'T RELY ON ME...

...BECAUSE I CAN'T HANDLE IT.

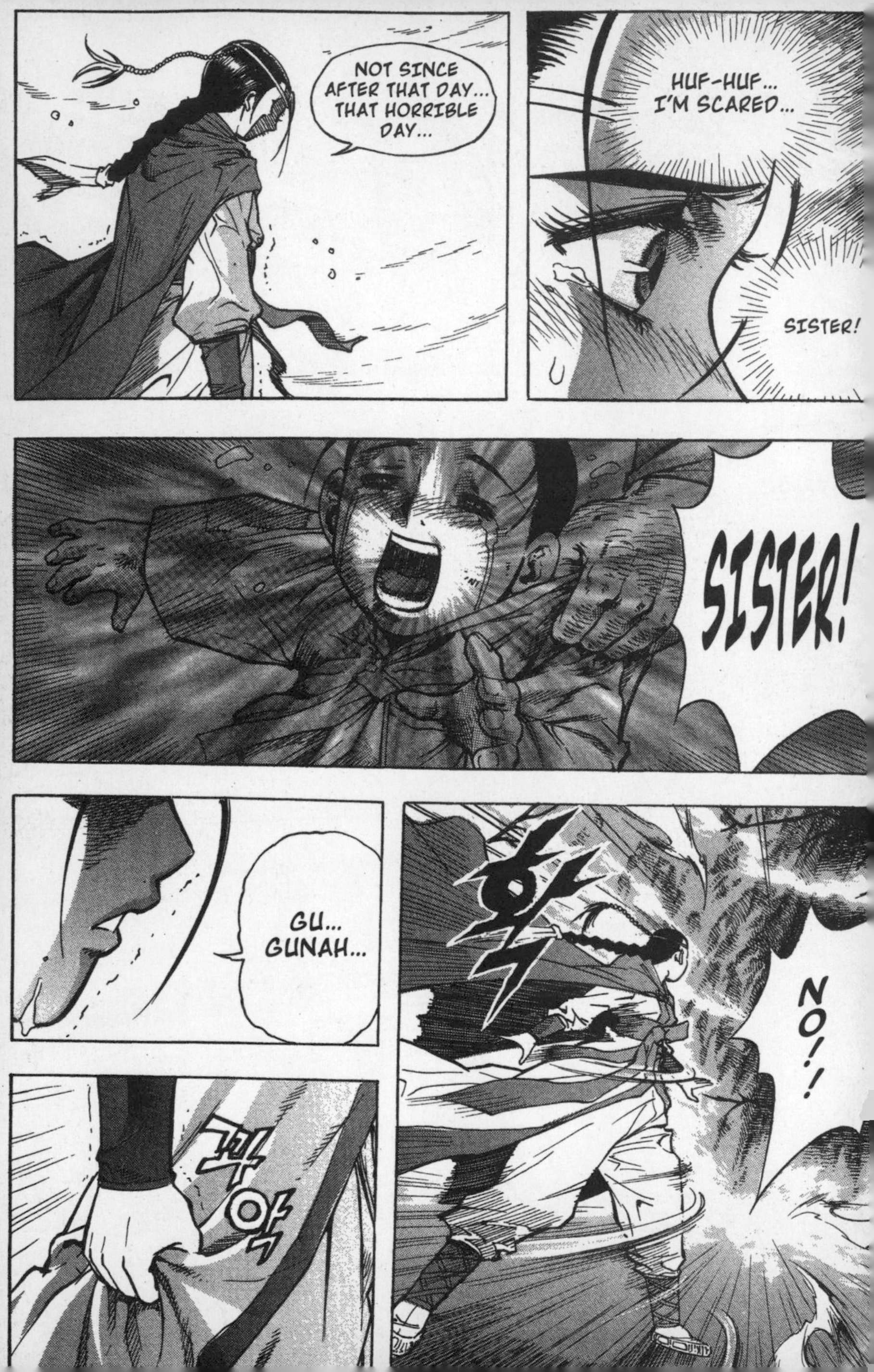
NOT SINCE AFTER THAT DAY... THAT HORRIBLE DAY...
HUF-HUF... I'M SCARED...
SISTER!
SISTER!
GU... GUNAH...
NO!!

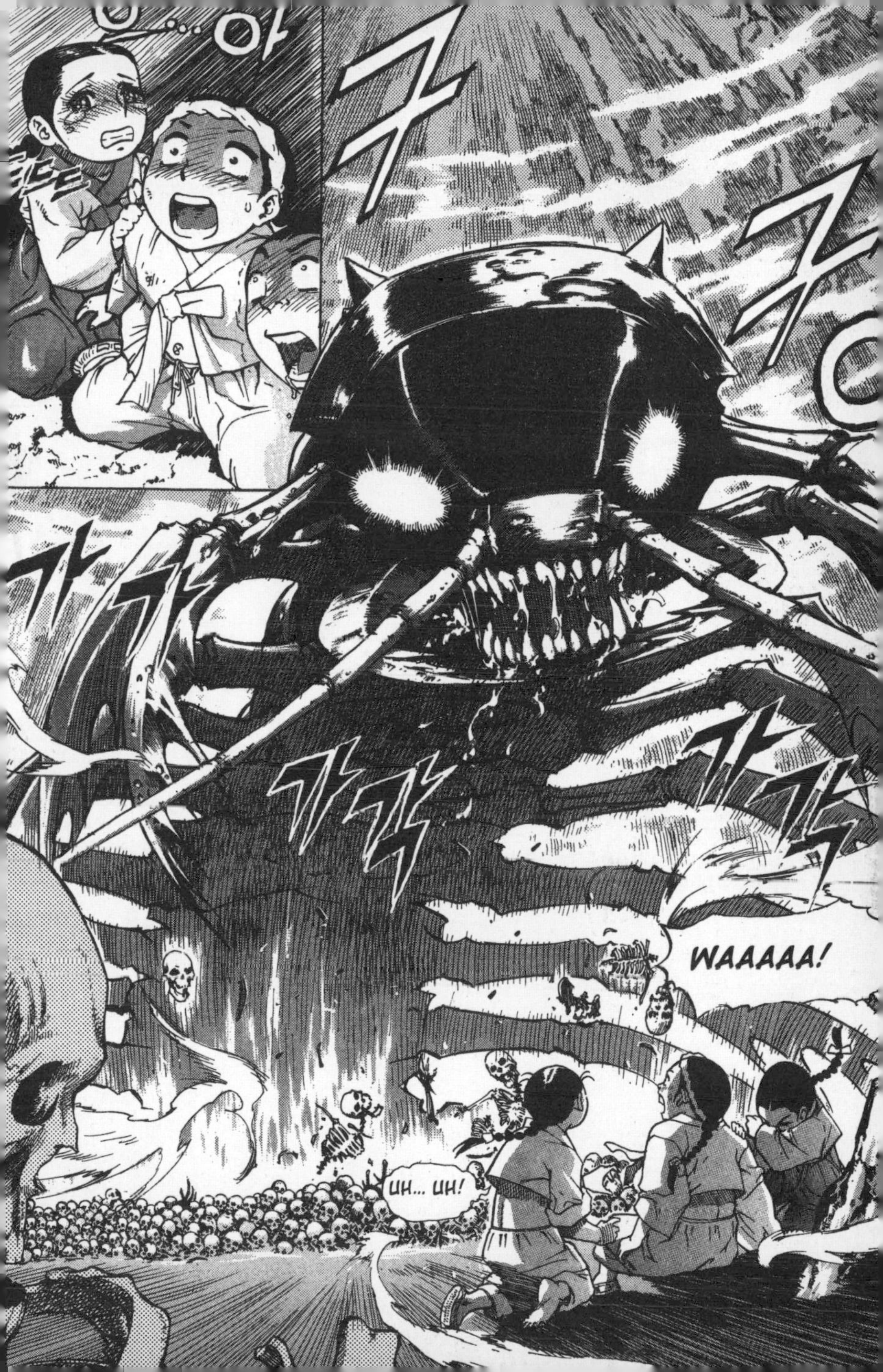
WAAAAA!
UH... UH!

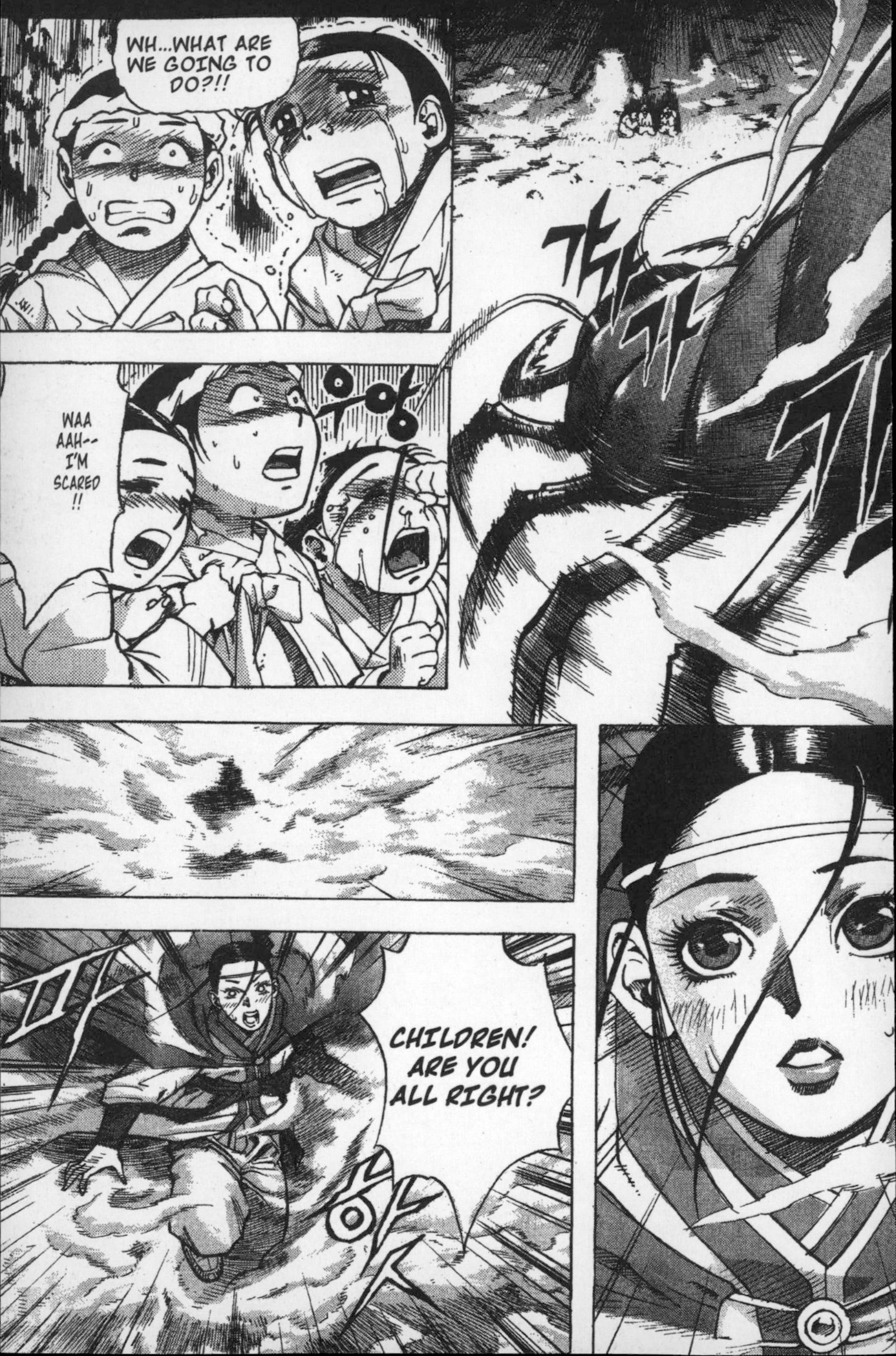
WH...WHAT ARE WE GOING TO DO?!!
WAA AAH-- I'M SCARED !!
CHILDREN! ARE YOU ALL RIGHT?

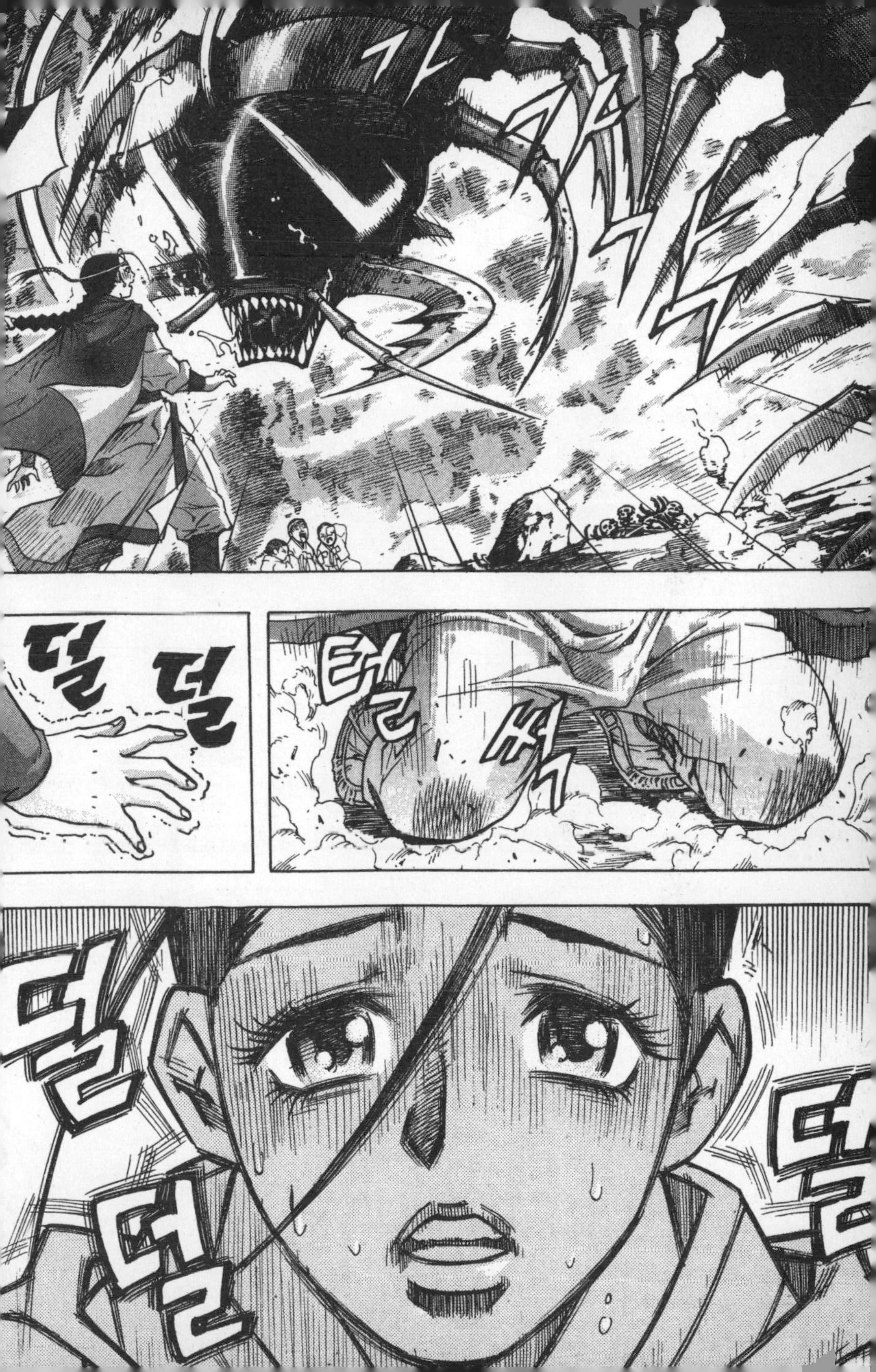
덜 덜
털썩
덜
덜
덜

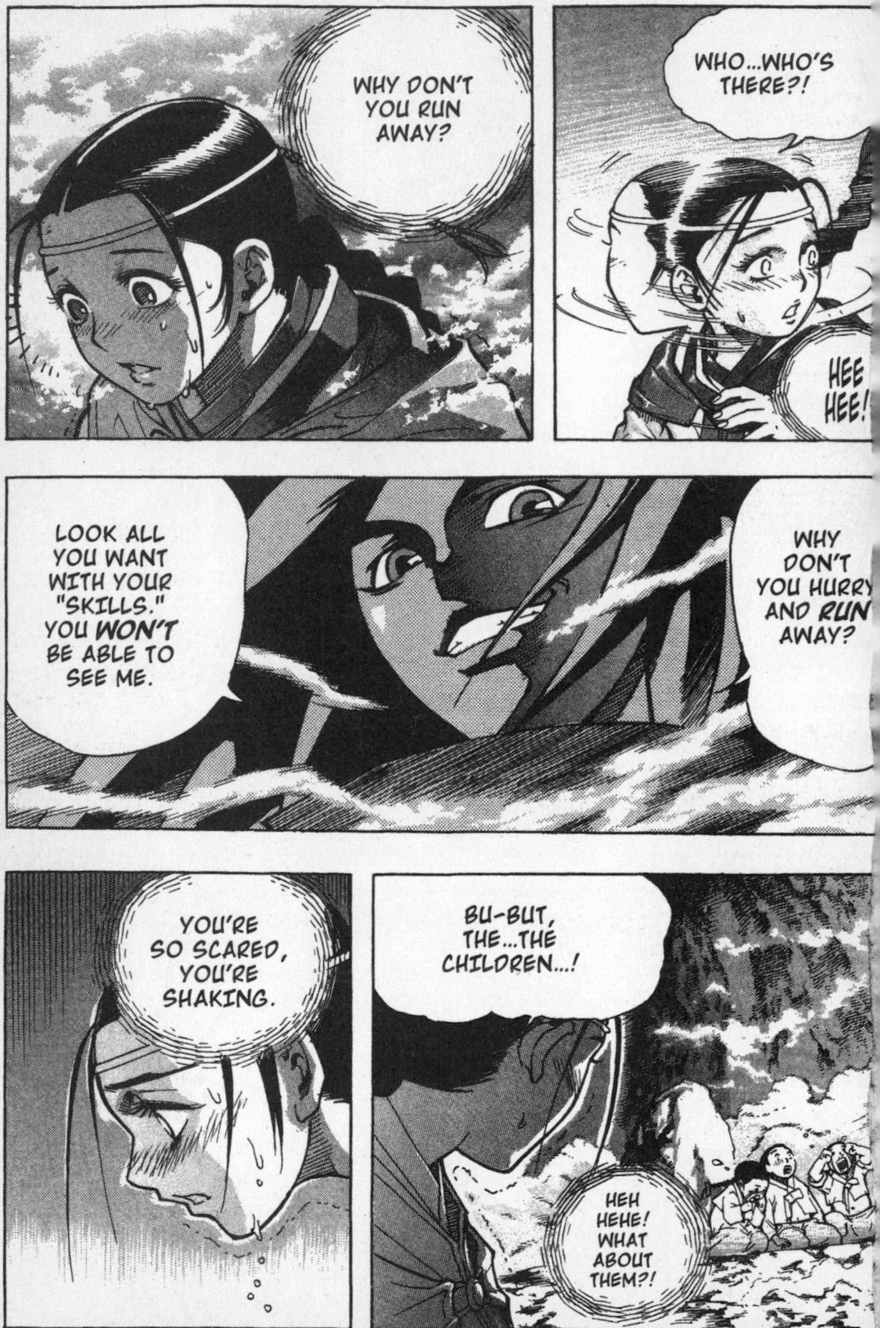
WHY DON'T YOU RUN AWAY?
WHO...WHO'S THERE?!
HEE HEE!
LOOK ALL YOU WANT WITH YOUR "SKILLS." YOU WON'T BE ABLE TO SEE ME.
WHY DON'T YOU HURRY AND RUN AWAY?
YOU'RE SO SCARED, YOU'RE SHAKING.
BU-BUT, THE...THE CHILDREN...!
HEH HEHE! WHAT ABOUT THEM?!

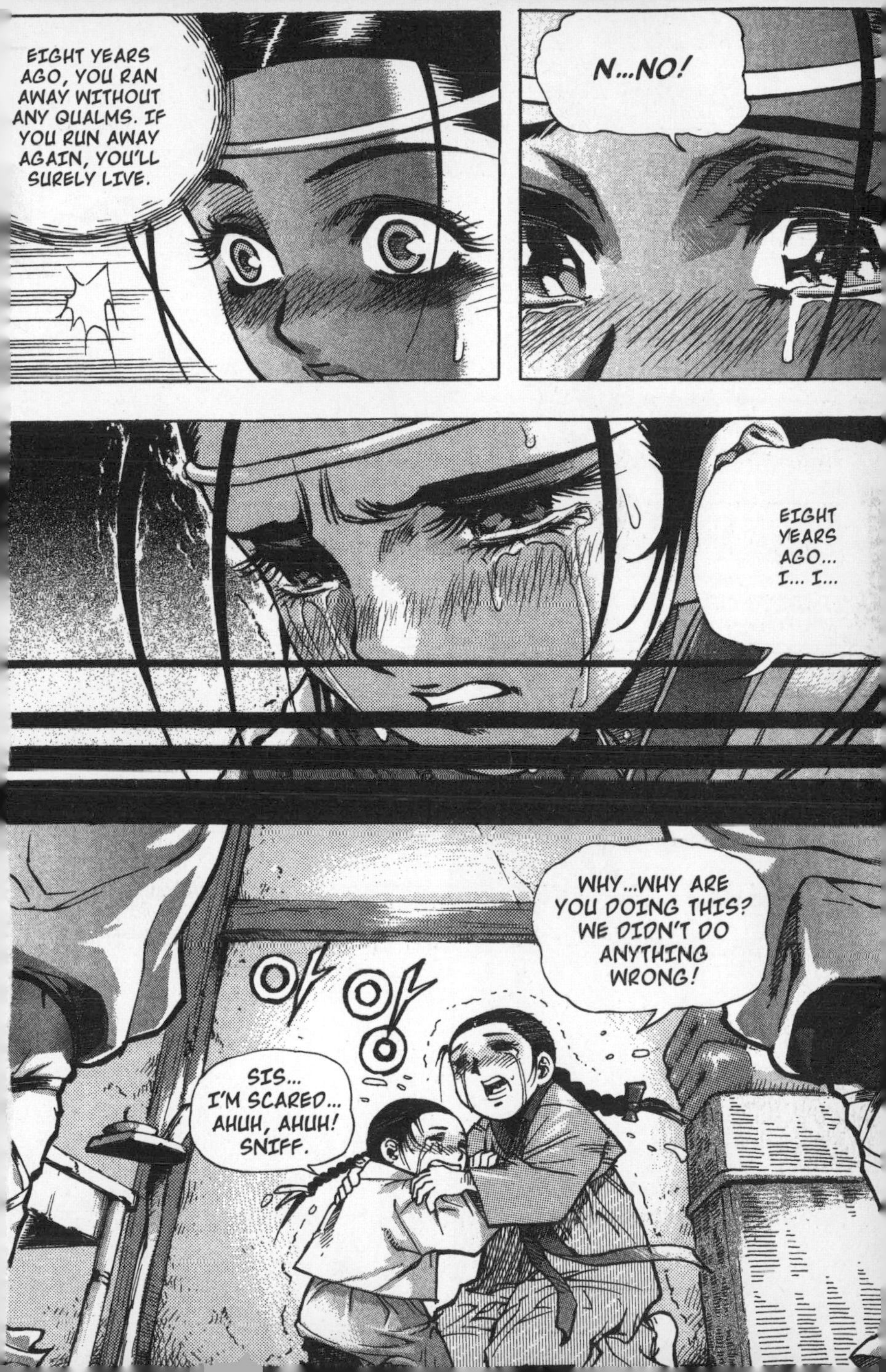
EIGHT YEARS AGO, YOU RAN AWAY WITHOUT ANY QUALMS. IF YOU RUN AWAY AGAIN, YOU'LL SURELY LIVE.
N...NO!
EIGHT YEARS AGO... I... I...
WHY...WHY ARE YOU DOING THIS? WE DIDN'T DO ANYTHING WRONG!
SIS... I'M SCARED... AHUH, AHUH! SNIFF.

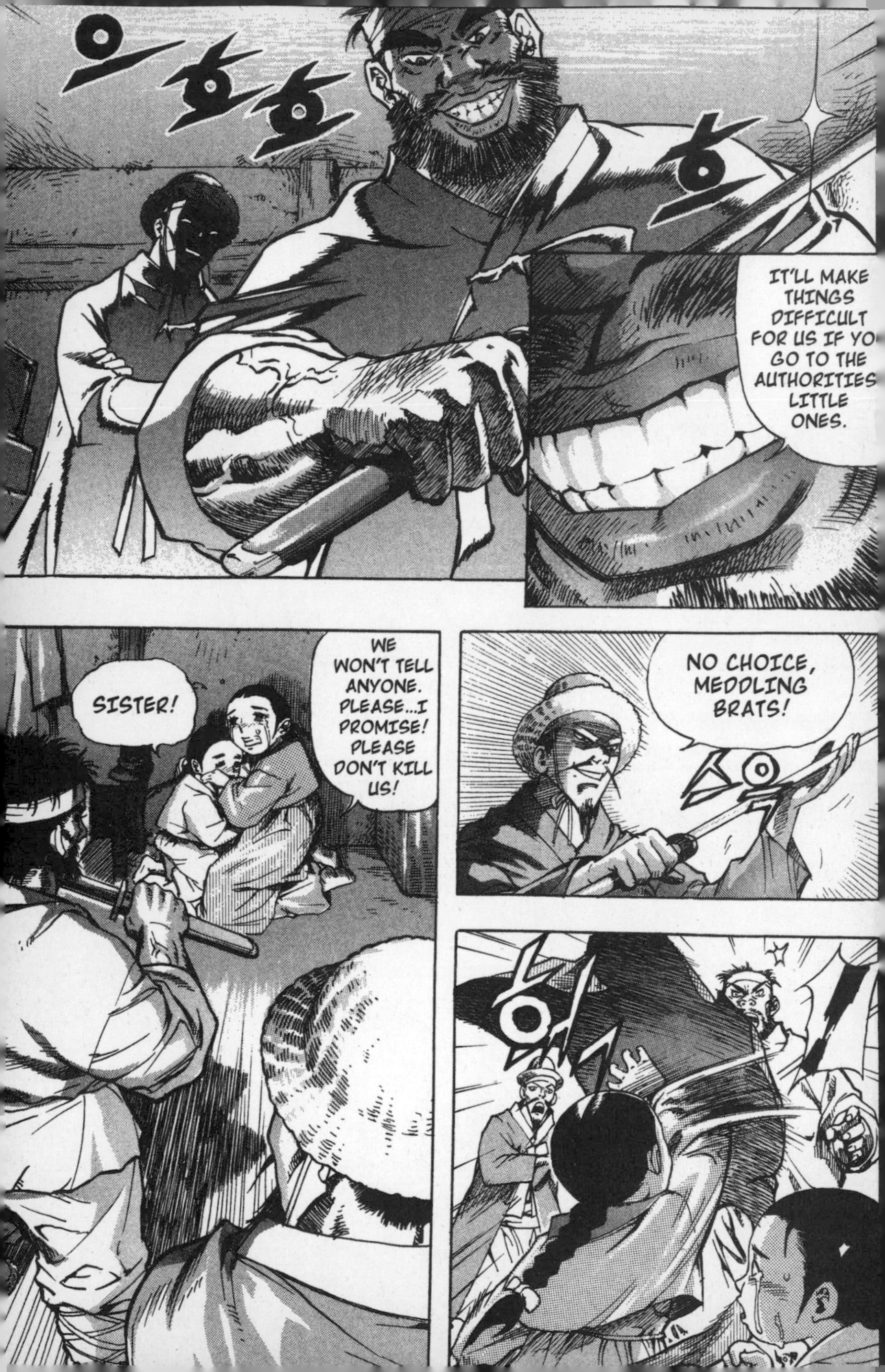
IT'LL MAKE THINGS DIFFICULT FOR US IF YO GO TO THE AUTHORITIES LITTLE ONES.
SISTER!
WE WON'T TELL ANYONE. PLEASE...I PROMISE! PLEASE DON'T KILL US!
NO CHOICE, MEDDLING BRATS!

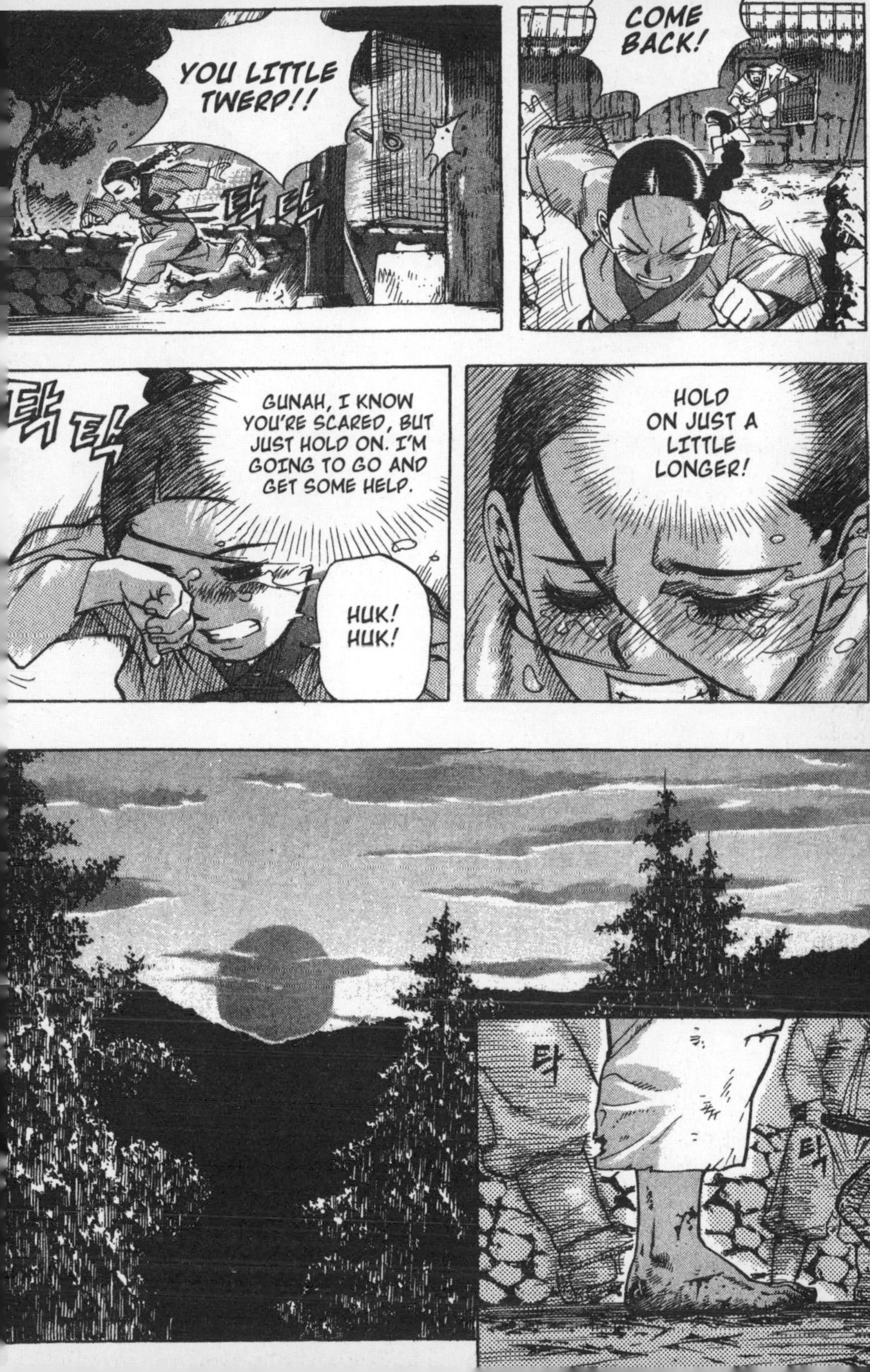
YOU LITTLE TWERP!!
탁 탁
COME BACK!
탁 탁
GUNAH, I KNOW YOU'RE SCARED, BUT JUST HOLD ON. I'M GOING TO GO AND GET SOME HELP.
HUK! HUK!
HOLD ON JUST A LITTLE LONGER!
탁
탁

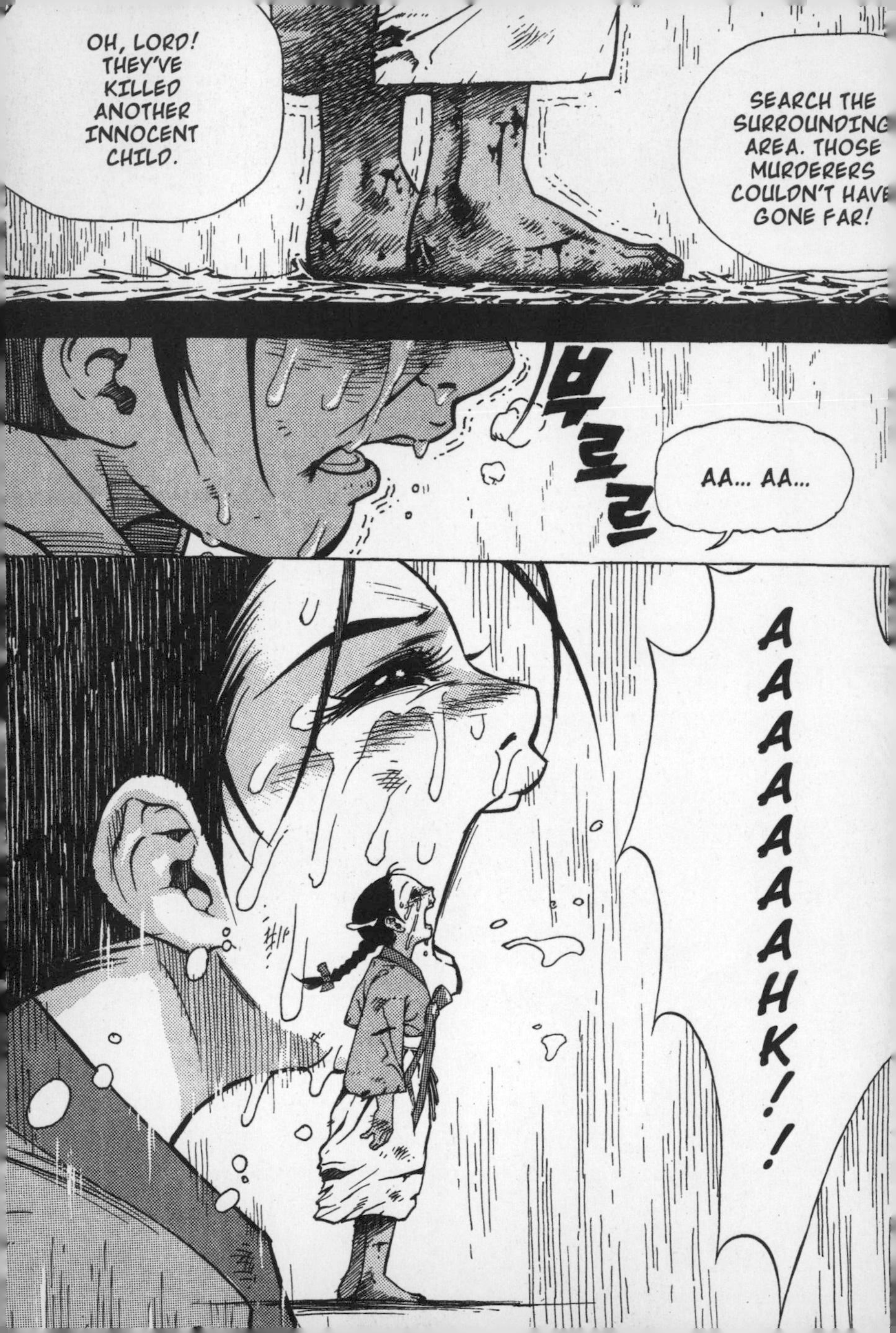
OH, LORD! THEY'VE KILLED ANOTHER INNOCENT CHILD.
SEARCH THE SURROUNDING AREA. THOSE MURDERERS COULDN'T HAVE GONE FAR!
부르르
AA... AA...
AAAAAAAHK!!

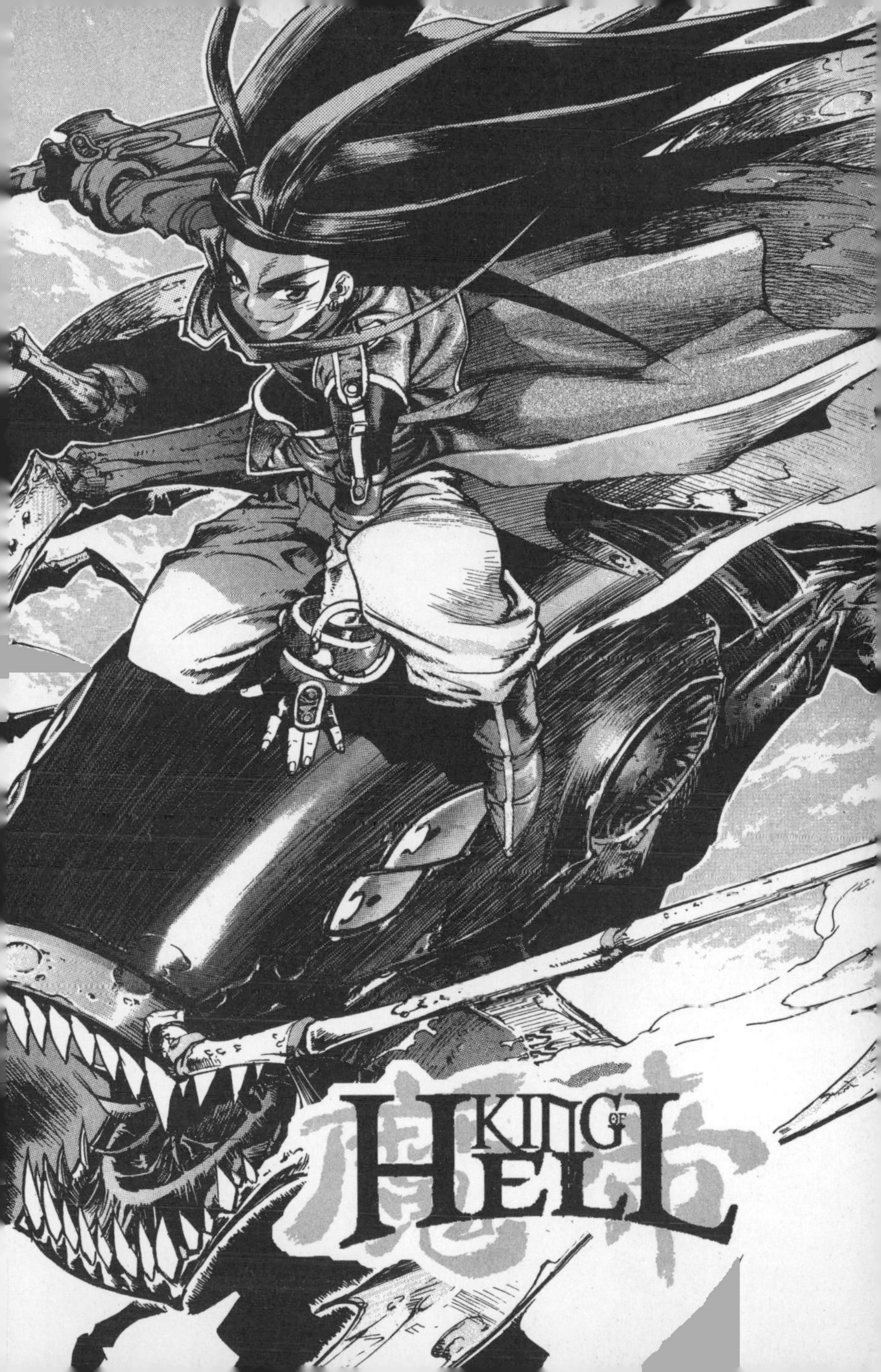
KING OF
HELL

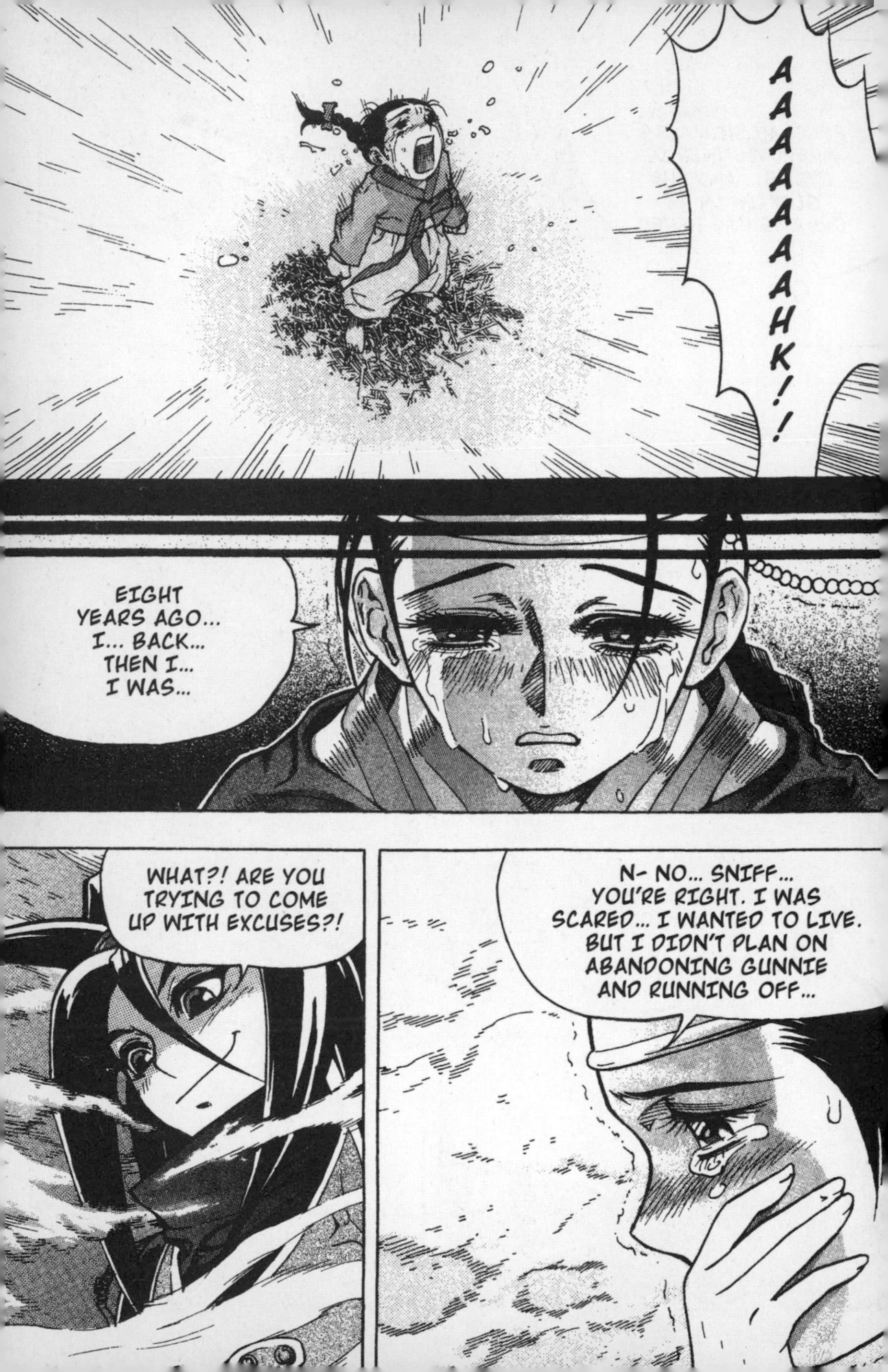
AAAAAAAAAHK!!
EIGHT YEARS AGO... I... BACK... THEN I... I WAS...
WHAT?! ARE YOU TRYING TO COME UP WITH EXCUSES?!
N- NO... SNIFF... YOU'RE RIGHT. I WAS SCARED... I WANTED TO LIVE. BUT I DIDN'T PLAN ON ABANDONING GUNNIE AND RUNNING OFF...

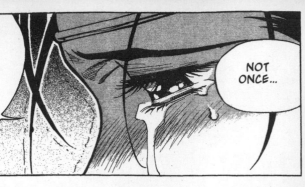

FOR THE PAST EIGHT YEARS, I'VE HATED MYSELF. I AWAKE FROM NIGHTMARES WHERE GUNNIE IS DYING... AND THE GUNNIE IN MY DREAMS HAS NEVER FORGIVEN ME.

NOT ONCE...

WE...WE'RE ALL GOING TO DIE! WHAHAH!

DON'T SAY THAT!

LO...LOOK OVER THERE.

NO ONE CAN ESCAPE FROM THIS PLACE. THAT'S WHY THERE ARE SO MANY SKELETONS.

UH... UH!

HUH?!! THAT'S...

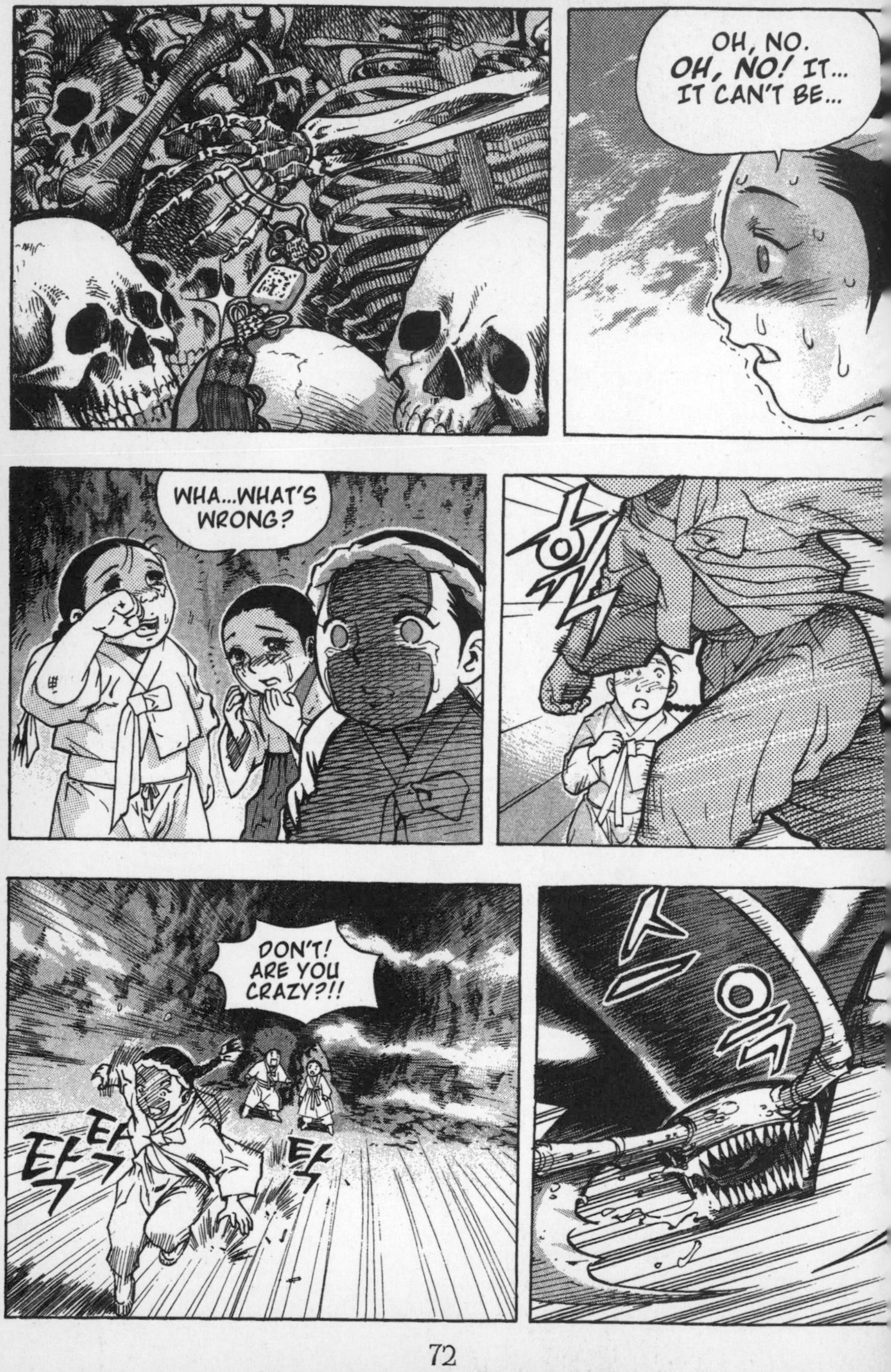
OH, NO. OH, NO! IT... IT CAN'T BE...
WHA...WHAT'S WRONG?
DON'T! ARE YOU CRAZY?!!

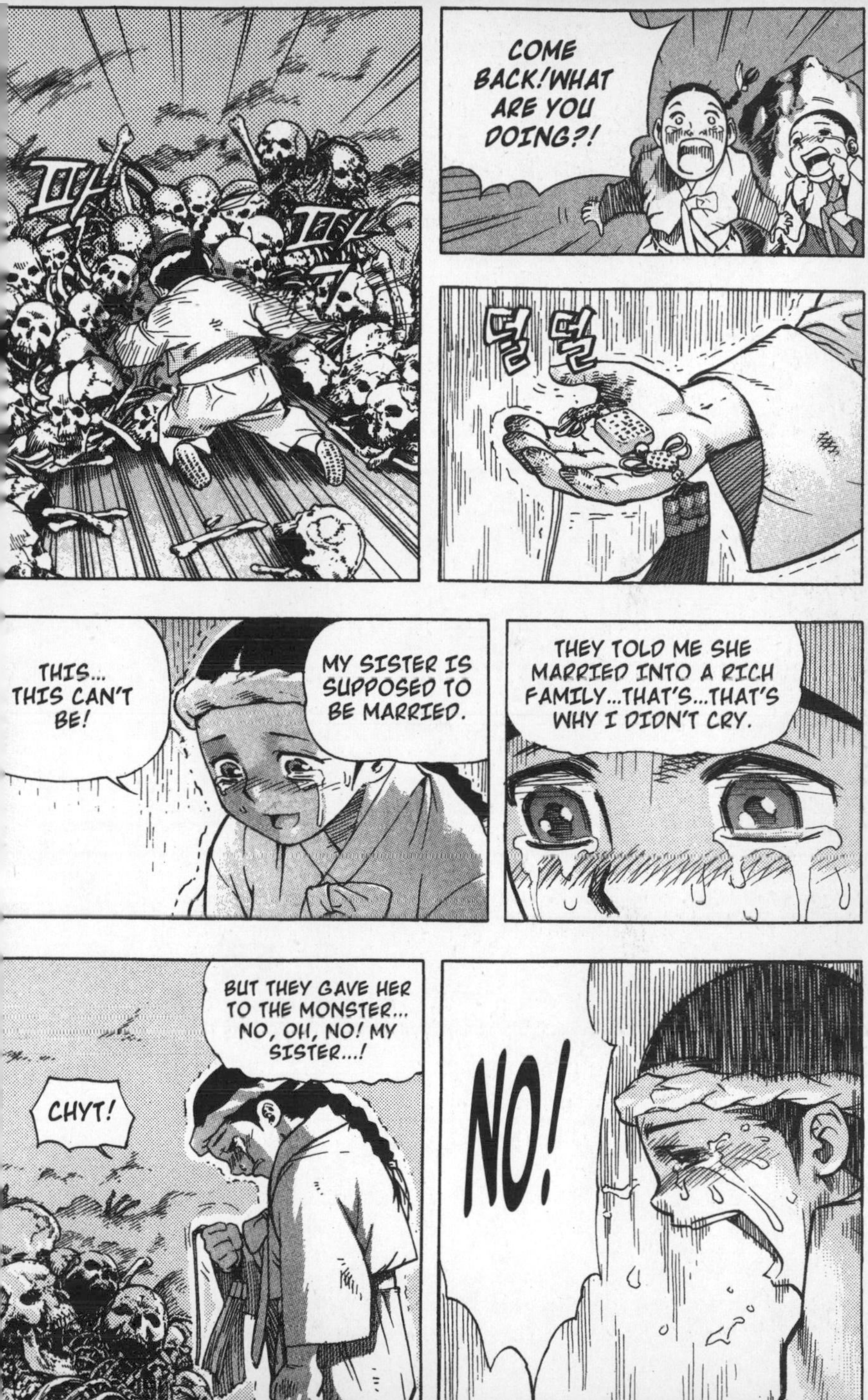
COME BACK! WHAT ARE YOU DOING?!
덜 덜
THIS... THIS CAN'T BE!
MY SISTER IS SUPPOSED TO BE MARRIED.
THEY TOLD ME SHE MARRIED INTO A RICH FAMILY...THAT'S...THAT'S WHY I DIDN'T CRY.
BUT THEY GAVE HER TO THE MONSTER... NO, OH, NO! MY SISTER...!
CHYT!
NO!

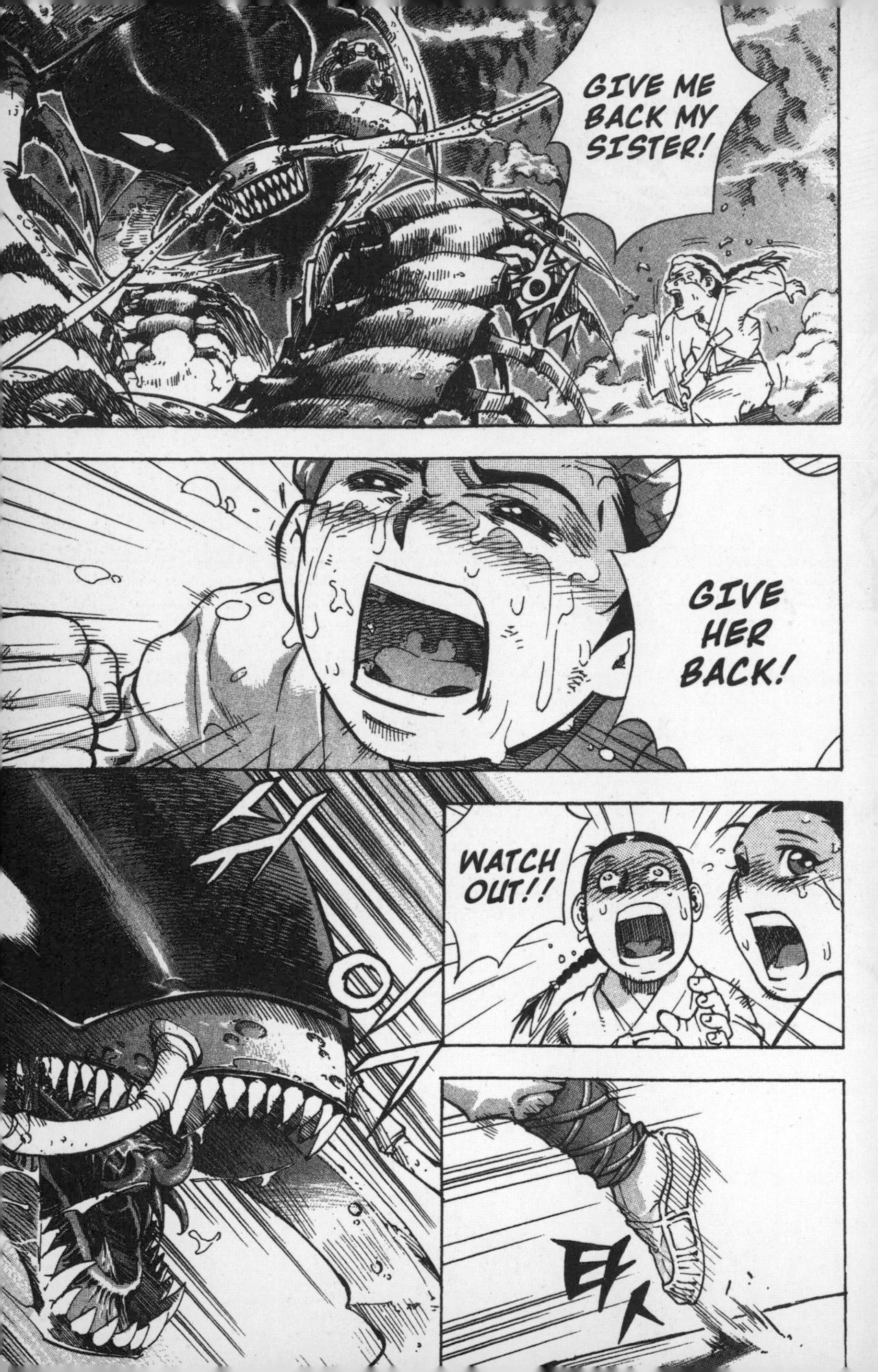
GIVE ME BACK MY SISTER!
GIVE HER BACK!
WATCH OUT!!

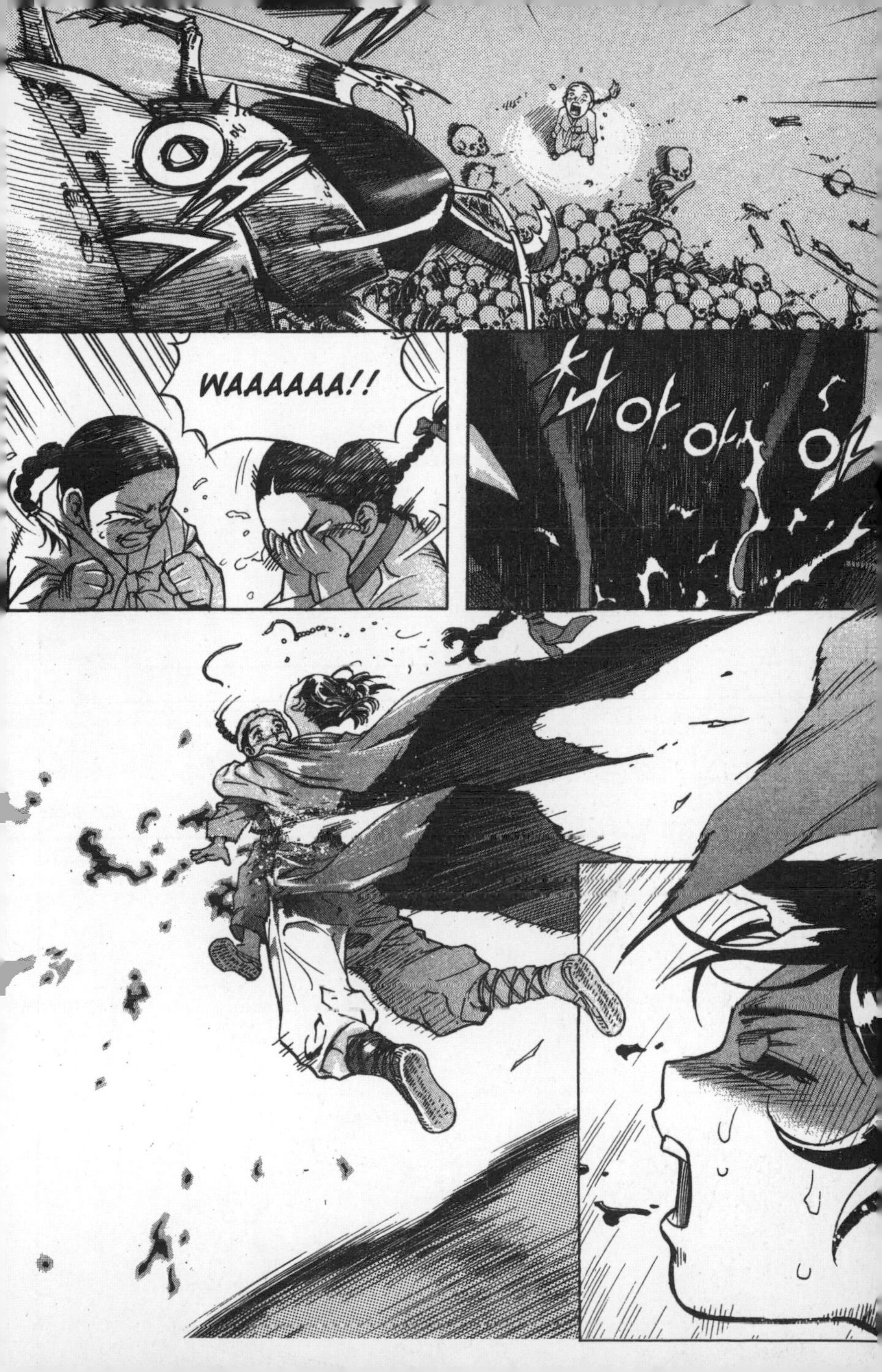
WAAAAAA!!

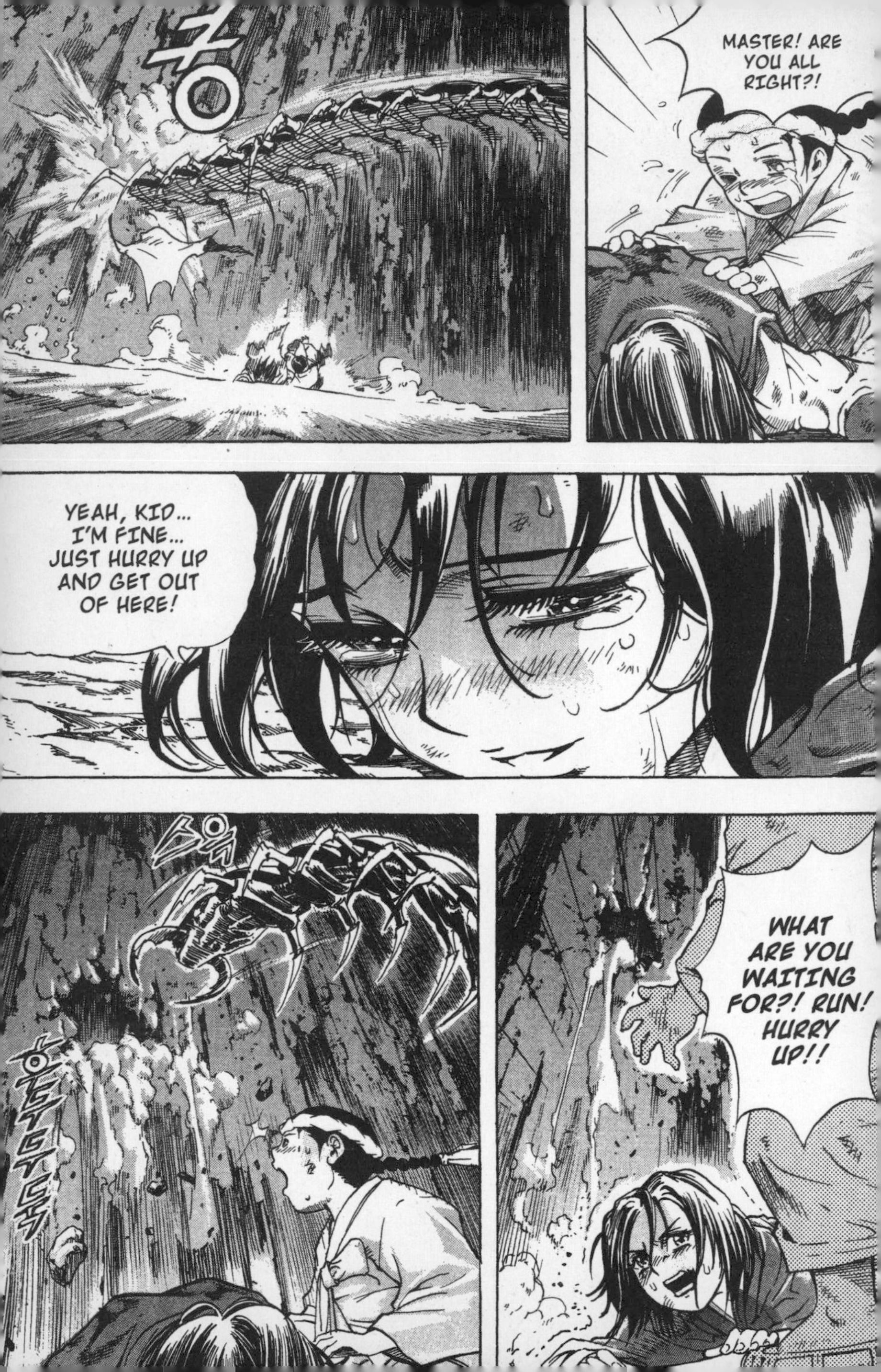
MASTER! ARE YOU ALL RIGHT?!
YEAH, KID... I'M FINE... JUST HURRY UP AND GET OUT OF HERE!
WHAT ARE YOU WAITING FOR?! RUN! HURRY UP!!

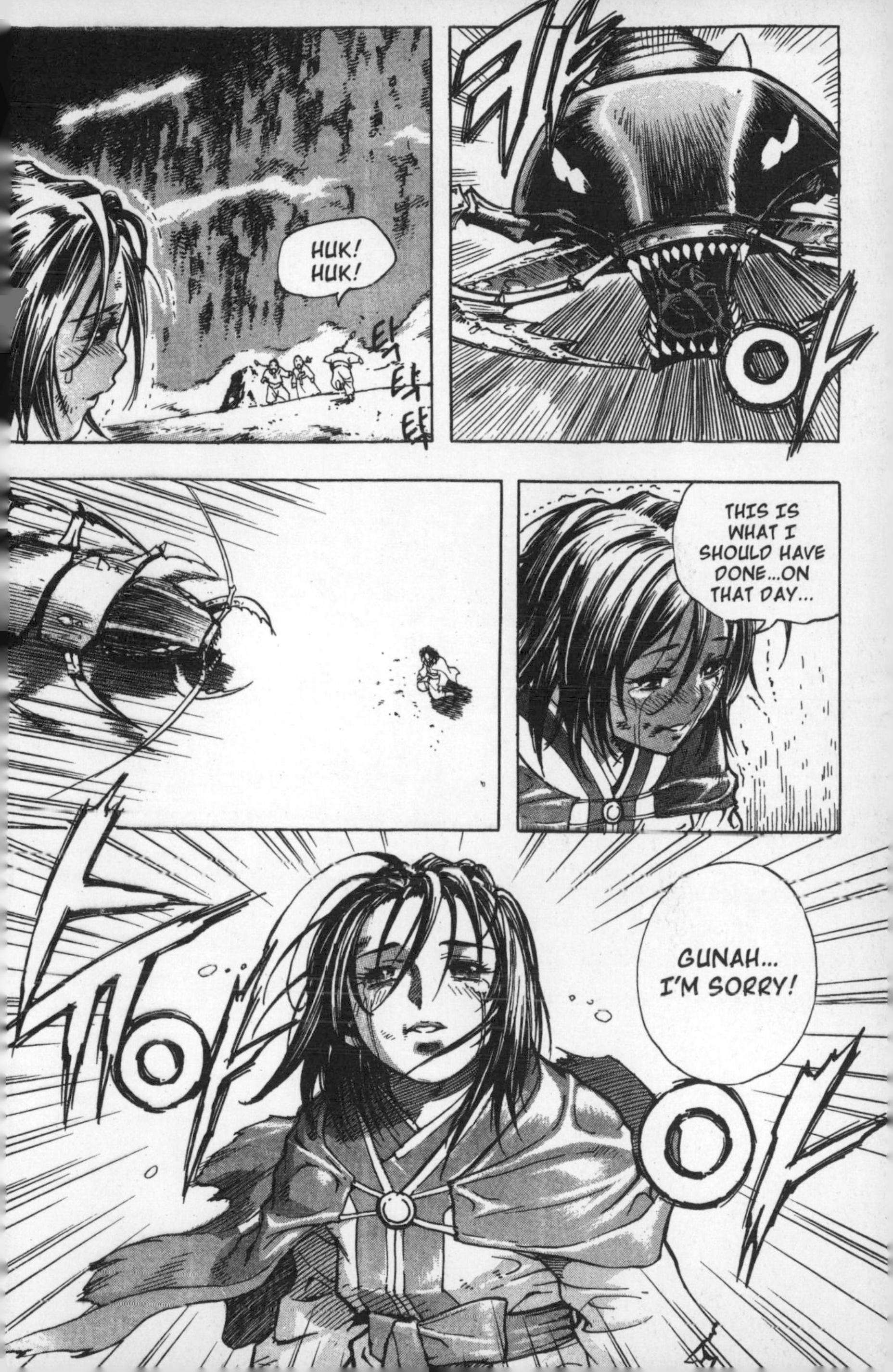
HUK! HUK!
탁 탁 탁
THIS IS WHAT I SHOULD HAVE DONE...ON THAT DAY...
GUNAH... I'M SORRY!

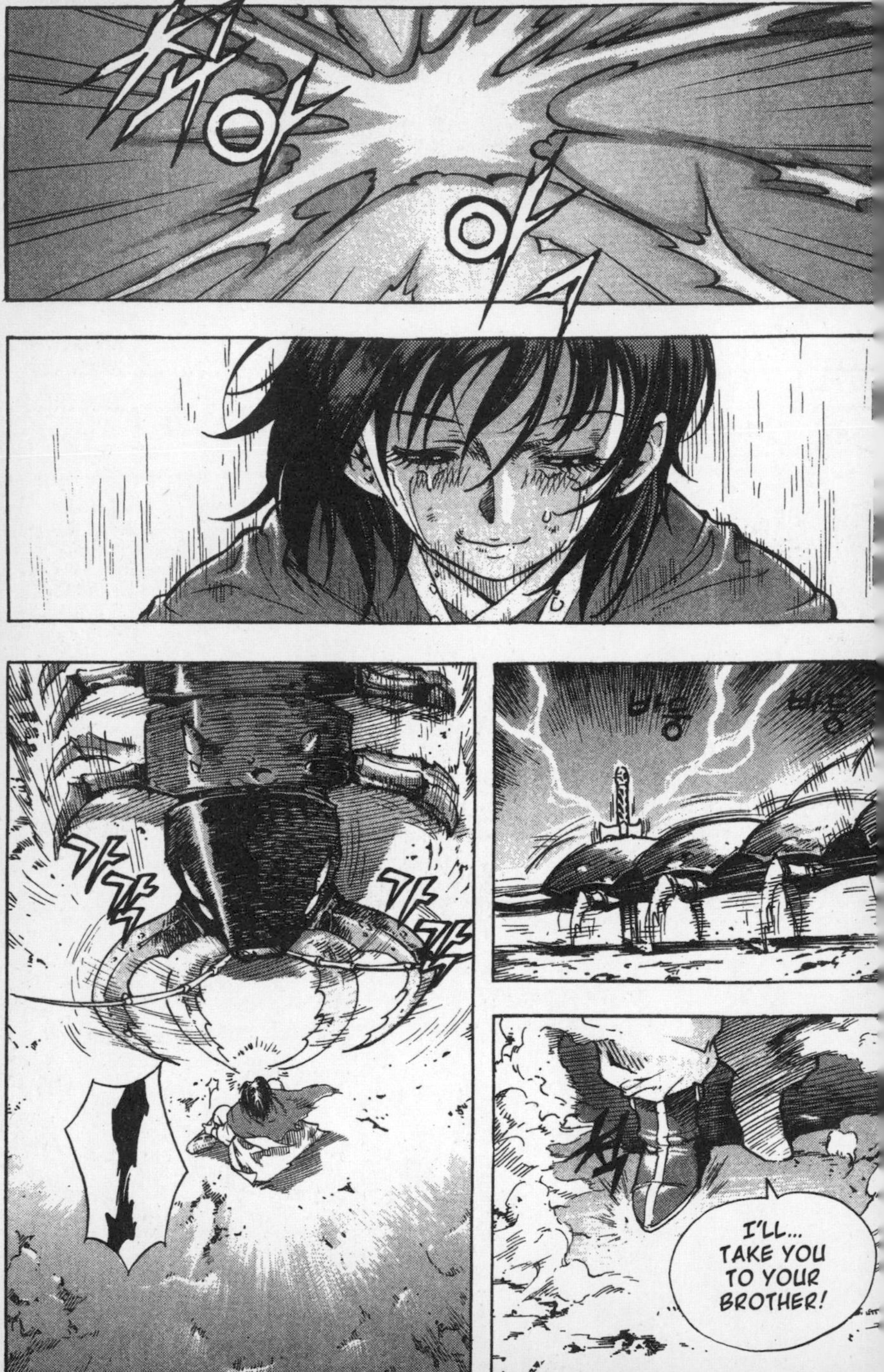
바둥 바둥
I'LL... TAKE YOU TO YOUR BROTHER!

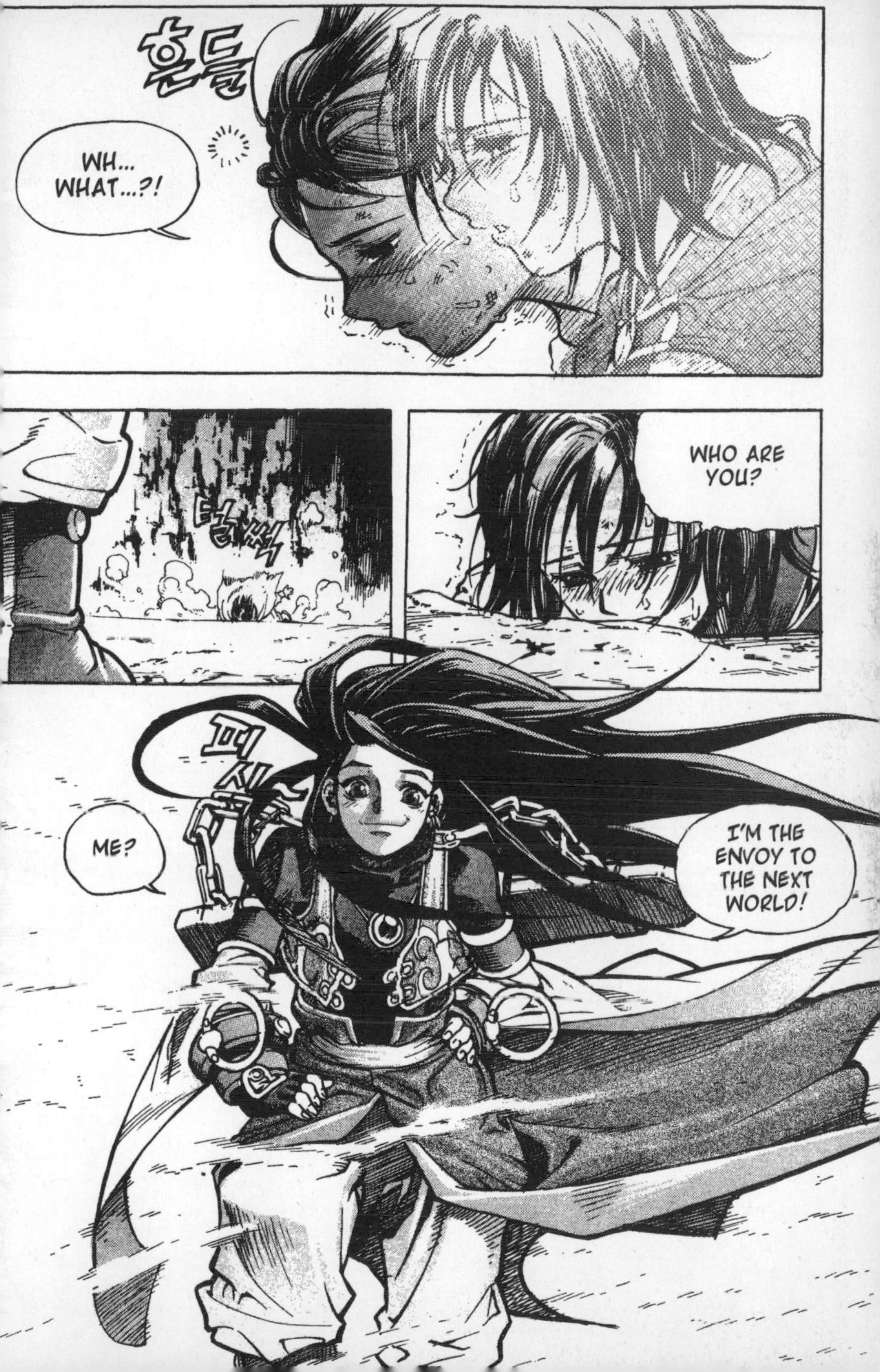
흔들
WH... WHAT...?!
WHO ARE YOU?
ME?
I'M THE ENVOY TO THE NEXT WORLD!

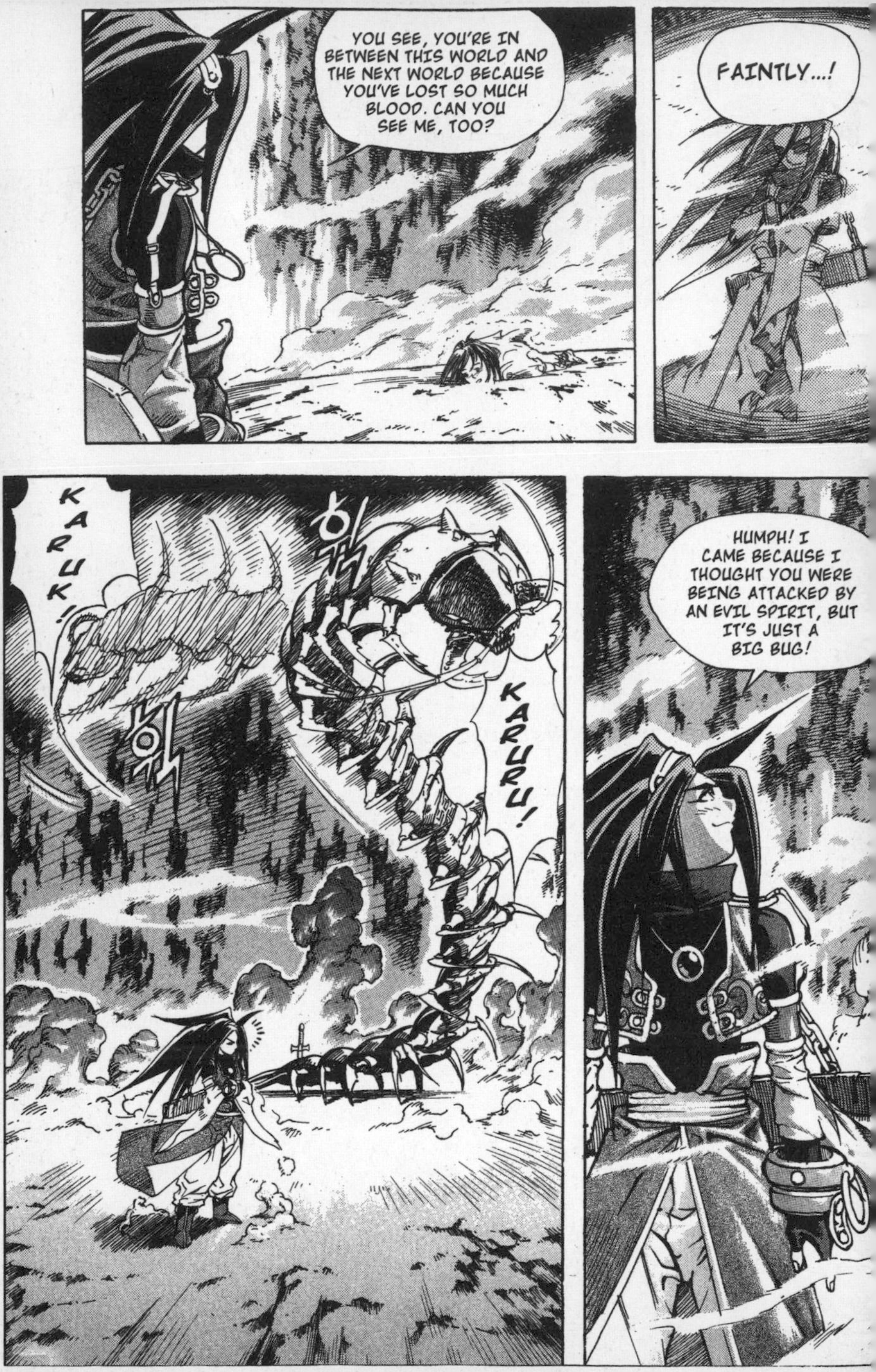
YOU SEE, YOU'RE IN BETWEEN THIS WORLD AND THE NEXT WORLD BECAUSE YOU'VE LOST SO MUCH BLOOD. CAN YOU SEE ME, TOO?
FAINTLY...!
KARUK!
KARURU!
HUMPH! I CAME BECAUSE I THOUGHT YOU WERE BEING ATTACKED BY AN EVIL SPIRIT, BUT IT'S JUST A BIG BUG!

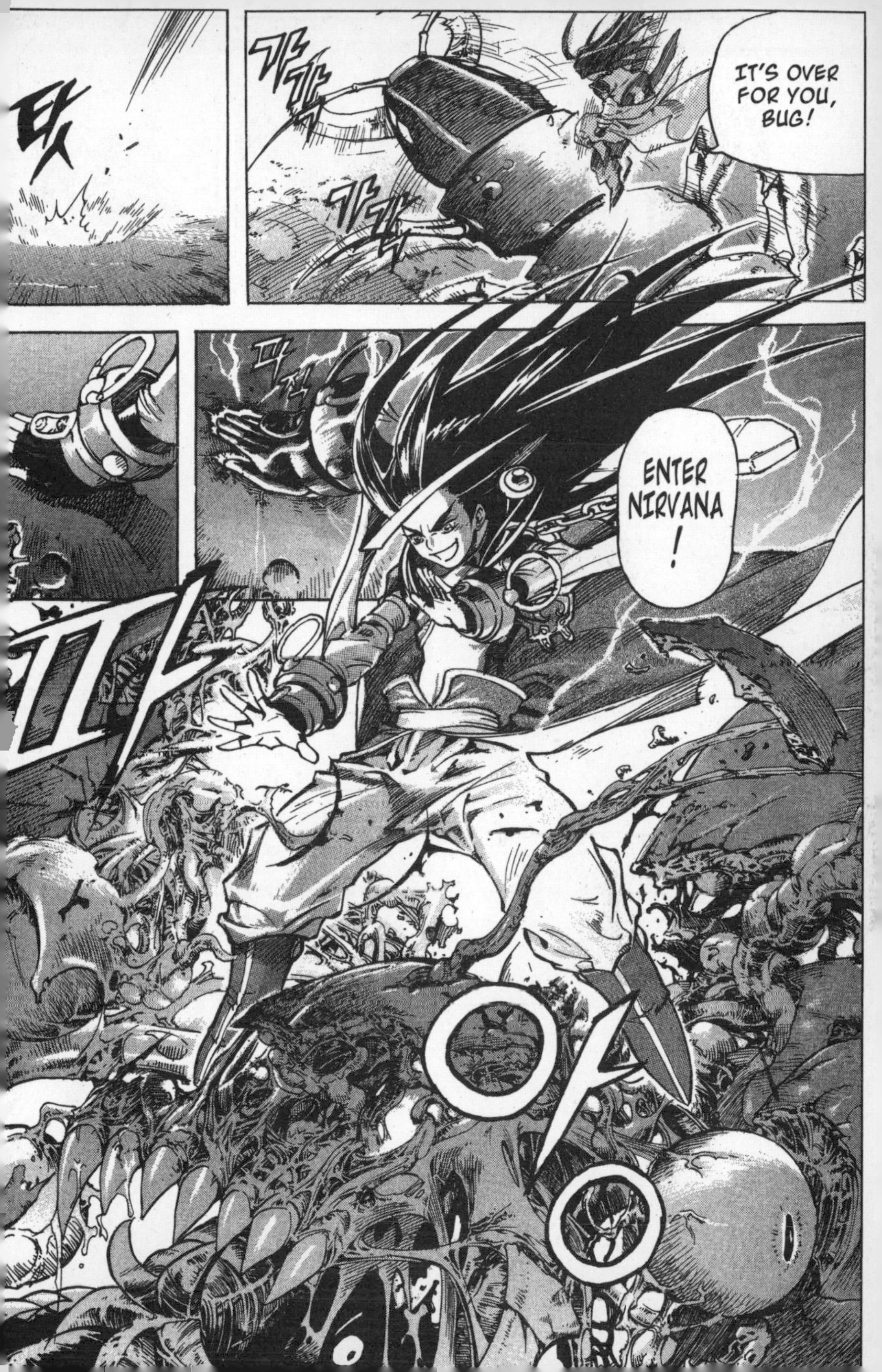
IT'S OVER FOR YOU, BUG!
ENTER NIRVANA !

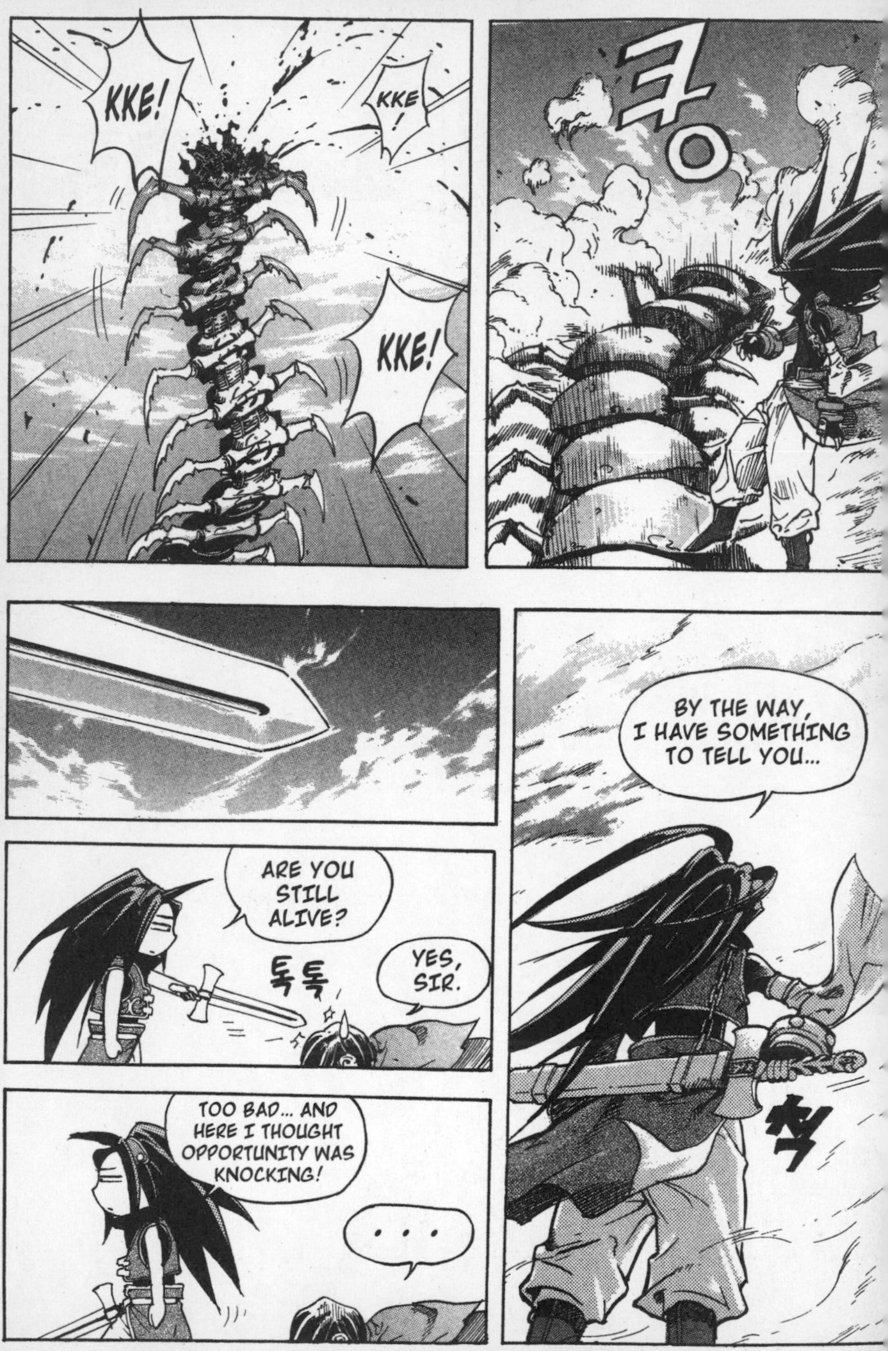
KKE!
KKE!
KKE!
ARE YOU STILL ALIVE?
톡톡
YES, SIR.
TOO BAD... AND HERE I THOUGHT OPPORTUNITY WAS KNOCKING!
. . .
BY THE WAY, I HAVE SOMETHING TO TELL YOU...

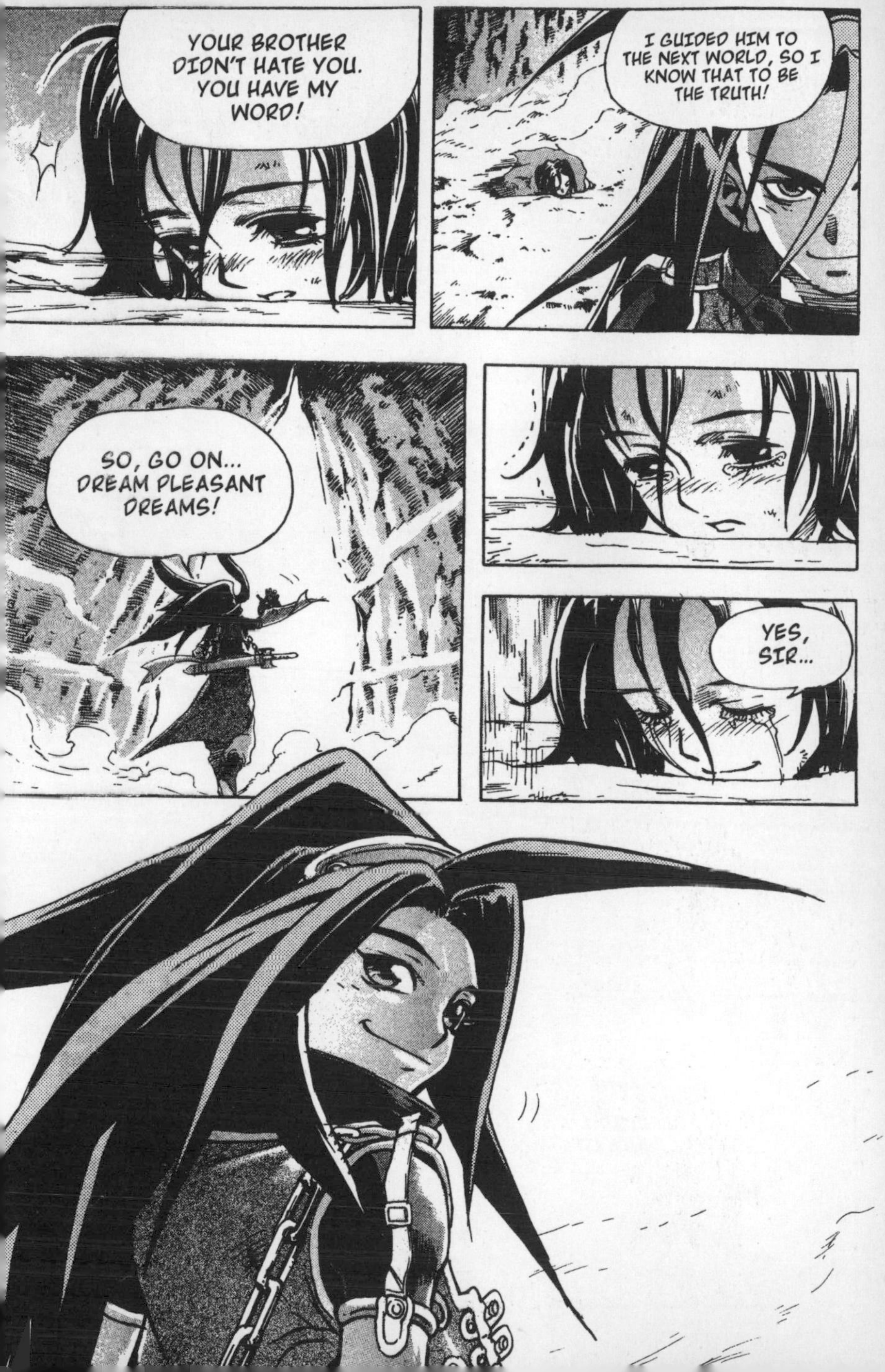
YOUR BROTHER DIDN'T HATE YOU. YOU HAVE MY WORD!
I GUIDED HIM TO THE NEXT WORLD, SO I KNOW THAT TO BE THE TRUTH!
SO, GO ON... DREAM PLEASANT DREAMS!
YES, SIR...

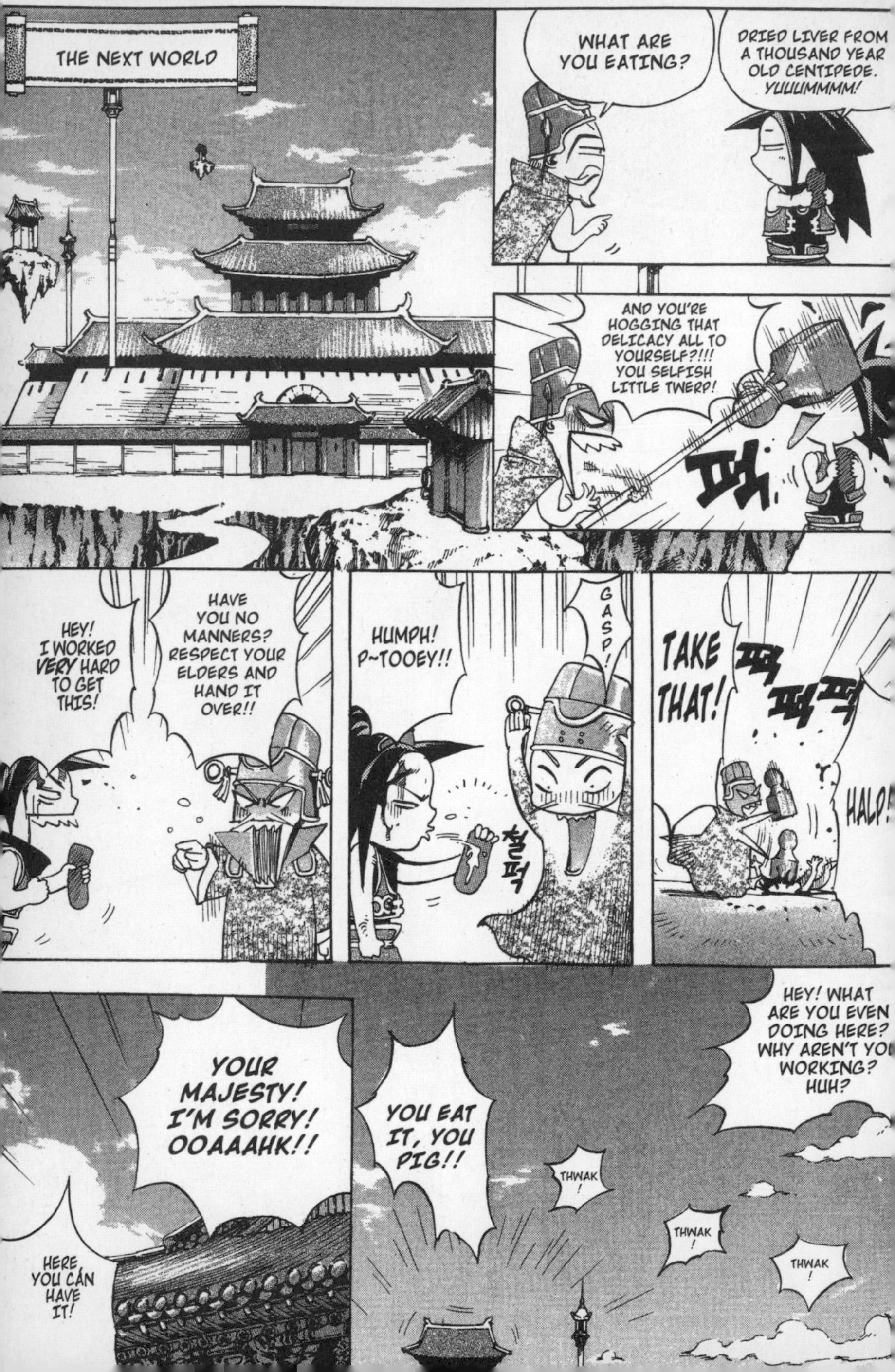
THE NEXT WORLD
WHAT ARE YOU EATING?
DRIED LIVER FROM A THOUSAND YEAR OLD CENTIPEDE. YUUUMMMM!
AND YOU'RE HOGGING THAT DELICACY ALL TO YOURSELF?!!! YOU SELFISH LITTLE TWERP!
퍽
HEY! I WORKED VERY HARD TO GET THIS!
HAVE YOU NO MANNERS? RESPECT YOUR ELDERS AND HAND IT OVER!!
HUMPH! P~TOOEY!!
GASP!
철퍽
TAKE THAT!
퍽
퍽퍽
HALP!
YOUR MAJESTY! I'M SORRY! OOAAAHK!!
HERE YOU CAN HAVE IT!
YOU EAT IT, YOU PIG!!
HEY! WHAT ARE YOU EVEN DOING HERE? WHY AREN'T YOU WORKING? HUH?
THWAK!
THWAK!
THWAK!

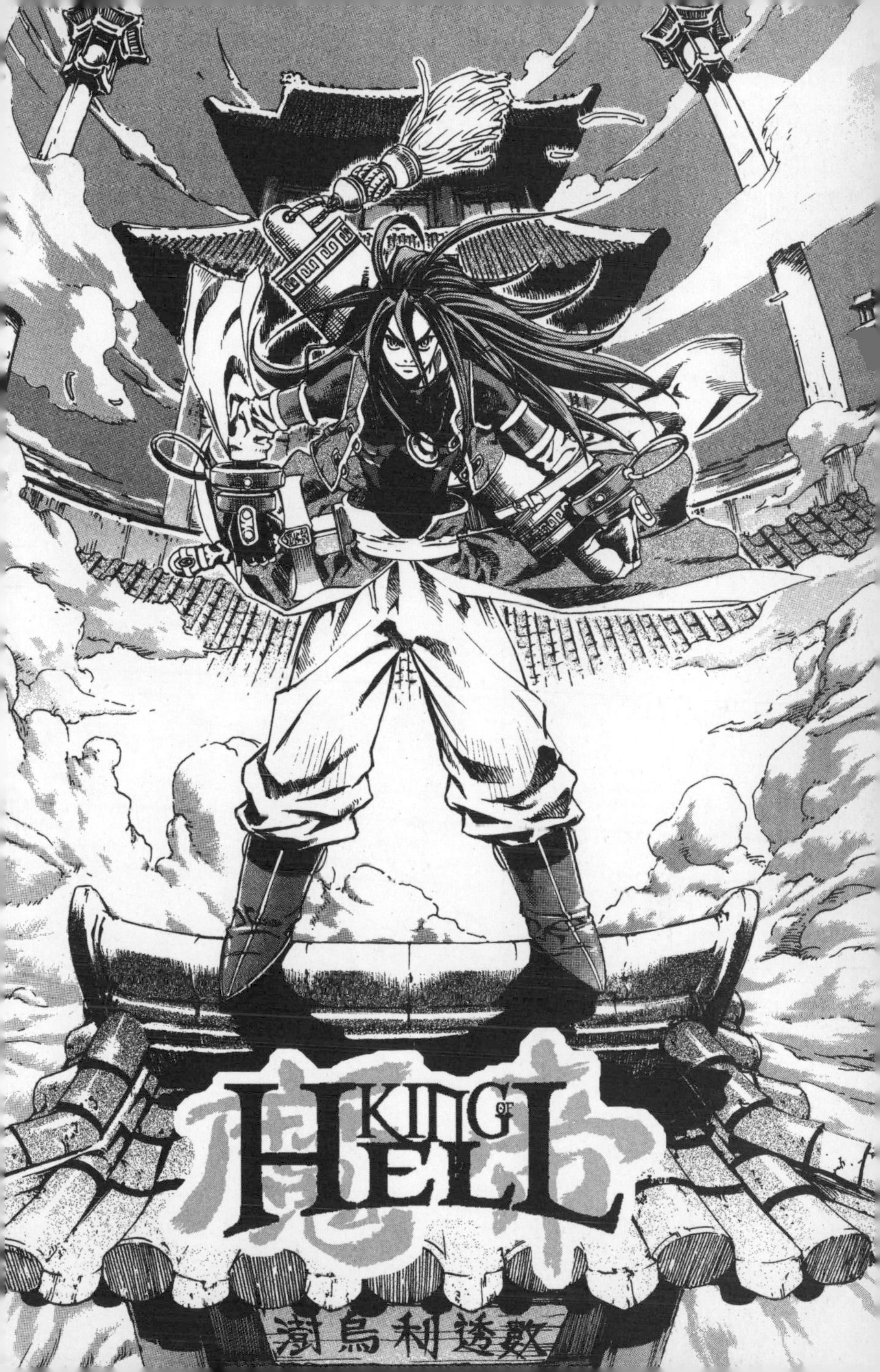
KING OF HELL

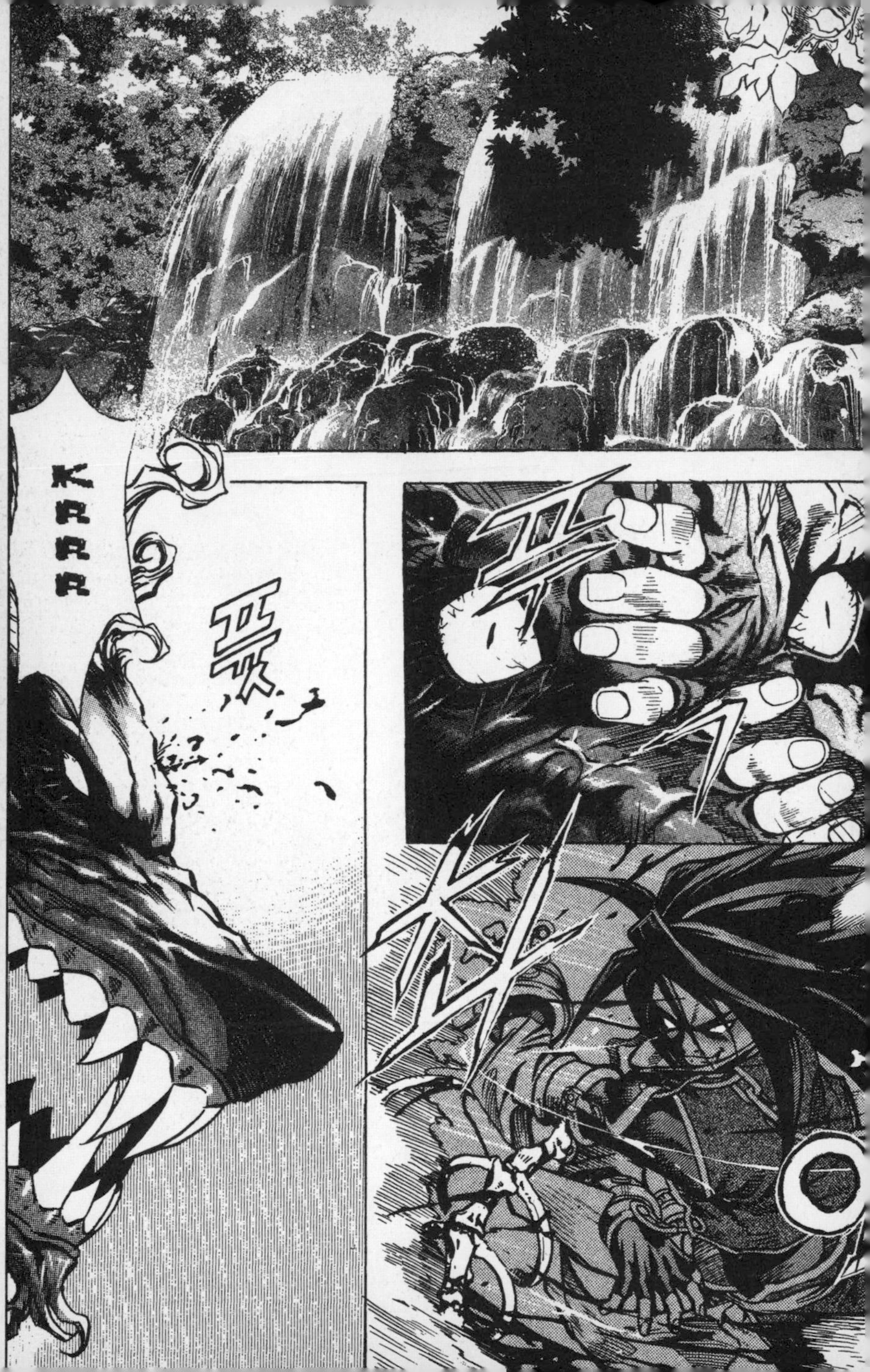
KRRRR

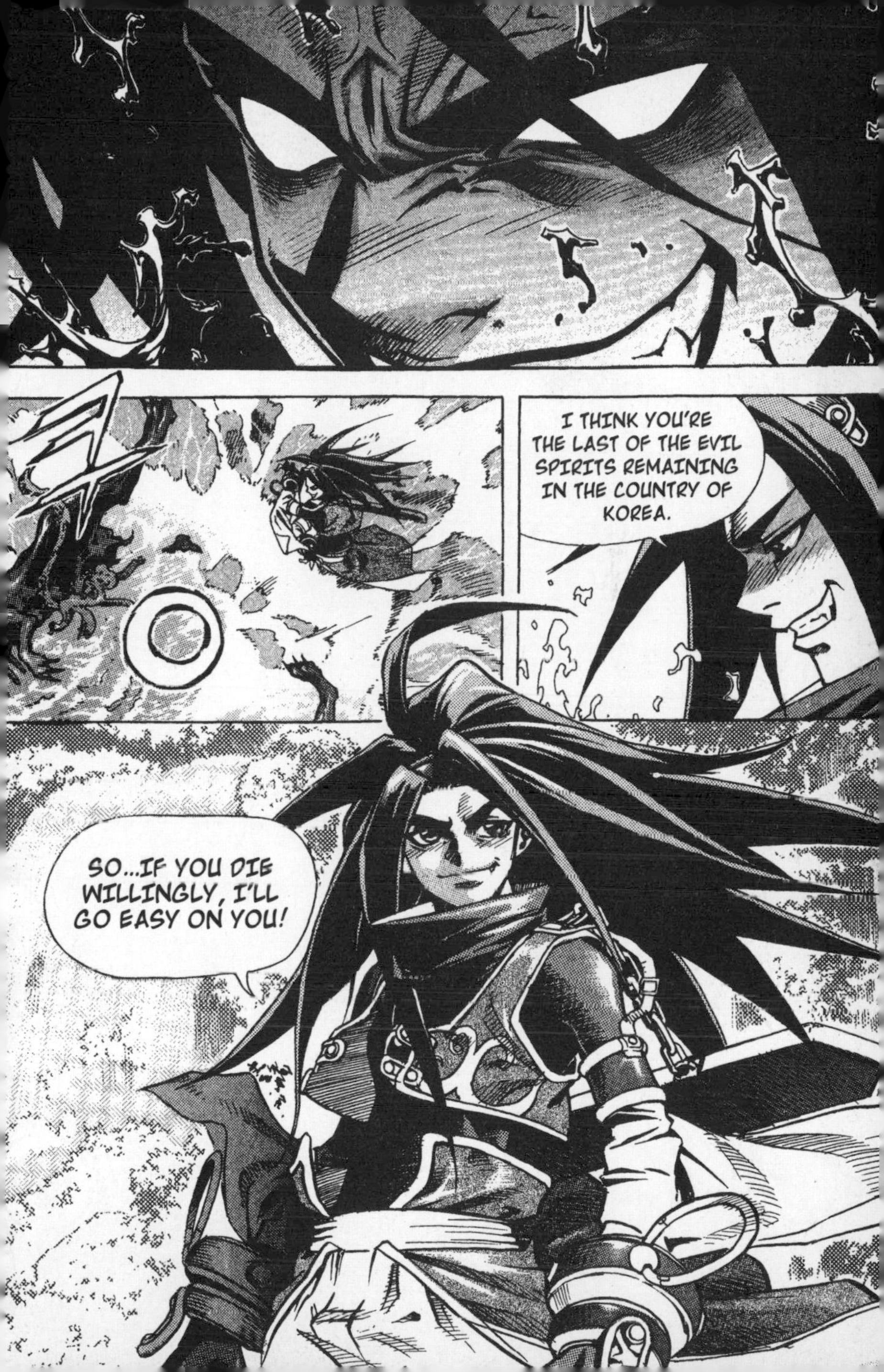
I THINK YOU'RE THE LAST OF THE EVIL SPIRITS REMAINING IN THE COUNTRY OF KOREA.
SO...IF YOU DIE WILLINGLY, I'LL GO EASY ON YOU!

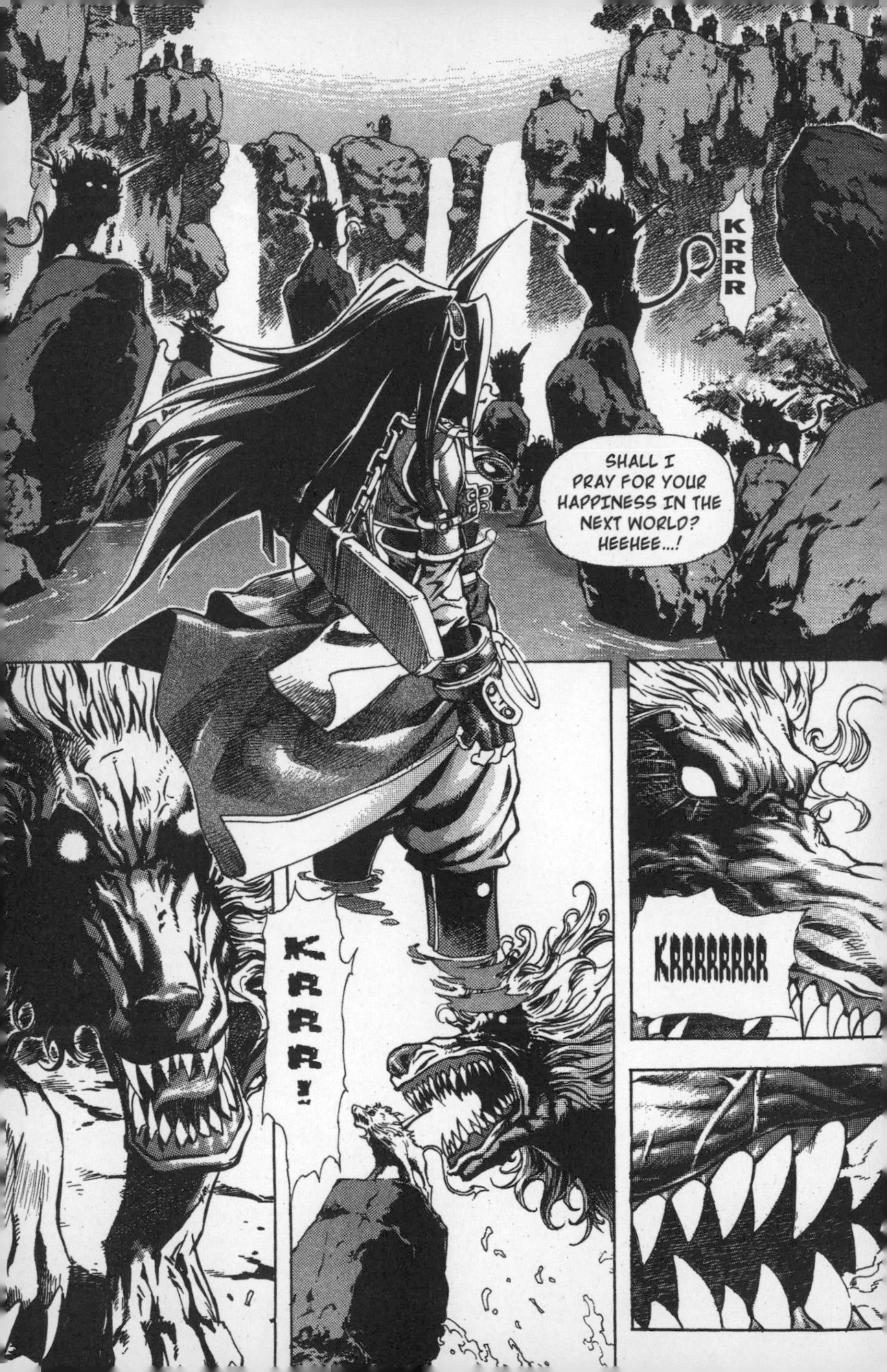
KRRR
SHALL I PRAY FOR YOUR HAPPINESS IN THE NEXT WORLD? HEEHEE...!
KRRRR!
KRRRRRRRR

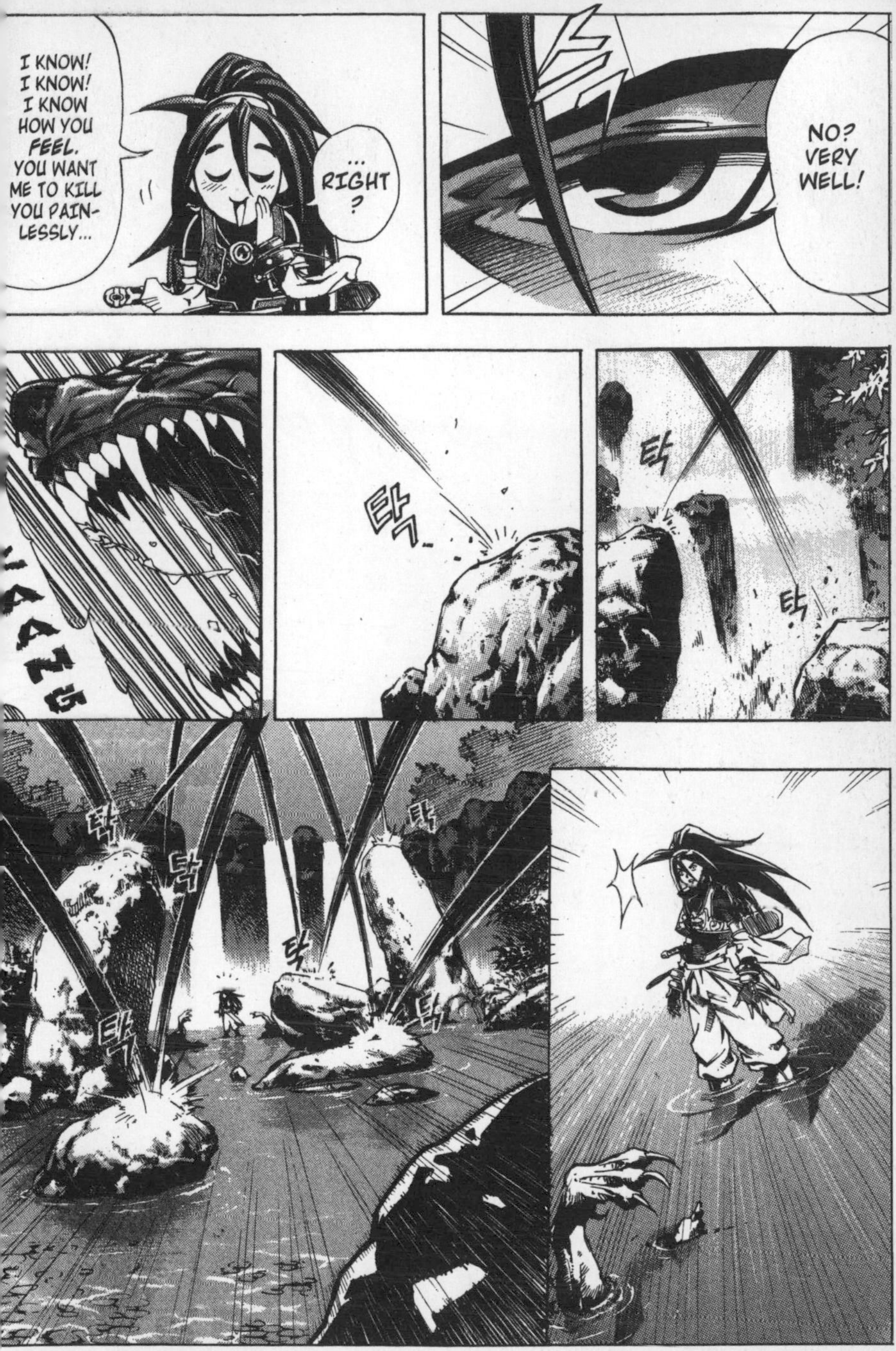
I KNOW! I KNOW! I KNOW HOW YOU FEEL. YOU WANT ME TO KILL YOU PAIN-LESSLY...
...RIGHT?
NO? VERY WELL!
AANG
탁
탁
탁
탁
탁
탁
탁
탁
탁

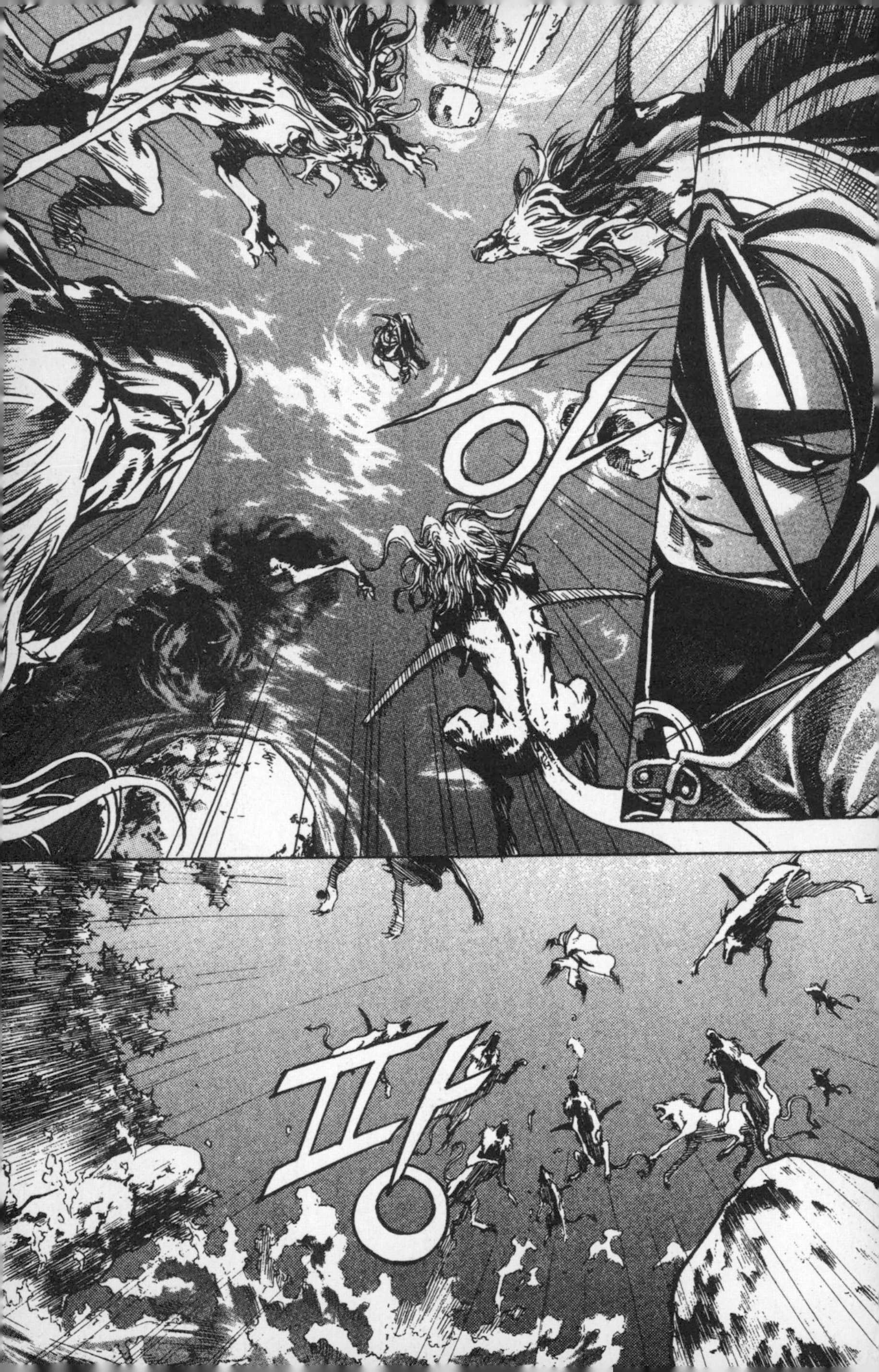
팡

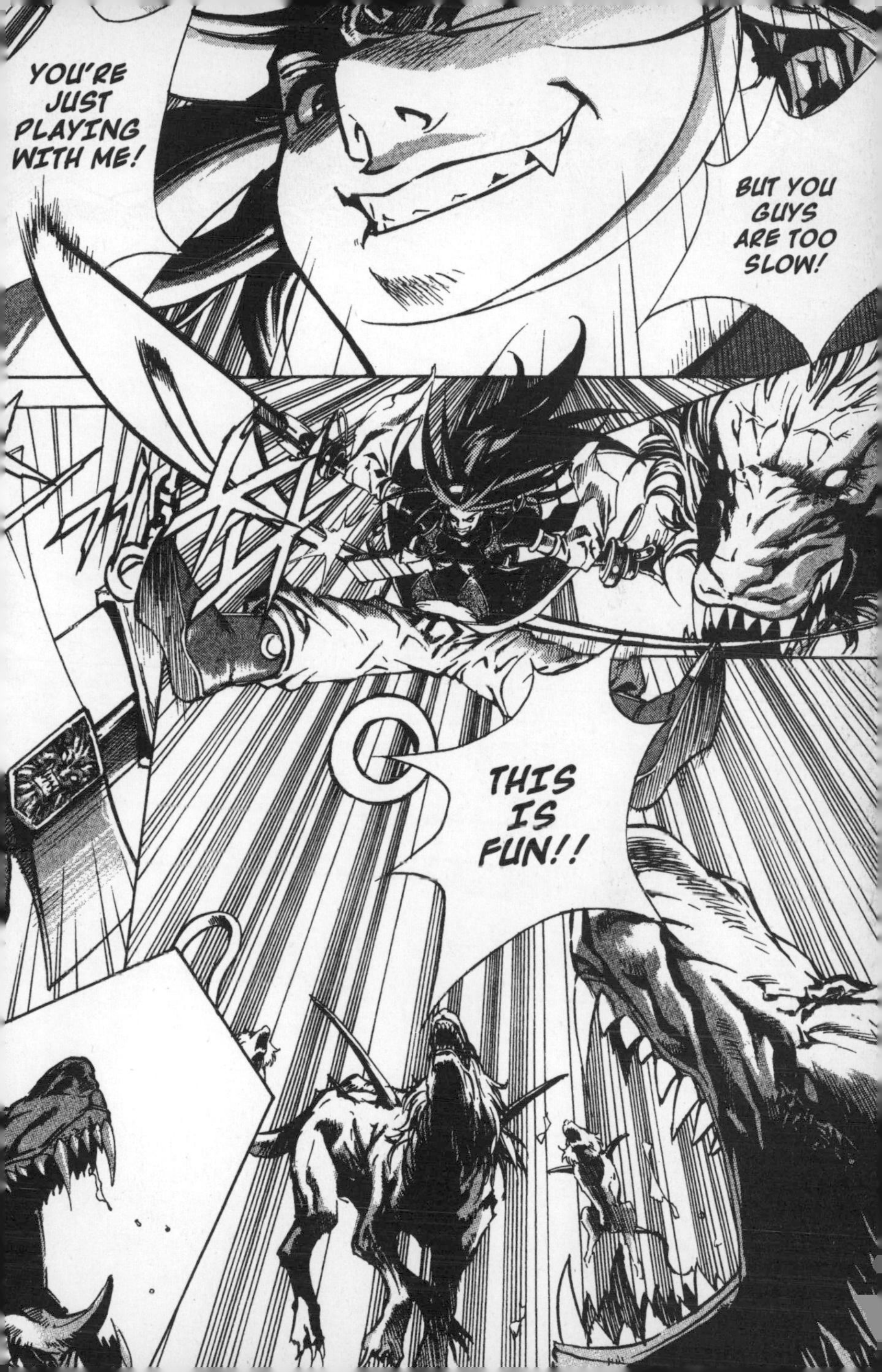
YOU'RE JUST PLAYING WITH ME!
BUT YOU GUYS ARE TOO SLOW!
THIS IS FUN!!

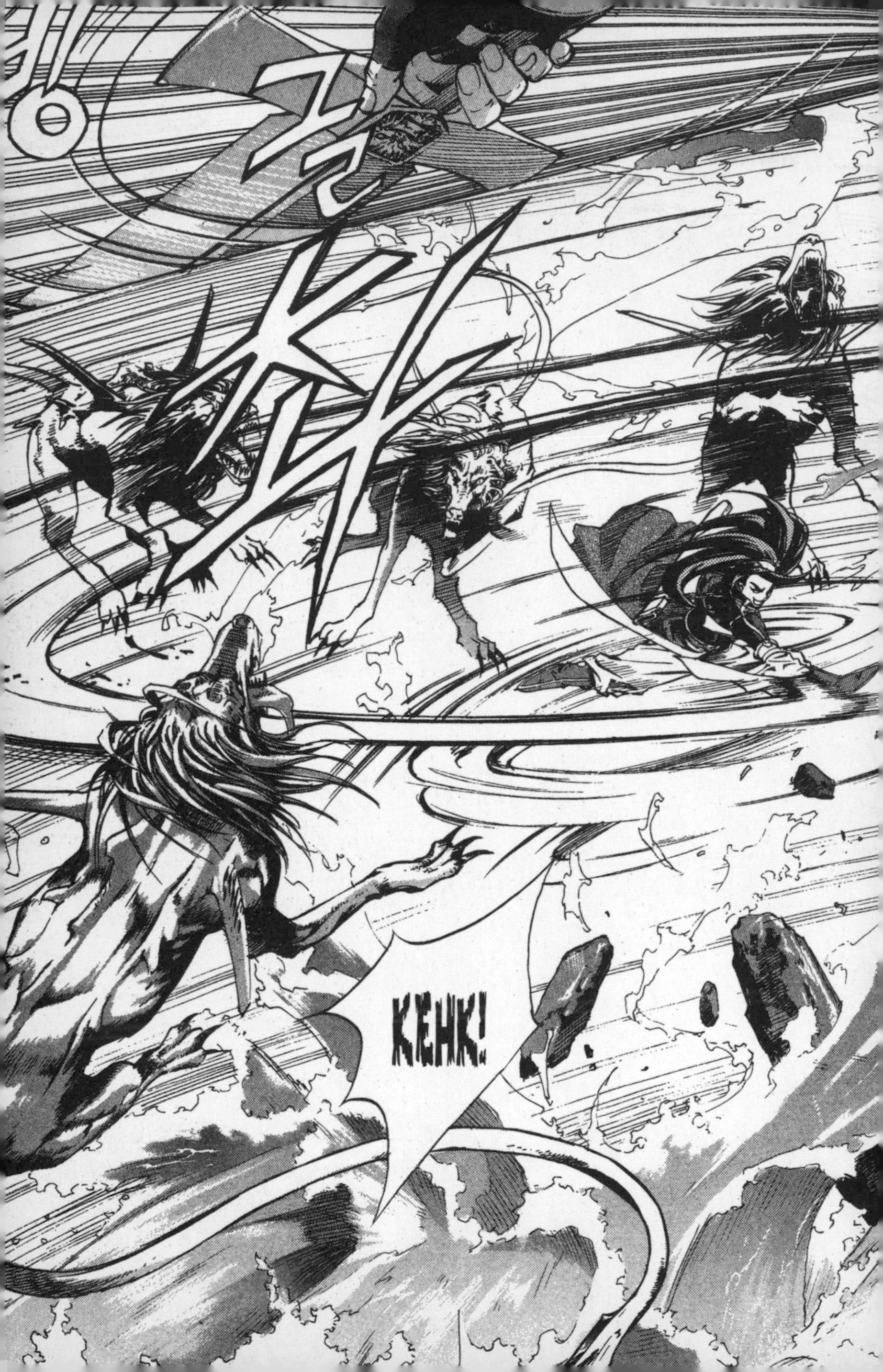
KEHK!

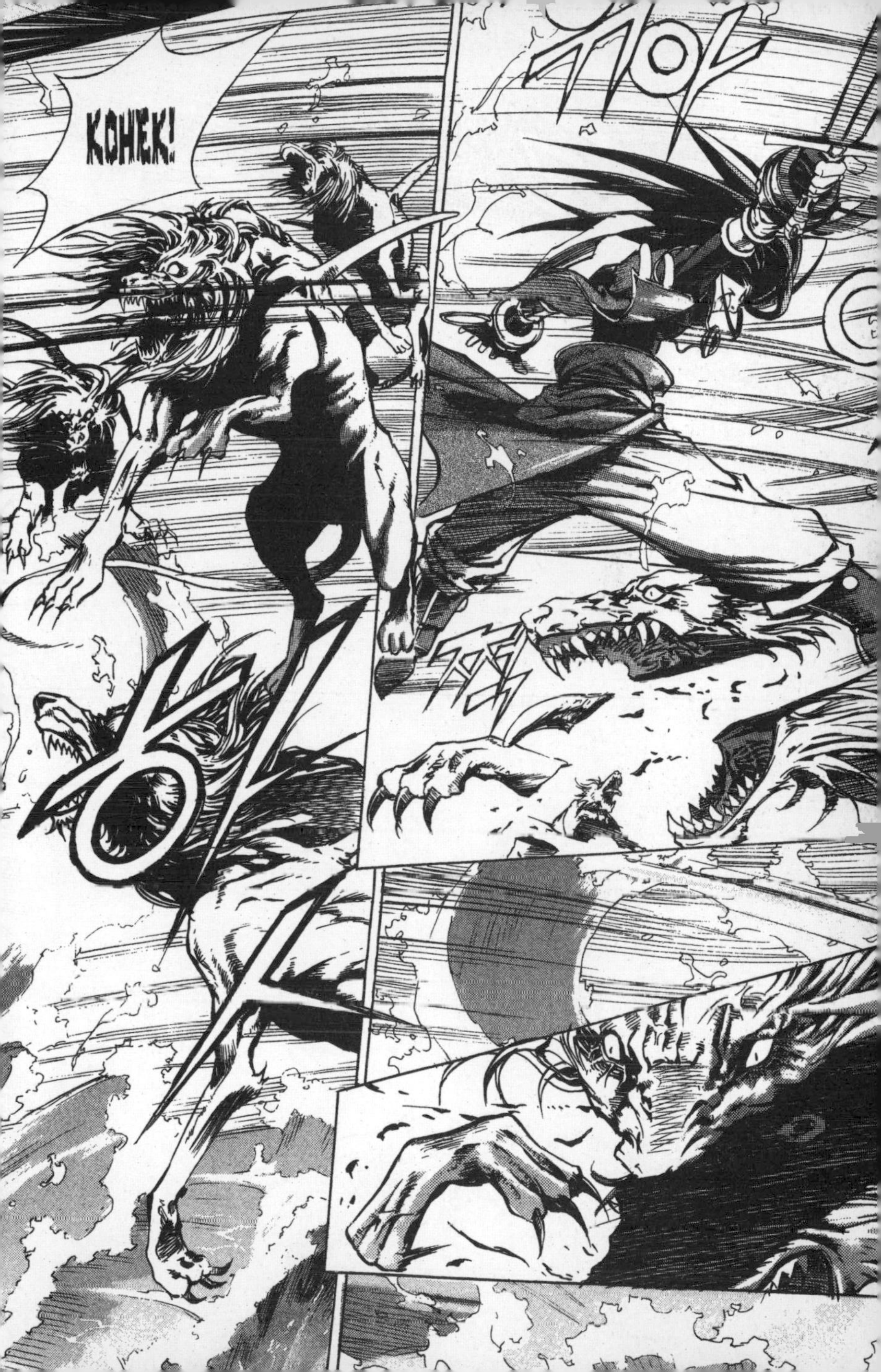
KOHEK!

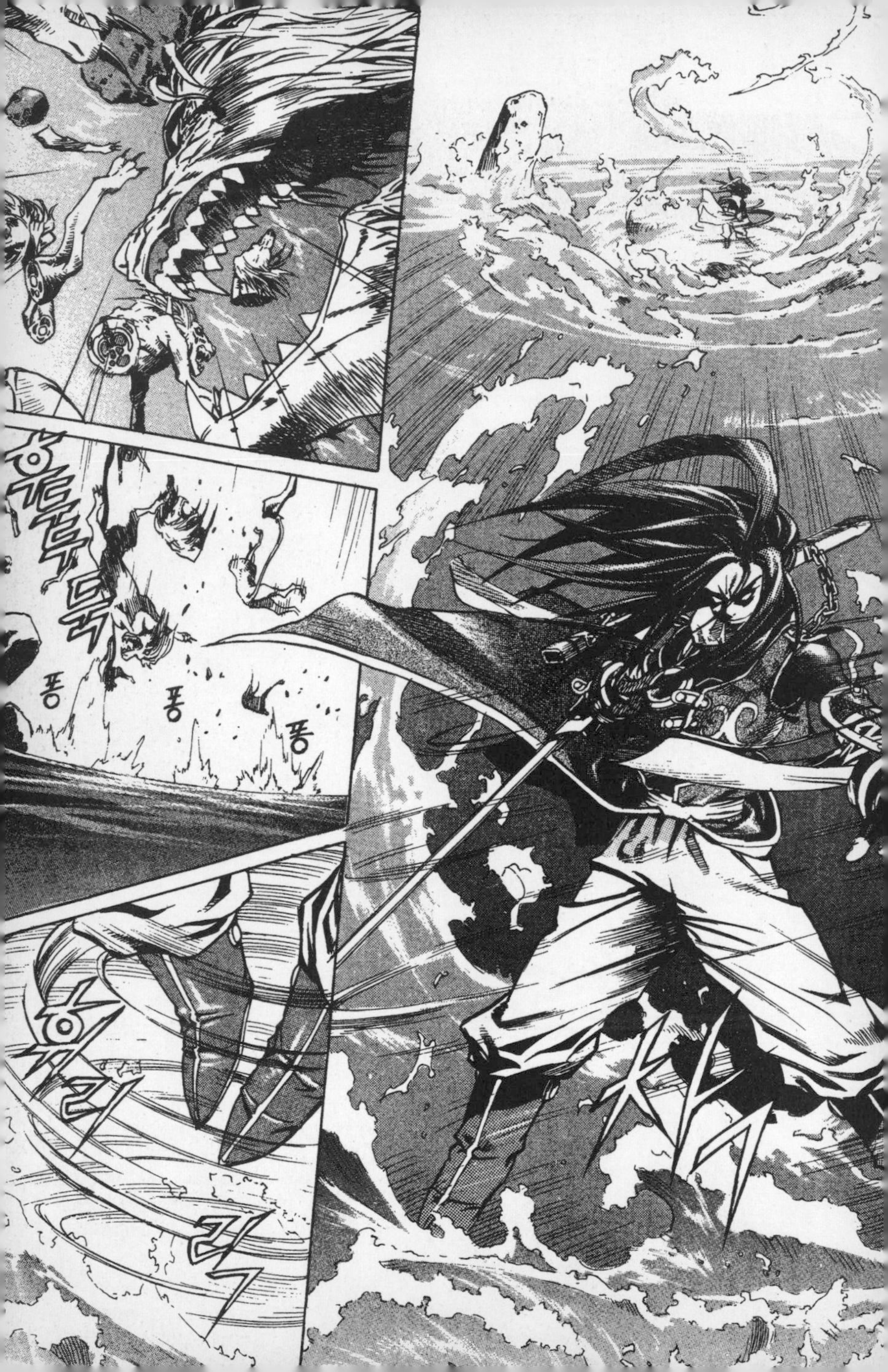
후드드득
퐁
퐁
퐁
휘리릭

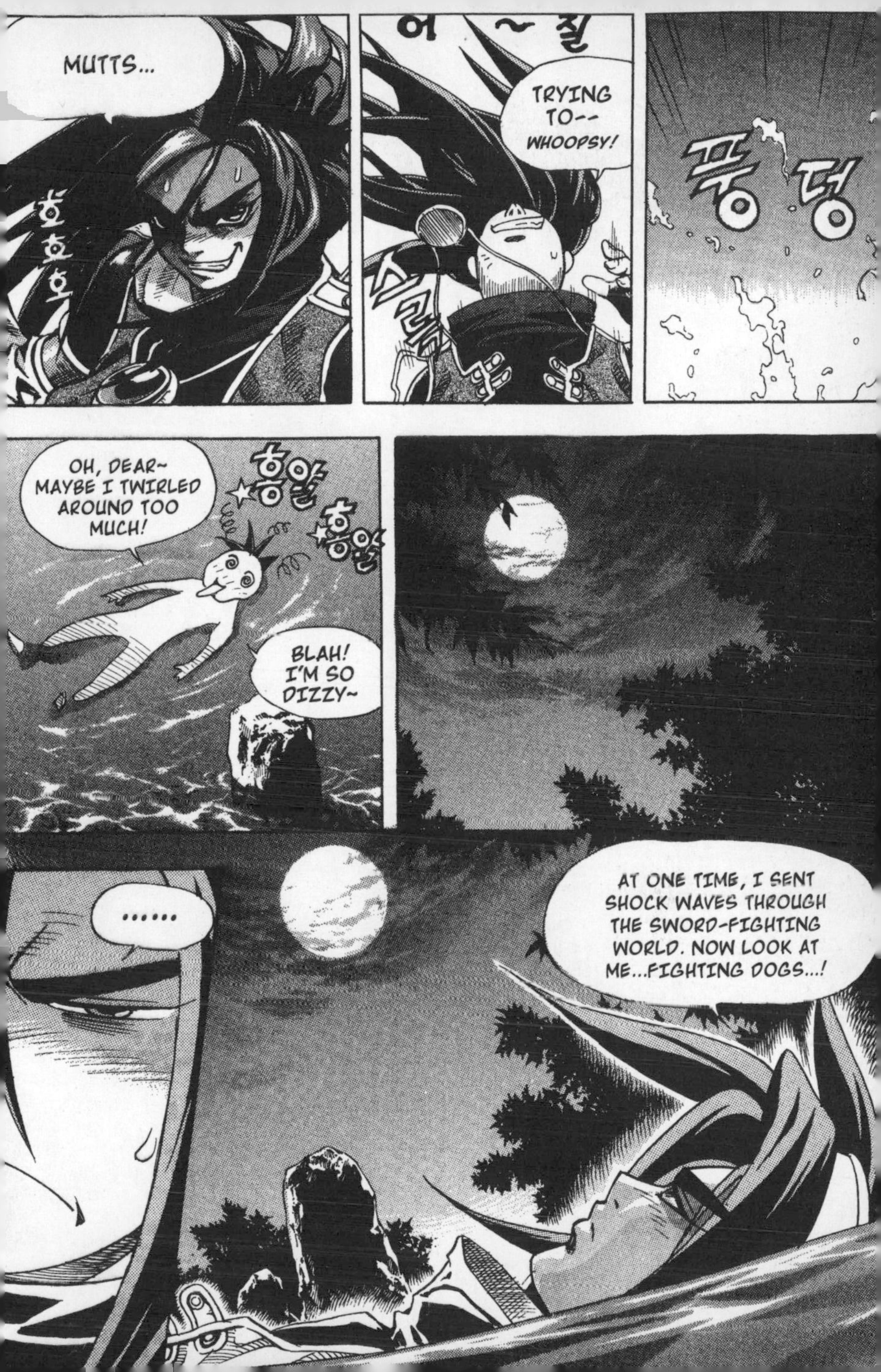
MUTTS...
호호호
어~찔
TRYING TO-- WHOOPSY!
풍덩
OH, DEAR~ MAYBE I TWIRLED AROUND TOO MUCH!
BLAH! I'M SO DIZZY~
......
AT ONE TIME, I SENT SHOCK WAVES THROUGH THE SWORD-FIGHTING WORLD. NOW LOOK AT ME...FIGHTING DOGS...!

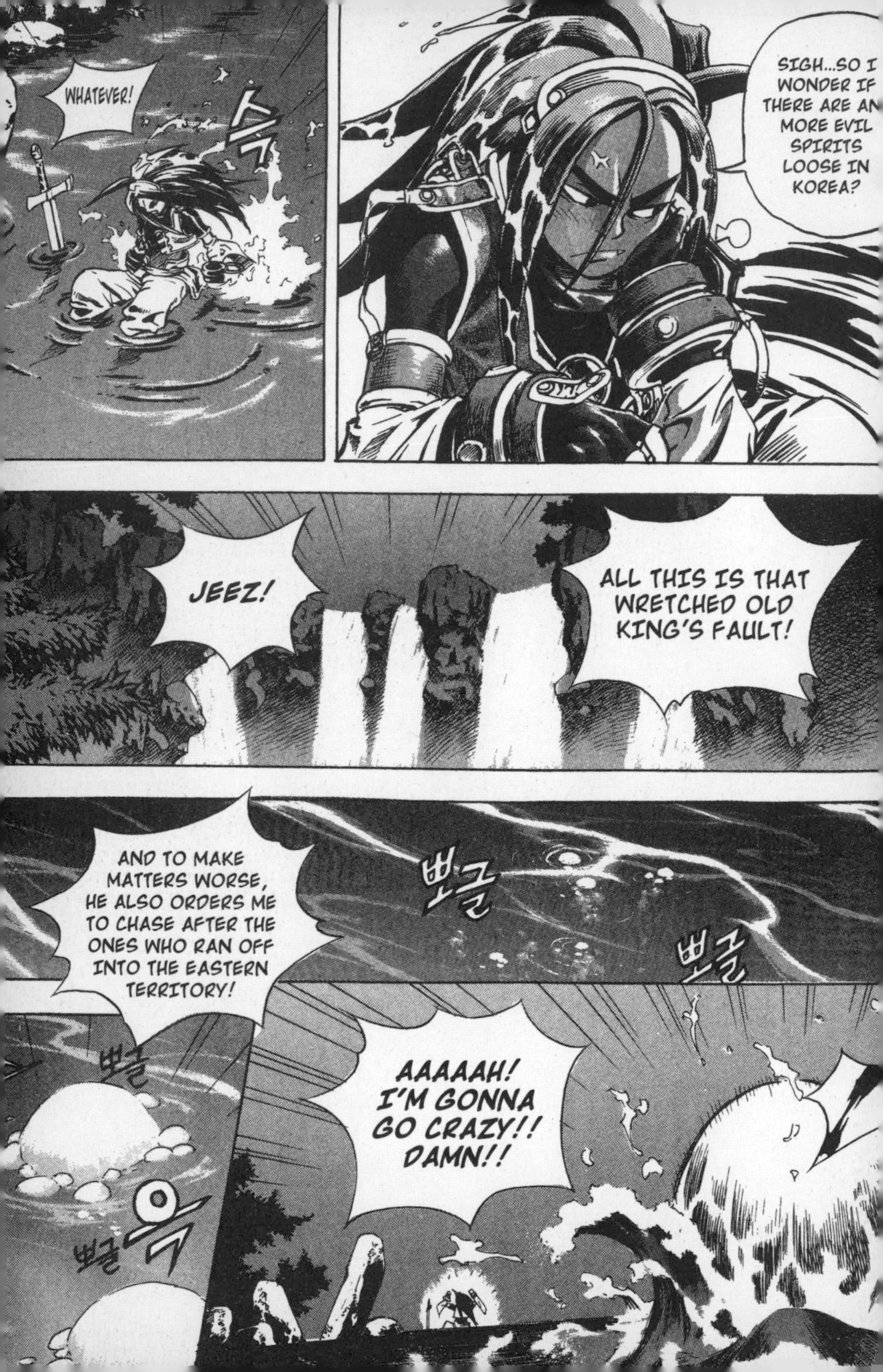
WHATEVER!
SIGH...SO I WONDER IF THERE ARE AN MORE EVIL SPIRITS LOOSE IN KOREA?
JEEZ!
ALL THIS IS THAT WRETCHED OLD KING'S FAULT!
AND TO MAKE MATTERS WORSE, HE ALSO ORDERS ME TO CHASE AFTER THE ONES WHO RAN OFF INTO THE EASTERN TERRITORY!
뽀글
뽀글
뽀글
뽀글
AAAAAH! I'M GONNA GO CRAZY!! DAMN!!

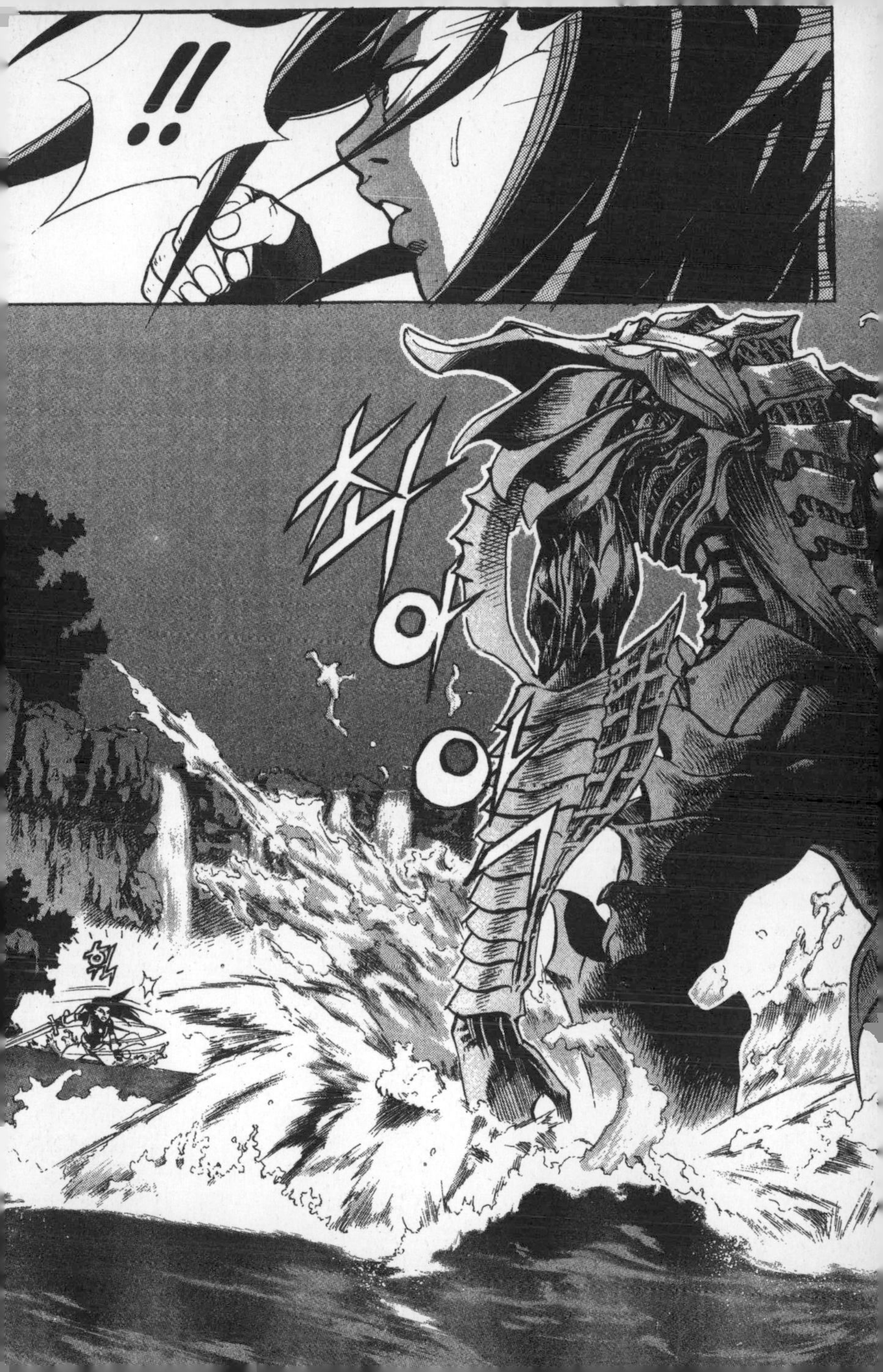
!!

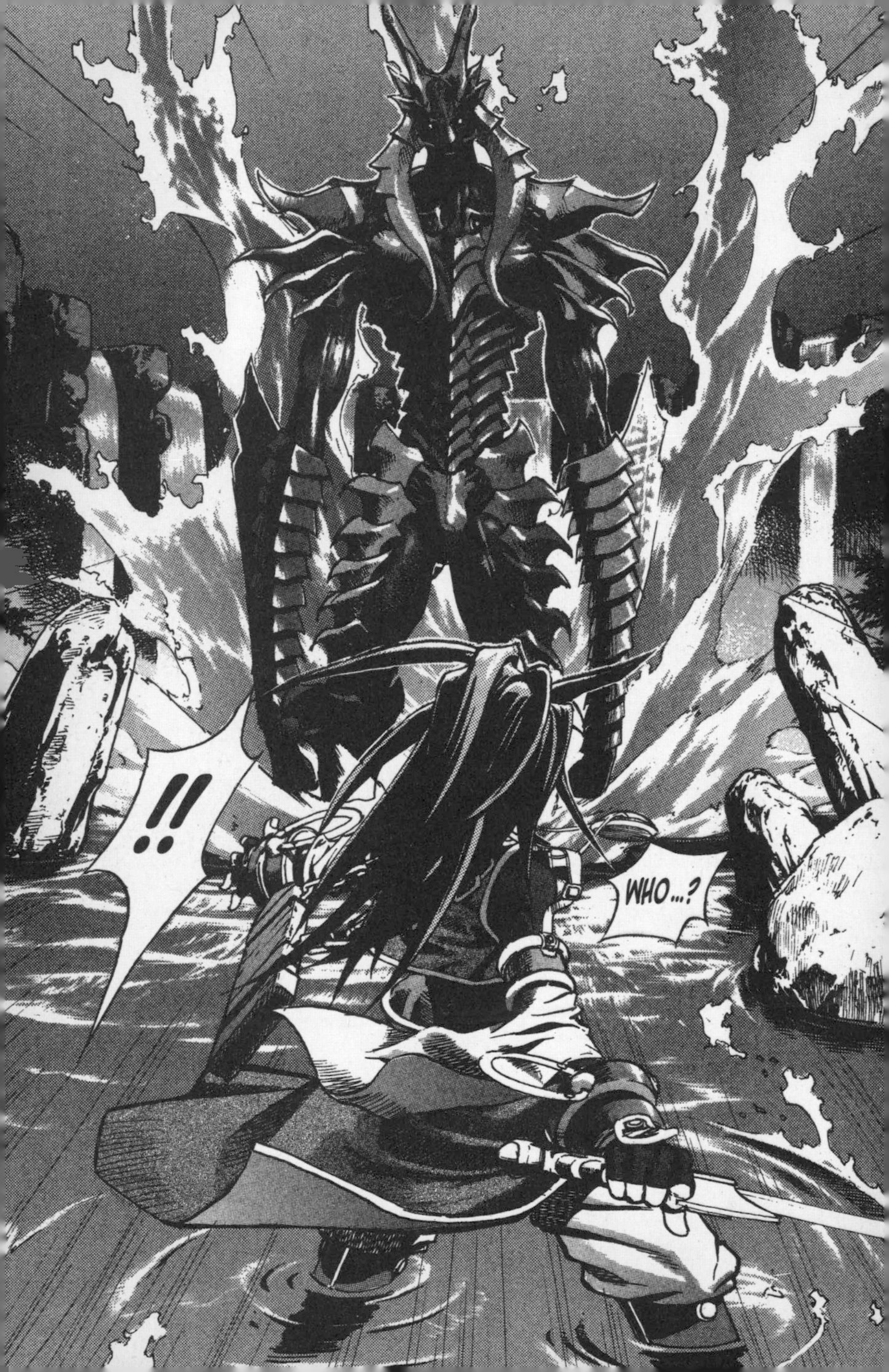
!!
WHO...?

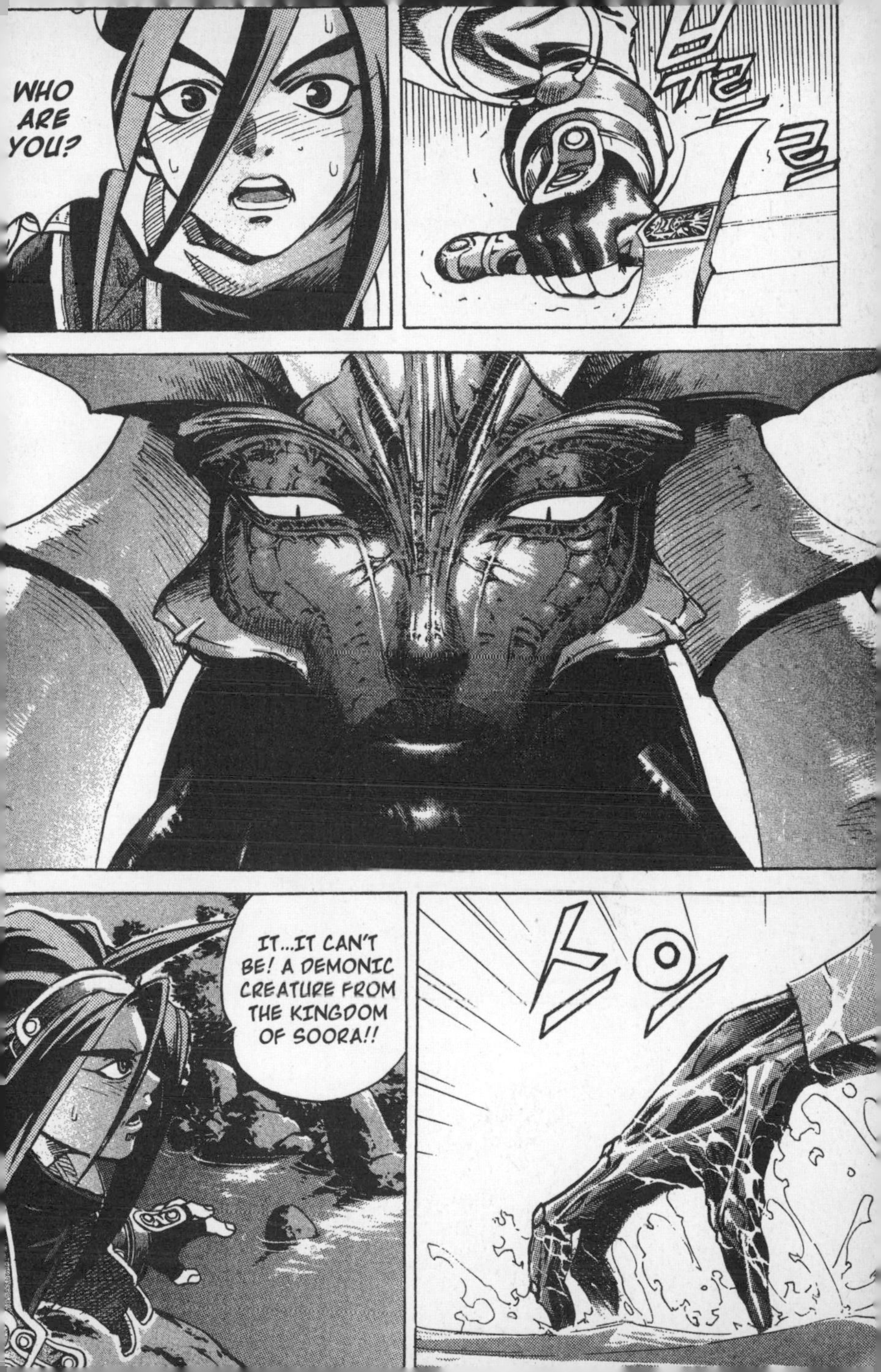
WHO ARE YOU?
IT...IT CAN'T BE! A DEMONIC CREATURE FROM THE KINGDOM OF SOORA!!

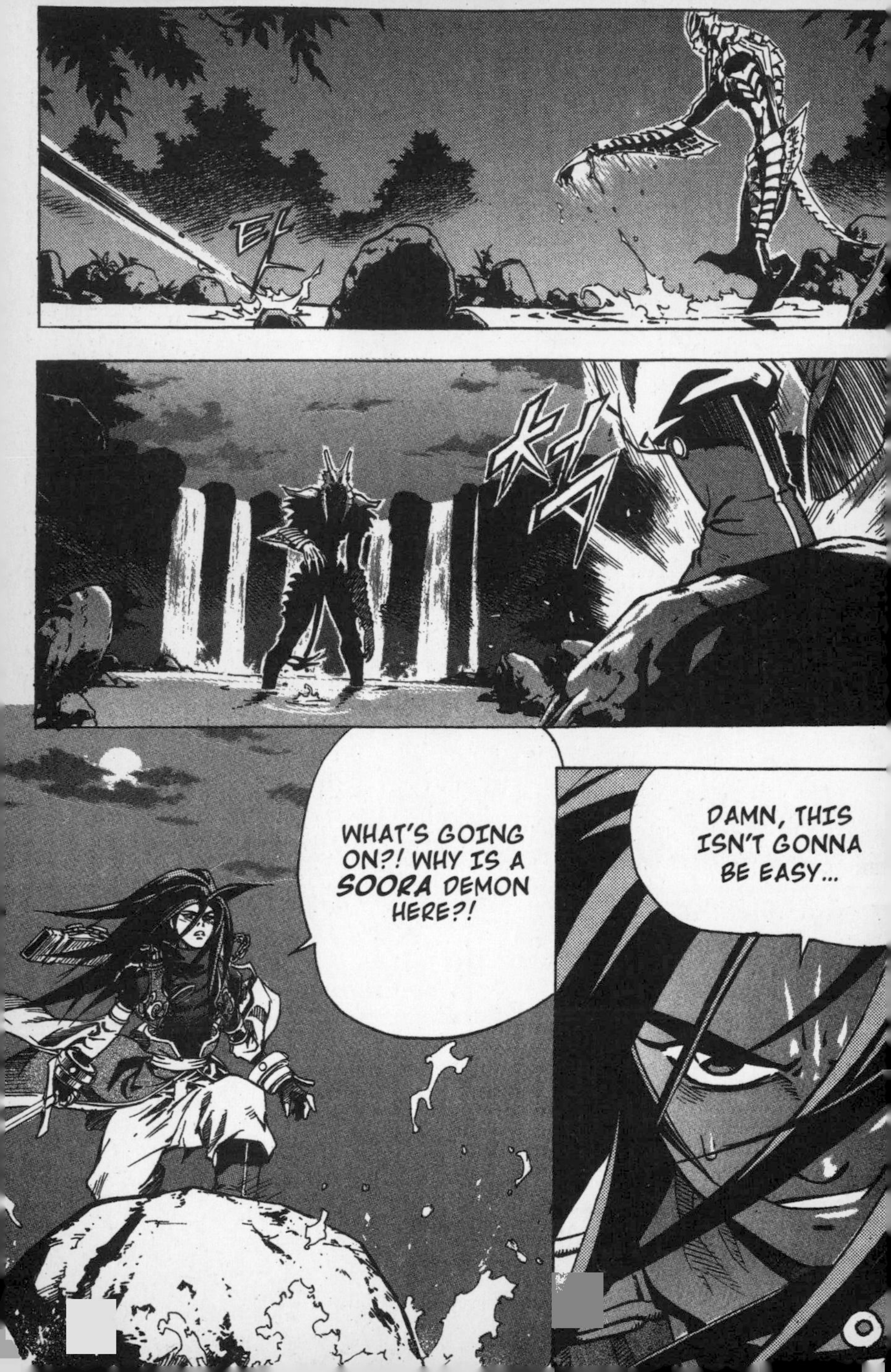
WHAT'S GOING ON?! WHY IS A SOORA DEMON HERE?!
DAMN, THIS ISN'T GONNA BE EASY...

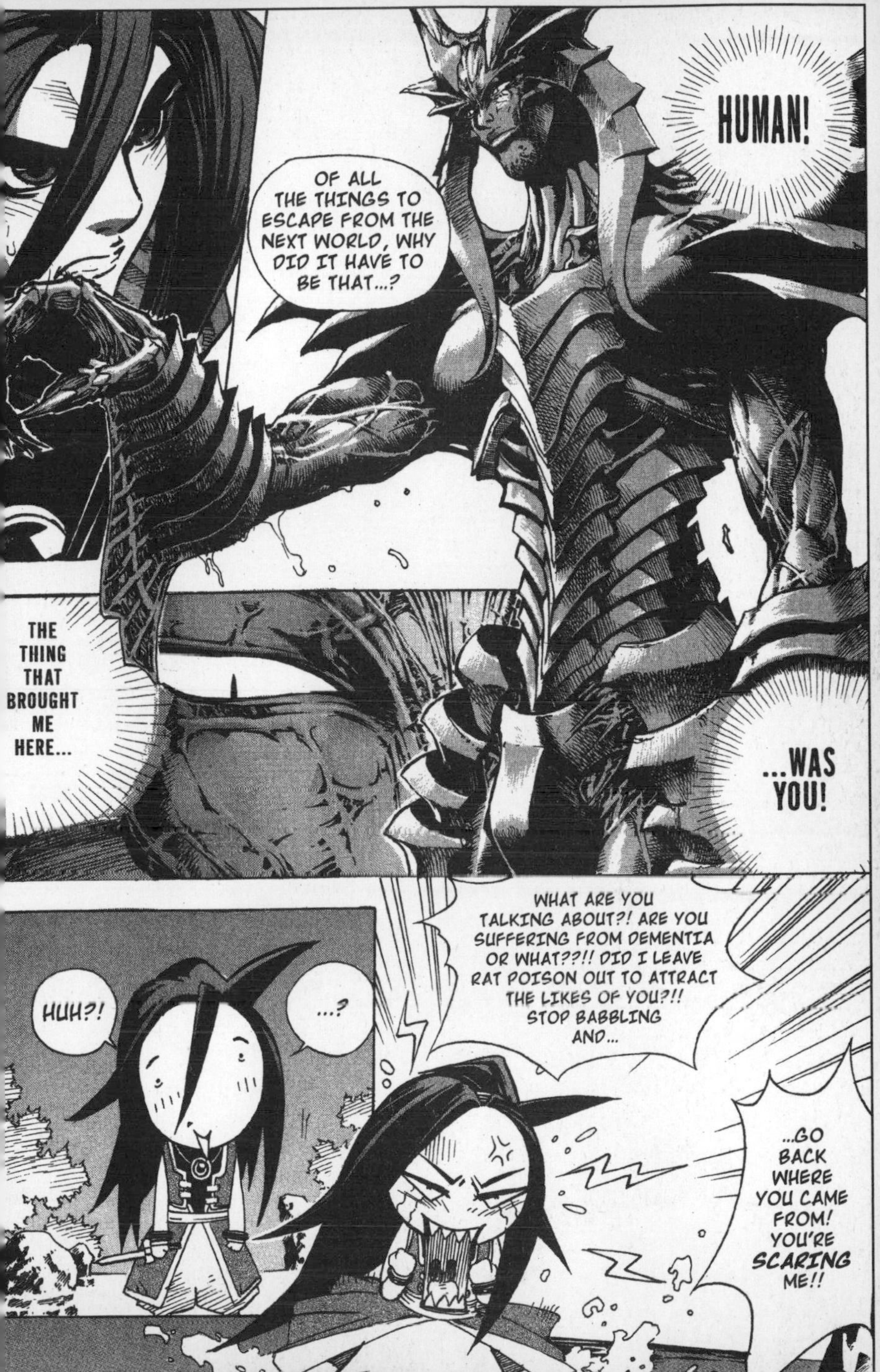
OF ALL THE THINGS TO ESCAPE FROM THE NEXT WORLD, WHY DID IT HAVE TO BE THAT...?
HUMAN!
THE THING THAT BROUGHT ME HERE...
...WAS YOU!
HUH?!
...?
WHAT ARE YOU TALKING ABOUT?! ARE YOU SUFFERING FROM DEMENTIA OR WHAT??!! DID I LEAVE RAT POISON OUT TO ATTRACT THE LIKES OF YOU?!! STOP BABBLING AND...
...GO BACK WHERE YOU CAME FROM! YOU'RE SCARING ME!!

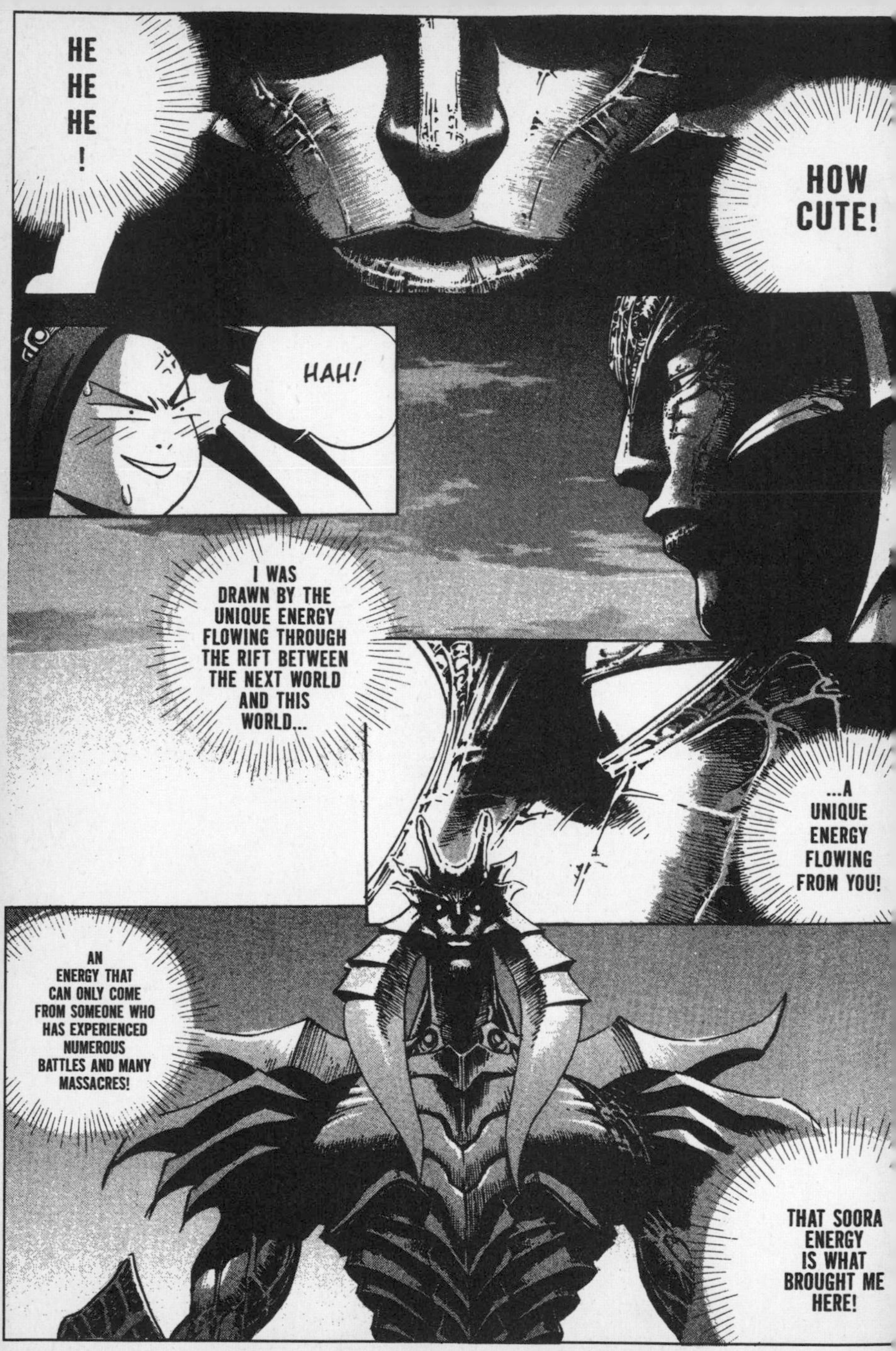
HE HE HE !
HOW CUTE!
HAH!
I WAS DRAWN BY THE UNIQUE ENERGY FLOWING THROUGH THE RIFT BETWEEN THE NEXT WORLD AND THIS WORLD...
...A UNIQUE ENERGY FLOWING FROM YOU!
AN ENERGY THAT CAN ONLY COME FROM SOMEONE WHO HAS EXPERIENCED NUMEROUS BATTLES AND MANY MASSACRES!
THAT SOORA ENERGY IS WHAT BROUGHT ME HERE!

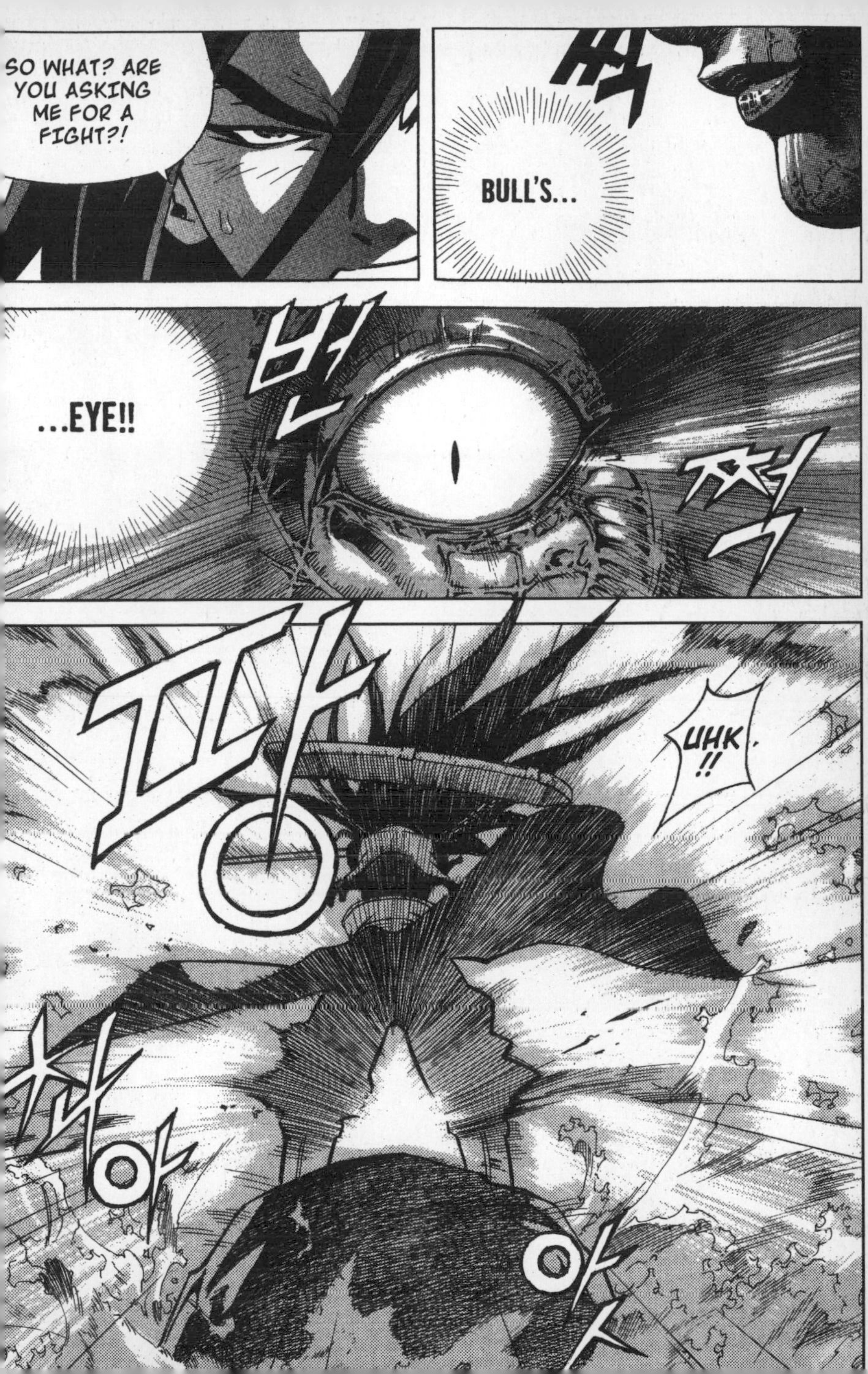
SO WHAT? ARE YOU ASKING ME FOR A FIGHT?!
BULL'S...
...EYE!!
UHK!!

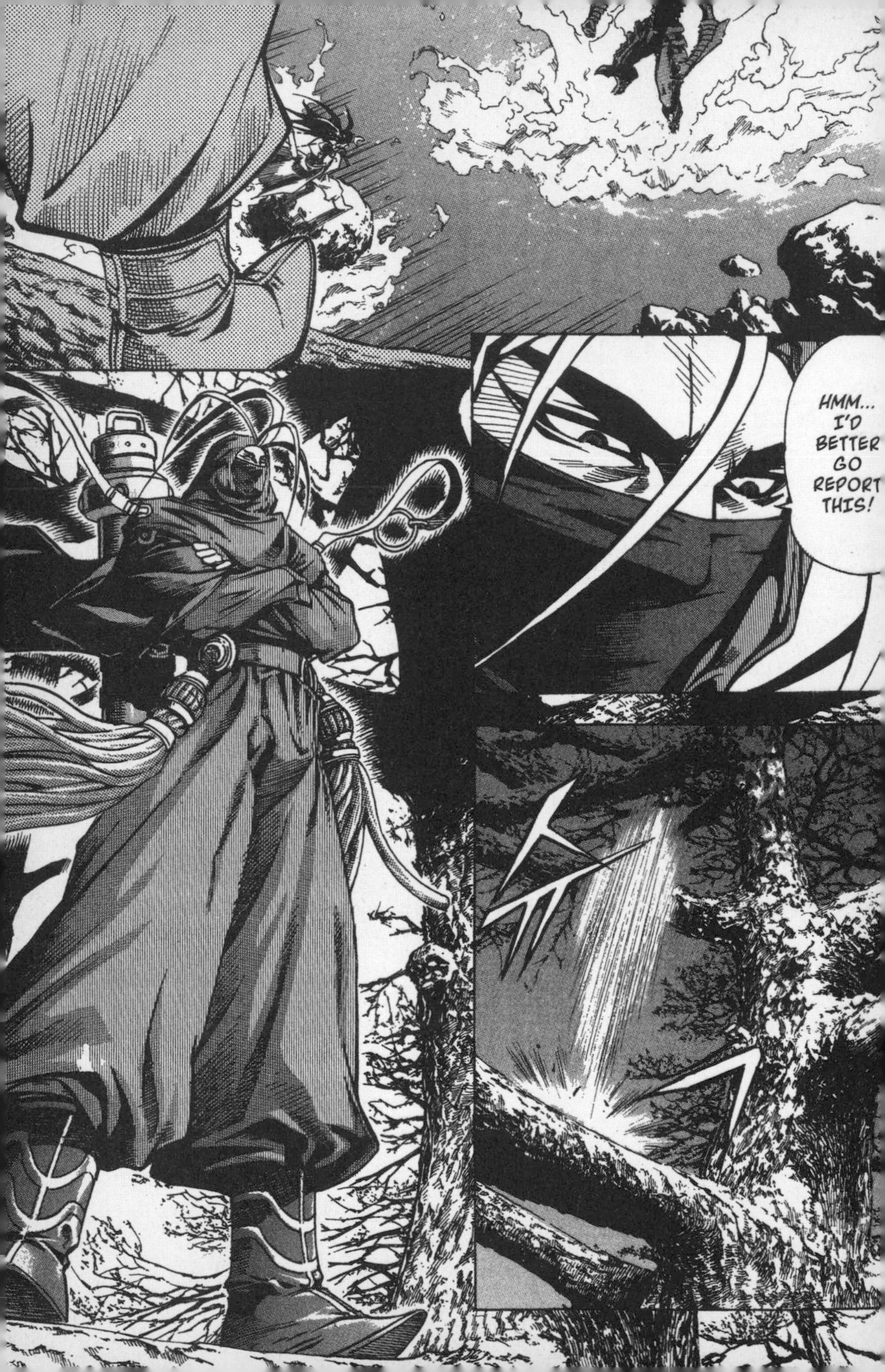
HMM... I'D BETTER GO REPORT THIS!

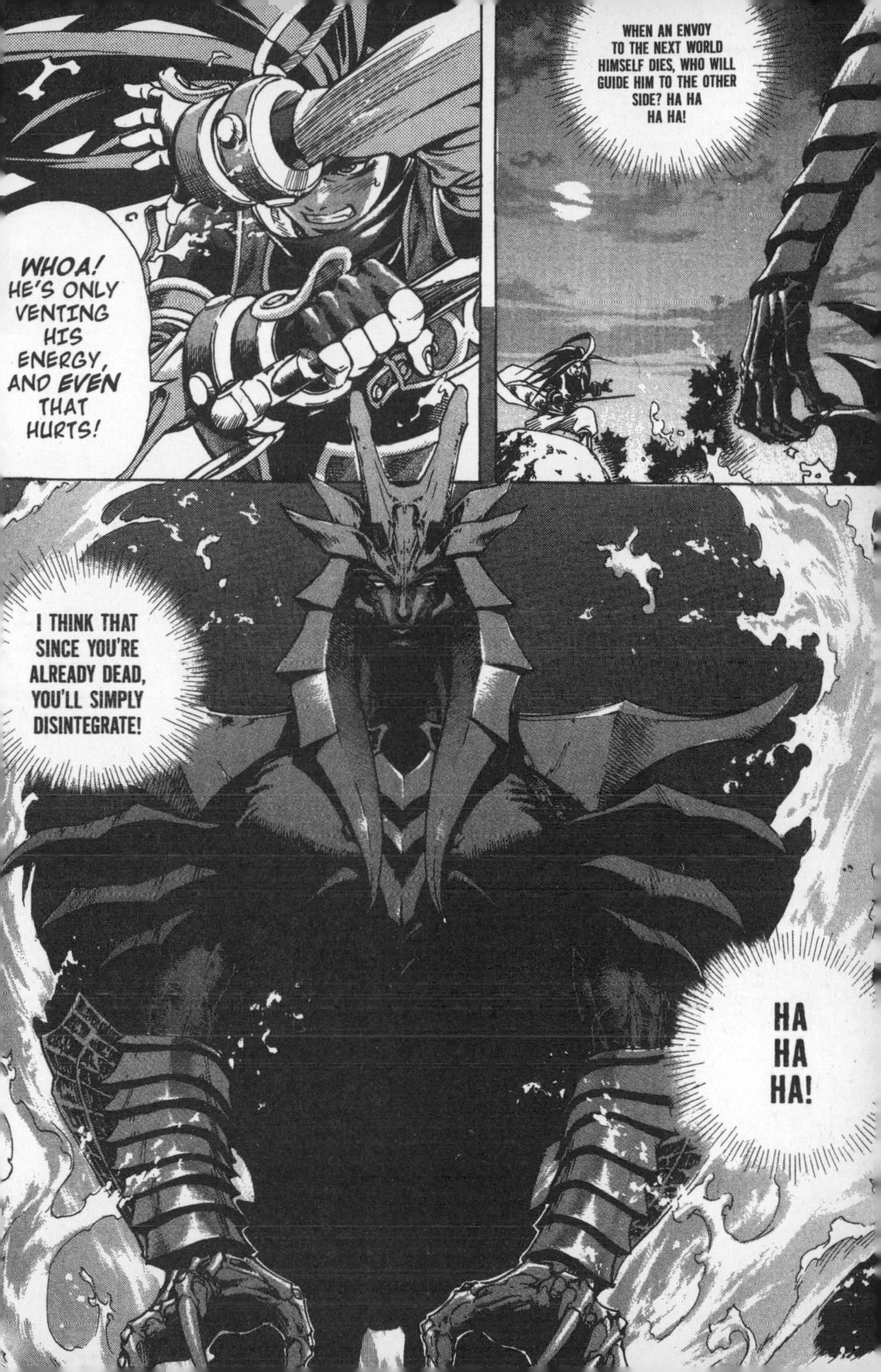
WHOA! HE'S ONLY VENTING HIS ENERGY, AND EVEN THAT HURTS!
WHEN AN ENVOY TO THE NEXT WORLD HIMSELF DIES, WHO WILL GUIDE HIM TO THE OTHER SIDE? HA HA HA HA!
I THINK THAT SINCE YOU'RE ALREADY DEAD, YOU'LL SIMPLY DISINTEGRATE!
HA HA HA!

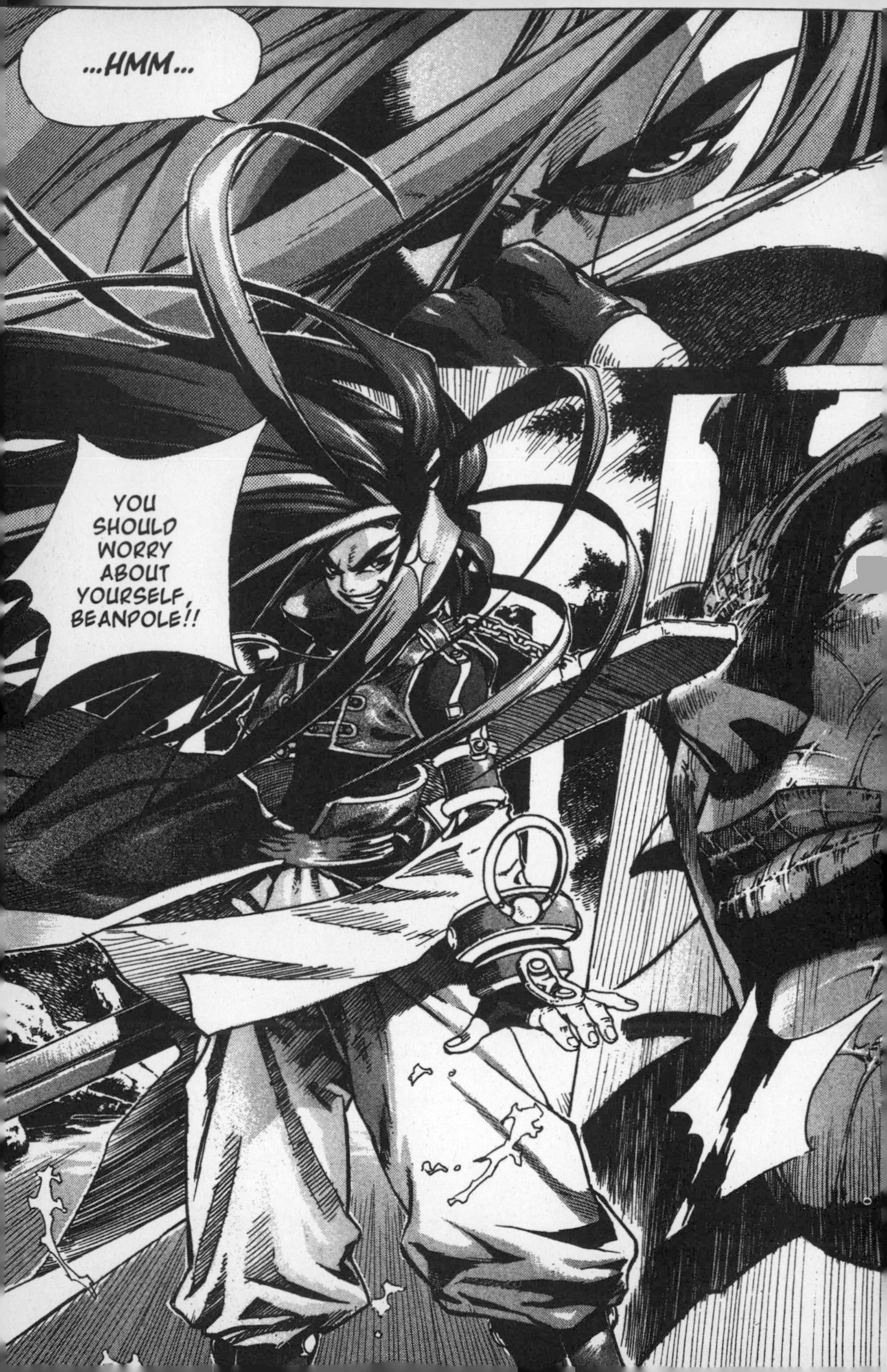
...HMM...
YOU SHOULD WORRY ABOUT YOURSELF, BEANPOLE!!

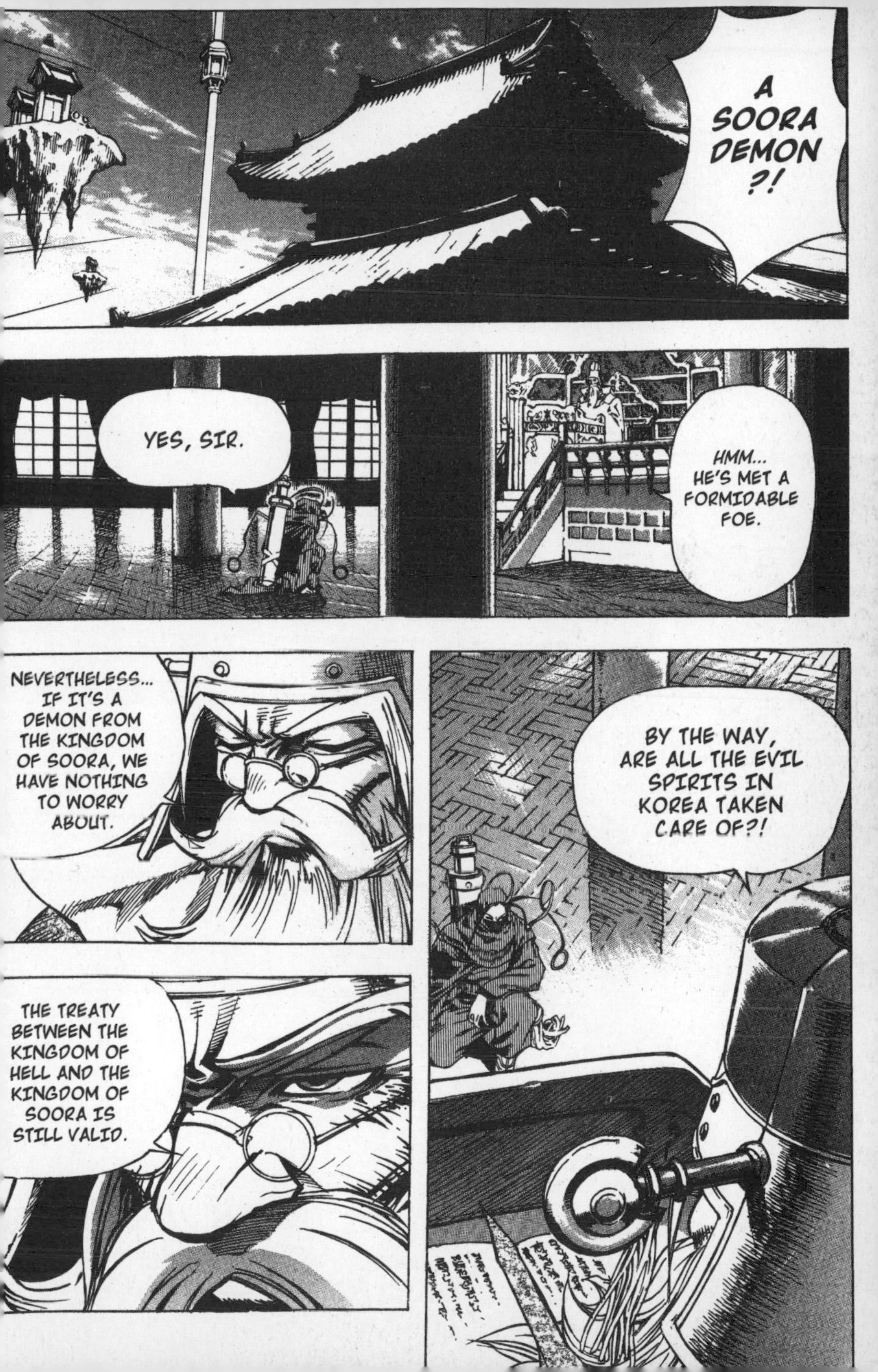
A SOORA DEMON ?!
YES, SIR.
HMM... HE'S MET A FORMIDABLE FOE.
NEVERTHELESS... IF IT'S A DEMON FROM THE KINGDOM OF SOORA, WE HAVE NOTHING TO WORRY ABOUT.
THE TREATY BETWEEN THE KINGDOM OF HELL AND THE KINGDOM OF SOORA IS STILL VALID.
BY THE WAY, ARE ALL THE EVIL SPIRITS IN KOREA TAKEN CARE OF?!

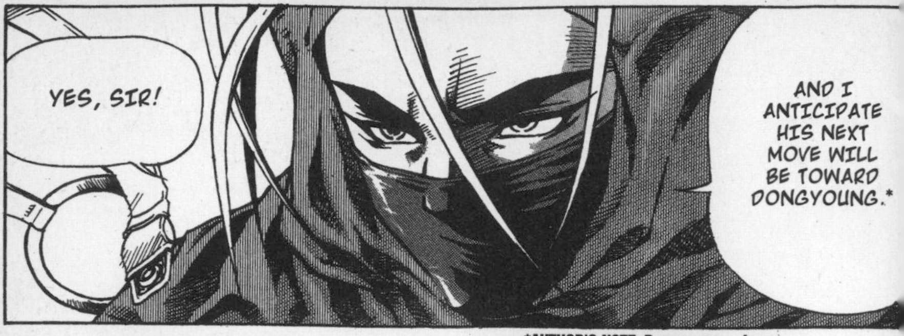
YES, SIR!
AND I ANTICIPATE HIS NEXT MOVE WILL BE TOWARD DONGYOUNG.*

*AUTHOR'S NOTE: Dongyoung = Japan

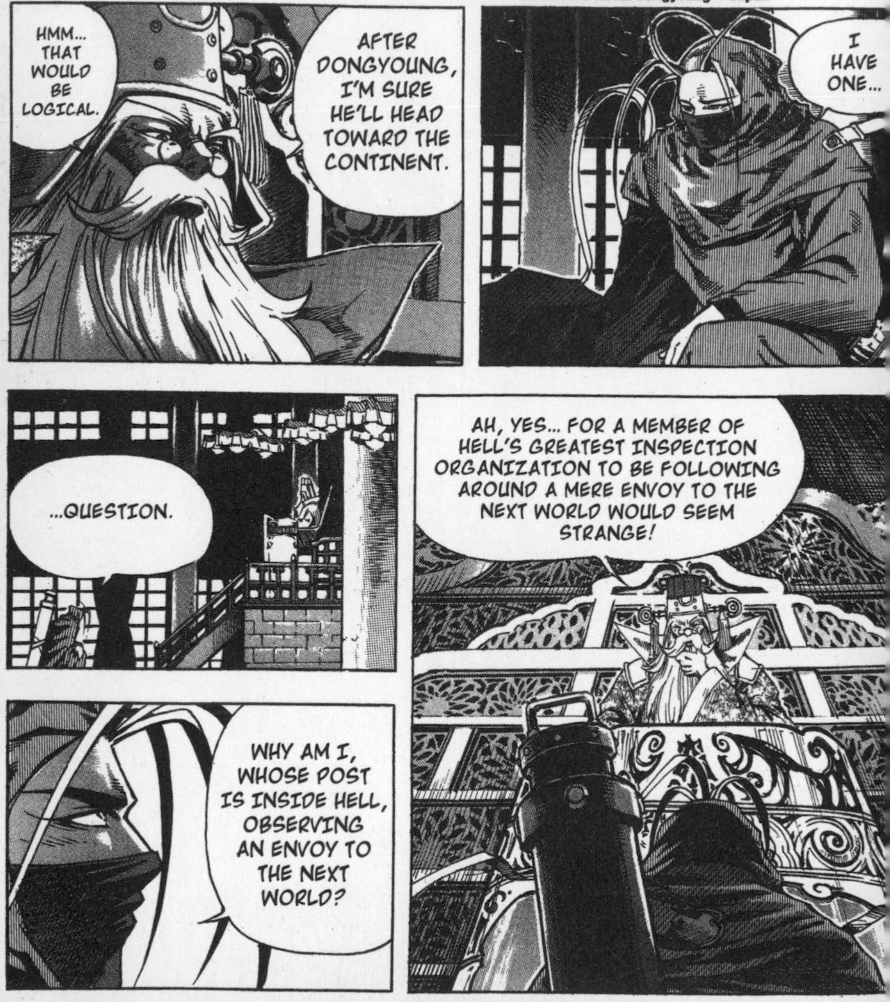
HMM... THAT WOULD BE LOGICAL.
AFTER DONGYOUNG, I'M SURE HE'LL HEAD TOWARD THE CONTINENT.
I HAVE ONE...
...QUESTION.
WHY AM I, WHOSE POST IS INSIDE HELL, OBSERVING AN ENVOY TO THE NEXT WORLD?
AH, YES... FOR A MEMBER OF HELL'S GREATEST INSPECTION ORGANIZATION TO BE FOLLOWING AROUND A MERE ENVOY TO THE NEXT WORLD WOULD SEEM STRANGE!

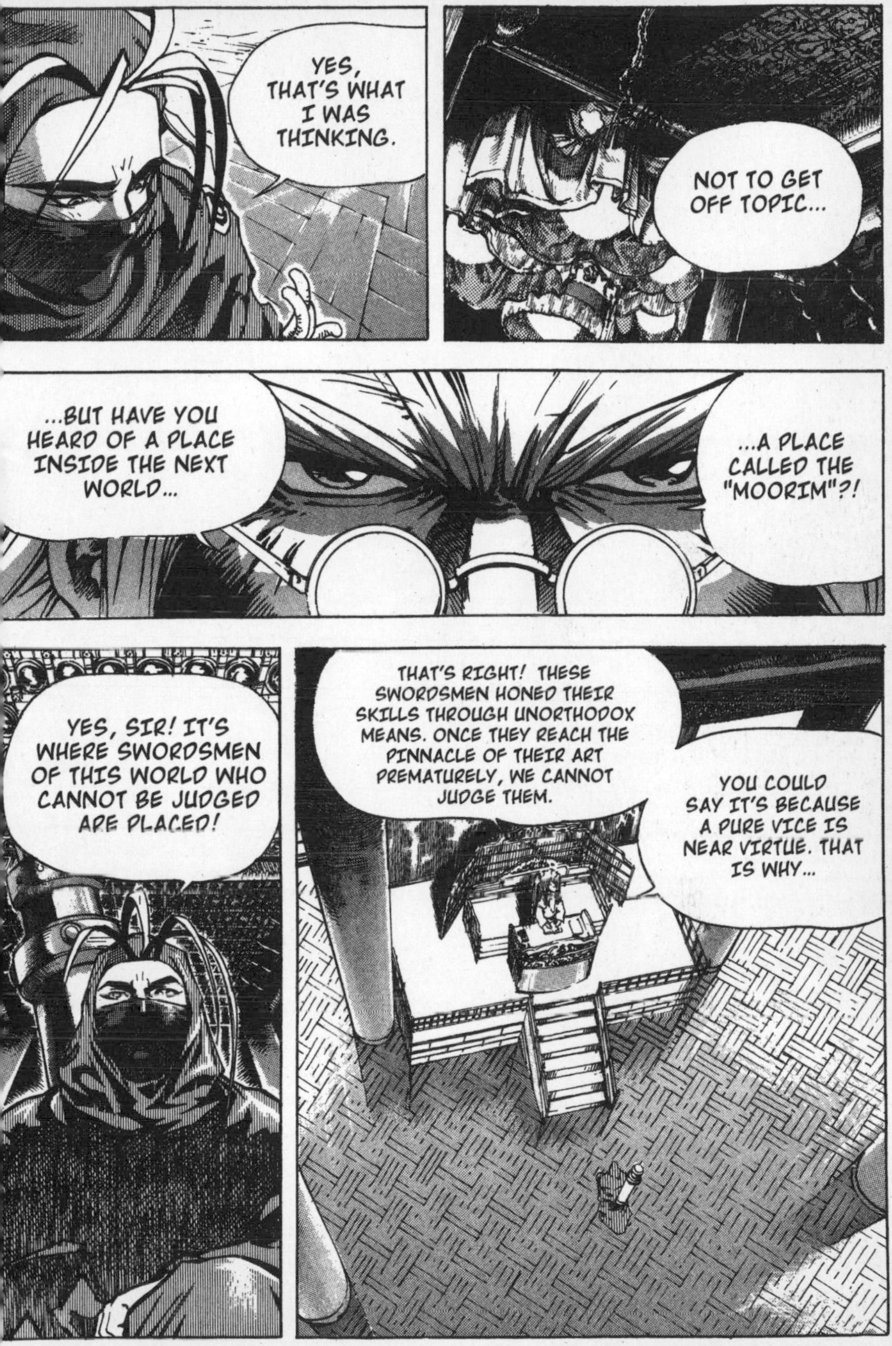
YES, THAT'S WHAT I WAS THINKING.
NOT TO GET OFF TOPIC...
...BUT HAVE YOU HEARD OF A PLACE INSIDE THE NEXT WORLD...
...A PLACE CALLED THE "MOORIM"?!
YES, SIR! IT'S WHERE SWORDSMEN OF THIS WORLD WHO CANNOT BE JUDGED ARE PLACED!
THAT'S RIGHT! THESE SWORDSMEN HONED THEIR SKILLS THROUGH UNORTHODOX MEANS. ONCE THEY REACH THE PINNACLE OF THEIR ART PREMATURELY, WE CANNOT JUDGE THEM.
YOU COULD SAY IT'S BECAUSE A PURE VICE IS NEAR VIRTUE. THAT IS WHY...

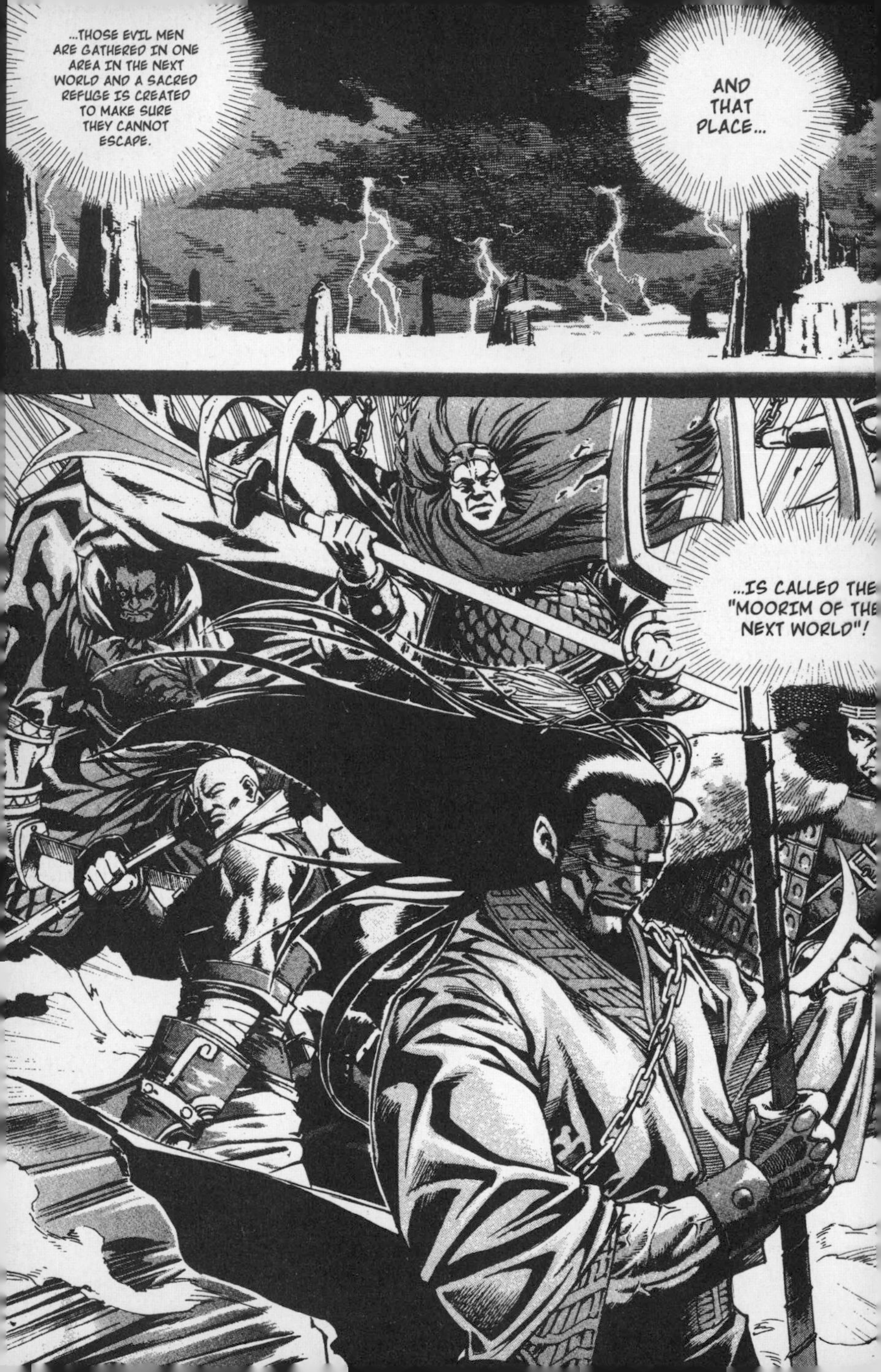
...THOSE EVIL MEN ARE GATHERED IN ONE AREA IN THE NEXT WORLD AND A SACRED REFUGE IS CREATED TO MAKE SURE THEY CANNOT ESCAPE.
AND THAT PLACE...
...IS CALLED THE "MOORIM OF THE NEXT WORLD"!

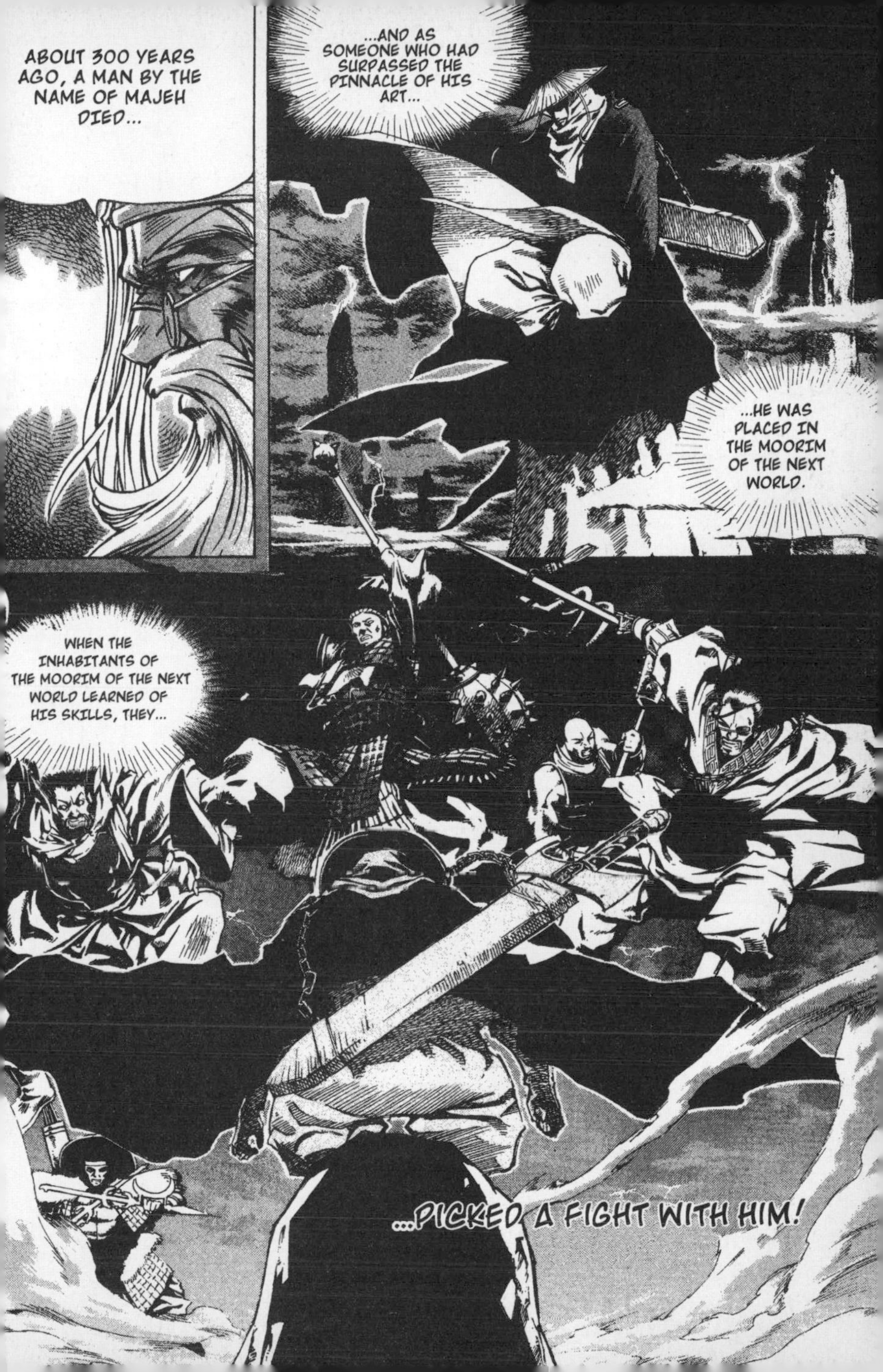
ABOUT 300 YEARS AGO, A MAN BY THE NAME OF MAJEH DIED...
...AND AS SOMEONE WHO HAD SURPASSED THE PINNACLE OF HIS ART...
...HE WAS PLACED IN THE MOORIM OF THE NEXT WORLD.
WHEN THE INHABITANTS OF THE MOORIM OF THE NEXT WORLD LEARNED OF HIS SKILLS, THEY...
...PICKED A FIGHT WITH HIM!

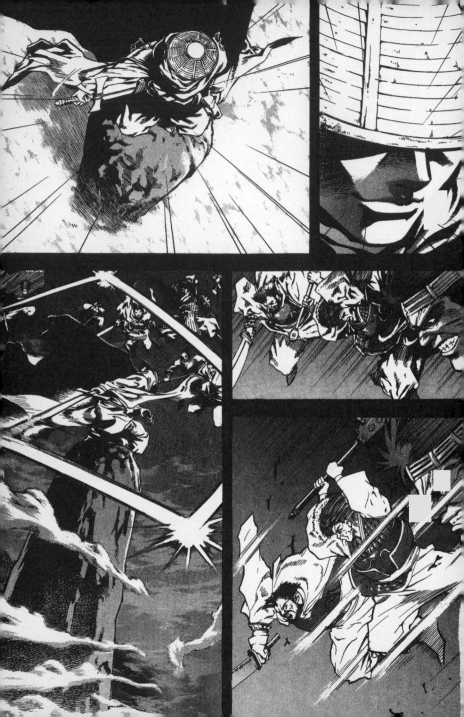

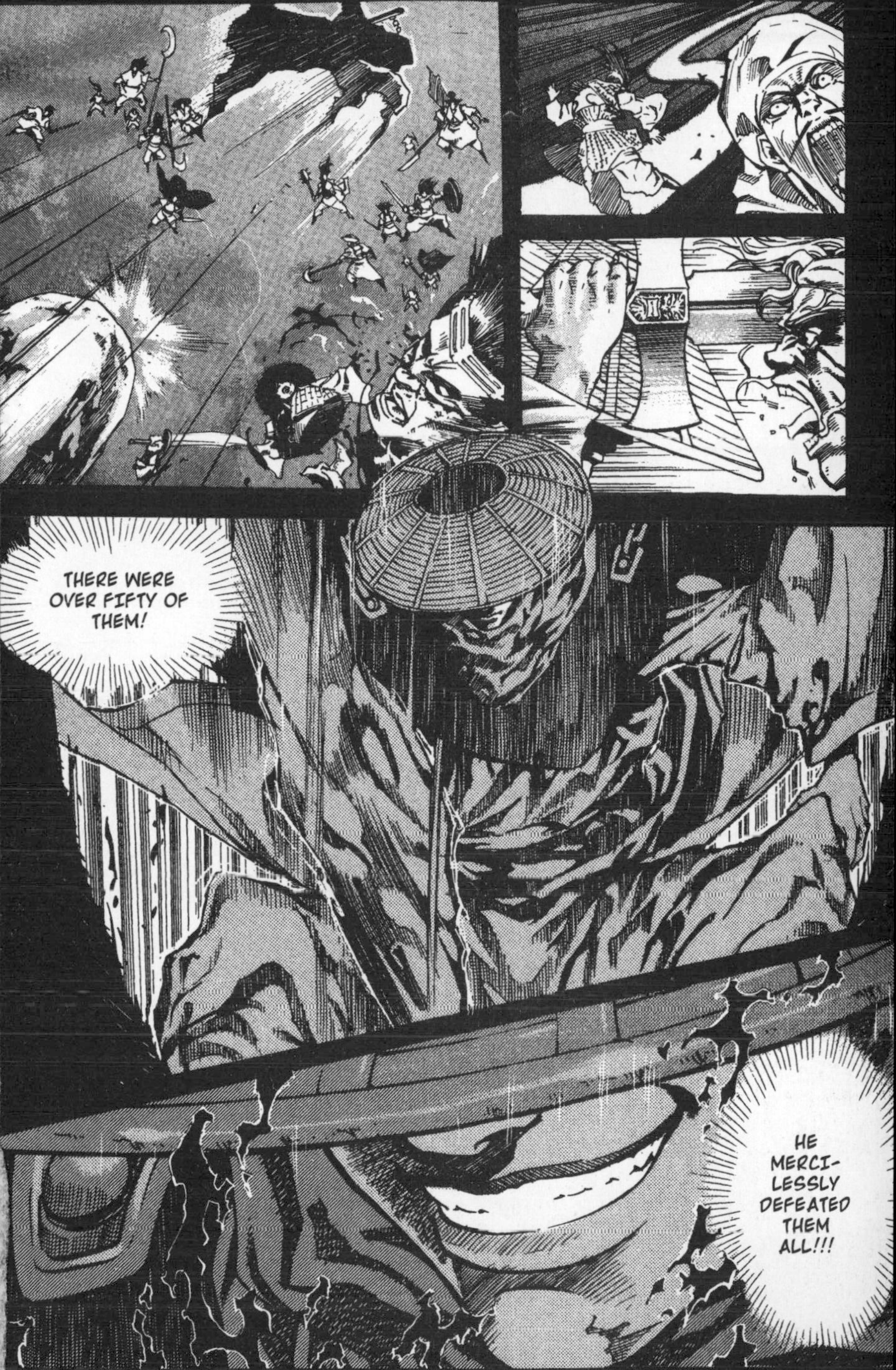
THERE WERE OVER FIFTY OF THEM!
HE MERCI-LESSLY DEFEATED THEM ALL!!!

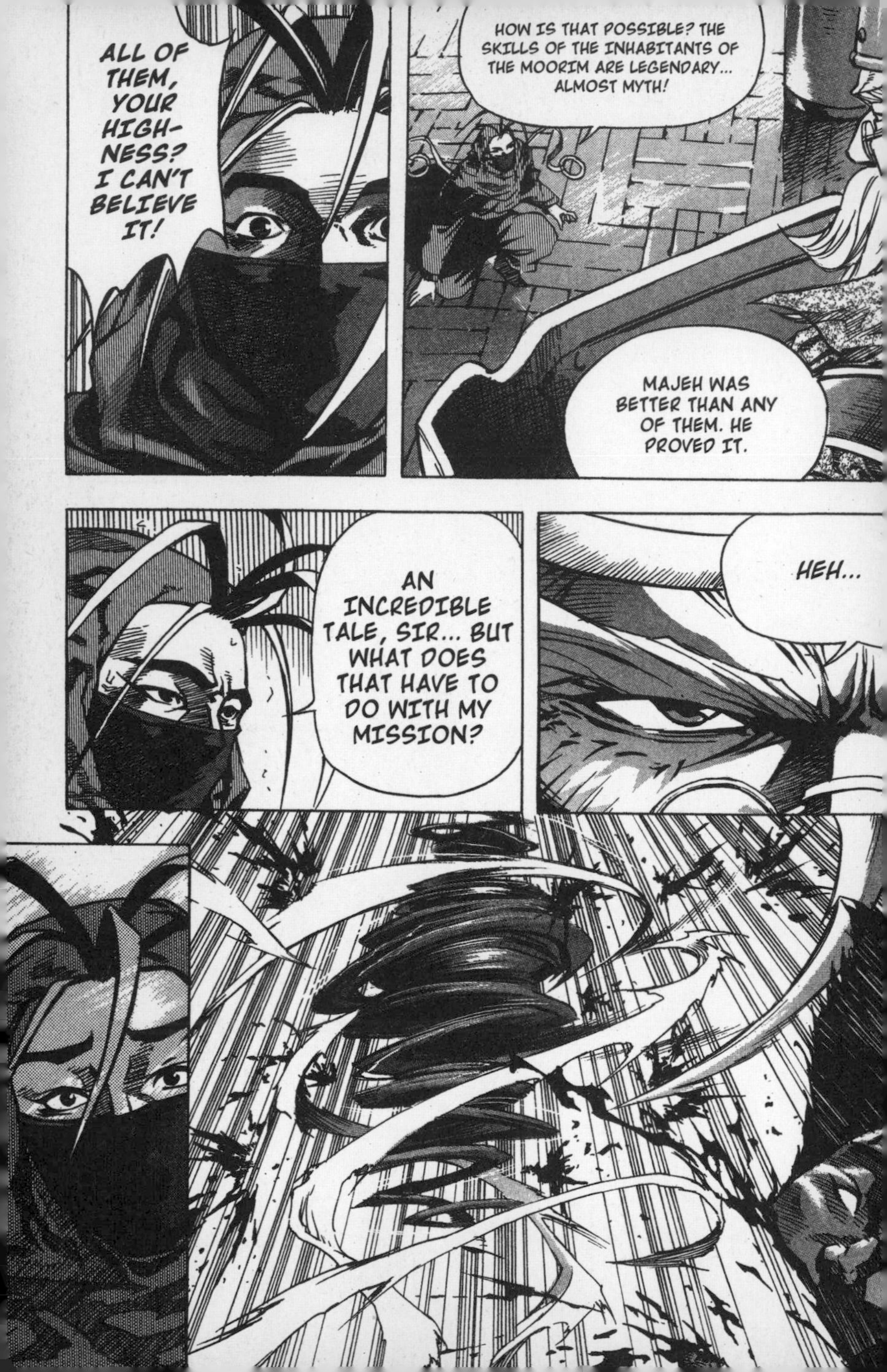
ALL OF THEM, YOUR HIGHNESS? I CAN'T BELIEVE IT!
HOW IS THAT POSSIBLE? THE SKILLS OF THE INHABITANTS OF THE MOORIM ARE LEGENDARY... ALMOST MYTH!
MAJEH WAS BETTER THAN ANY OF THEM. HE PROVED IT.
AN INCREDIBLE TALE, SIR... BUT WHAT DOES THAT HAVE TO DO WITH MY MISSION?
HEH...

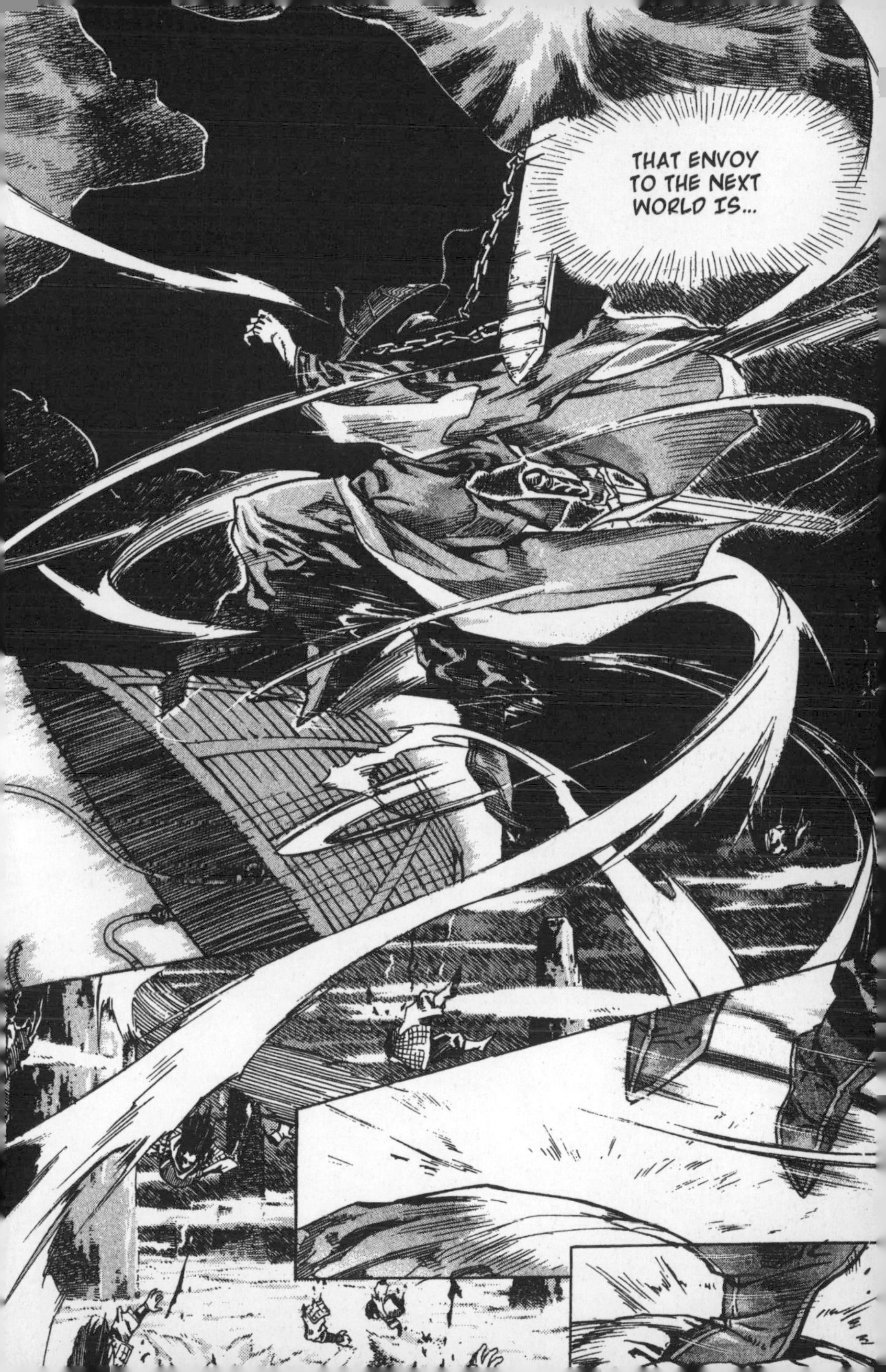
THAT ENVOY TO THE NEXT WORLD IS...

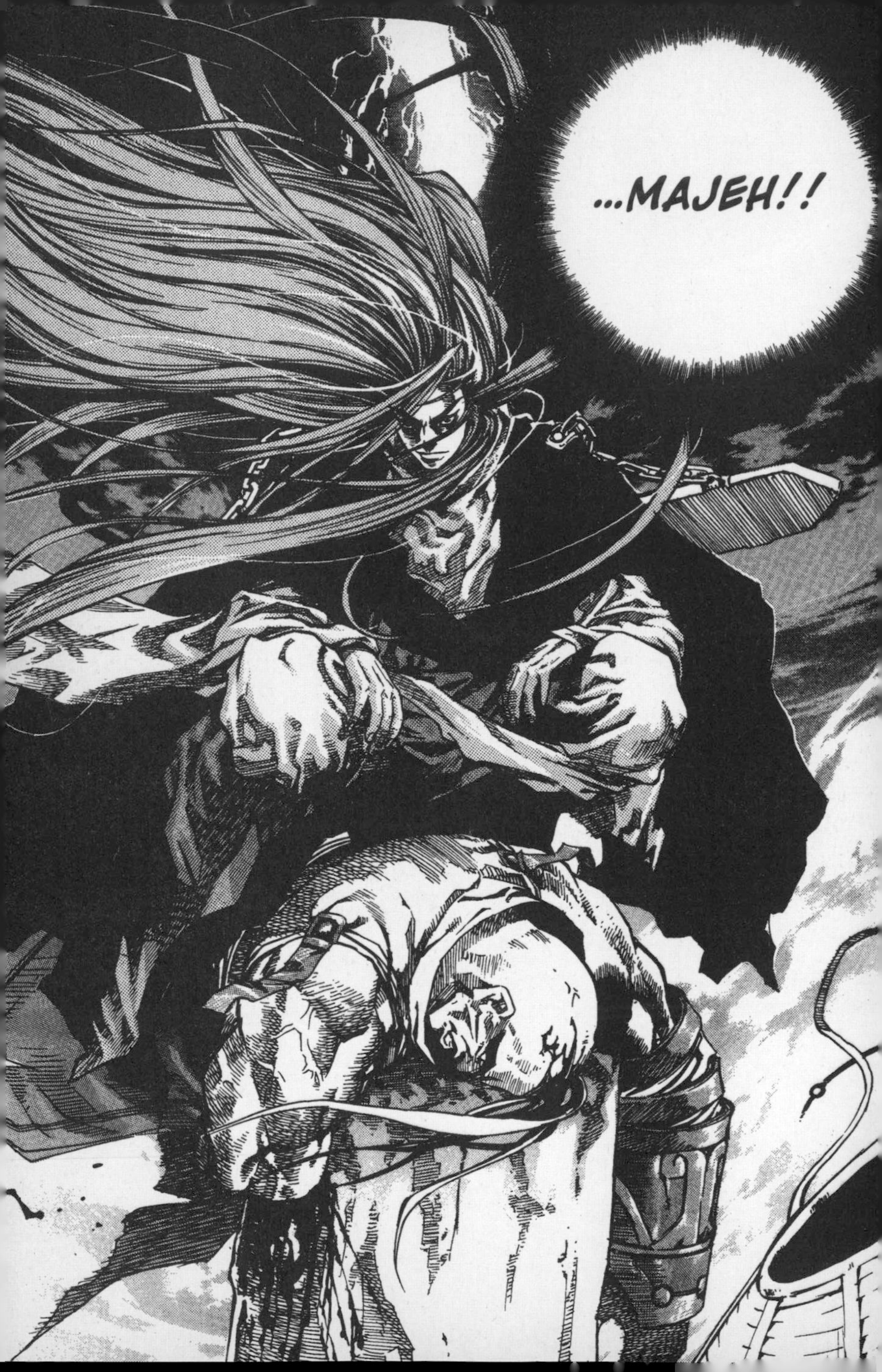
...MAJEH!!

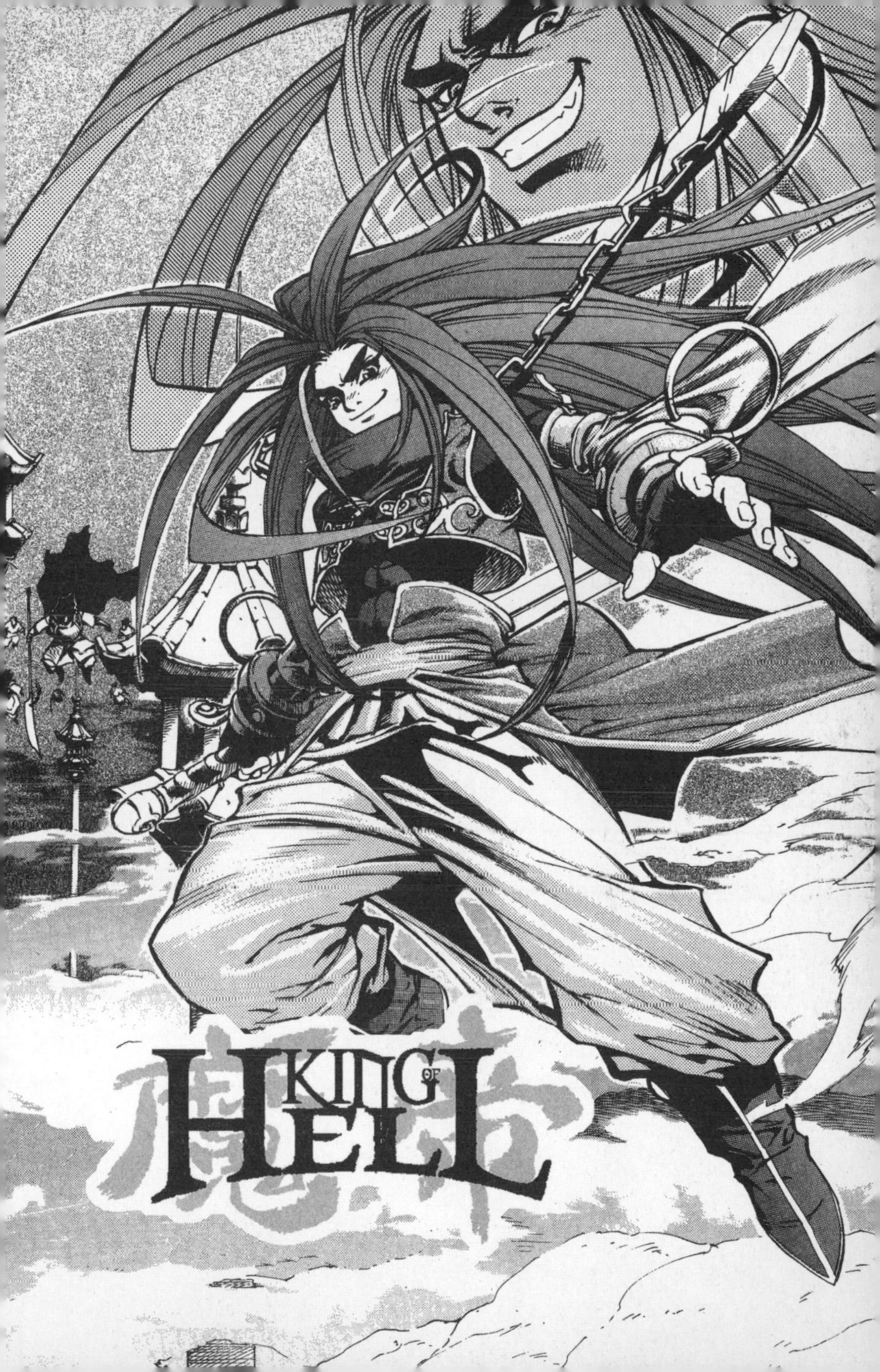
KING OF HELL

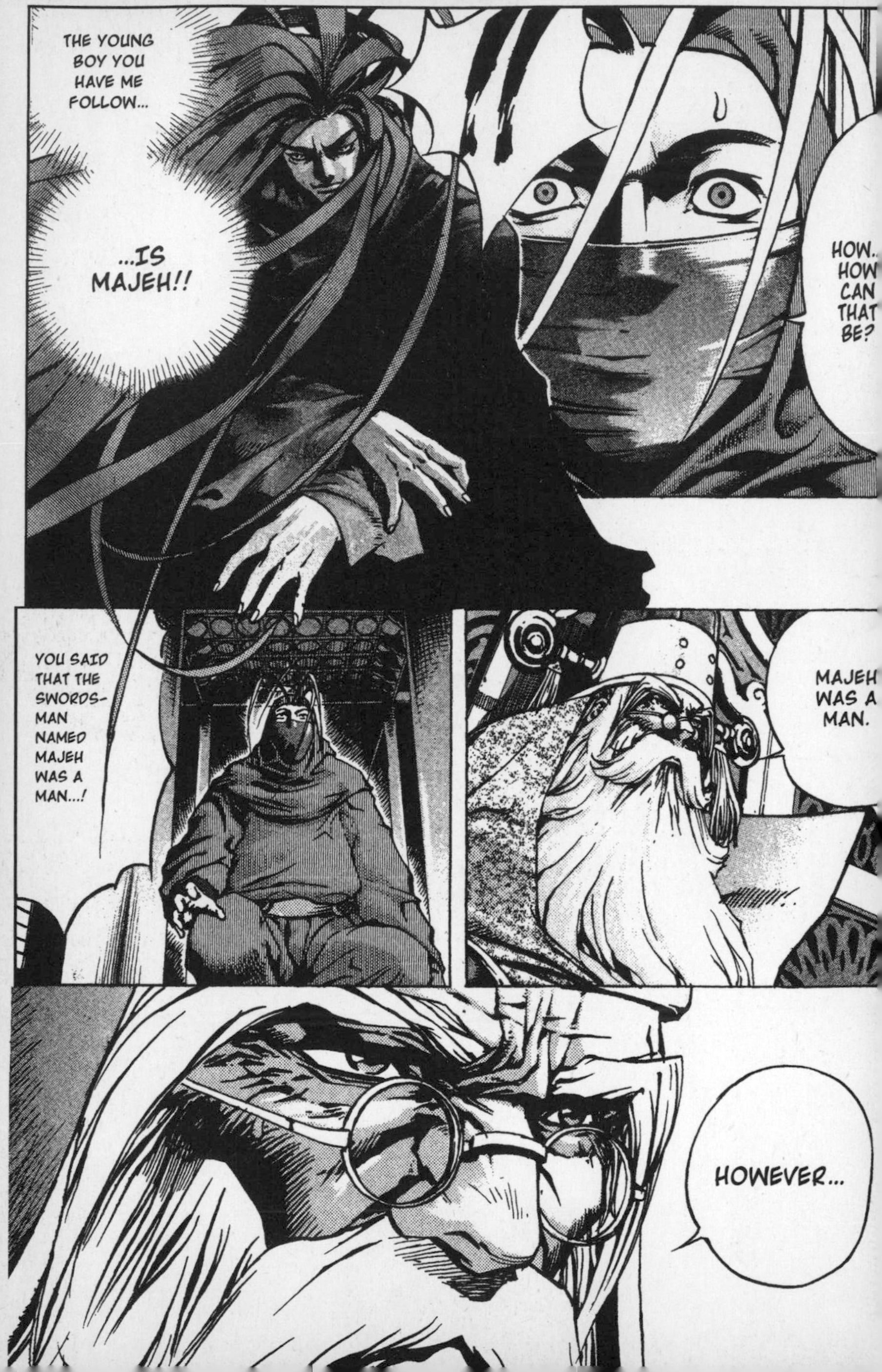
THE YOUNG BOY YOU HAVE ME FOLLOW...
...IS MAJEH!!
HOW.. HOW CAN THAT BE?
YOU SAID THAT THE SWORDS-MAN NAMED MAJEH WAS A MAN...!
MAJEH WAS A MAN.
HOWEVER...

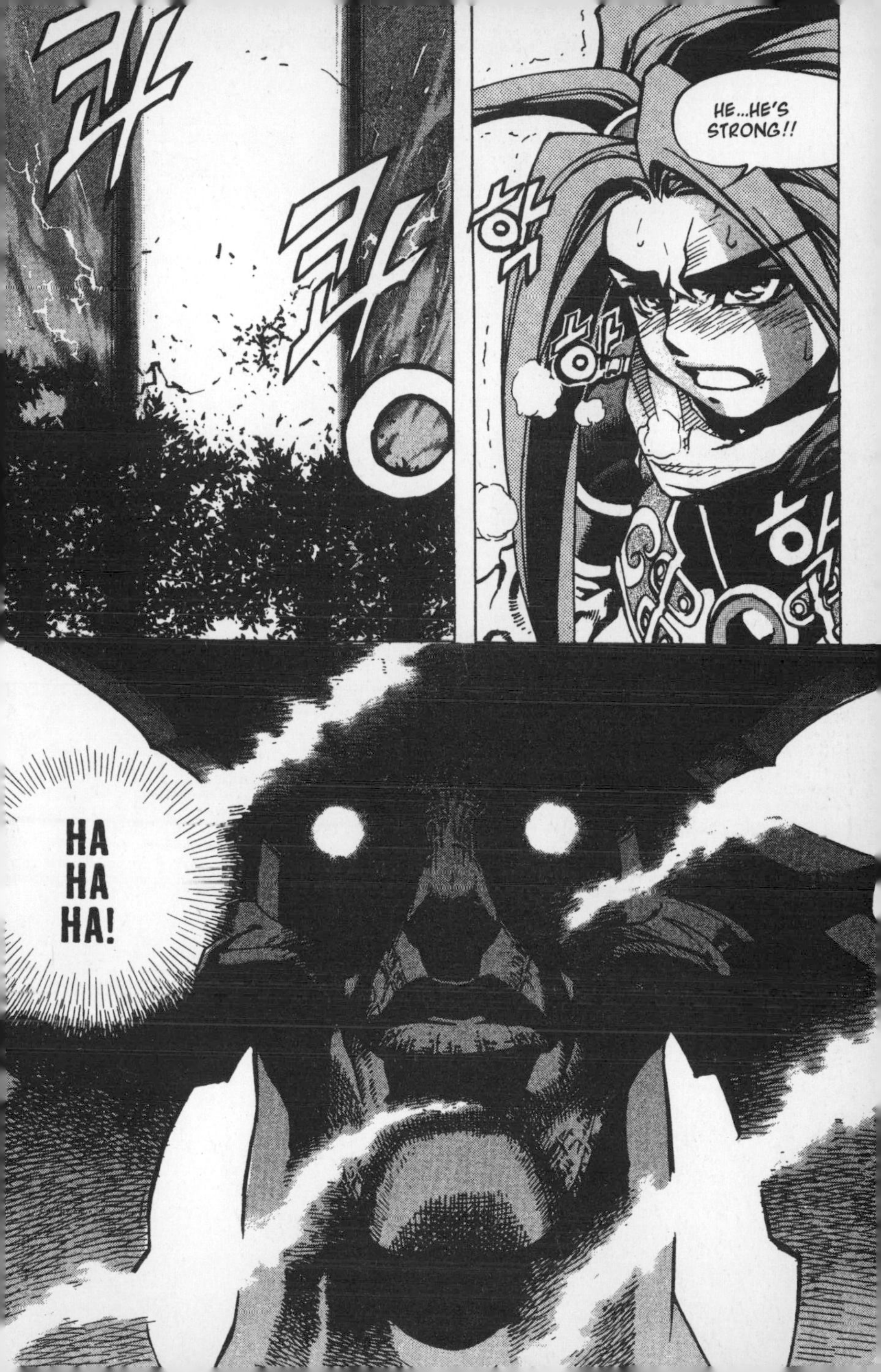

HE...HE'S STRONG!!
학
학
학
HA HA HA!

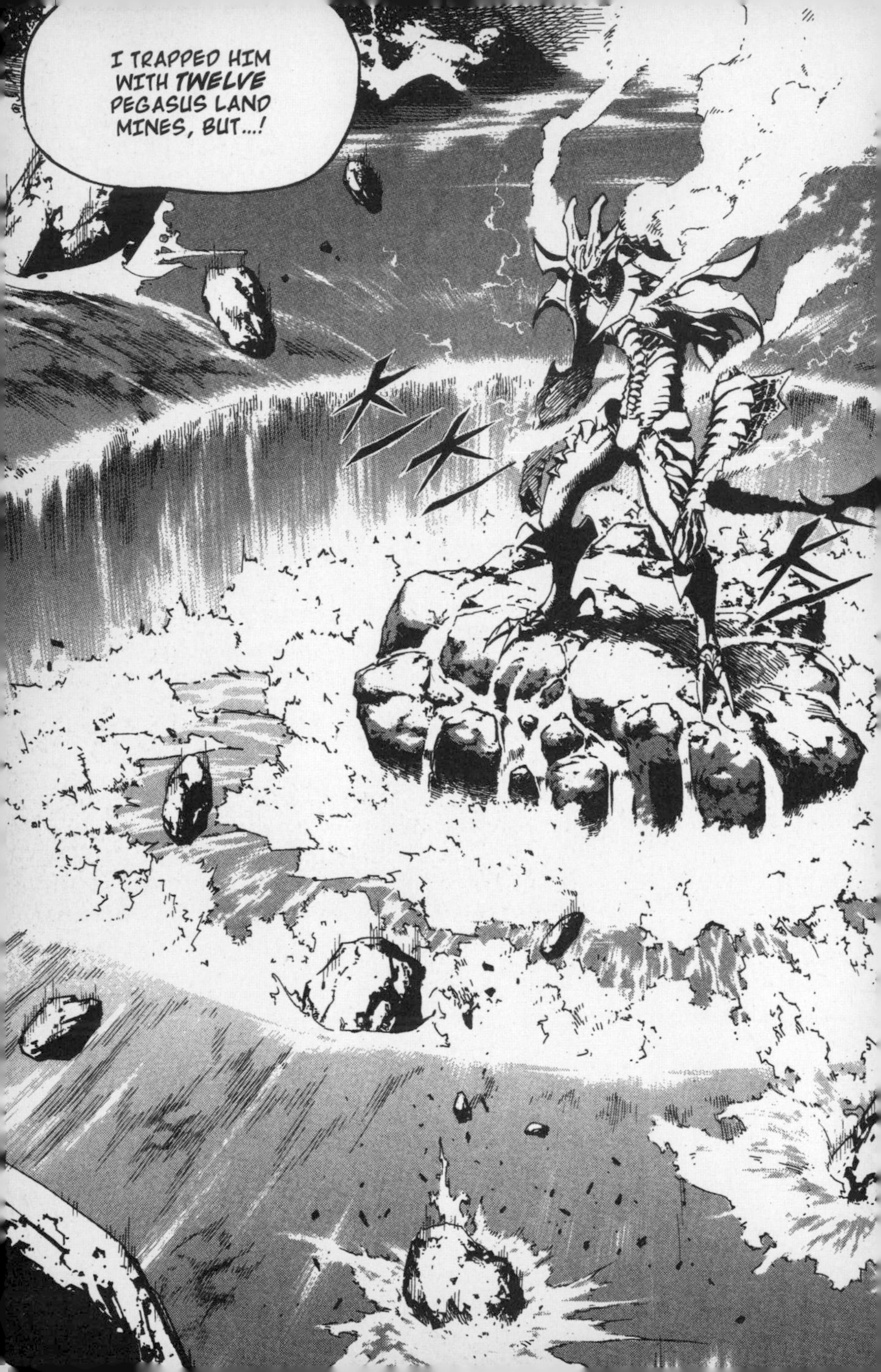
I TRAPPED HIM WITH *TWELVE* PEGASUS LAND MINES, BUT...!

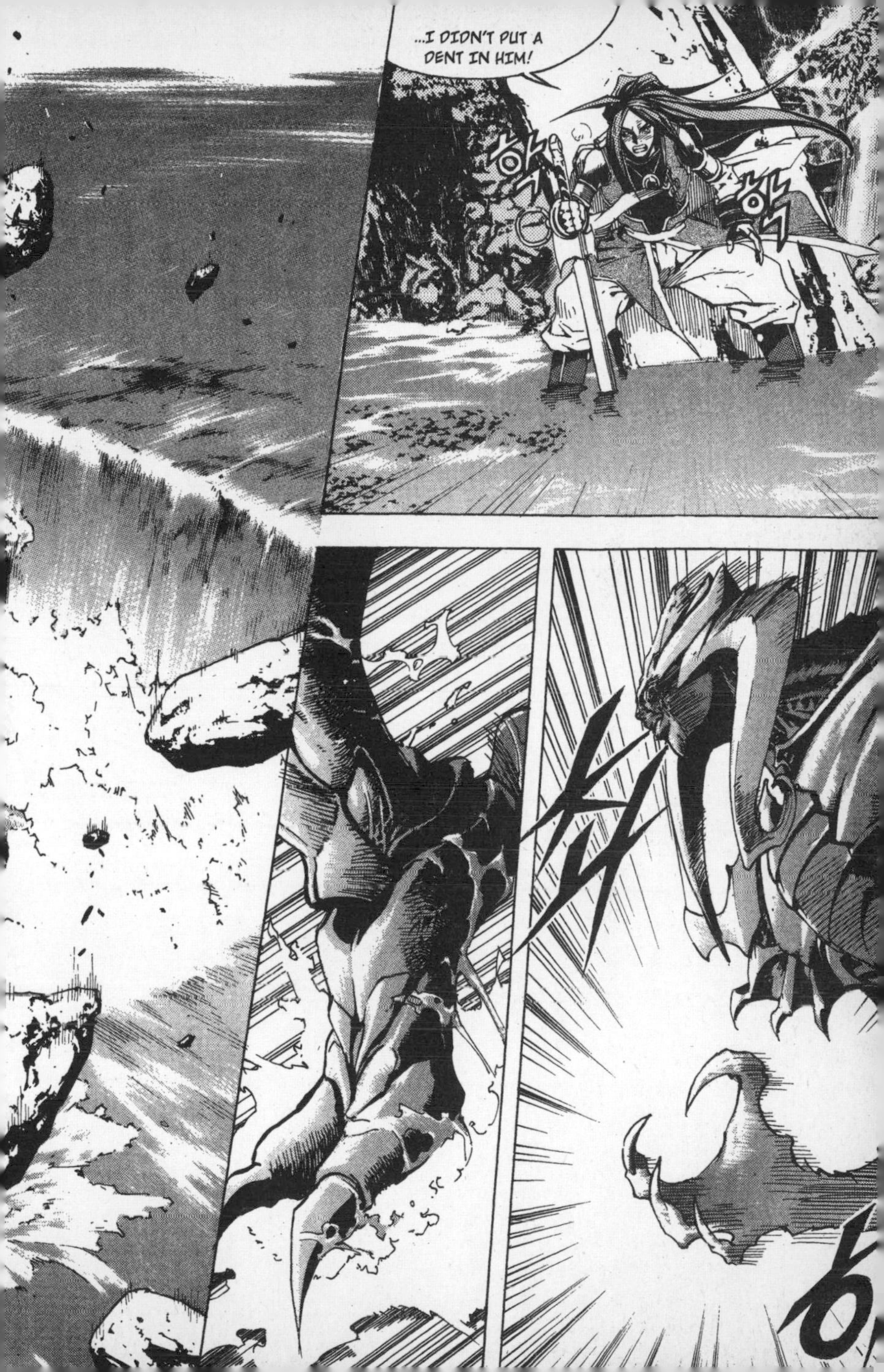
...I DIDN'T PUT A DENT IN HIM!

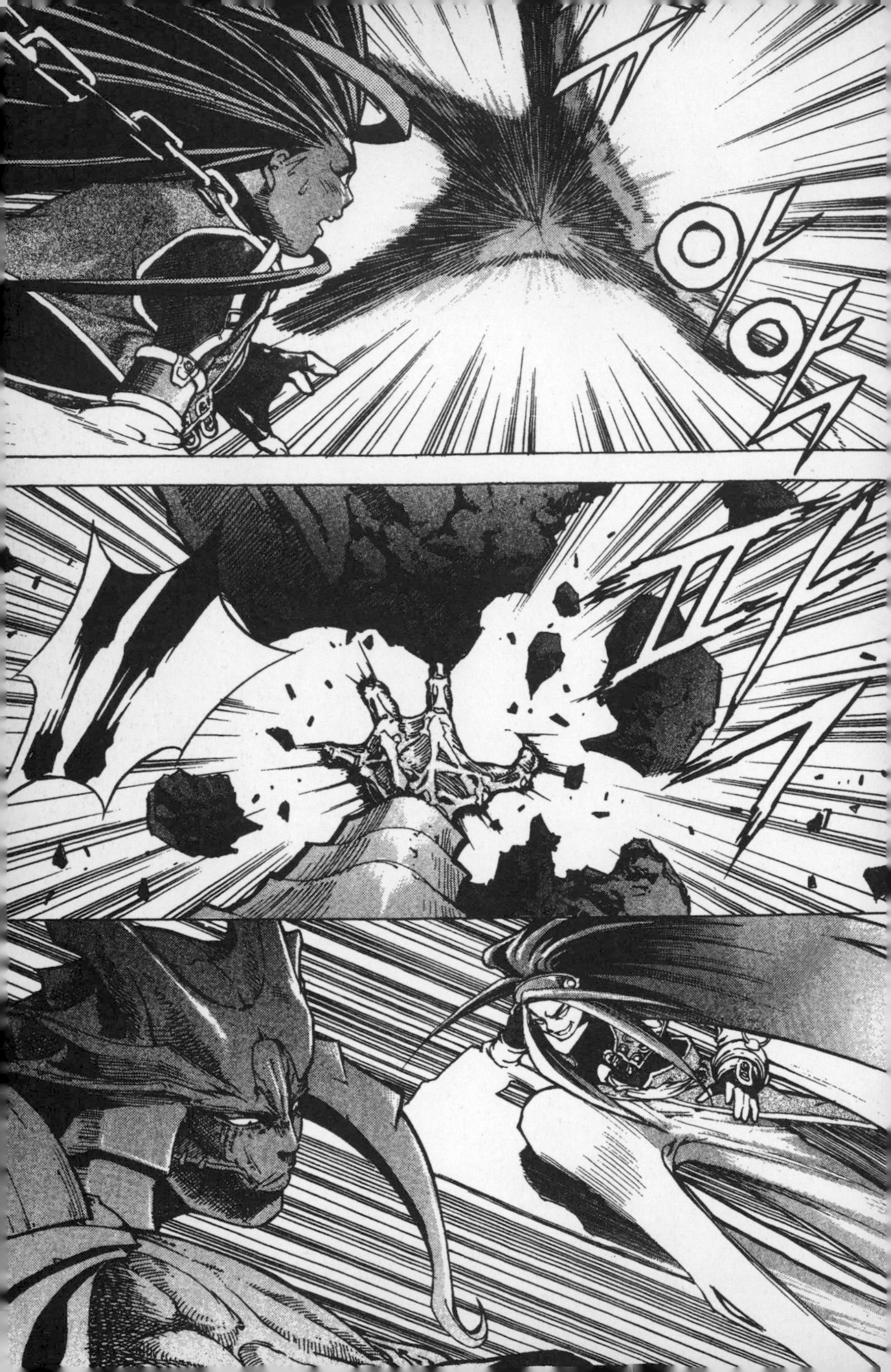
끼야얏

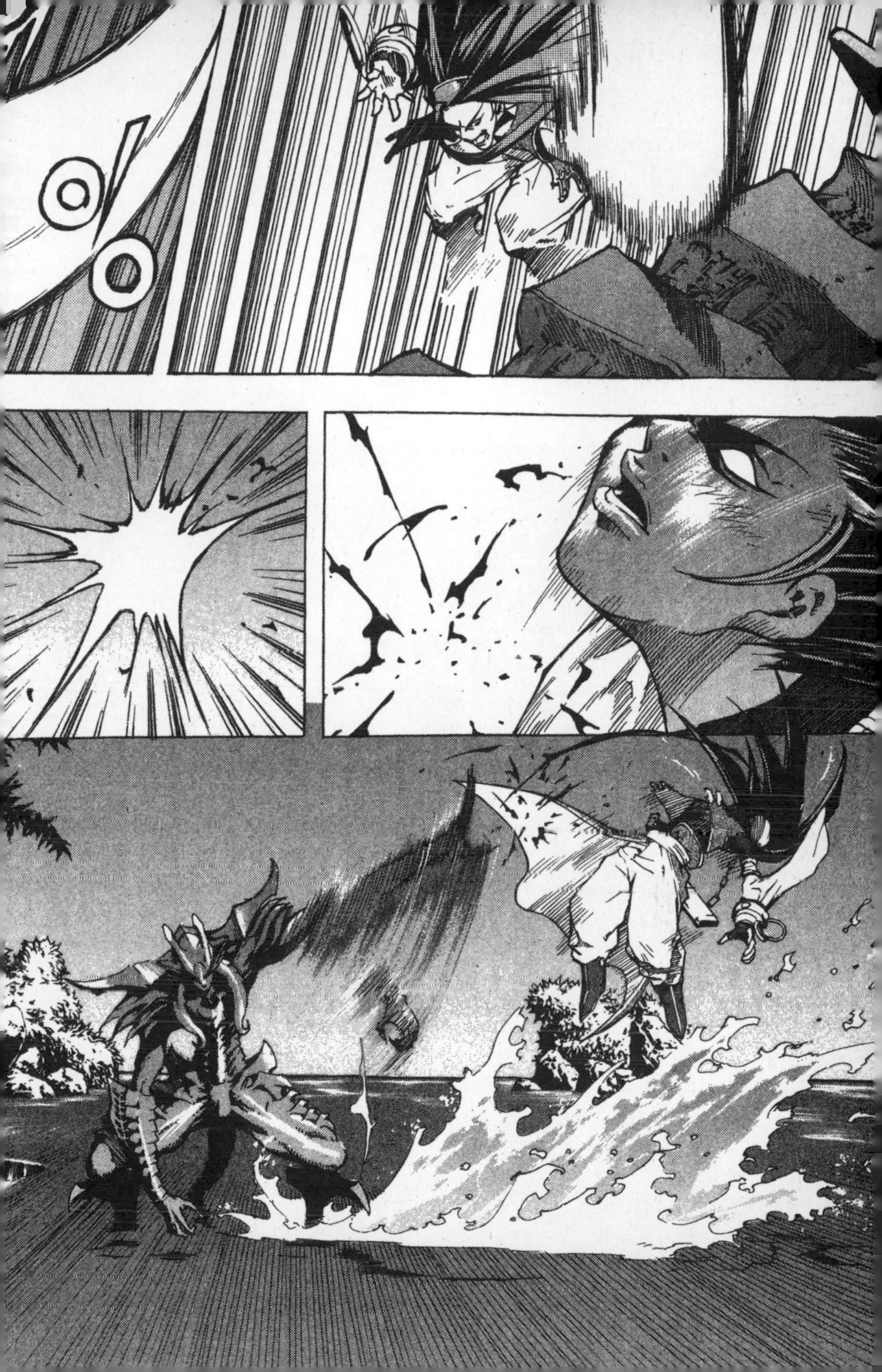

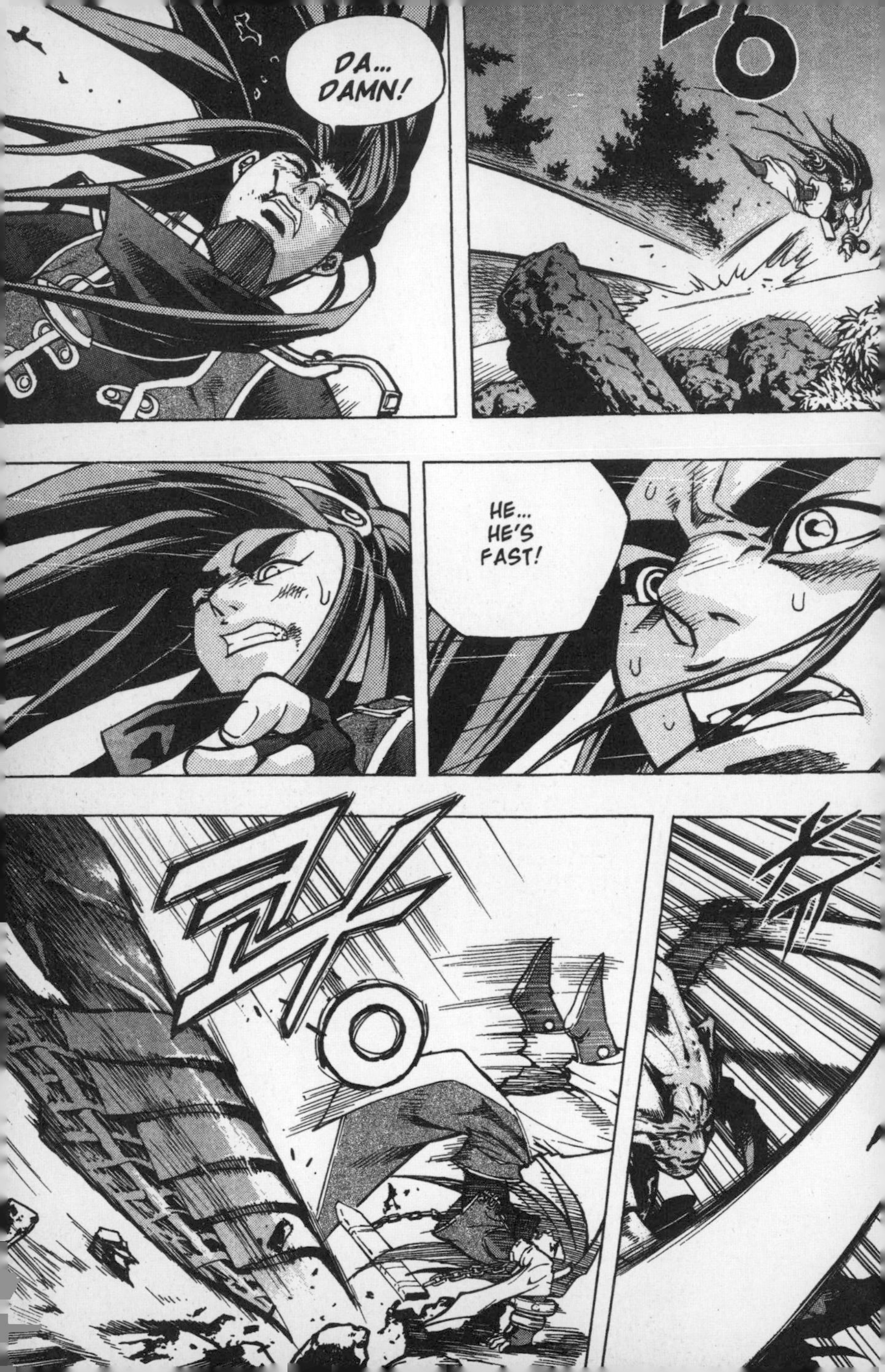
DA... DAMN!
HE... HE'S FAST!

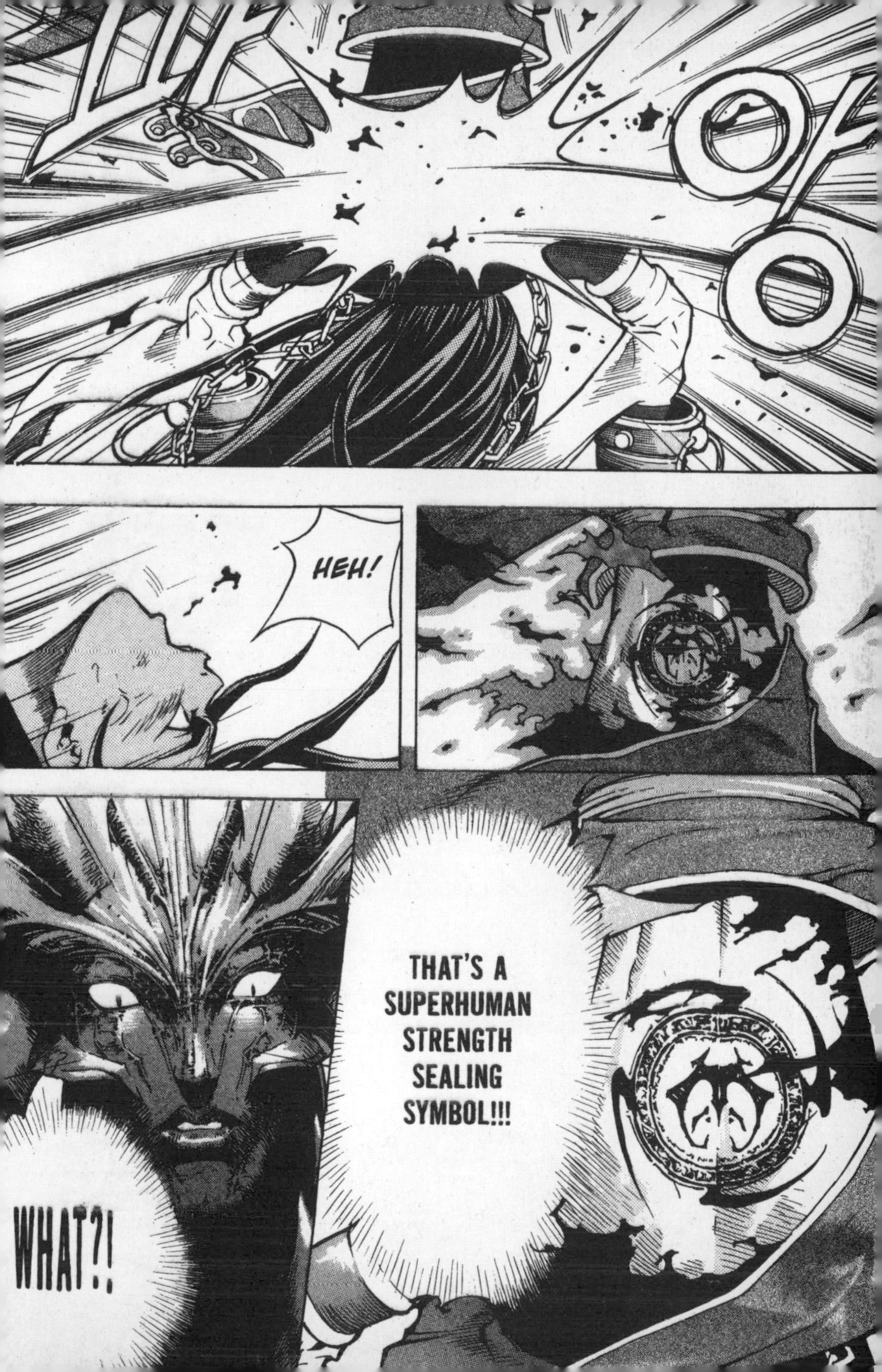
HEH!
WHAT?!
THAT'S A SUPERHUMAN STRENGTH SEALING SYMBOL!!!

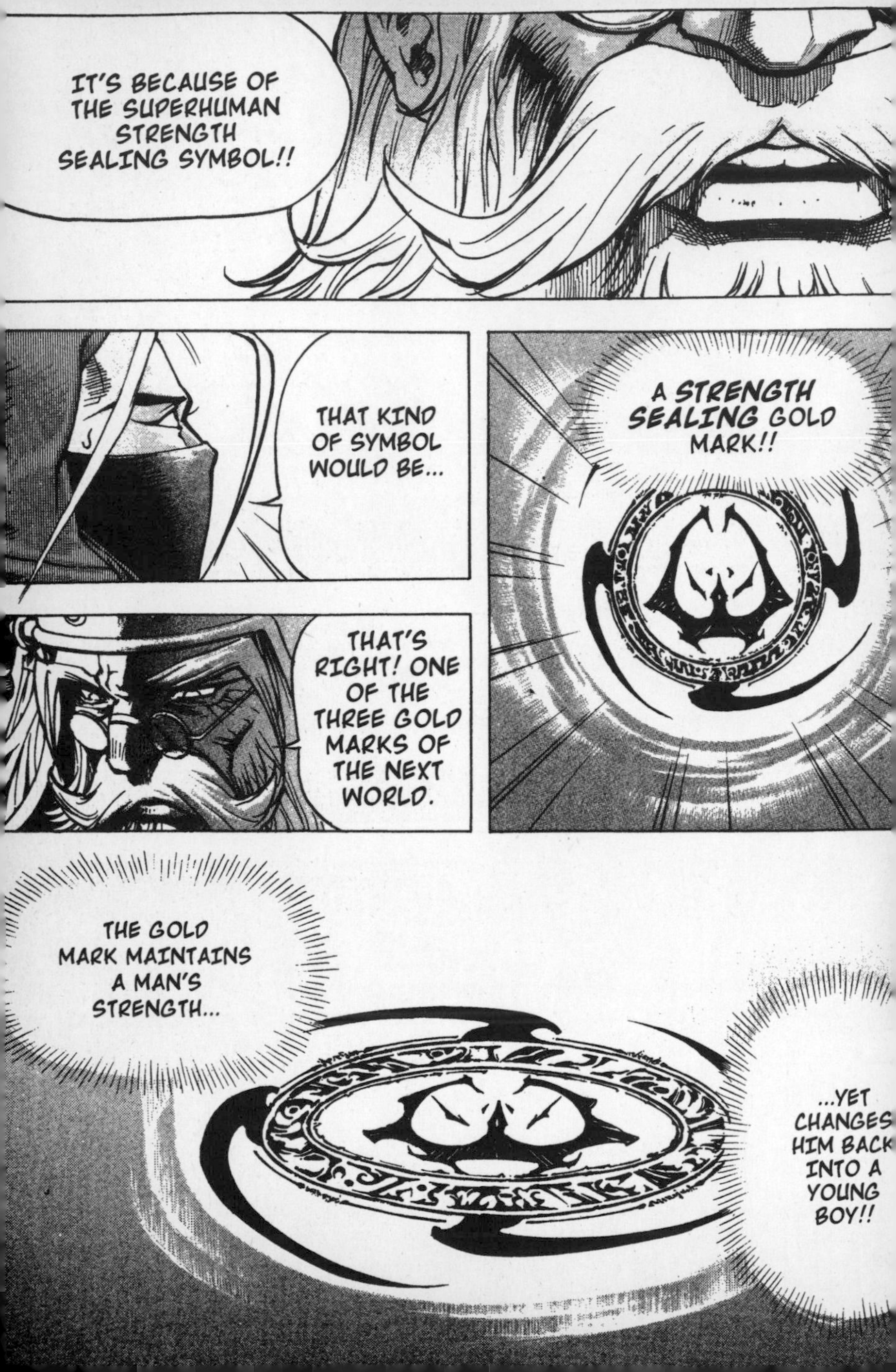
IT'S BECAUSE OF THE SUPERHUMAN STRENGTH SEALING SYMBOL!!
THAT KIND OF SYMBOL WOULD BE...
A STRENGTH SEALING GOLD MARK!!
THAT'S RIGHT! ONE OF THE THREE GOLD MARKS OF THE NEXT WORLD.
THE GOLD MARK MAINTAINS A MAN'S STRENGTH...
...YET CHANGES HIM BACK INTO A YOUNG BOY!!

AFTER THE INCIDENT IN MOORIM OCCURRED...

...A COMMITTEE MEETING WAS HELD FOR THE FIRST TIME IN 500 YEARS.

IN ORDER TO SEAL THE STRENGTH OF MAJEH, A STRENGTH NOT TO BE UNDER-ESTIMATED...

...SEVEN ELDERS PLACED THE GOLD MARK ON HIM!

THEN... THEN YOU'RE TELLING ME THAT THE YOUNG BOY I'M OBSERVING IS THIS **MAJEH?!!**

I CAN'T BELIEVE I'VE BEEN SPYING ON SUCH A DANGEROUS ENTITY.

YES! THAT IS WHY I'VE HAD HIM UNDER **CLOSE** OBSERVATION...

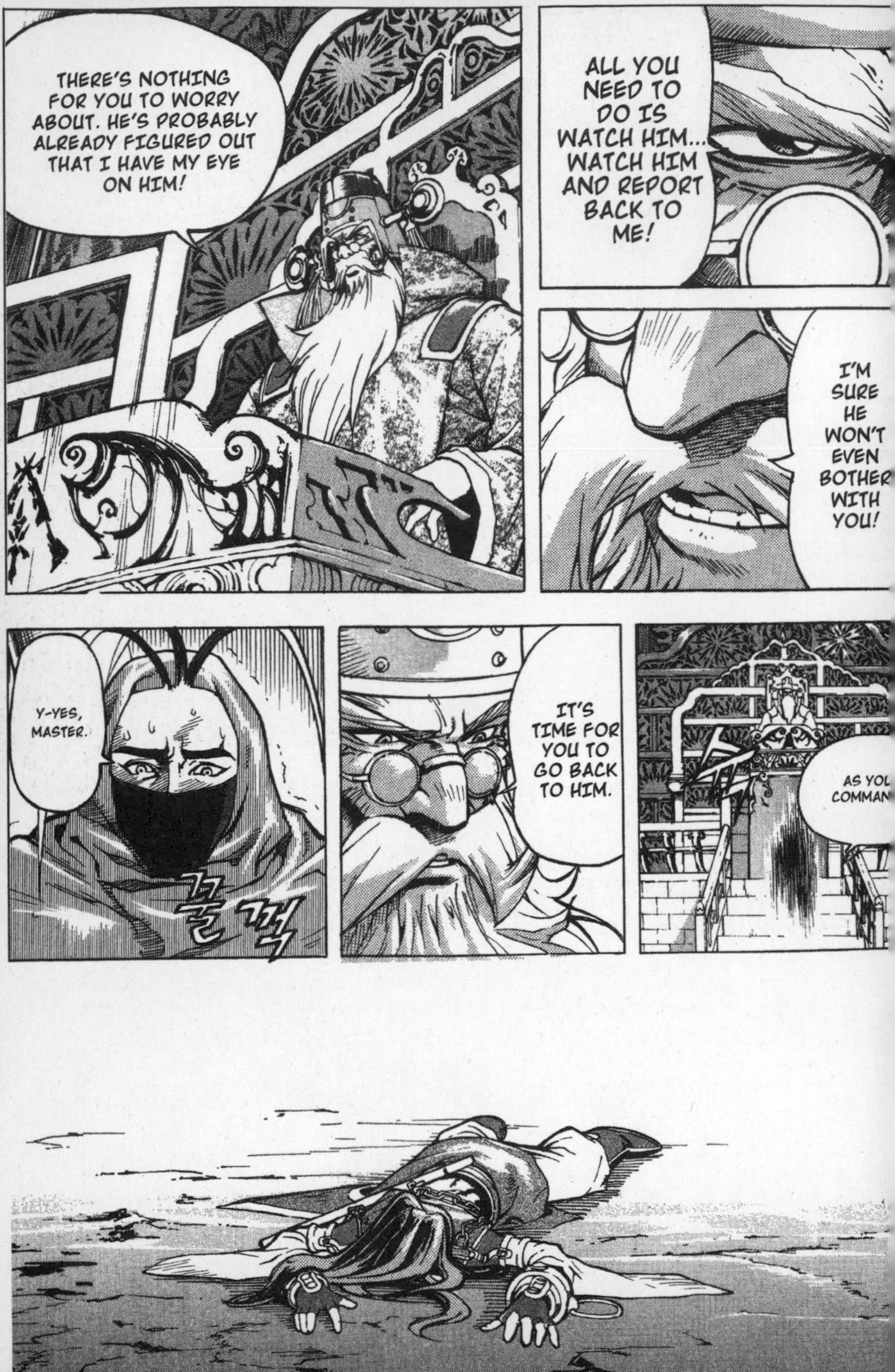
THERE'S NOTHING FOR YOU TO WORRY ABOUT. HE'S PROBABLY ALREADY FIGURED OUT THAT I HAVE MY EYE ON HIM!
ALL YOU NEED TO DO IS WATCH HIM... WATCH HIM AND REPORT BACK TO ME!
I'M SURE HE WON'T EVEN BOTHER WITH YOU!
Y-YES, MASTER.
꿀꺽
IT'S TIME FOR YOU TO GO BACK TO HIM.
AS YO COMMAN

I SEE YOU'VE FAINTED... YOU ARE WEAKER THAN I EXPECTED... HEHE!

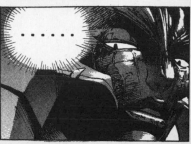

......

DEFEATING YOU WHILE YOU BEAR THE GOLD MARK ISN'T SOMETHING TO BE PROUD OF...

...SO, I'LL LEAVE YOU FOR ANOTHER DAY.

HEHEHE...!

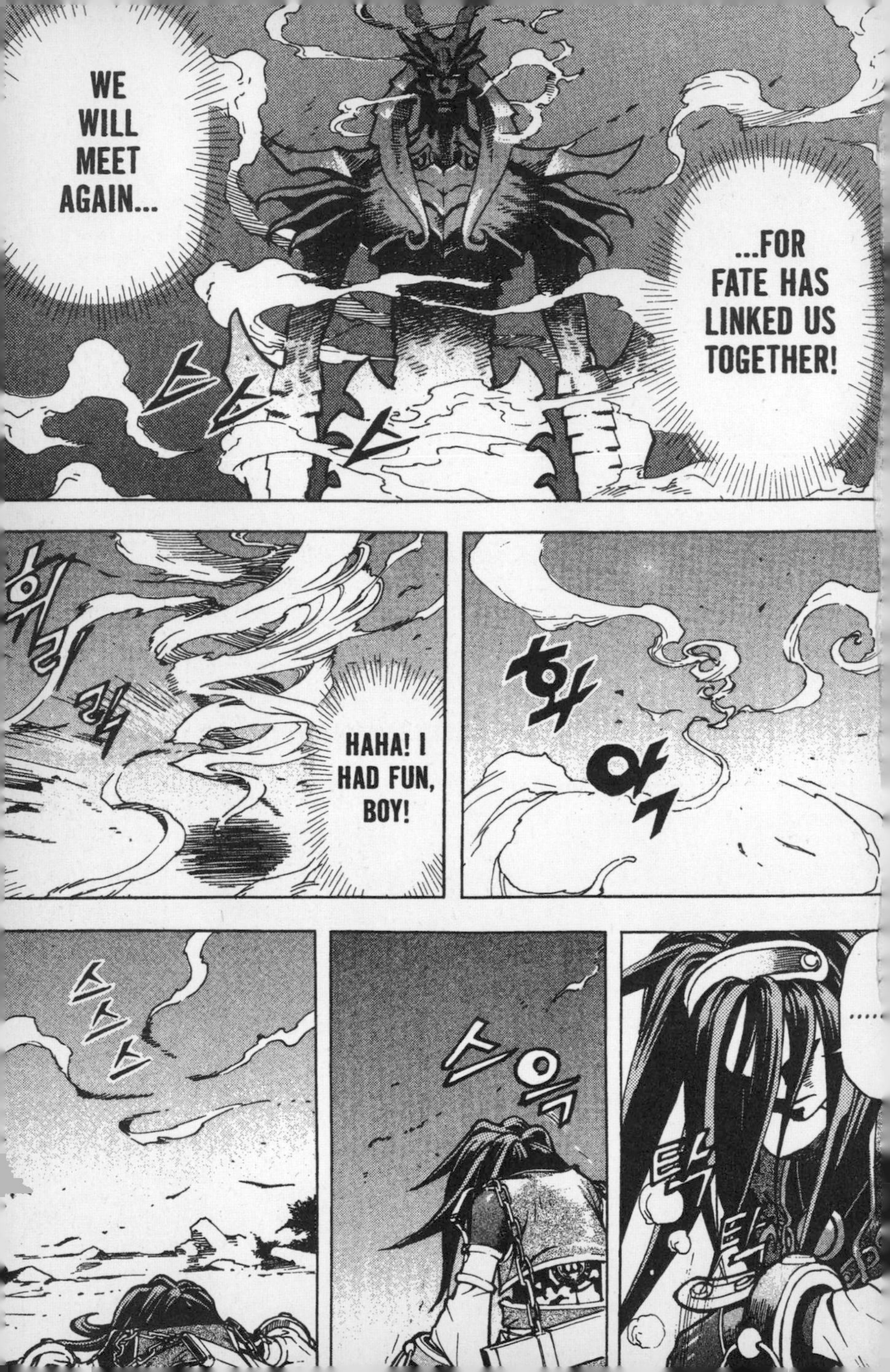

WE WILL MEET AGAIN...
...FOR FATE HAS LINKED US TOGETHER!
HAHA! I HAD FUN, BOY!
.....

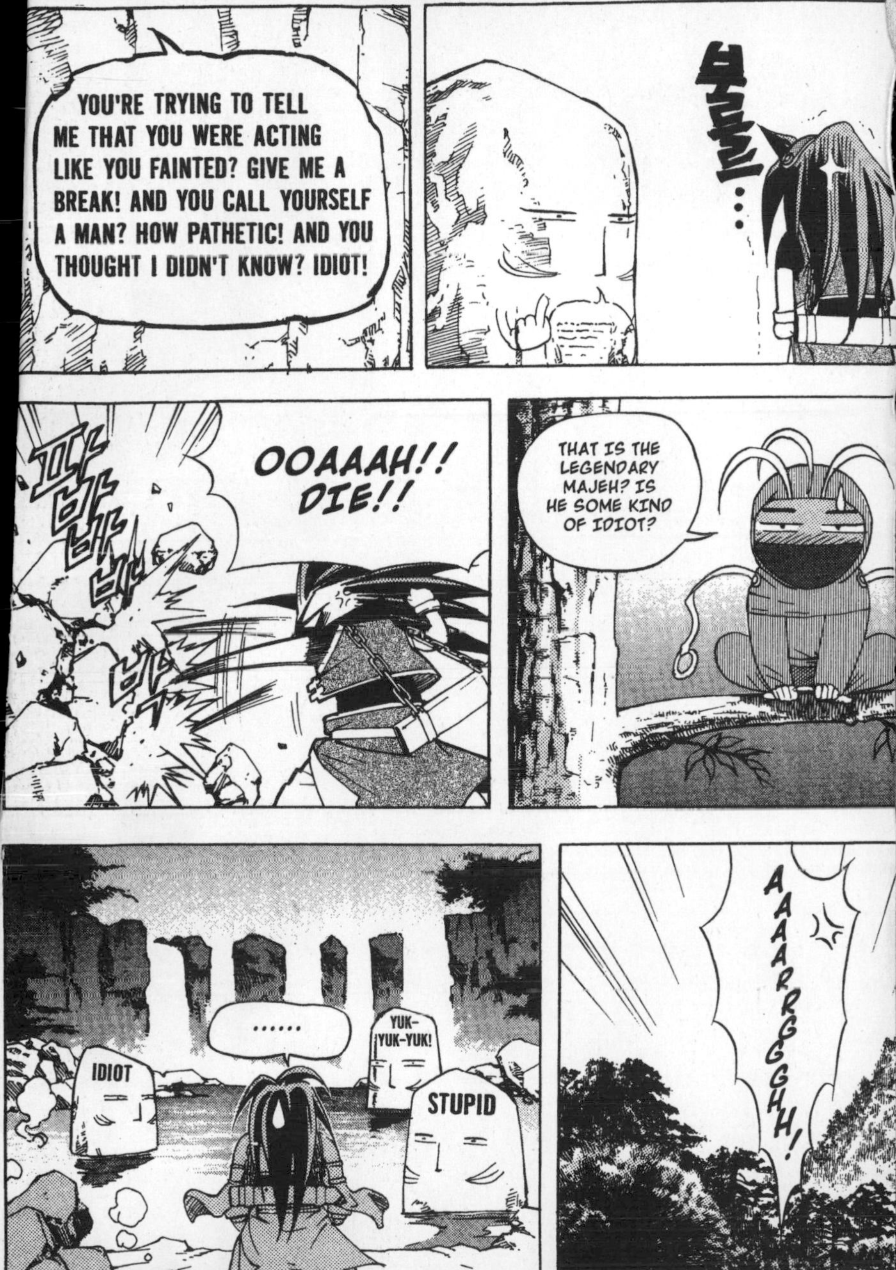
YOU'RE TRYING TO TELL ME THAT YOU WERE ACTING LIKE YOU FAINTED? GIVE ME A BREAK! AND YOU CALL YOURSELF A MAN? HOW PATHETIC! AND YOU THOUGHT I DIDN'T KNOW? IDIOT!
OOAAAH!! DIE!!
THAT IS THE LEGENDARY MAJEH? IS HE SOME KIND OF IDIOT?
......
IDIOT
YUK-YUK-YUK!
STUPID
AAAARRGGGHH!

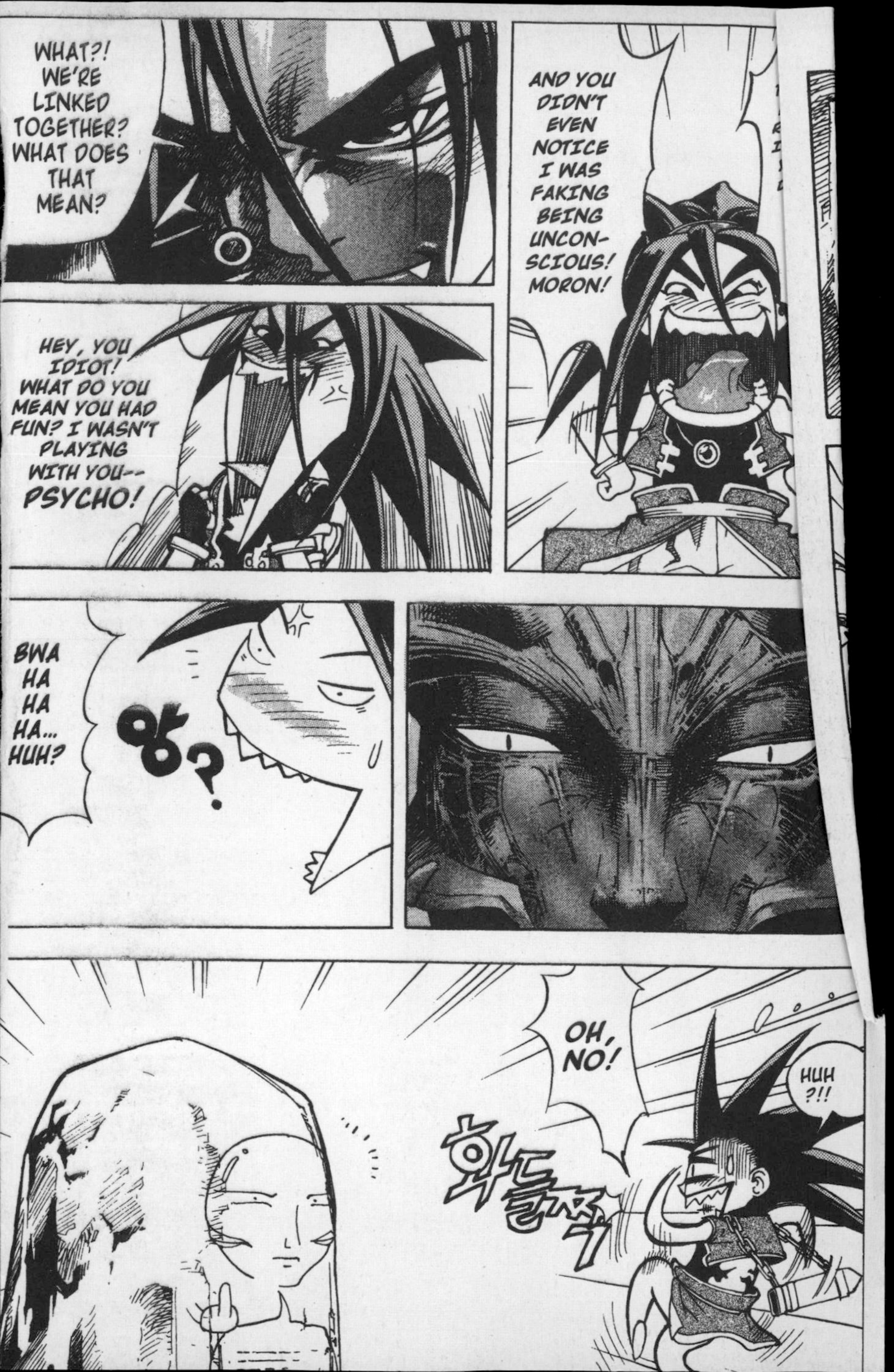
WHAT?! WE'RE LINKED TOGETHER? WHAT DOES THAT MEAN?
HEY, YOU IDIOT! WHAT DO YOU MEAN YOU HAD FUN? I WASN'T PLAYING WITH YOU-- PSYCHO!
AND YOU DIDN'T EVEN NOTICE I WAS FAKING BEING UNCON-SCIOUS! MORON!
BWA HA HA HA... HUH?
OH, NO!
HUH ?!!
화들짝

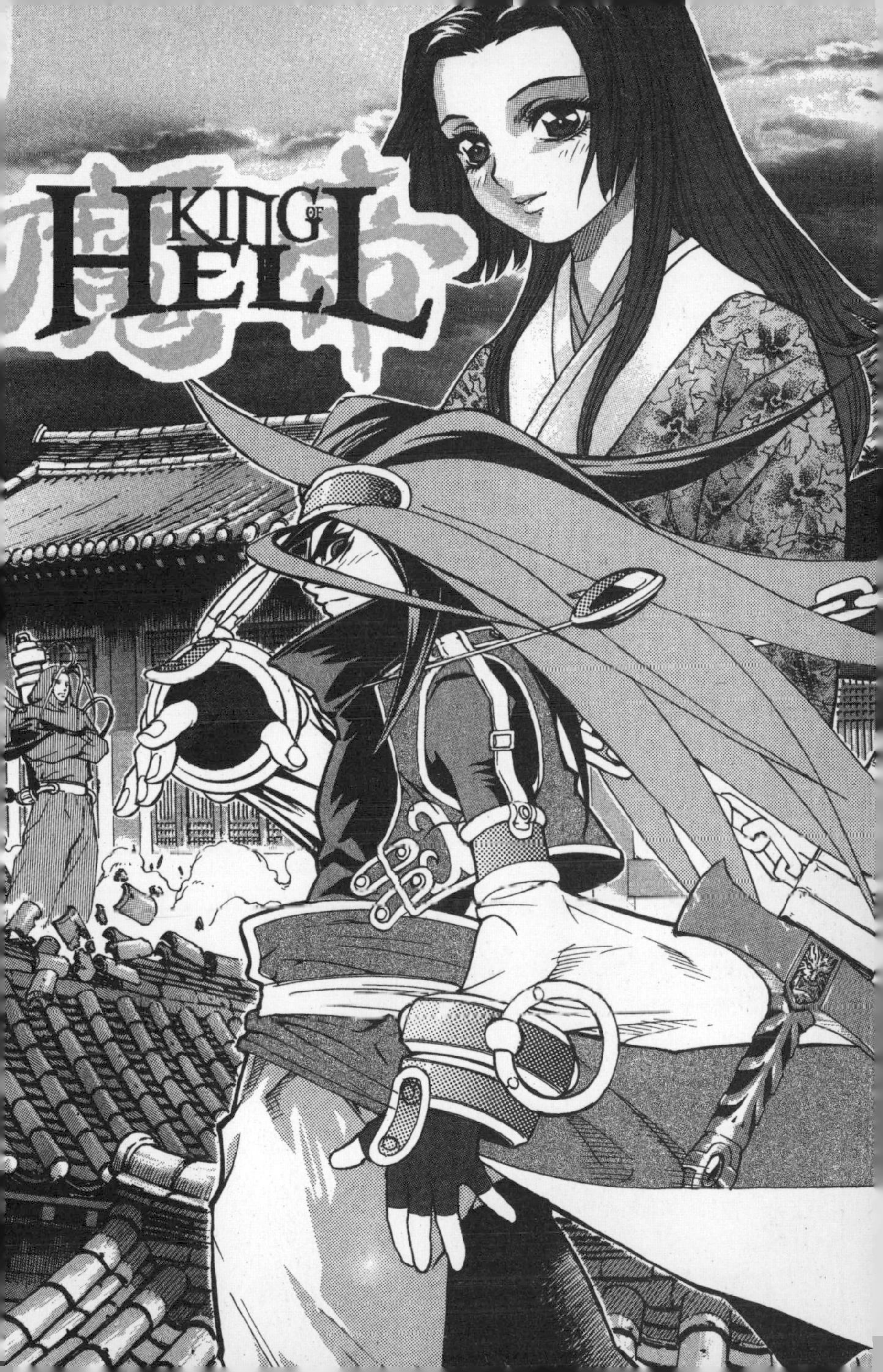
KING OF HELL

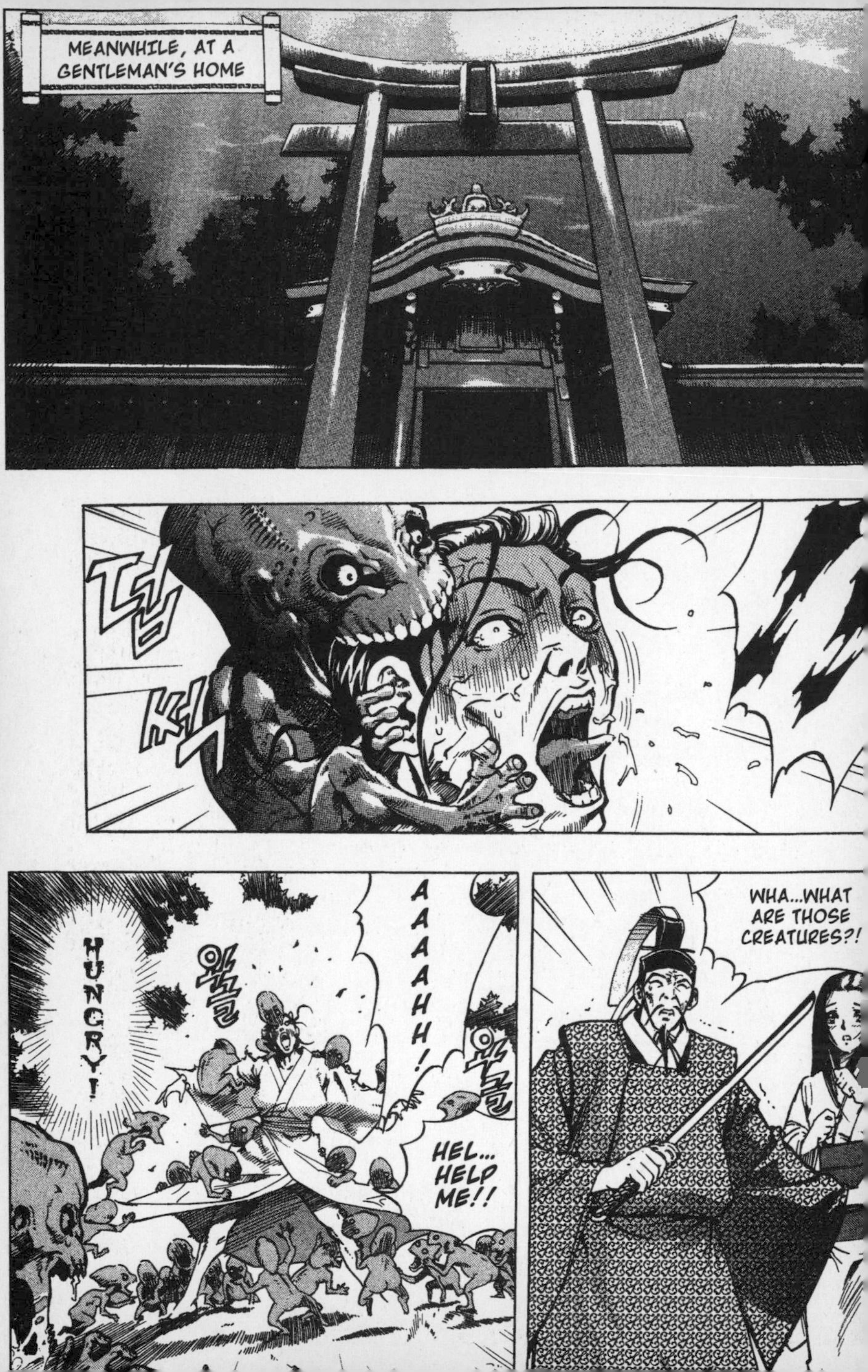
MEANWHILE, AT A GENTLEMAN'S HOME
덥석
HUNGRY!
와글
AAAAAHH!
와글
HEL... HELP ME!!
WHA...WHAT ARE THOSE CREATURES?!

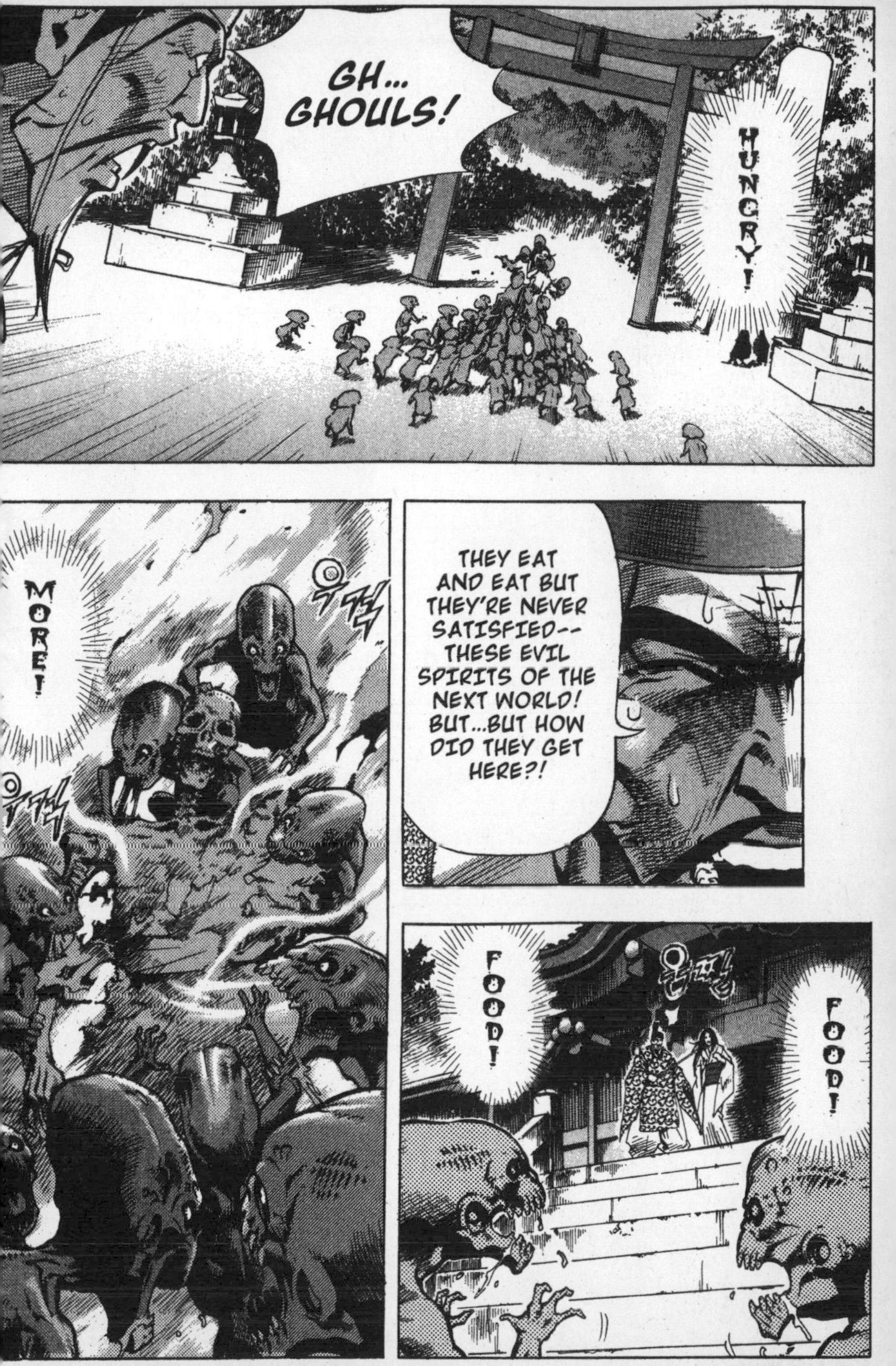
GH... GHOULS!
HUNGRY!
MORE!
THEY EAT AND EAT BUT THEY'RE NEVER SATISFIED-- THESE EVIL SPIRITS OF THE NEXT WORLD! BUT...BUT HOW DID THEY GET HERE?!
FOOD!
FOOD!

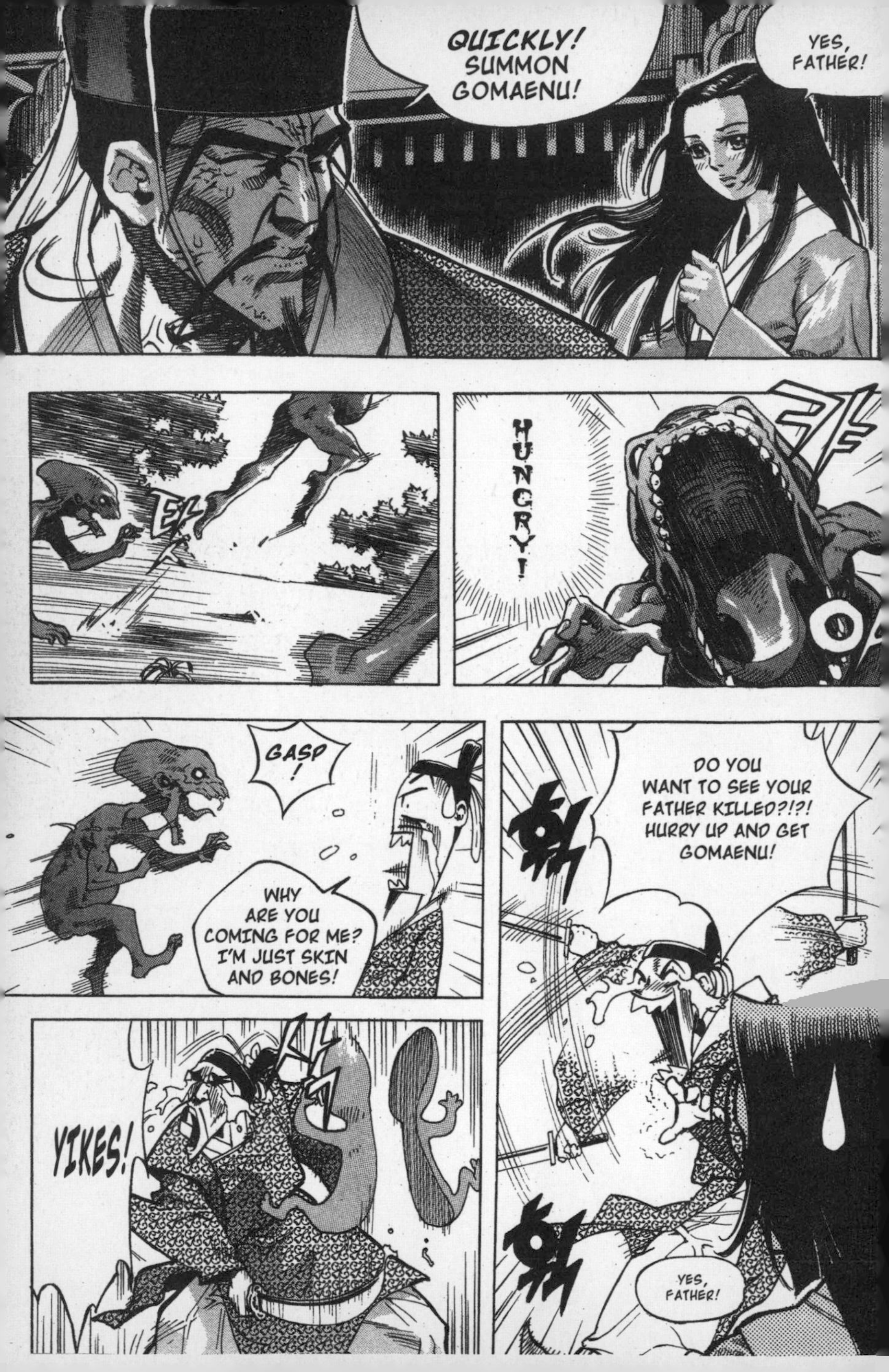
QUICKLY! SUMMON GOMAENU!
YES, FATHER!
HUNGRY!
GASP!
WHY ARE YOU COMING FOR ME? I'M JUST SKIN AND BONES!
YIKES!
DO YOU WANT TO SEE YOUR FATHER KILLED?!?! HURRY UP AND GET GOMAENU!
YES, FATHER!

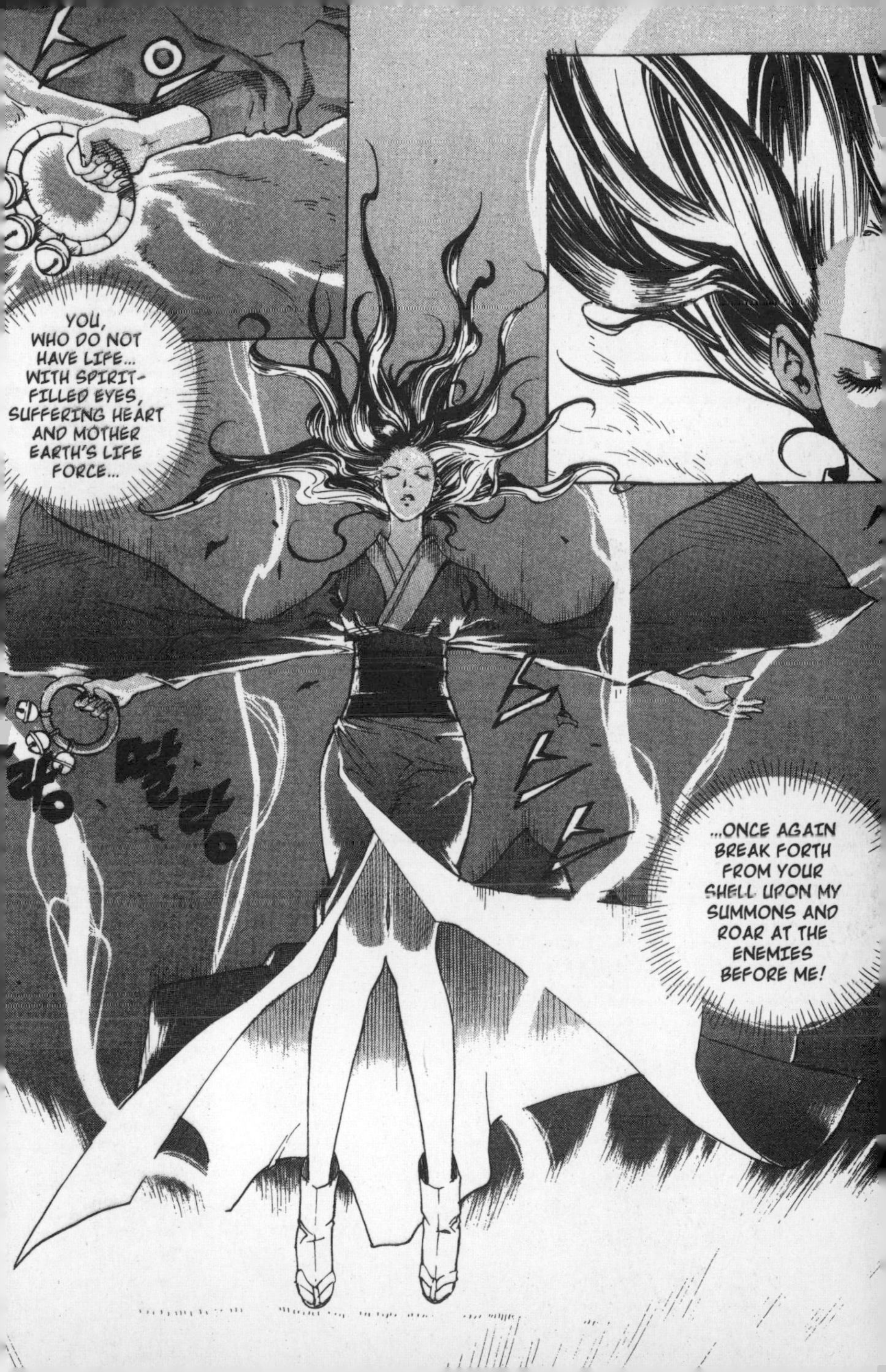
YOU, WHO DO NOT HAVE LIFE... WITH SPIRIT-FILLED EYES, SUFFERING HEART AND MOTHER EARTH'S LIFE FORCE...
...ONCE AGAIN BREAK FORTH FROM YOUR SHELL UPON MY SUMMONS AND ROAR AT THE ENEMIES BEFORE ME!

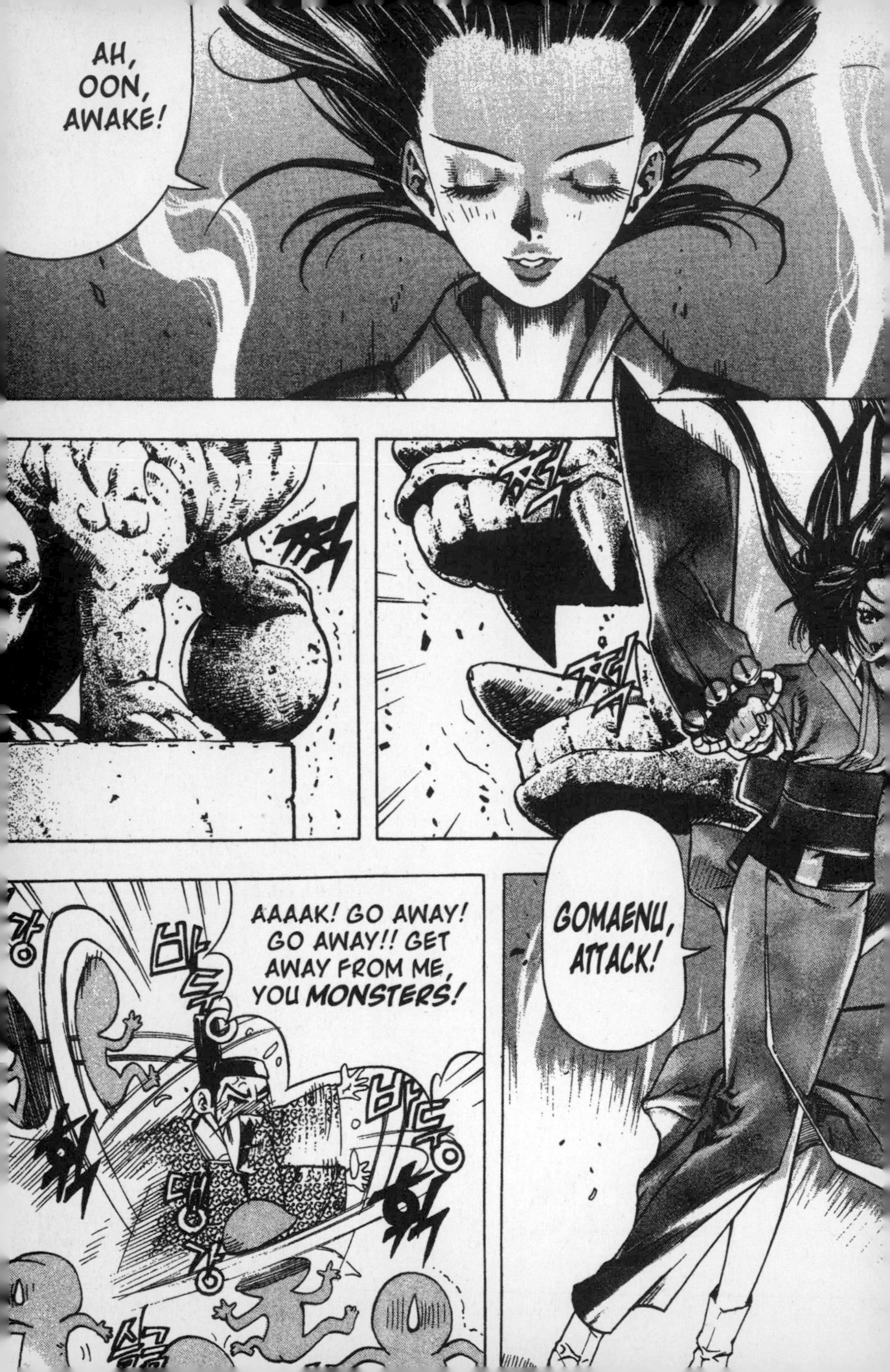
AH, OON, AWAKE!
AAAAK! GO AWAY! GO AWAY!! GET AWAY FROM ME, YOU MONSTERS!
GOMAENU, ATTACK!

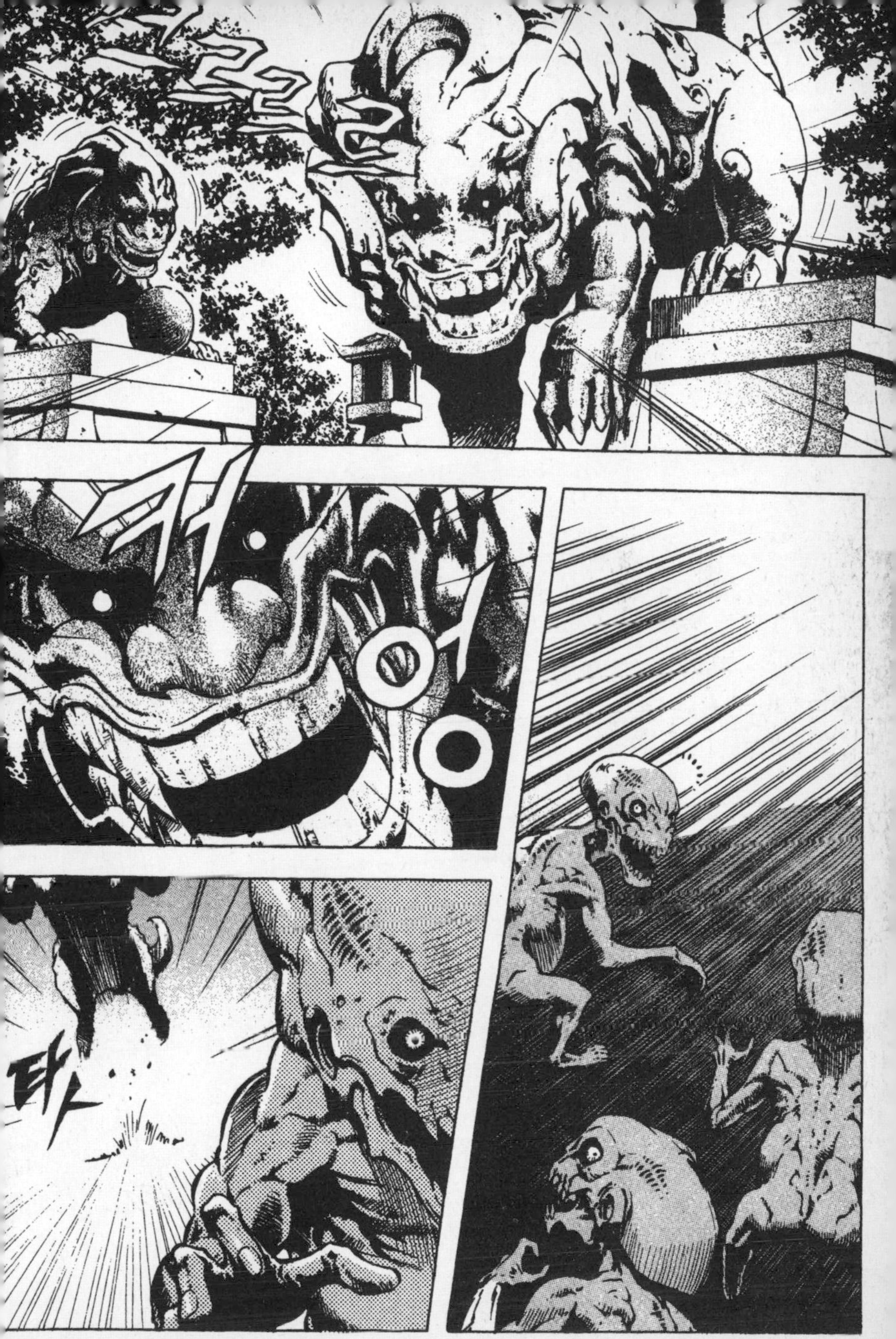
탓

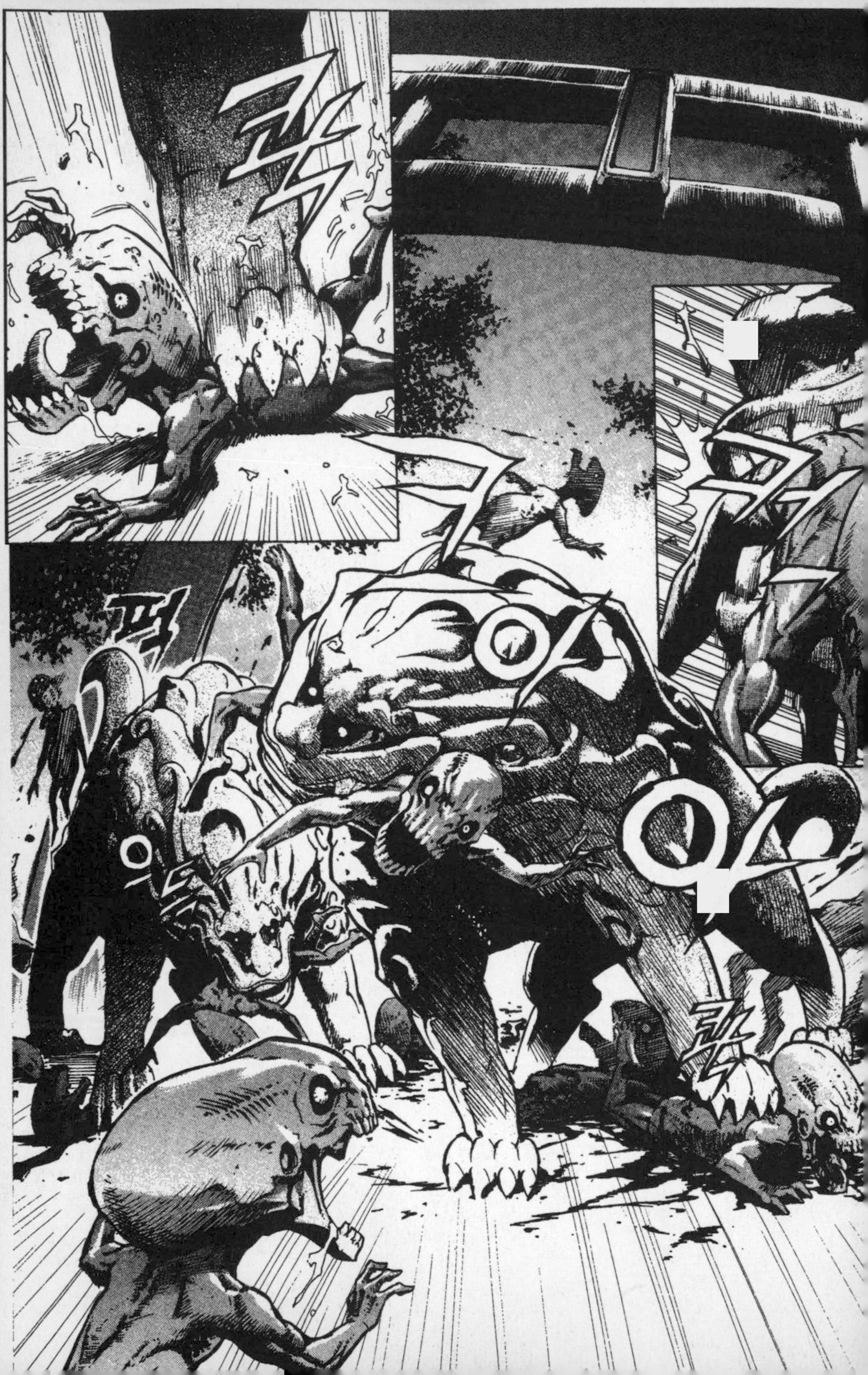
콰직
크아
파

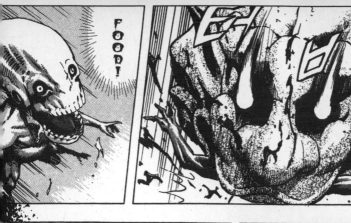

FOOD!

KKEEK!

FATHER... WHERE DID THOSE GHOULS COME FROM?

HAAHK... HAAHK... I DON'T KNOW. ANYWAY, IT LOOKS LIKE IT'S OVER.

THOUGHT I WAS GONNA DIE BEFORE I GOT A NEW WIFE...

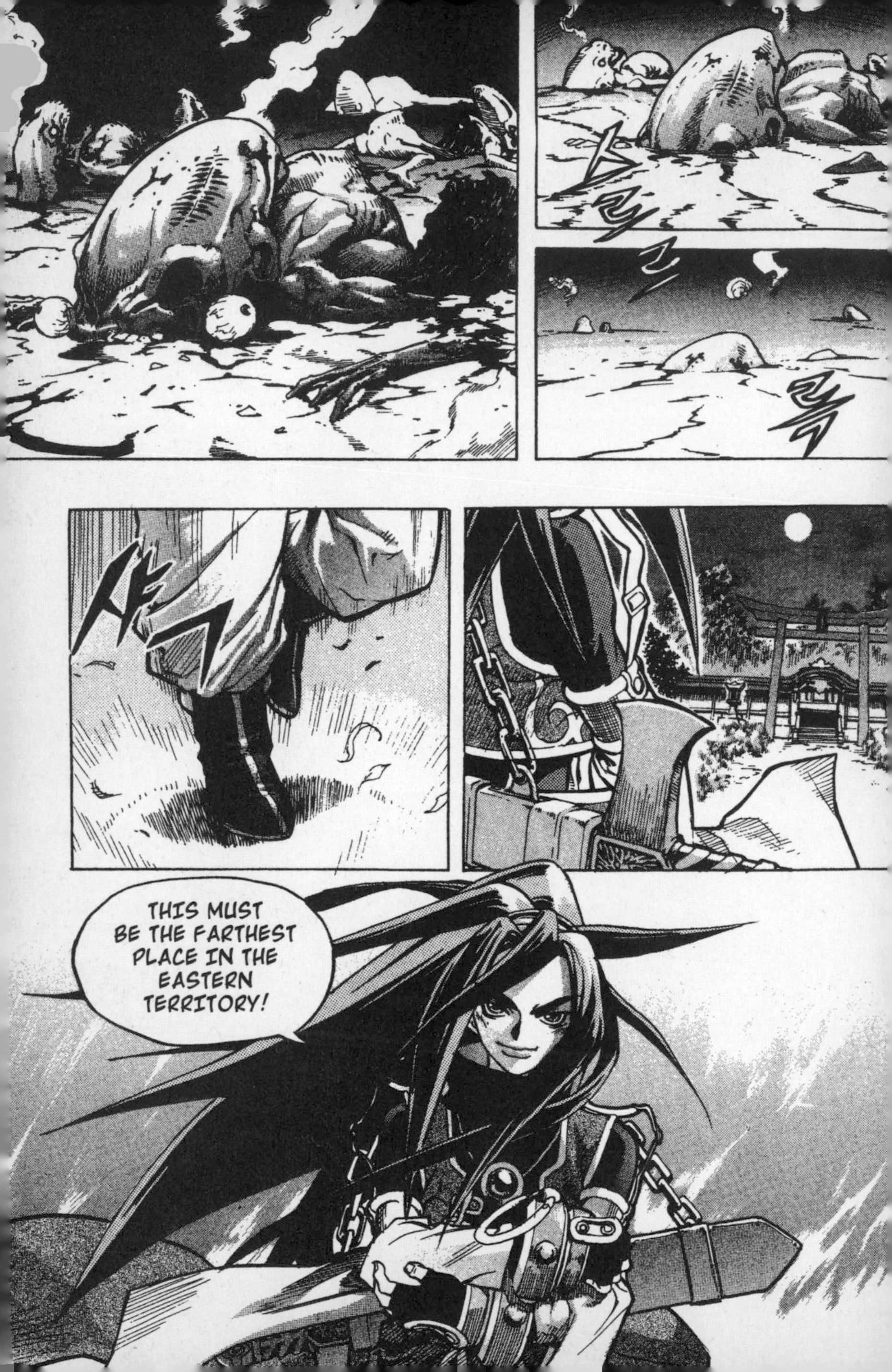
THIS MUST BE THE FARTHEST PLACE IN THE EASTERN TERRITORY!

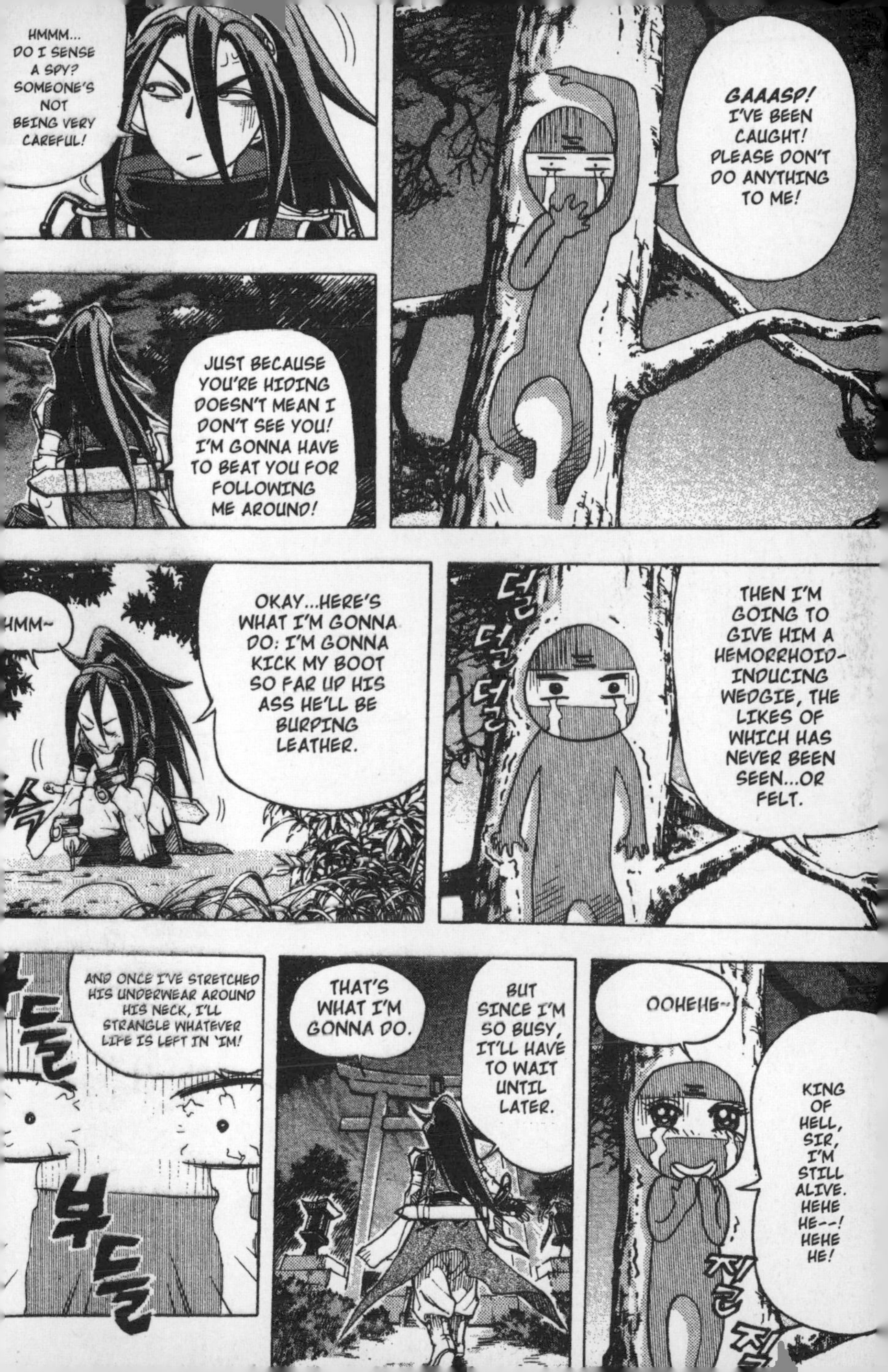
HMMM... DO I SENSE A SPY? SOMEONE'S NOT BEING VERY CAREFUL!
JUST BECAUSE YOU'RE HIDING DOESN'T MEAN I DON'T SEE YOU! I'M GONNA HAVE TO BEAT YOU FOR FOLLOWING ME AROUND!
GAAASP! I'VE BEEN CAUGHT! PLEASE DON'T DO ANYTHING TO ME!
HMM~
OKAY...HERE'S WHAT I'M GONNA DO: I'M GONNA KICK MY BOOT SO FAR UP HIS ASS HE'LL BE BURPING LEATHER.
THEN I'M GOING TO GIVE HIM A HEMORRHOID-INDUCING WEDGIE, THE LIKES OF WHICH HAS NEVER BEEN SEEN...OR FELT.
AND ONCE I'VE STRETCHED HIS UNDERWEAR AROUND HIS NECK, I'LL STRANGLE WHATEVER LIFE IS LEFT IN 'IM!
THAT'S WHAT I'M GONNA DO.
BUT SINCE I'M SO BUSY, IT'LL HAVE TO WAIT UNTIL LATER.
OOHEHE~
KING OF HELL, SIR, I'M STILL ALIVE. HEHE HE--! HEHE HE!

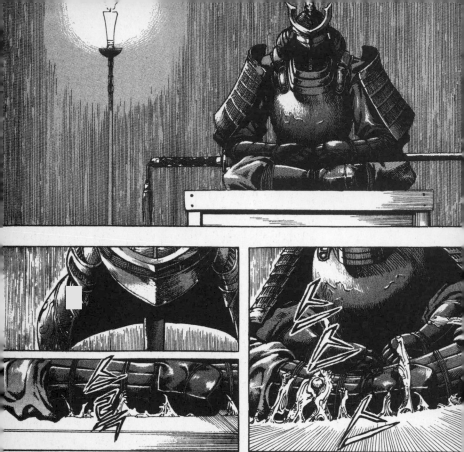

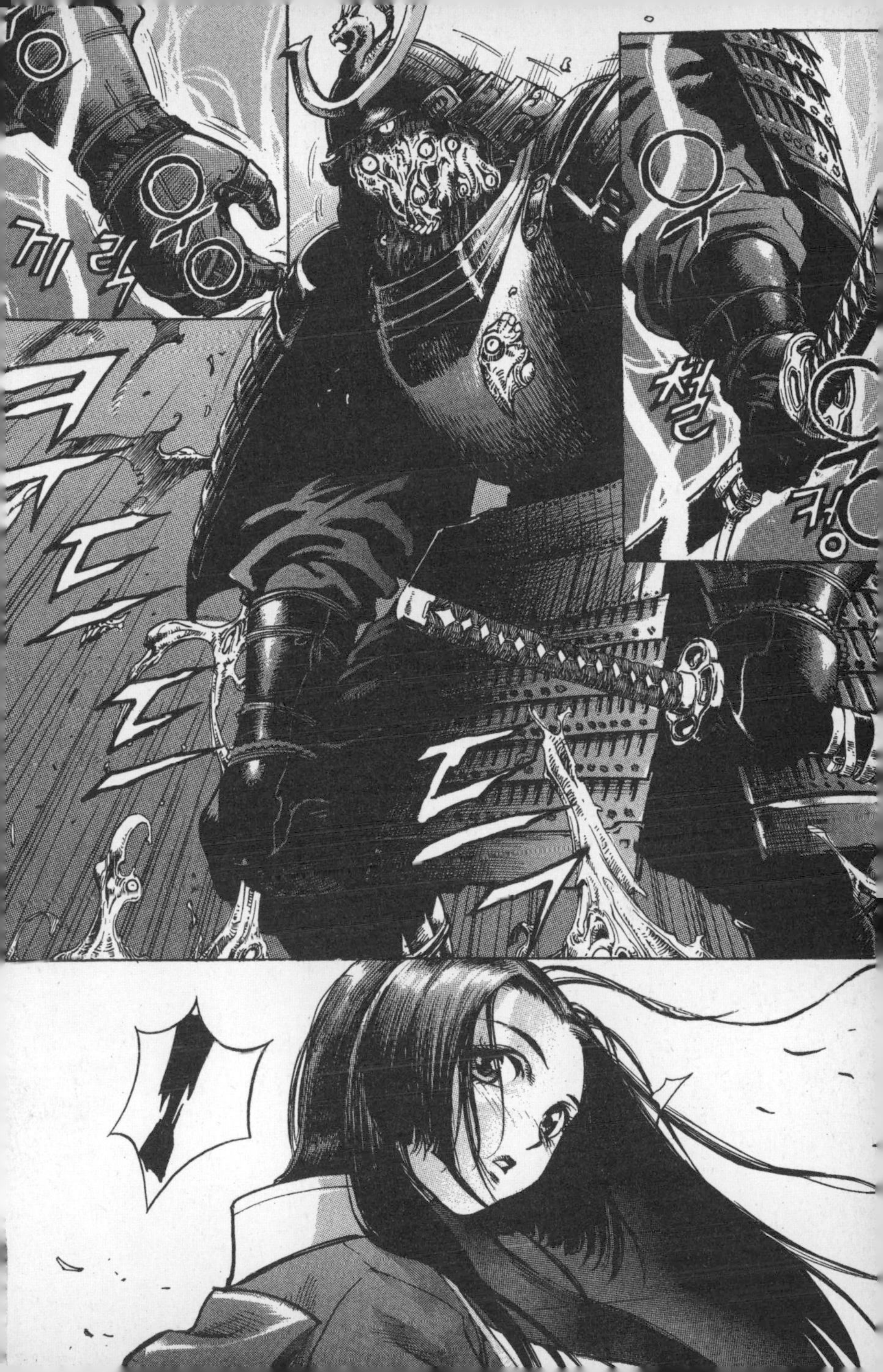
철컹

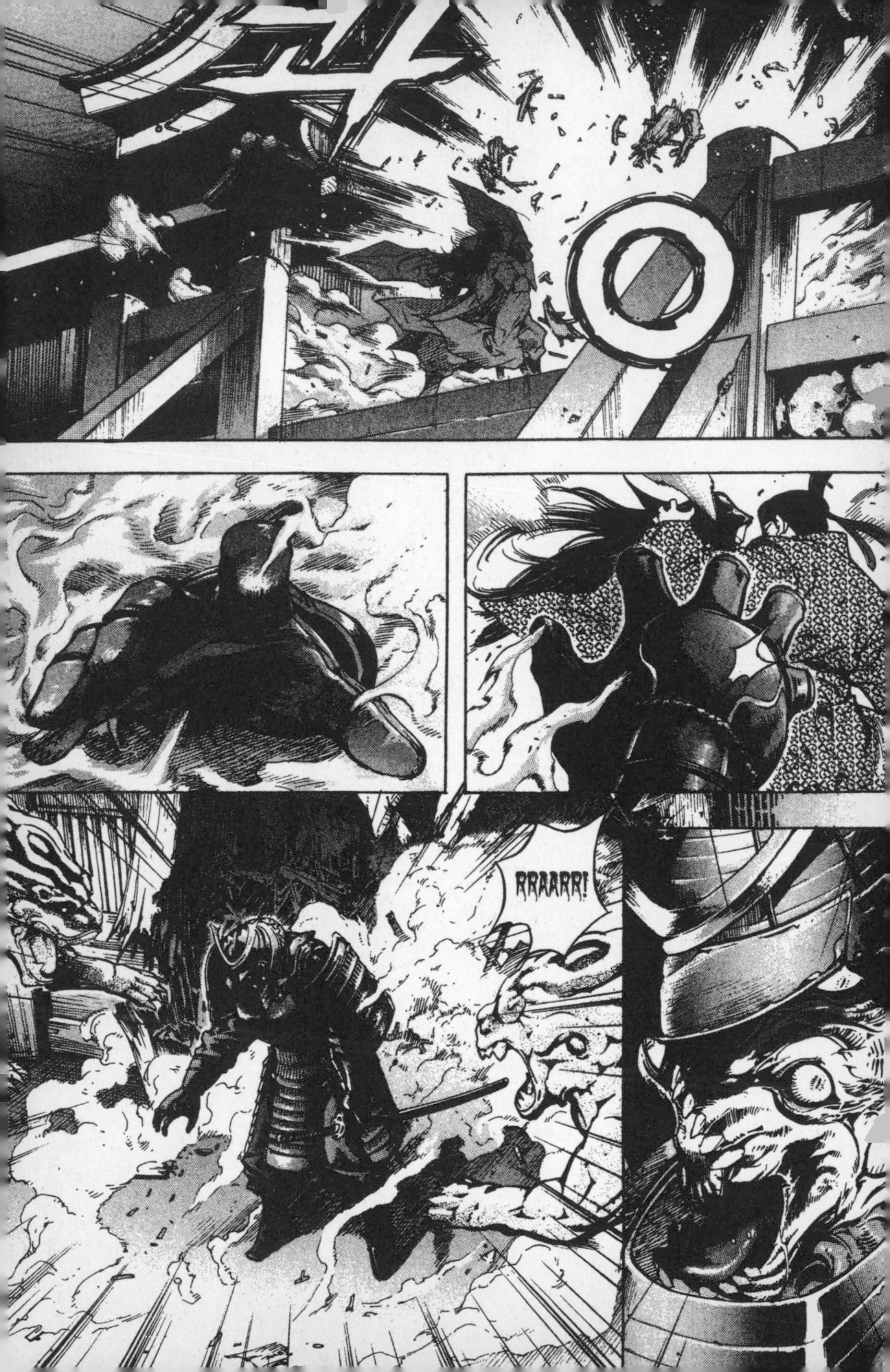
RRAARR!

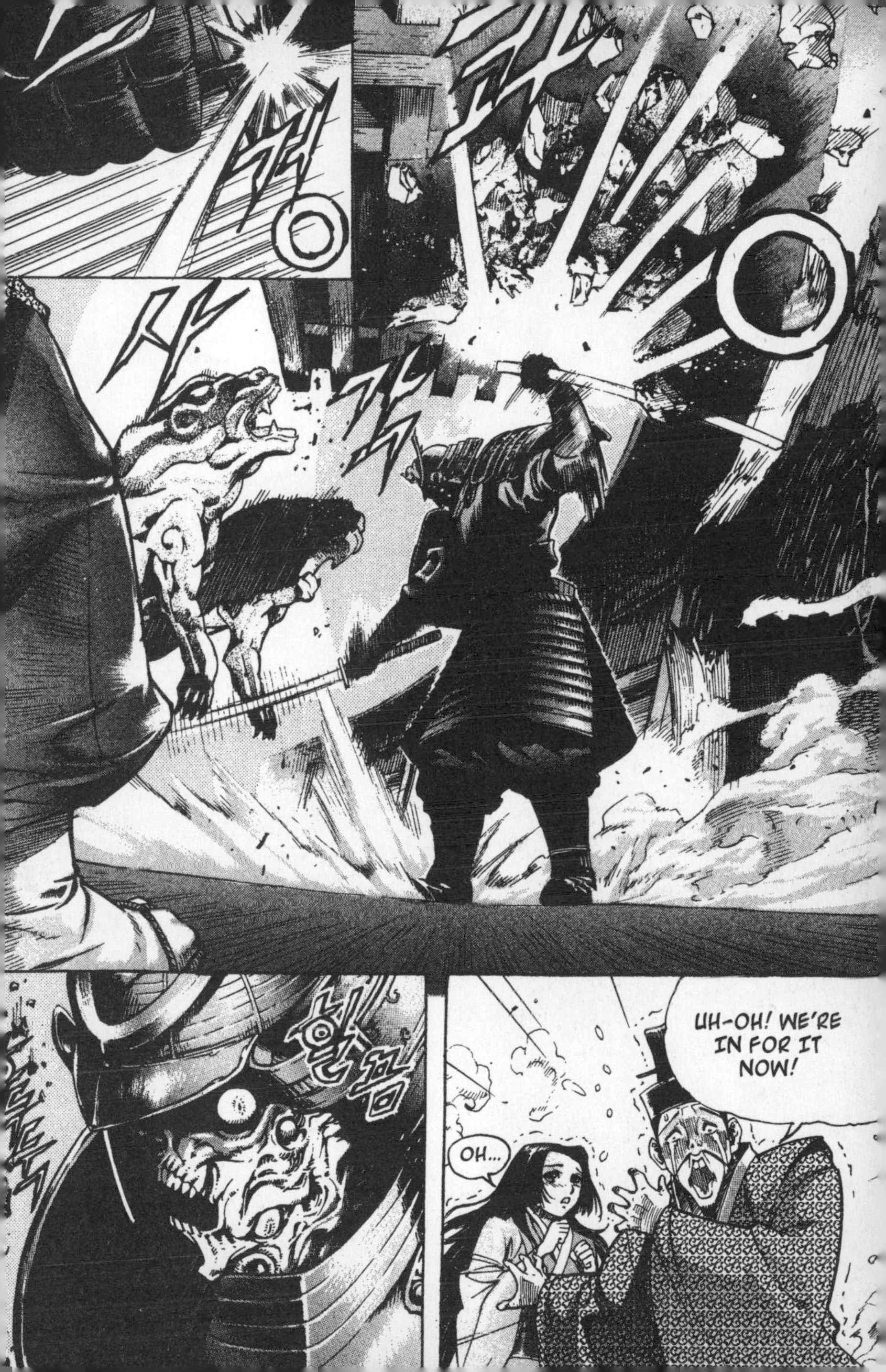
OH...
UH-OH! WE'RE IN FOR IT NOW!

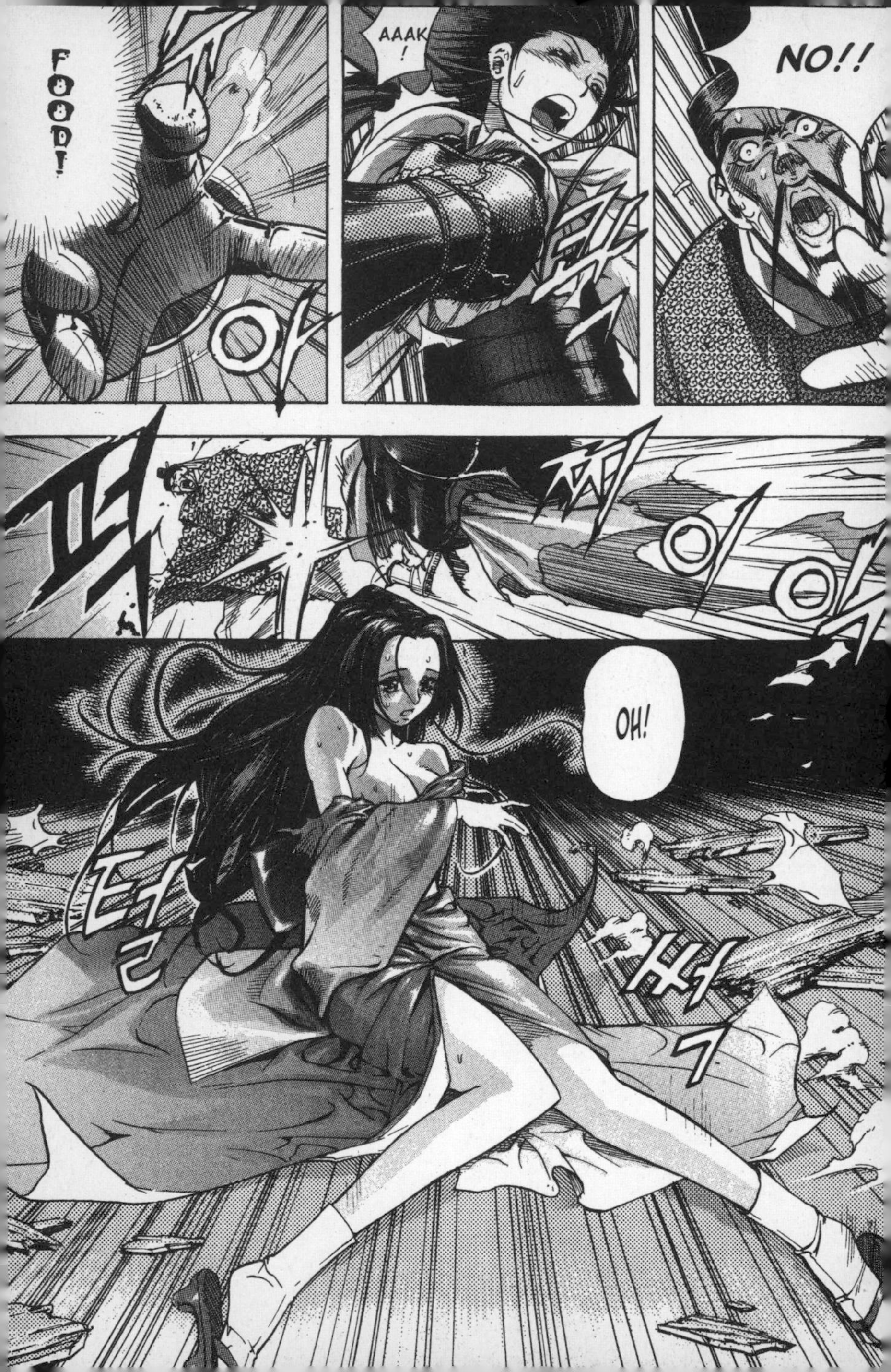
FOOD!
AAAK!
NO!!
OH!

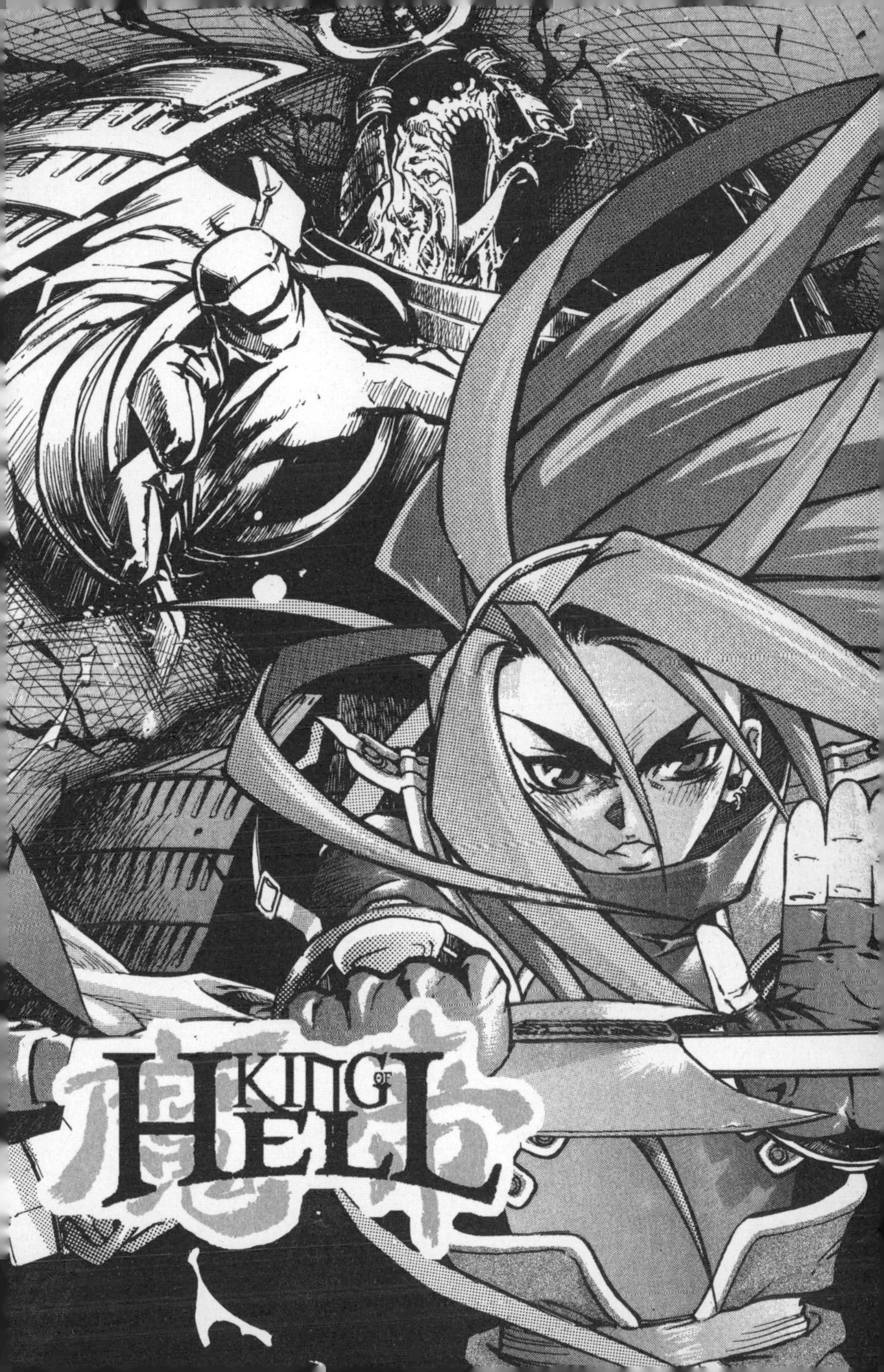
KING OF HELL

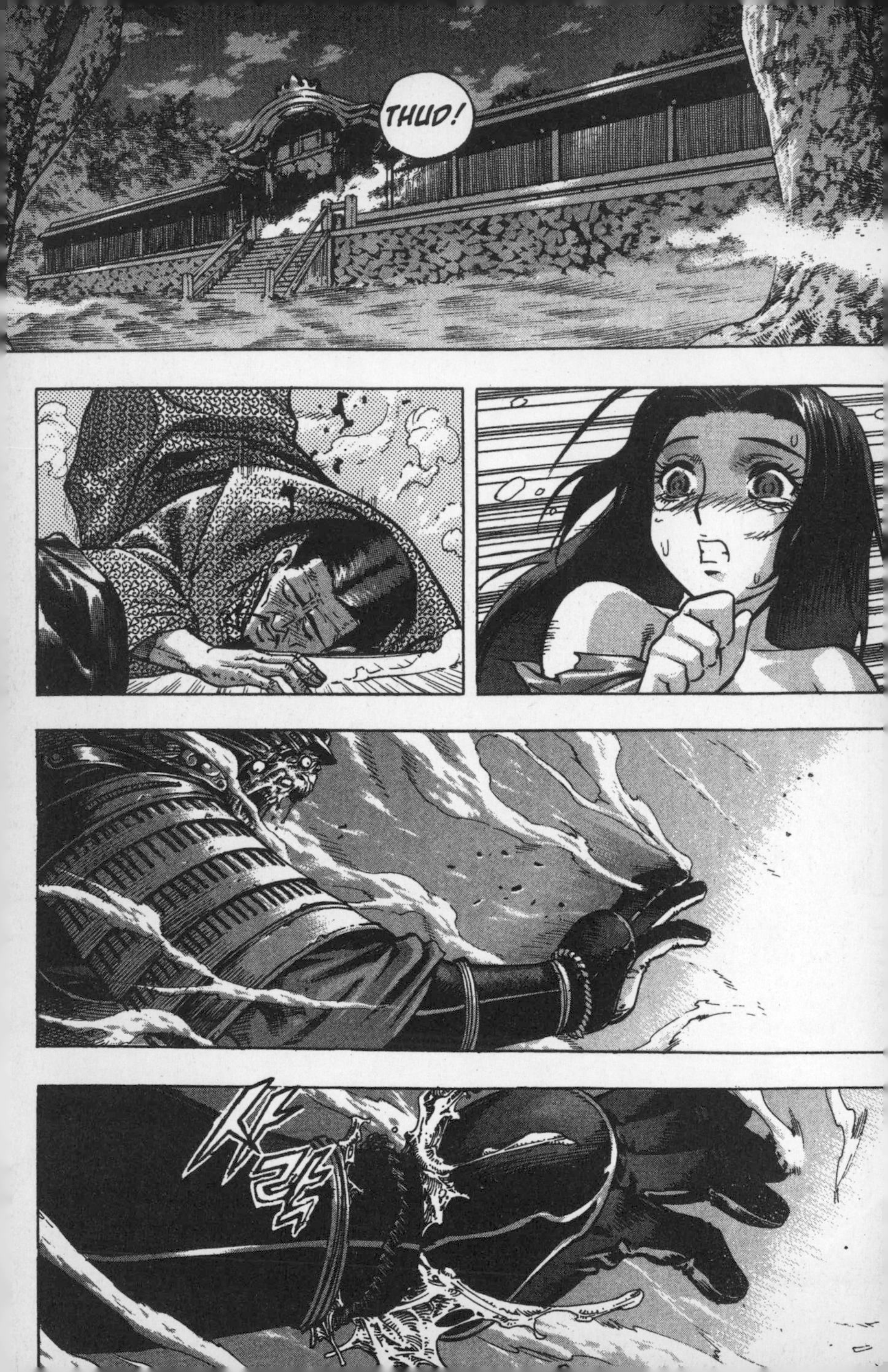
THUD!

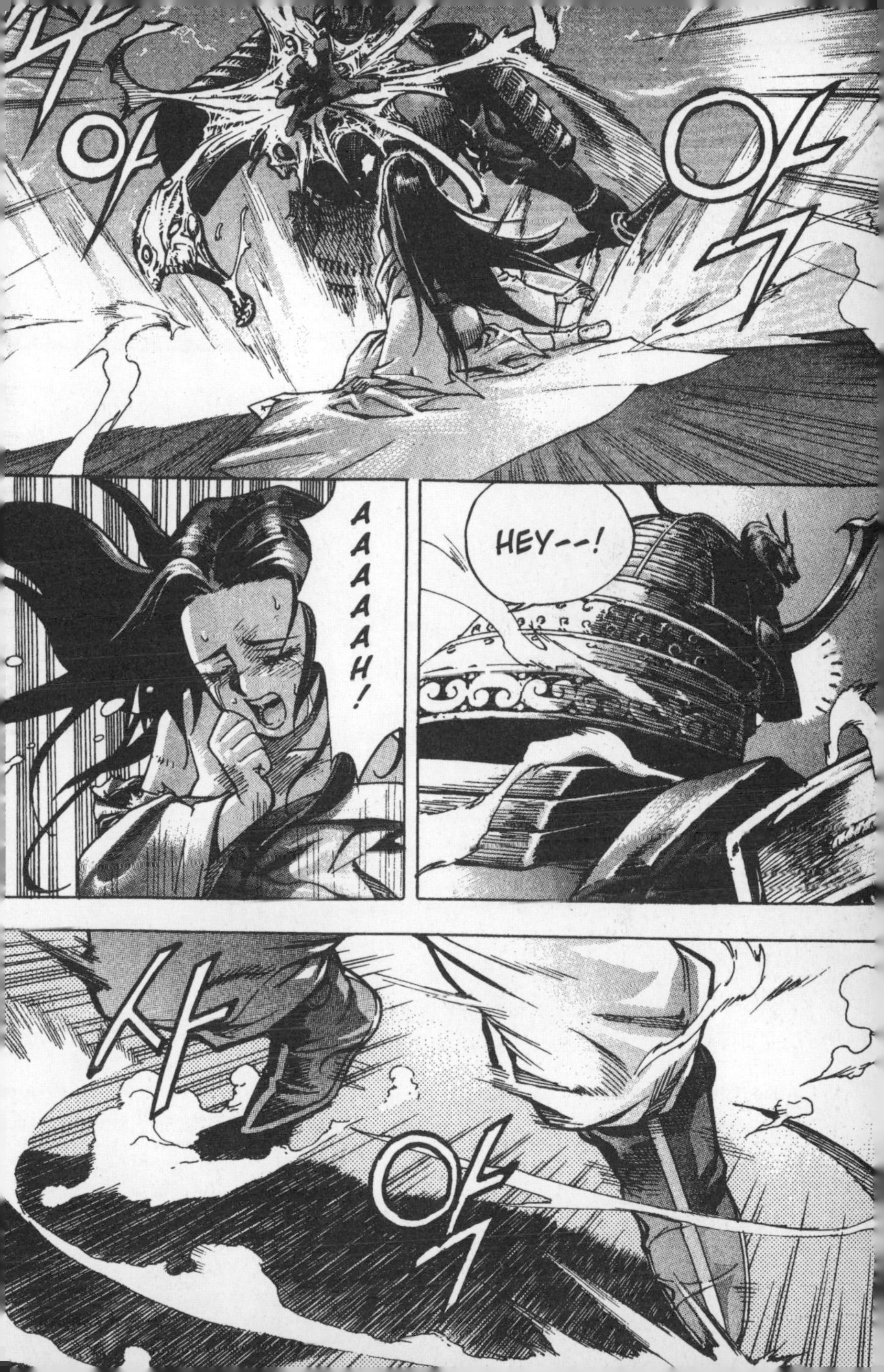
AAAAAH!
HEY--!

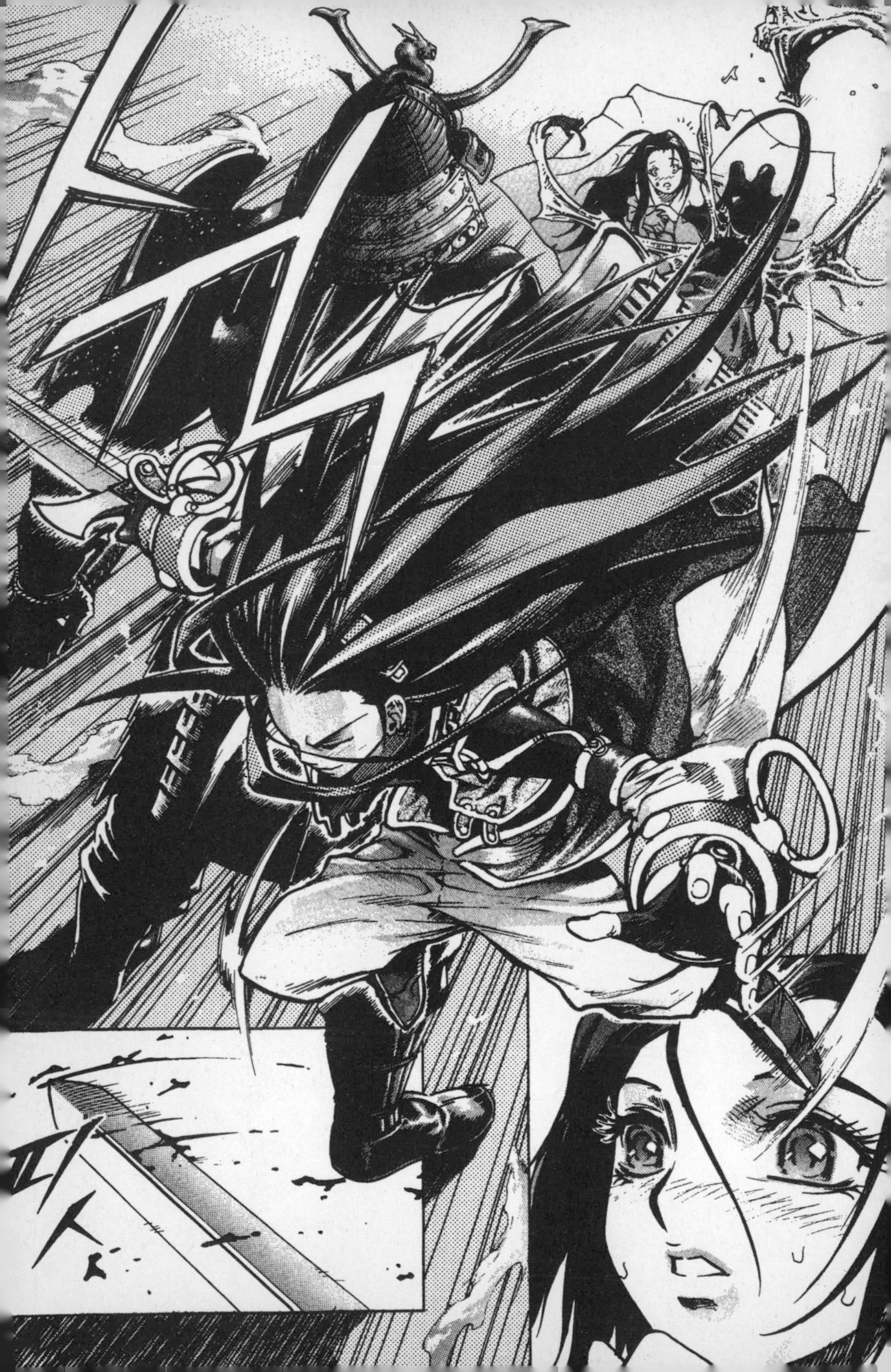

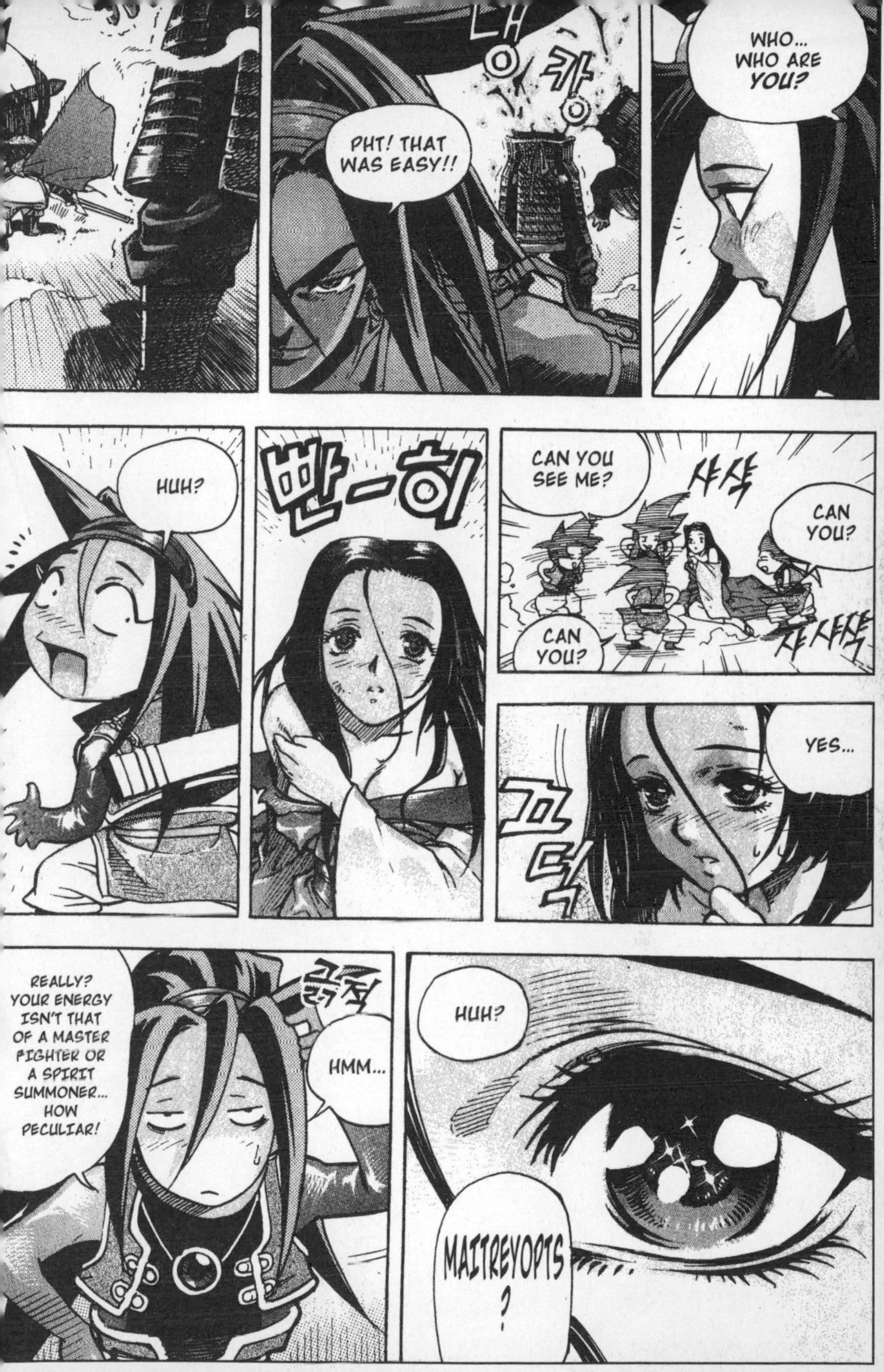
PHT! THAT WAS EASY!!
WHO... WHO ARE YOU?
HUH?
빤-히
CAN YOU SEE ME?
샤샥
CAN YOU?
CAN YOU?
샤샤샥
YES...
끄덕
REALLY? YOUR ENERGY ISN'T THAT OF A MASTER FIGHTER OR A SPIRIT SUMMONER... HOW PECULIAR!
HMM...
HUH?
MAITREYOPTS ?

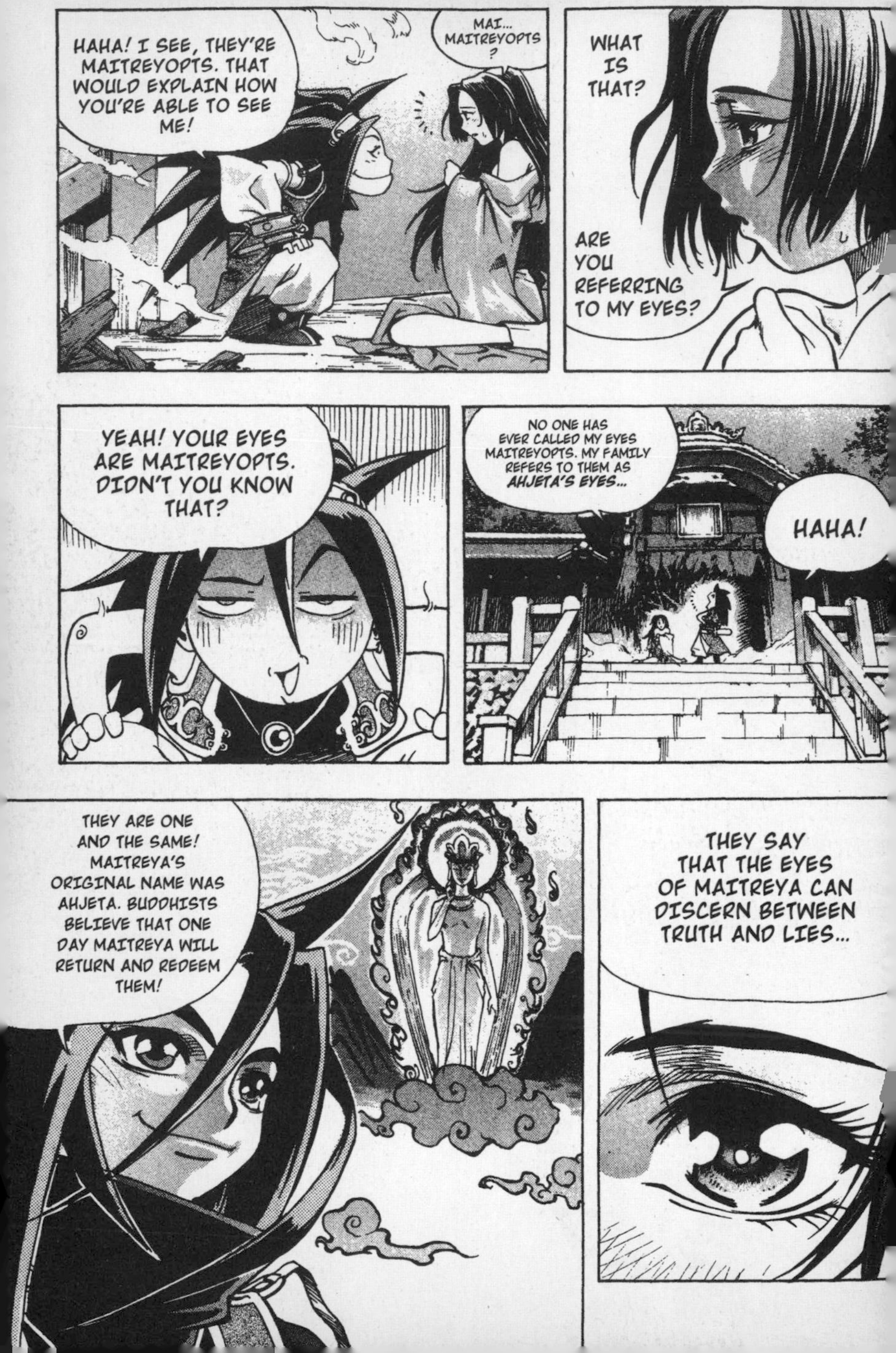
HAHA! I SEE, THEY'RE MAITREYOPTS. THAT WOULD EXPLAIN HOW YOU'RE ABLE TO SEE ME!
MAI... MAITREYOPTS?
WHAT IS THAT?
ARE YOU REFERRING TO MY EYES?
YEAH! YOUR EYES ARE MAITREYOPTS. DIDN'T YOU KNOW THAT?
NO ONE HAS EVER CALLED MY EYES MAITREYOPTS. MY FAMILY REFERS TO THEM AS AHJETA'S EYES...
HAHA!
THEY ARE ONE AND THE SAME! MAITREYA'S ORIGINAL NAME WAS AHJETA. BUDDHISTS BELIEVE THAT ONE DAY MAITREYA WILL RETURN AND REDEEM THEM!
THEY SAY THAT THE EYES OF MAITREYA CAN DISCERN BETWEEN TRUTH AND LIES...

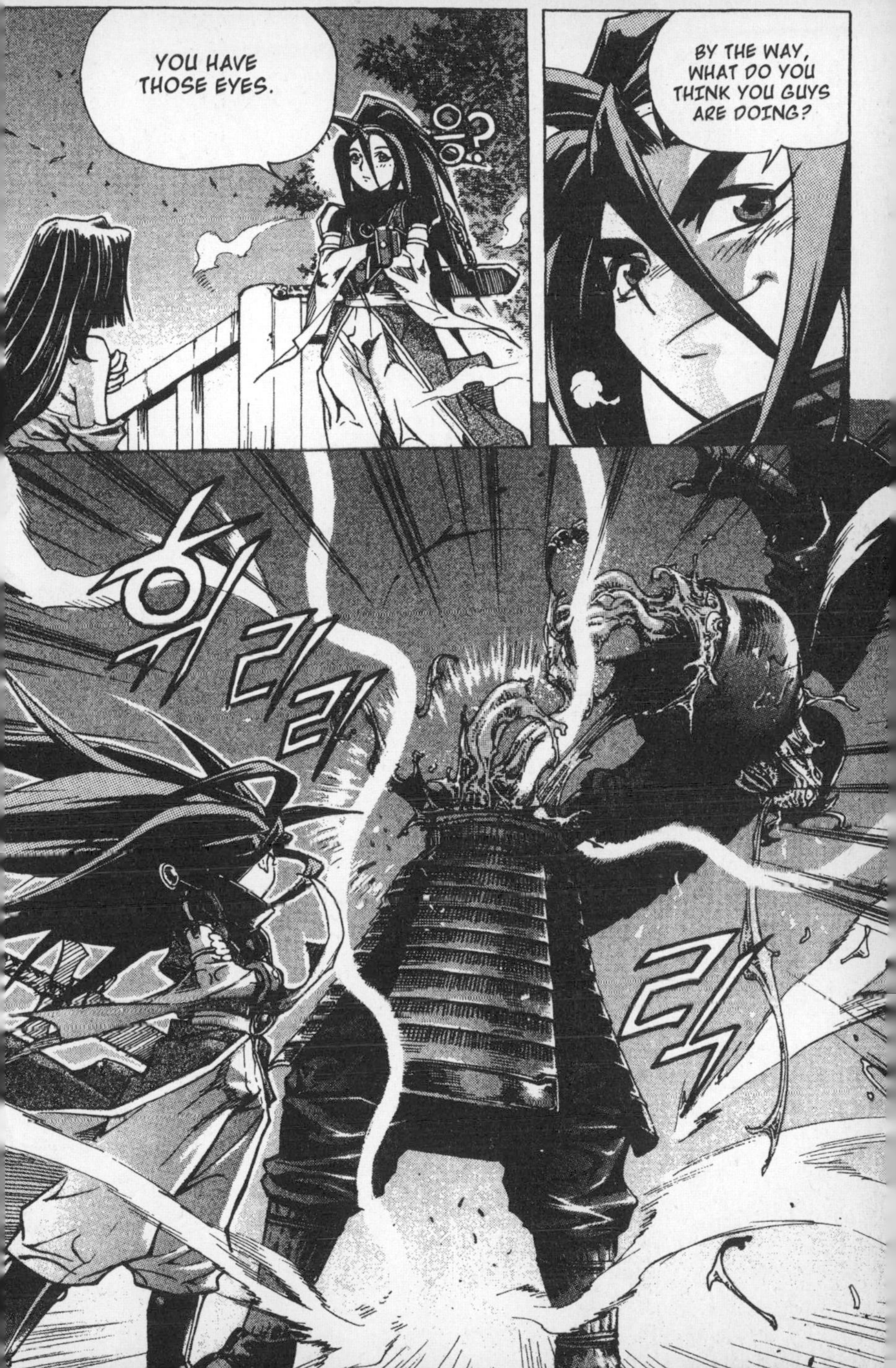
YOU HAVE THOSE EYES.
BY THE WAY, WHAT DO YOU THINK YOU GUYS ARE DOING?

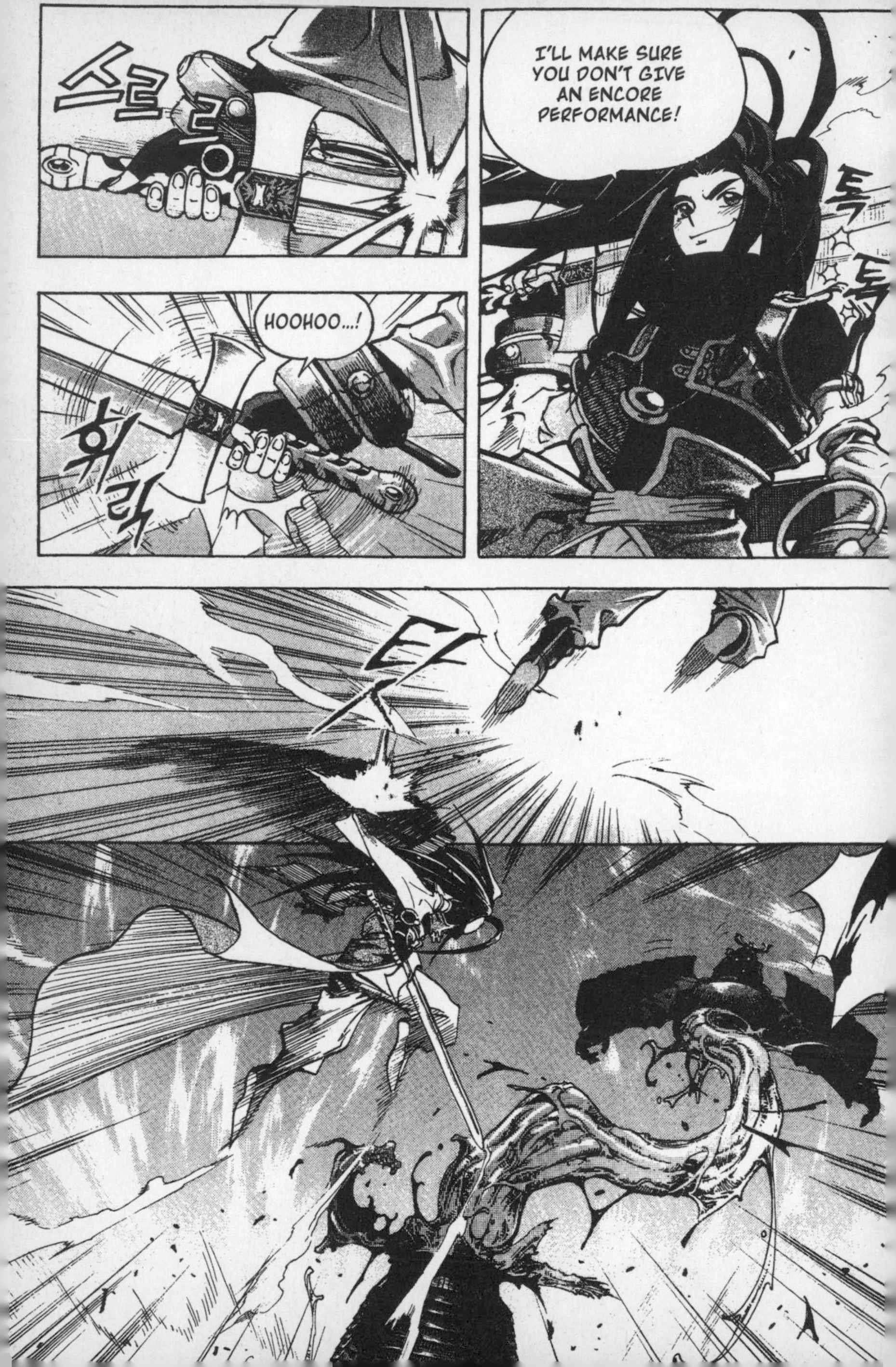
HOOHOO...!
I'LL MAKE SURE YOU DON'T GIVE AN ENCORE PERFORMANCE!
톡
톡

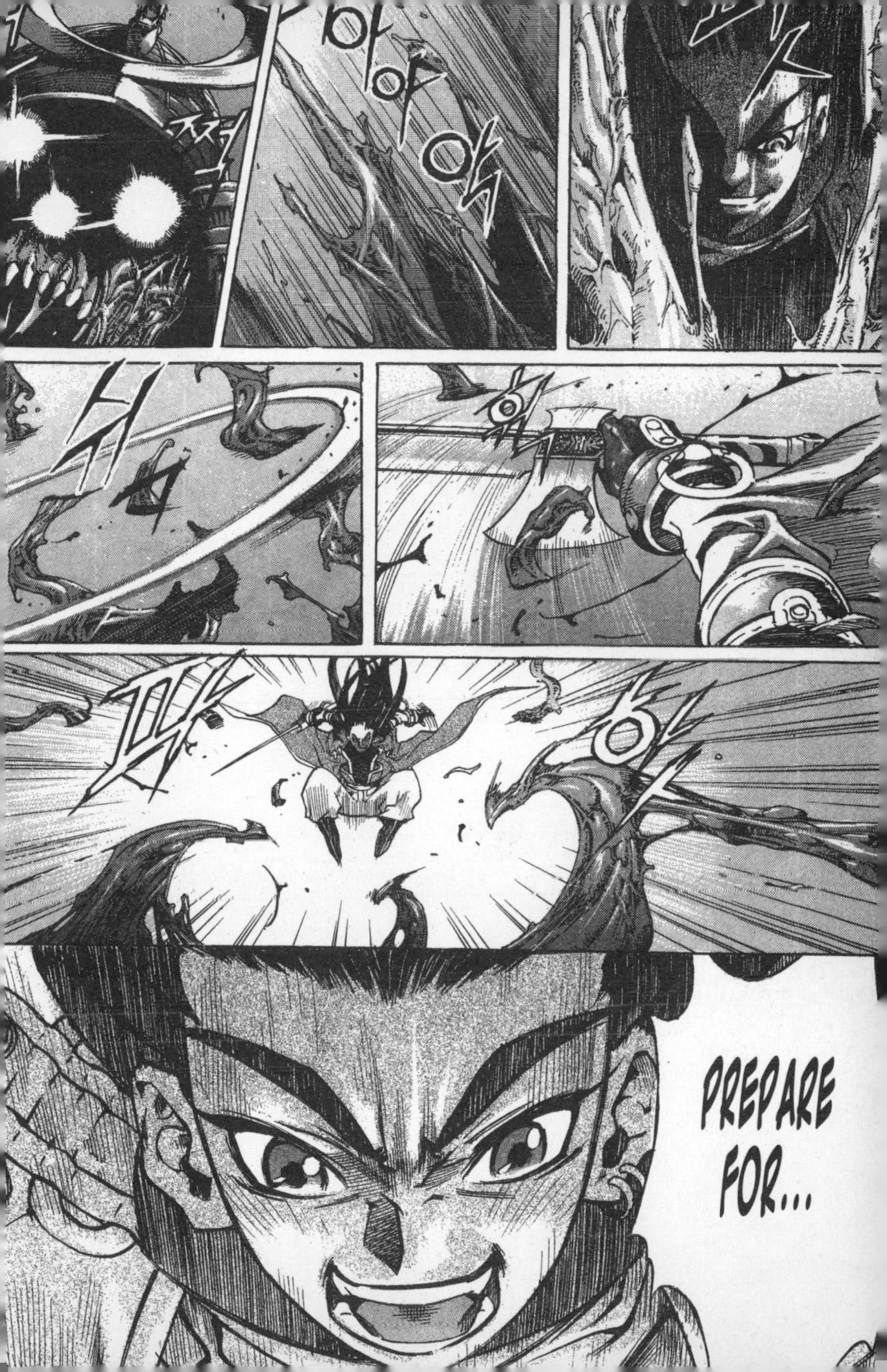
PREPARE FOR...

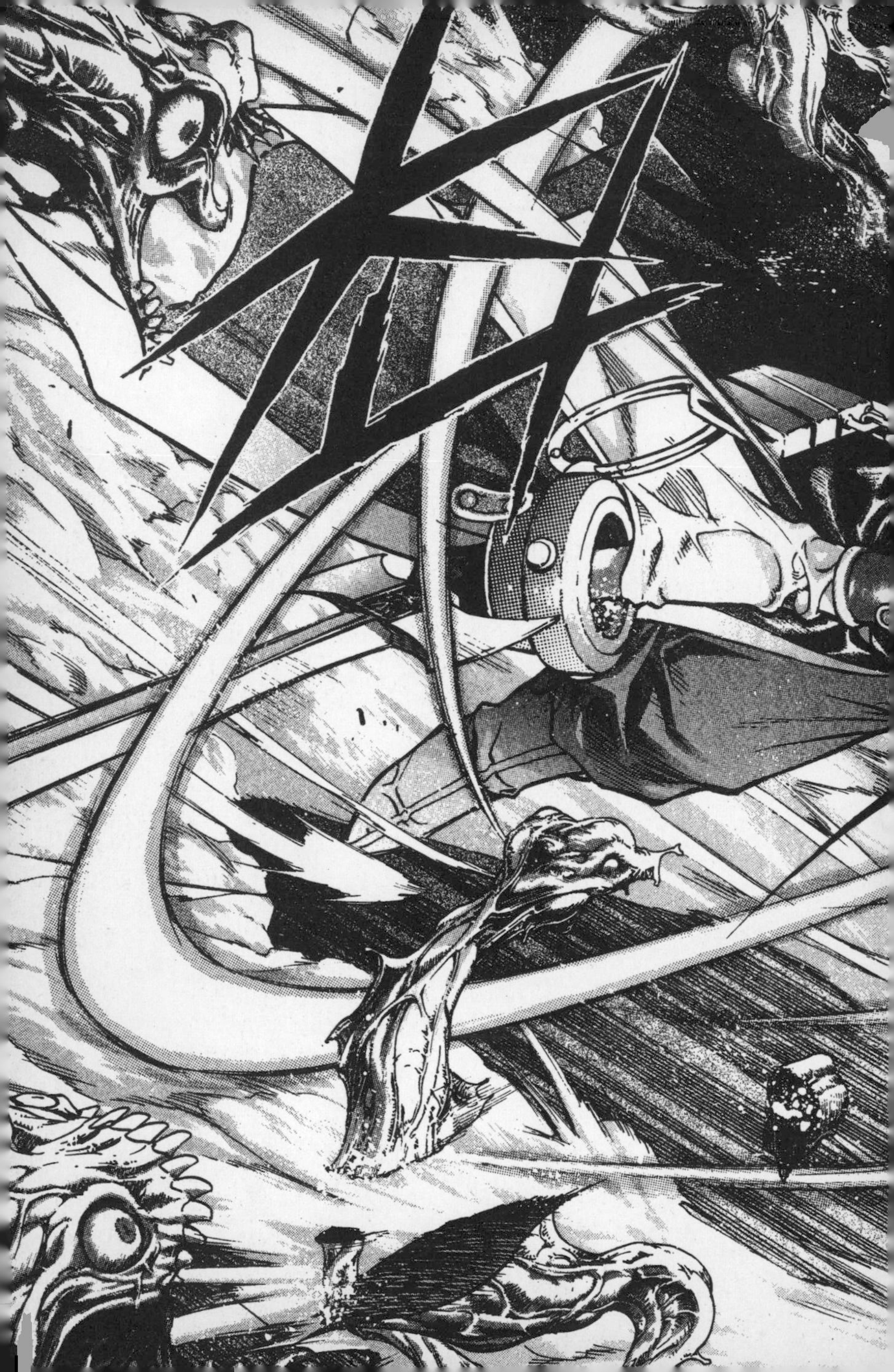

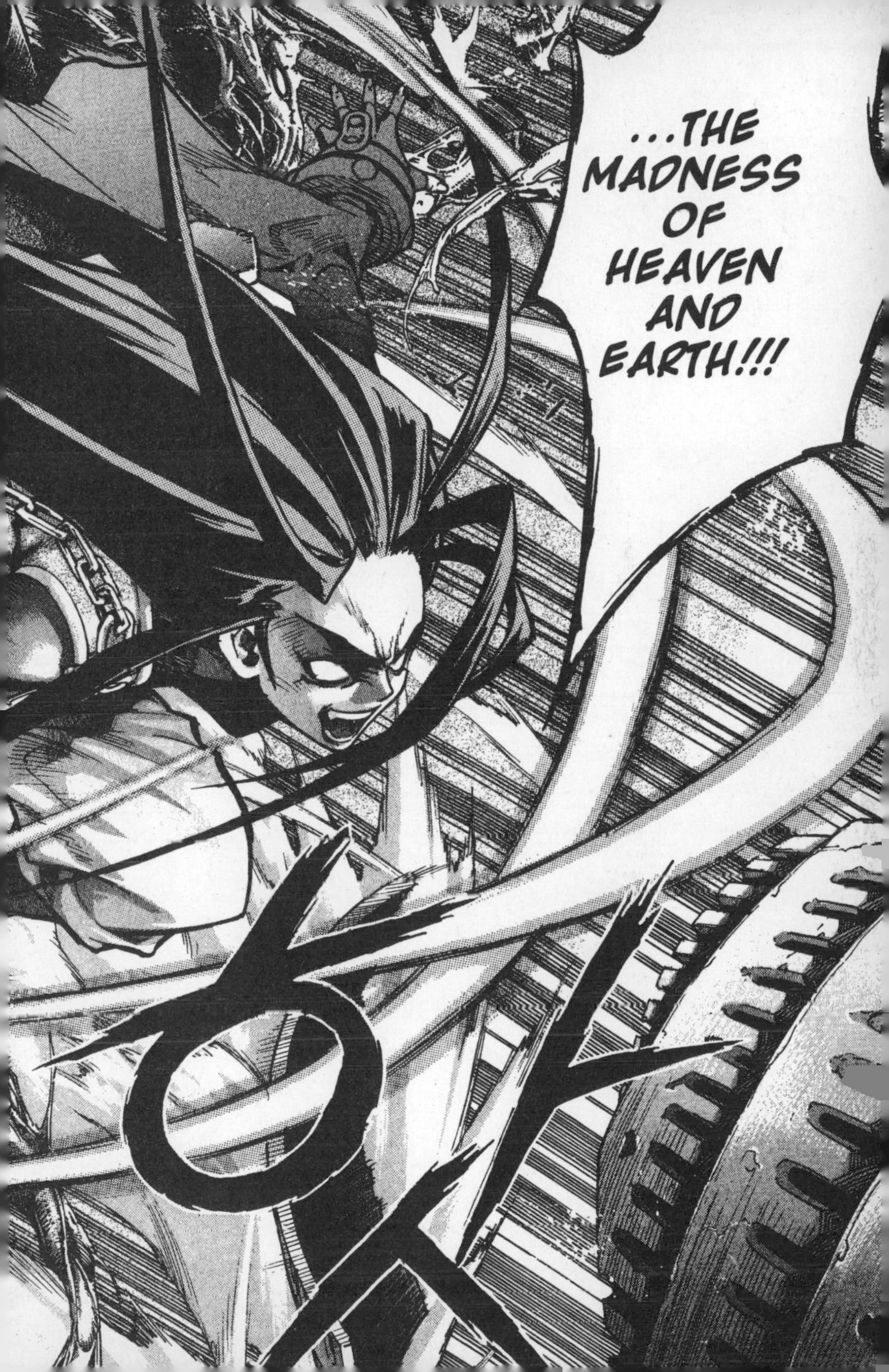
...THE MADNESS OF HEAVEN AND EARTH!!!

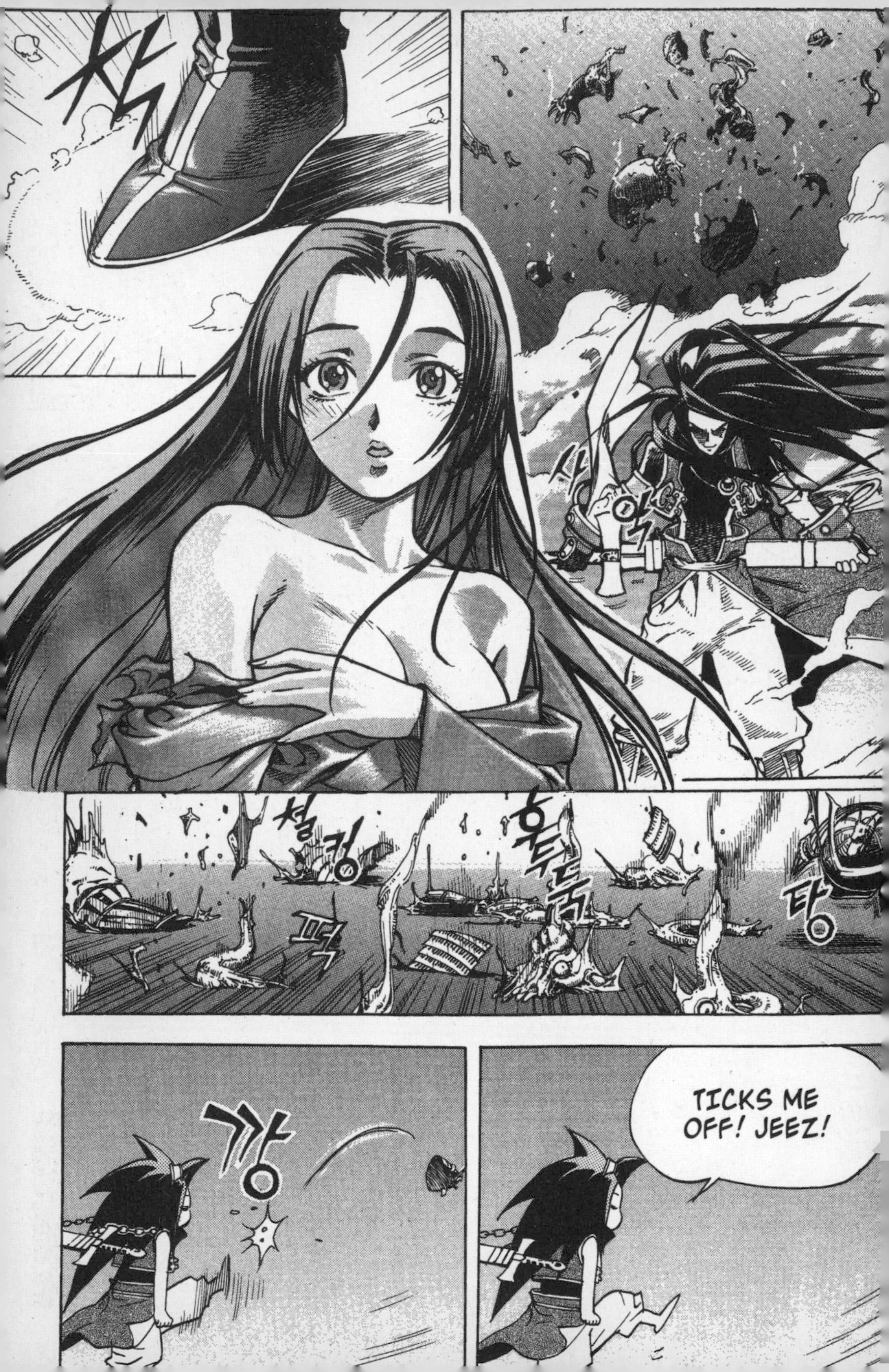
철컹
퍽
후두둑
탕
깡
TICKS ME OFF! JEEZ!

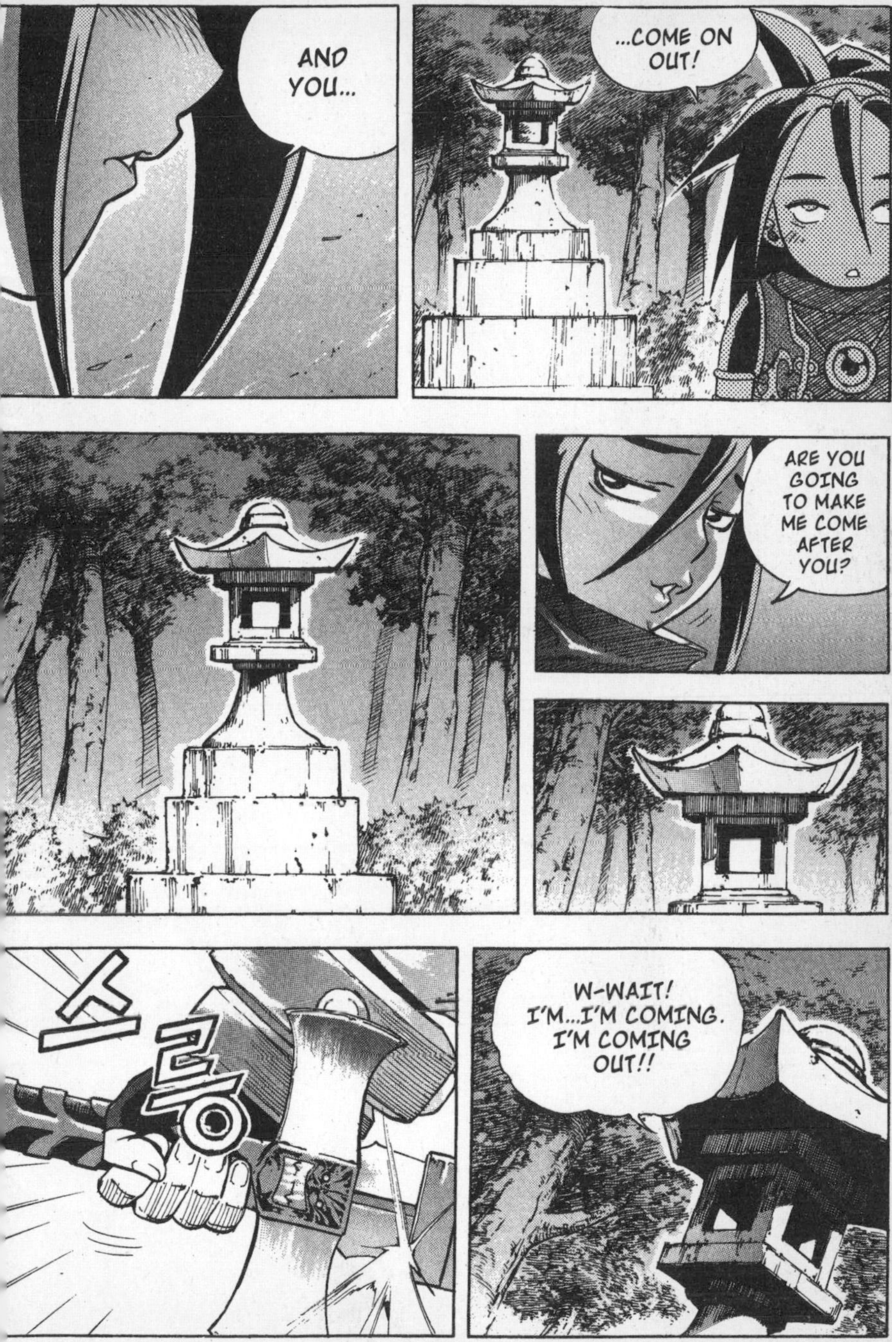
AND YOU...
...COME ON OUT!
ARE YOU GOING TO MAKE ME COME AFTER YOU?
W-WAIT! I'M...I'M COMING. I'M COMING OUT!!

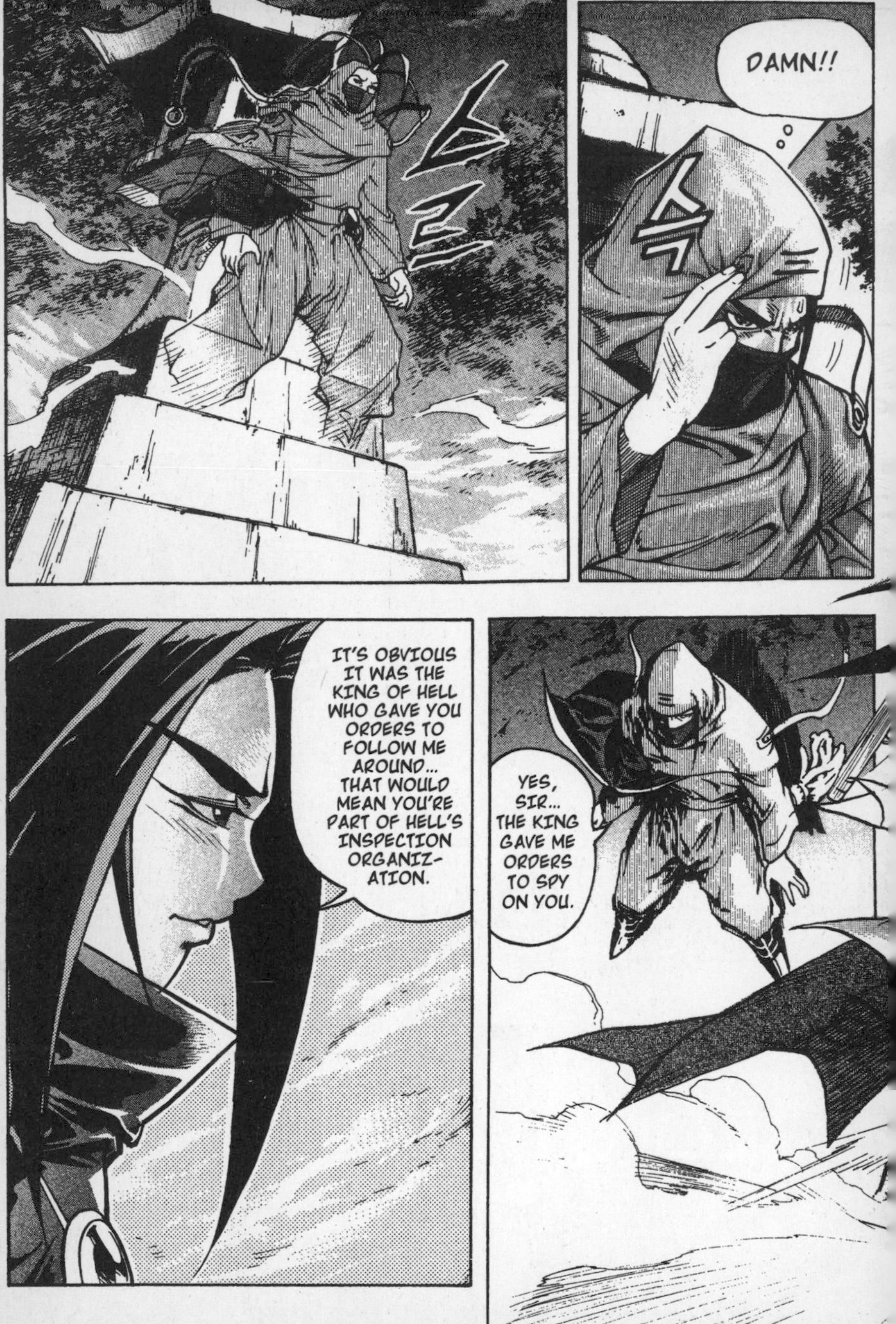
DAMN!!
IT'S OBVIOUS IT WAS THE KING OF HELL WHO GAVE YOU ORDERS TO FOLLOW ME AROUND... THAT WOULD MEAN YOU'RE PART OF HELL'S INSPECTION ORGANIZ-ATION.
YES, SIR... THE KING GAVE ME ORDERS TO SPY ON YOU.

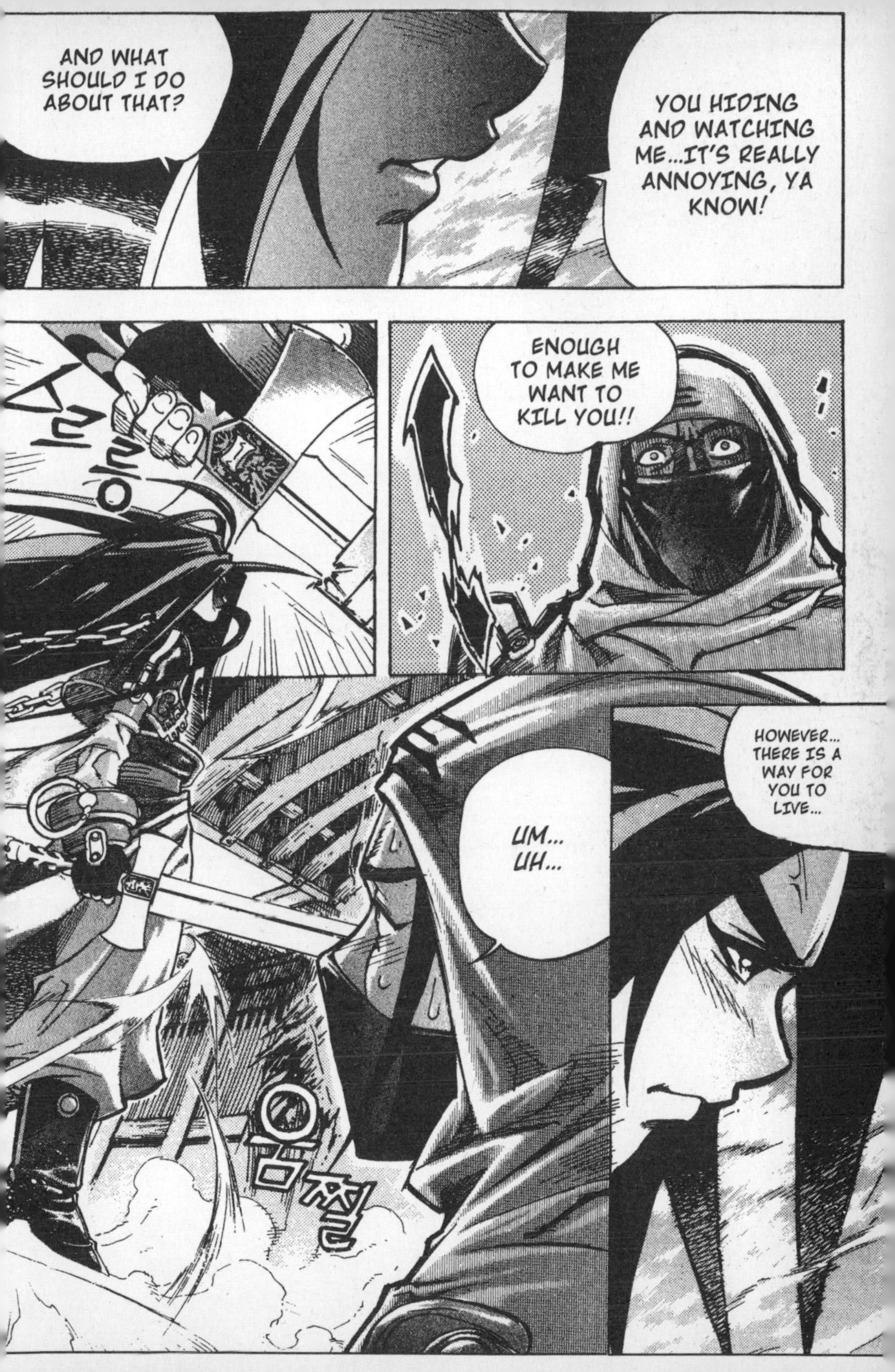
AND WHAT SHOULD I DO ABOUT THAT?
YOU HIDING AND WATCHING ME...IT'S REALLY ANNOYING, YA KNOW!
ENOUGH TO MAKE ME WANT TO KILL YOU!!
!
UM... UH...
움찔
HOWEVER... THERE IS A WAY FOR YOU TO LIVE...

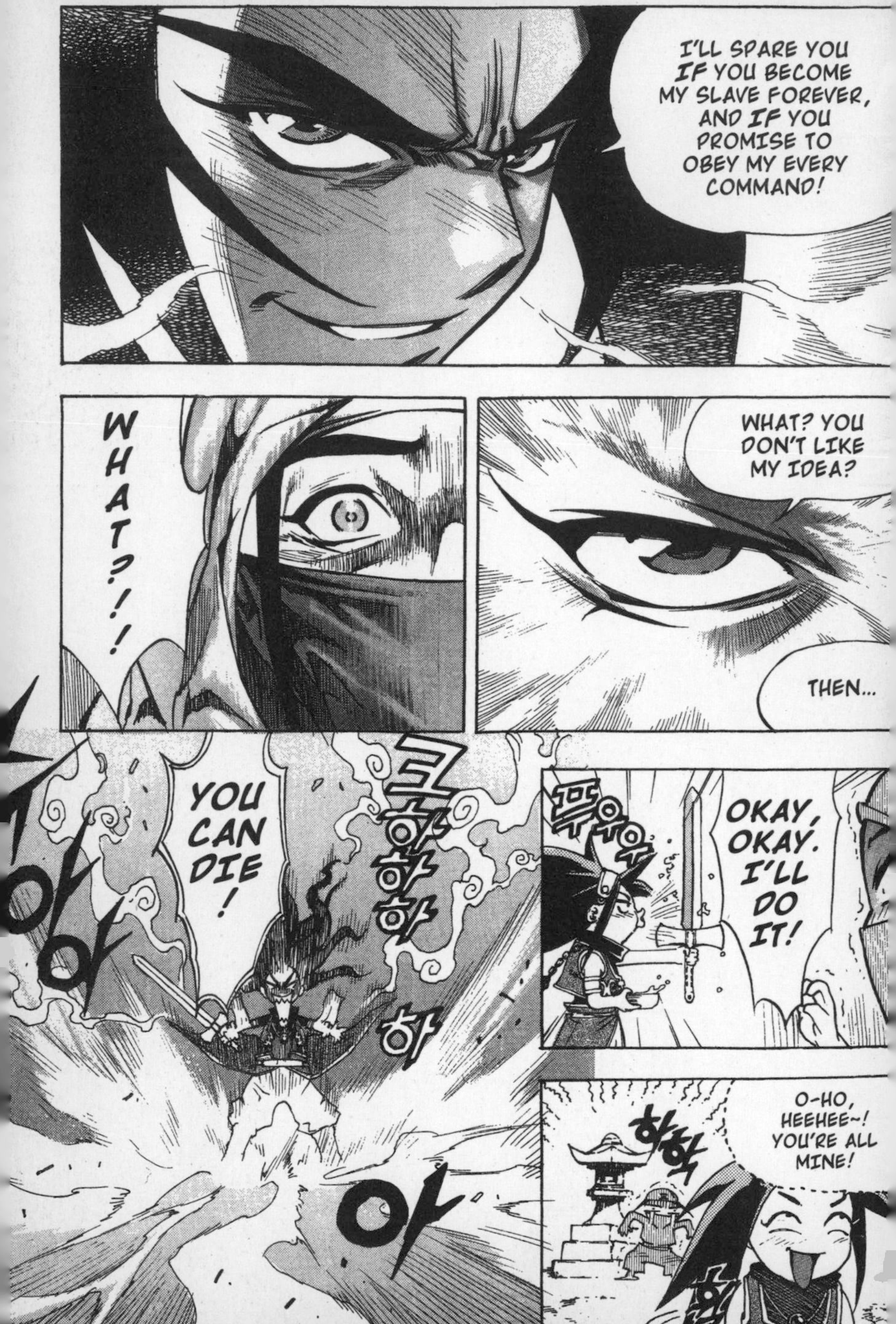

I'LL SPARE YOU IF YOU BECOME MY SLAVE FOREVER, AND IF YOU PROMISE TO OBEY MY EVERY COMMAND!
WHAT?!!
WHAT? YOU DON'T LIKE MY IDEA?
THEN...
YOU CAN DIE!
크하하하
하
아
OKAY, OKAY. I'LL DO IT!
O-HO, HEEHEE~! YOU'RE ALL MINE!

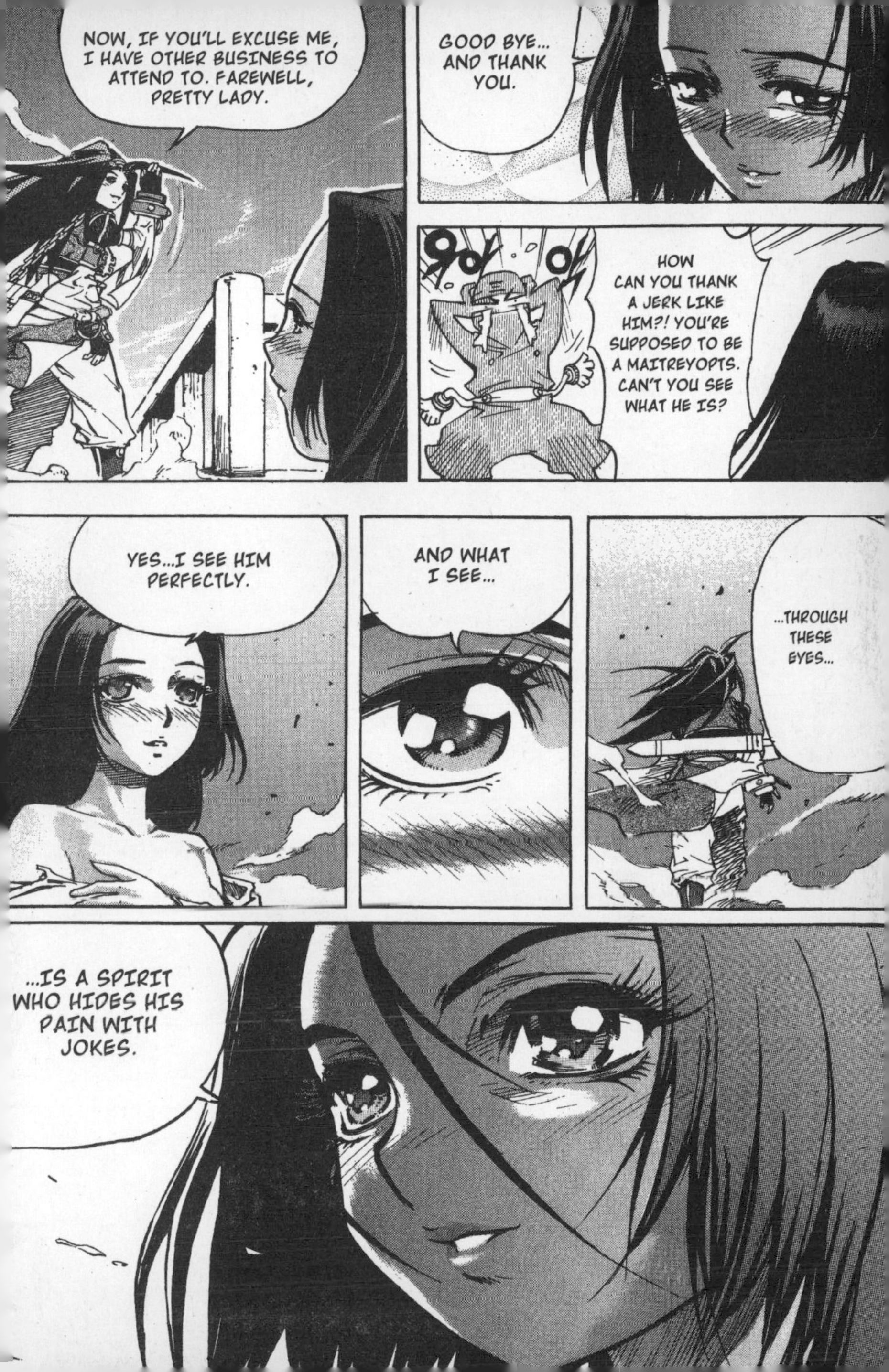
NOW, IF YOU'LL EXCUSE ME, I HAVE OTHER BUSINESS TO ATTEND TO. FAREWELL, PRETTY LADY.
GOOD BYE... AND THANK YOU.
HOW CAN YOU THANK A JERK LIKE HIM?! YOU'RE SUPPOSED TO BE A MAITREYOPTS. CAN'T YOU SEE WHAT HE IS?
YES...I SEE HIM PERFECTLY.
AND WHAT I SEE...
...THROUGH THESE EYES...
...IS A SPIRIT WHO HIDES HIS PAIN WITH JOKES.

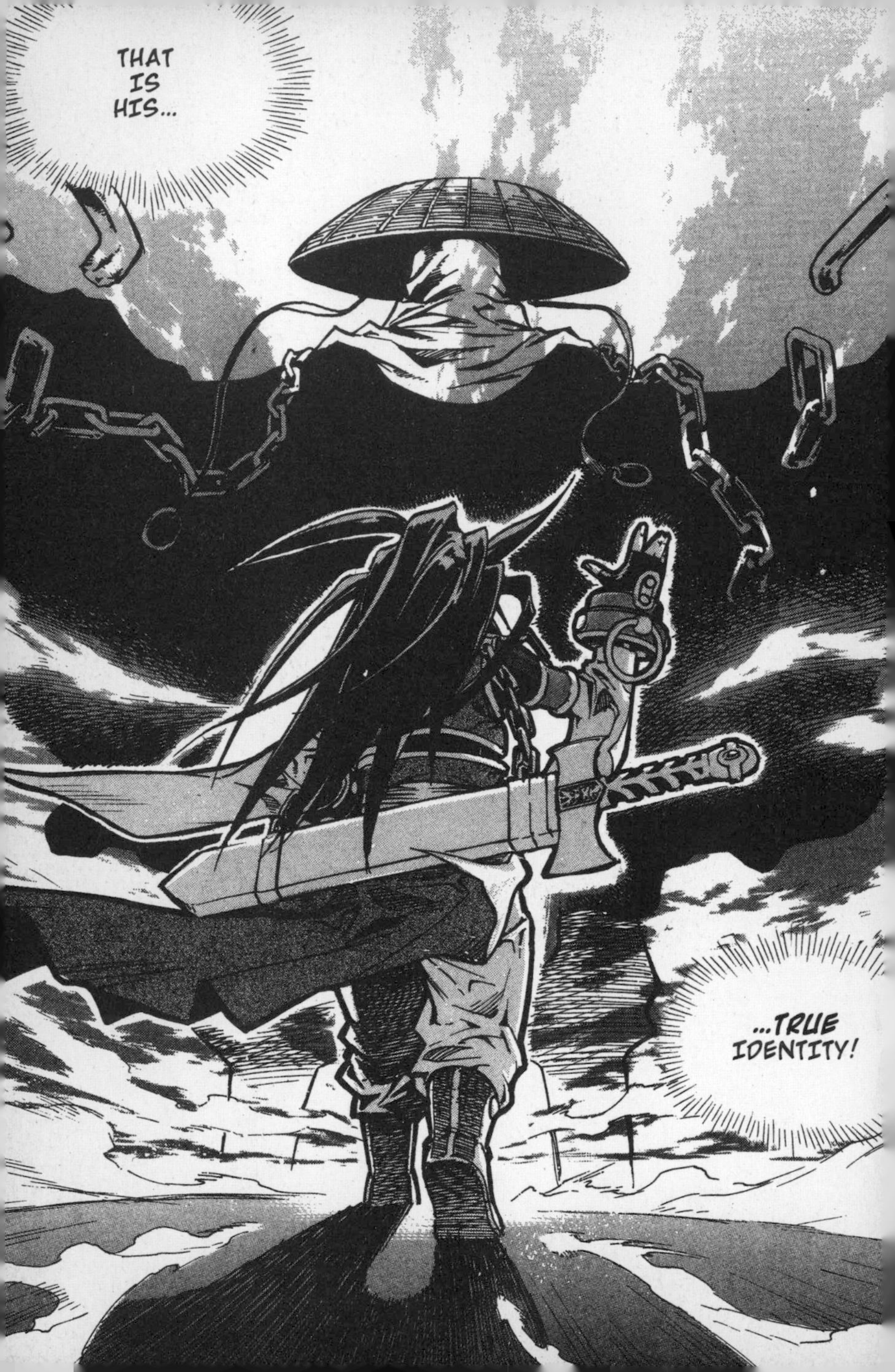
THAT IS HIS...
...TRUE IDENTITY!

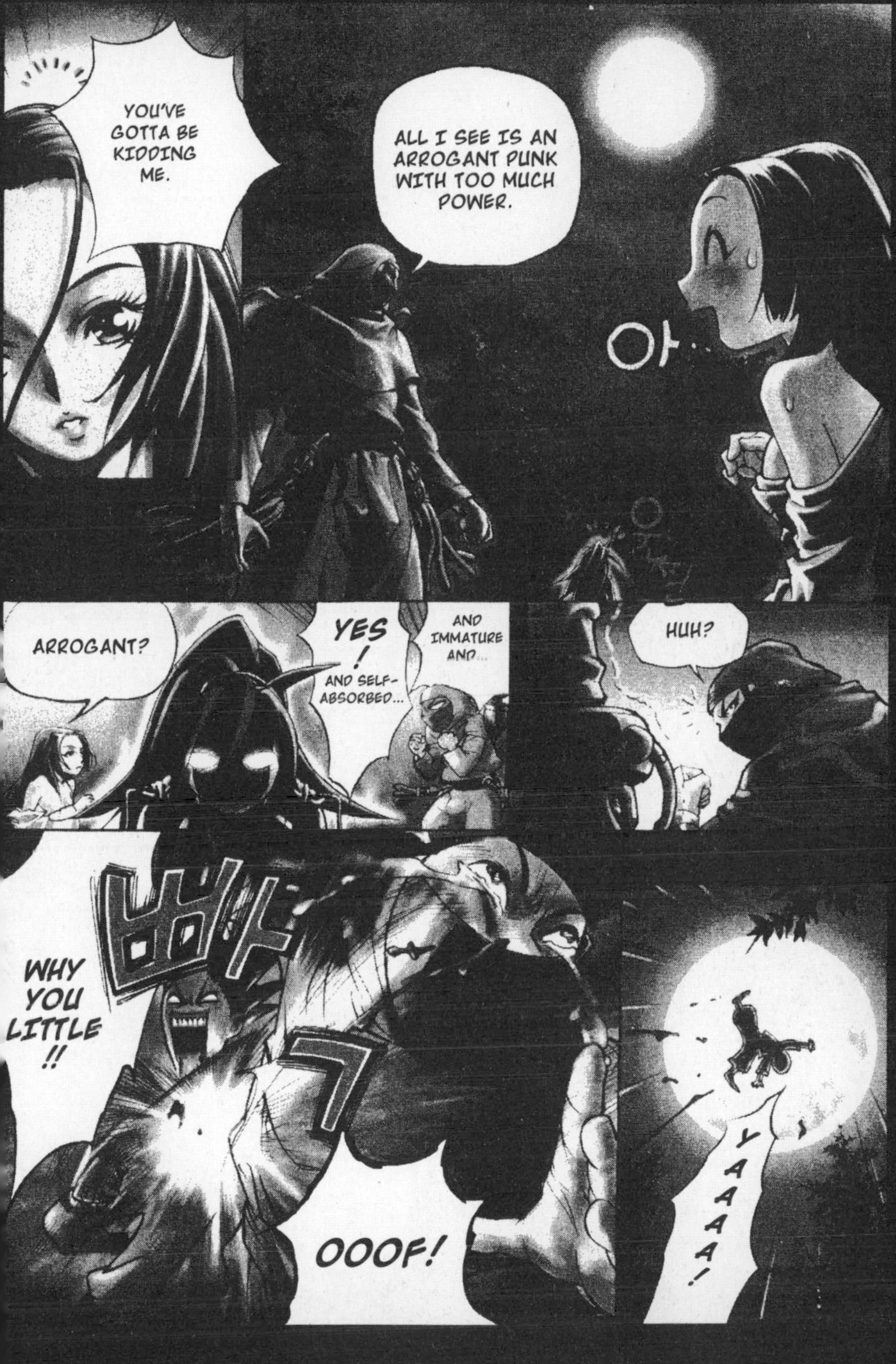

YOU'VE GOTTA BE KIDDING ME.
ALL I SEE IS AN ARROGANT PUNK WITH TOO MUCH POWER.
아...
ARROGANT?
YES! AND SELF-ABSORBED...
AND IMMATURE AND...
HUH?
빡
WHY YOU LITTLE!!
OOOF!
YAAAAA!

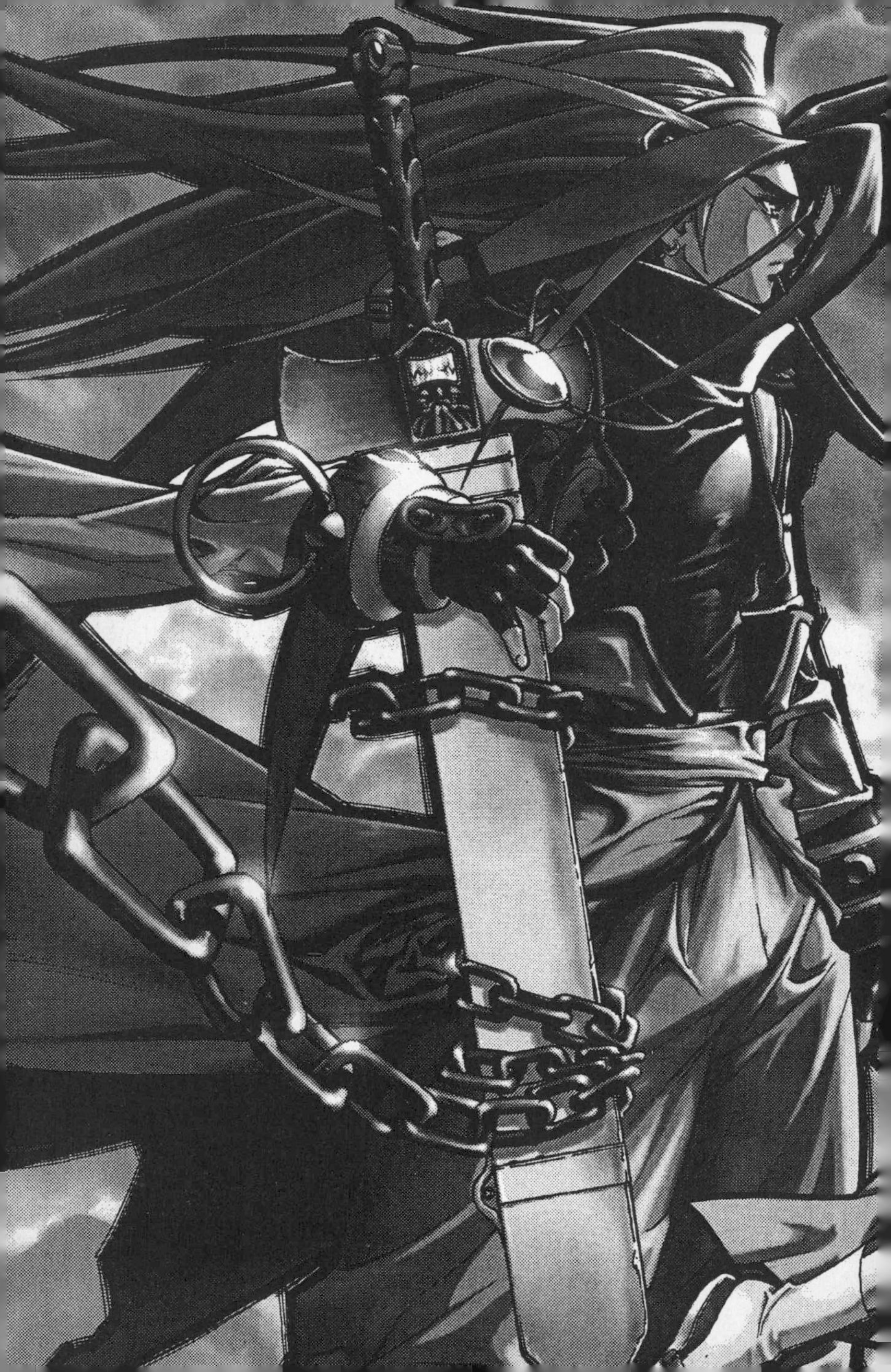

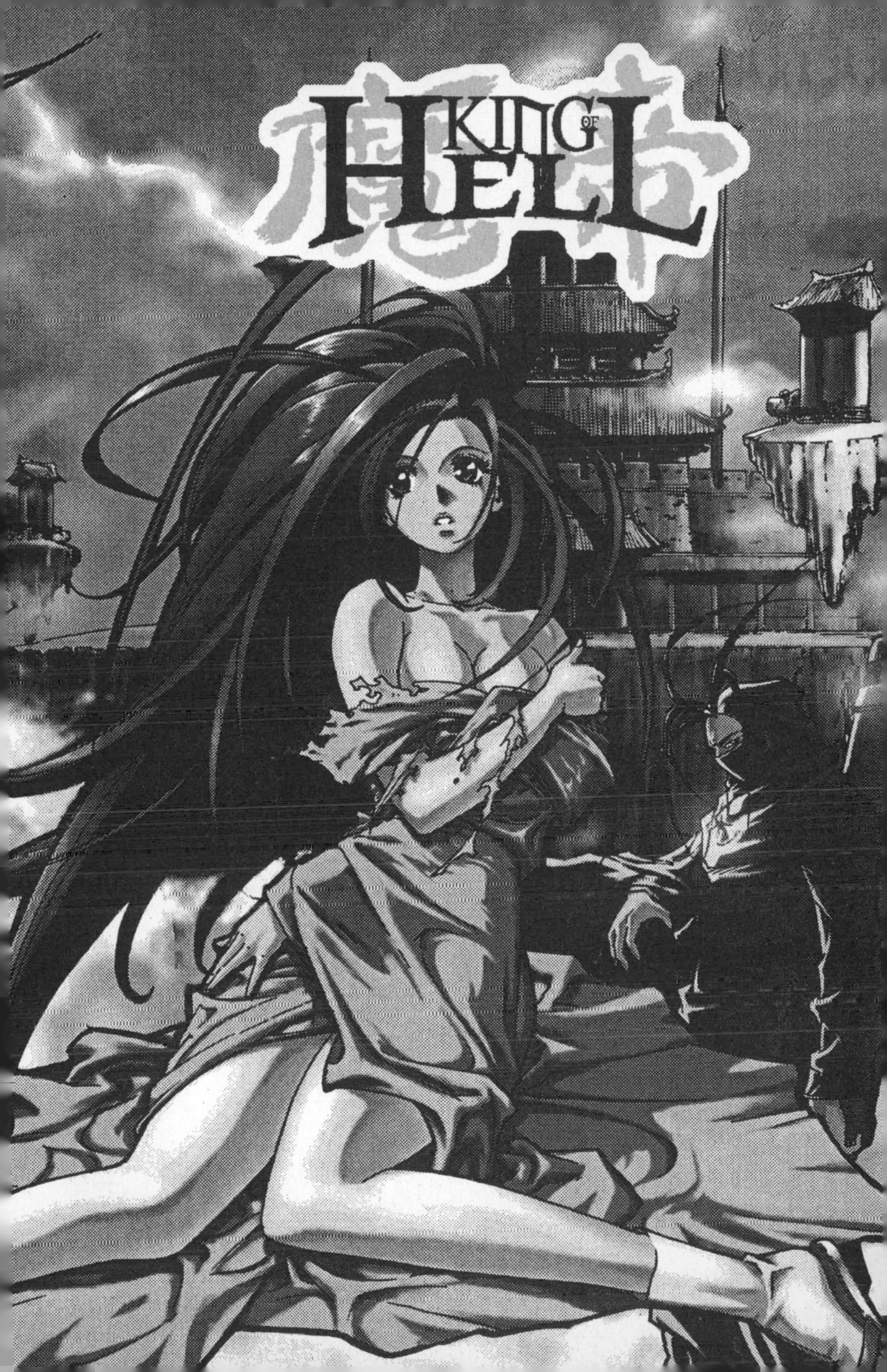
KING OF HELL

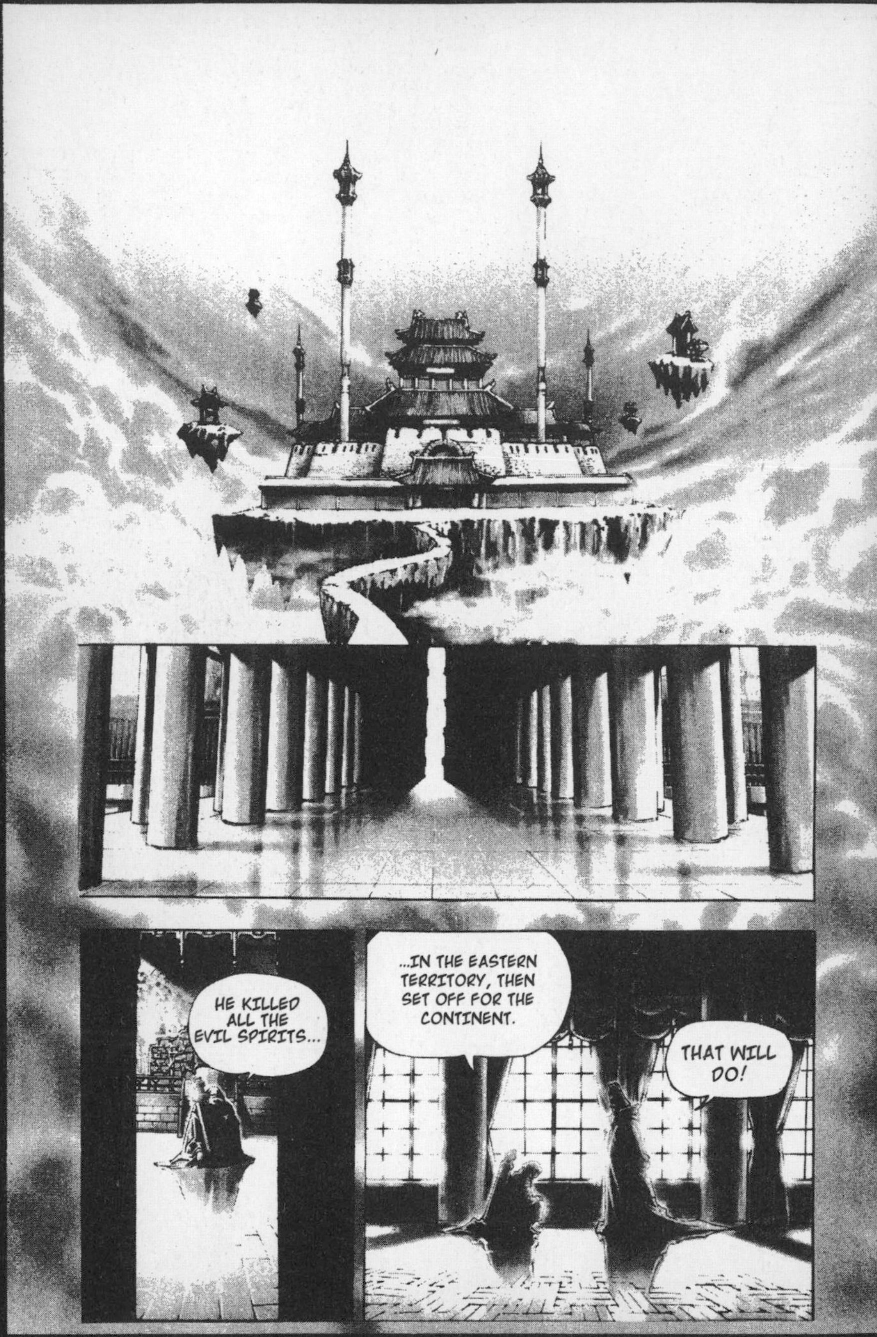
HE KILLED ALL THE EVIL SPIRITS...
...IN THE EASTERN TERRITORY, THEN SET OFF FOR THE CONTINENT.
THAT WILL DO!

UH... ER... UM...

WHAT IS IT?

WOULD IT BE POSSIBLE TO REQUEST A TRANSFER?

WHAT ?!

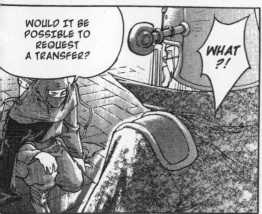

GIVE ME A DIFFERENT DUTY... *PLEASE?!* NOW HE CALLS ME AT ALL HOURS OF THE NIGHT AND MAKES ME DO ALL KINDS OF MENIAL AND DEGRADING TASKS...

...HE MAKES ME DANCE AND SING, AND I'M GOING OUT OF MY MIND! *CHOKE!*

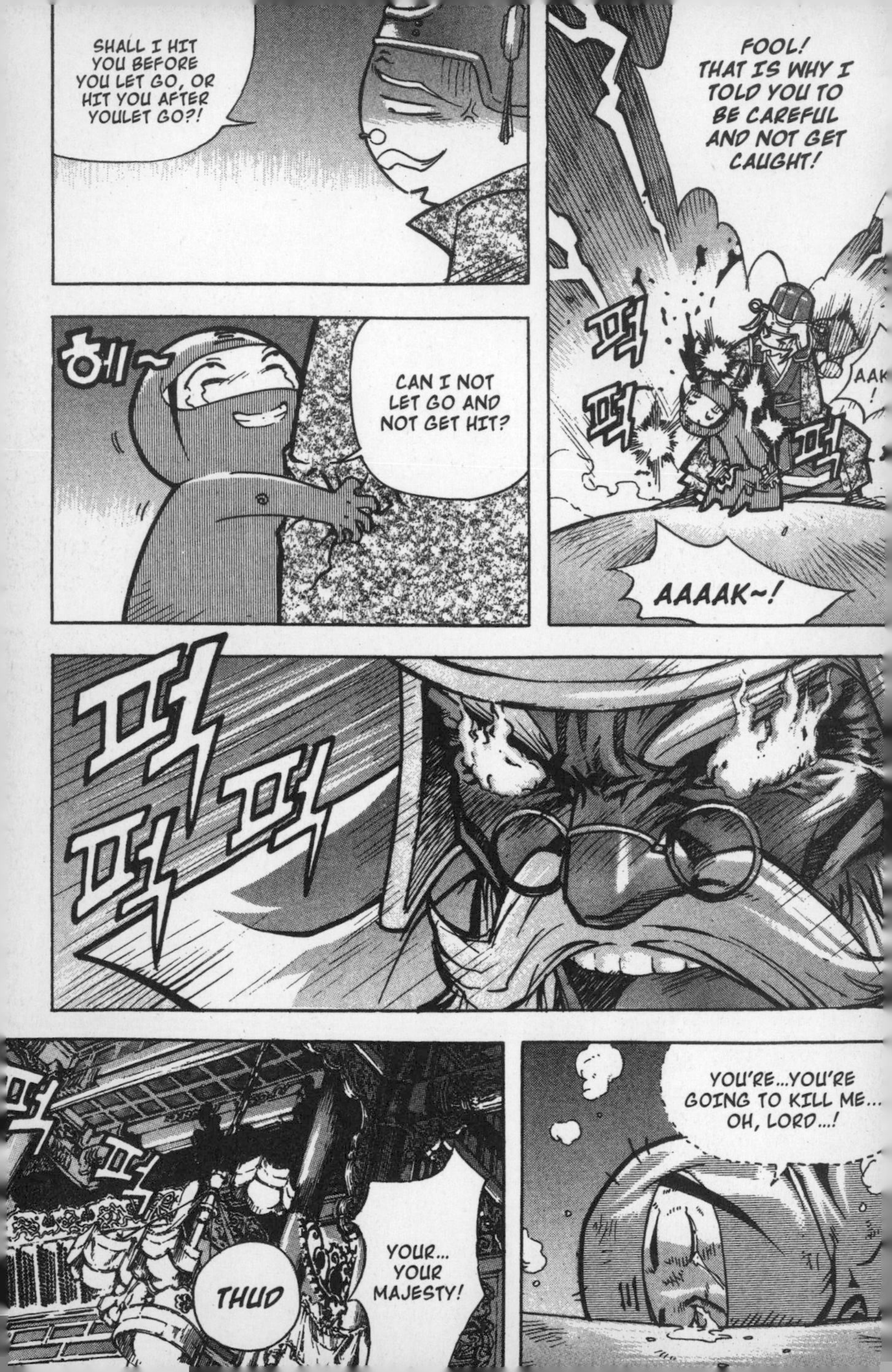
SHALL I HIT YOU BEFORE YOU LET GO, OR HIT YOU AFTER YOULET GO?!
헤~
CAN I NOT LET GO AND NOT GET HIT?
FOOL! THAT IS WHY I TOLD YOU TO BE CAREFUL AND NOT GET CAUGHT!
퍽
퍽
AAK!
퍽
AAAAK~!
퍽
퍽 퍽
퍽
THUD
YOUR... YOUR MAJESTY!
YOU'RE...YOU'RE GOING TO KILL ME... OH, LORD...!

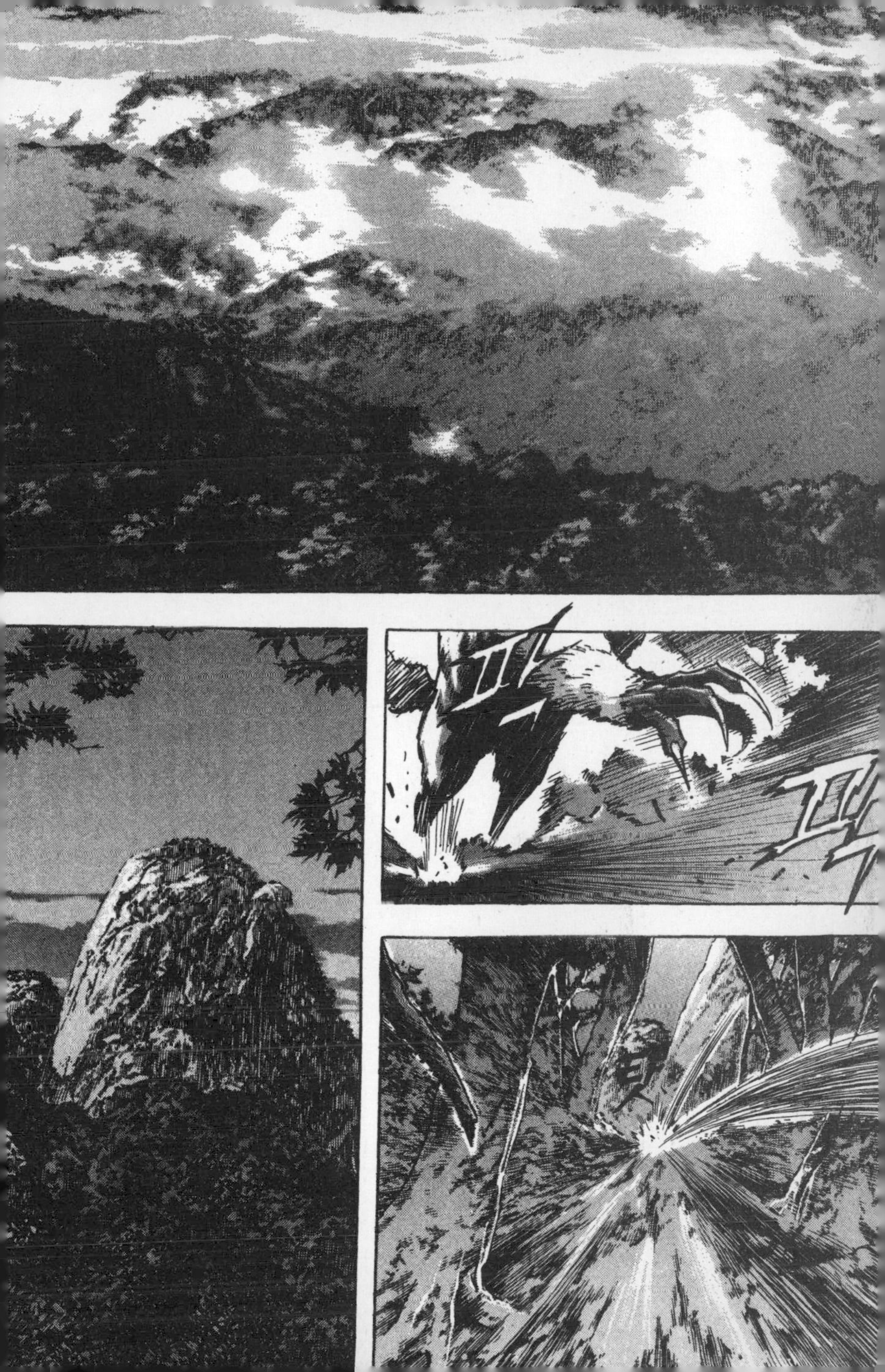

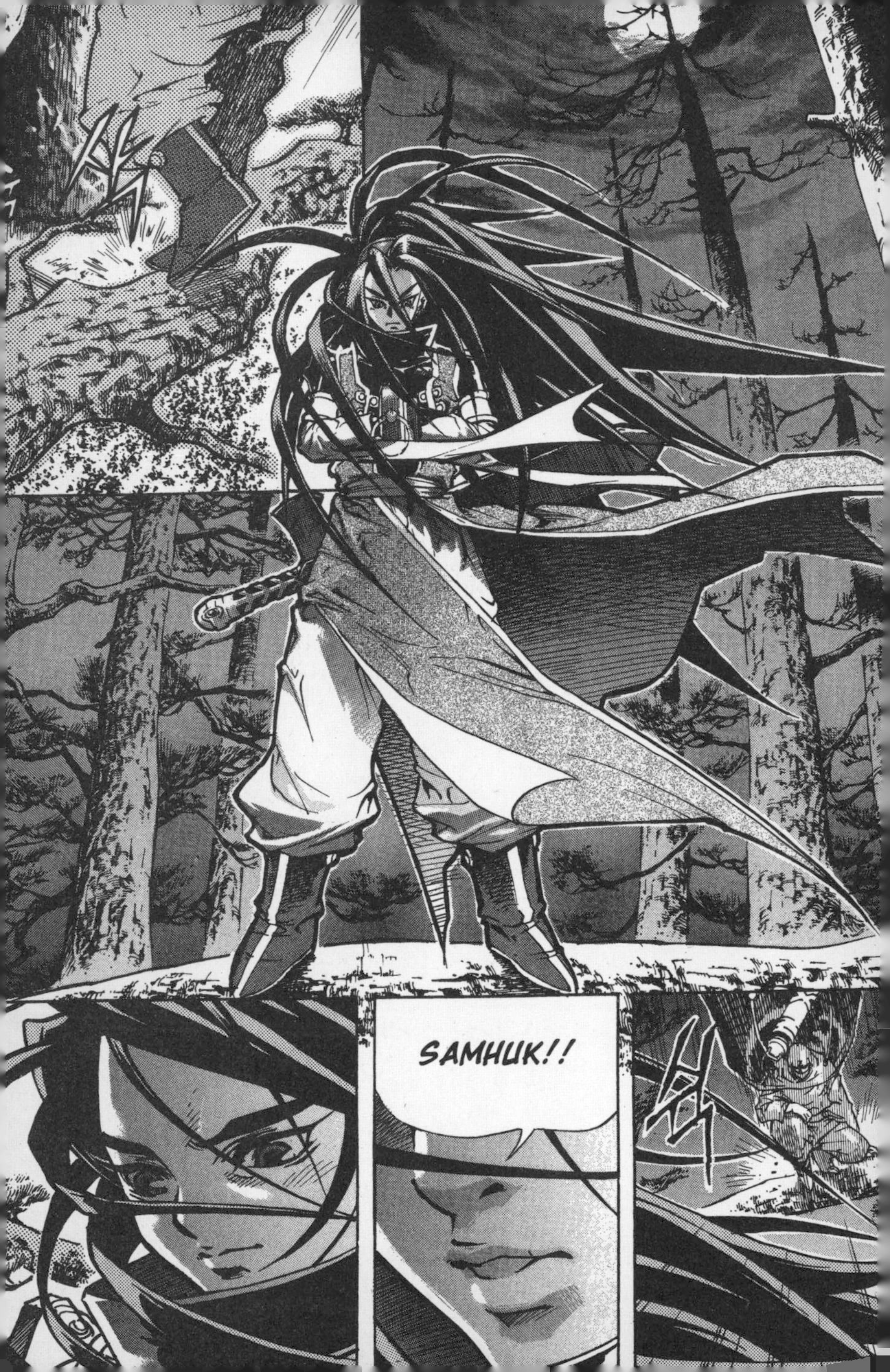
SAMHUK!!

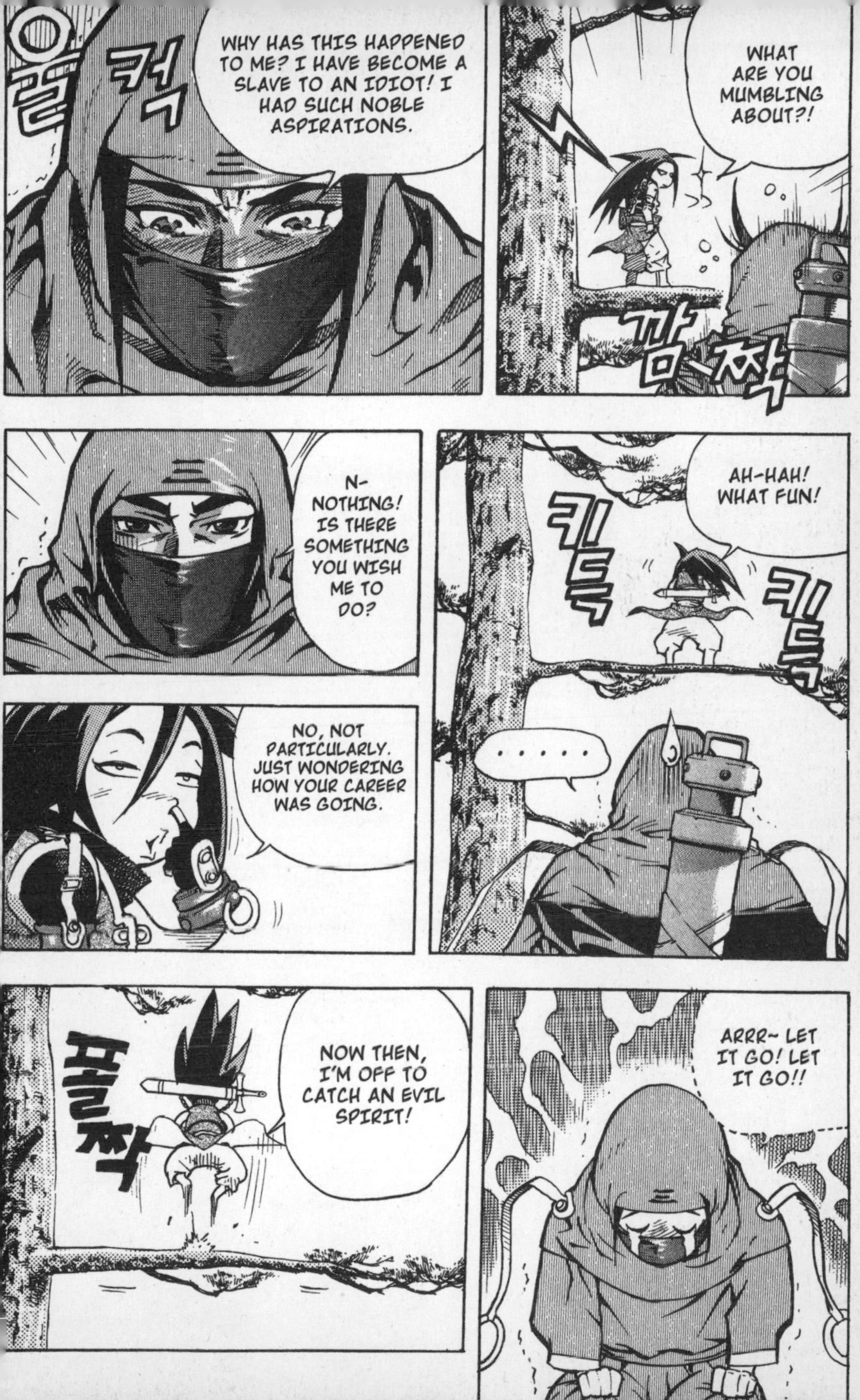
울컥
WHY HAS THIS HAPPENED TO ME? I HAVE BECOME A SLAVE TO AN IDIOT! I HAD SUCH NOBLE ASPIRATIONS.
WHAT ARE YOU MUMBLING ABOUT?!
깜~짝
N-NOTHING! IS THERE SOMETHING YOU WISH ME TO DO?
NO, NOT PARTICULARLY. JUST WONDERING HOW YOUR CAREER WAS GOING.
AH-HAH! WHAT FUN!
키득
키득
.....
폴짝
NOW THEN, I'M OFF TO CATCH AN EVIL SPIRIT!
ARRR~ LET IT GO! LET IT GO!!

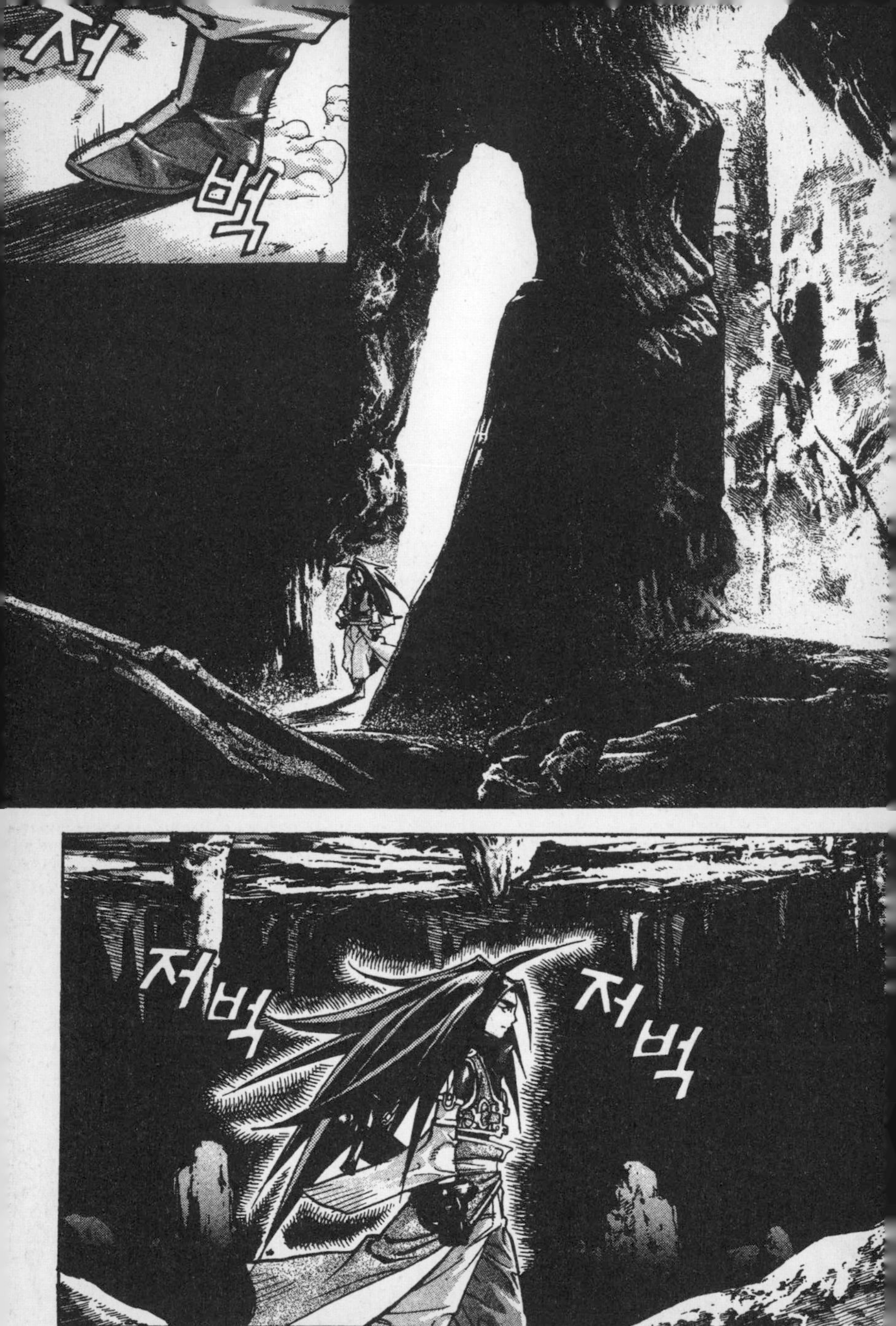
저벅
저벅
저벅

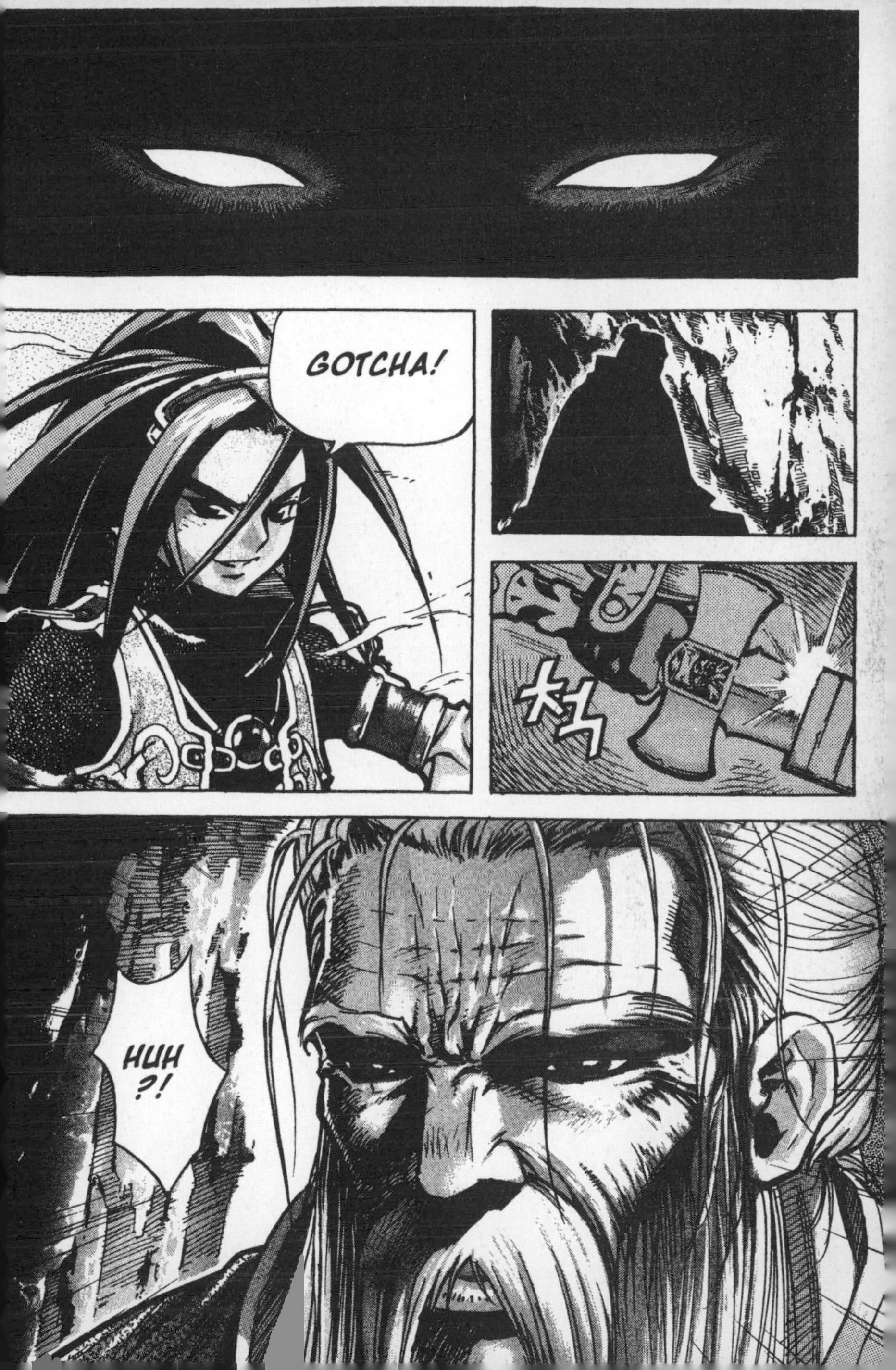
GOTCHA!
HUH ?!

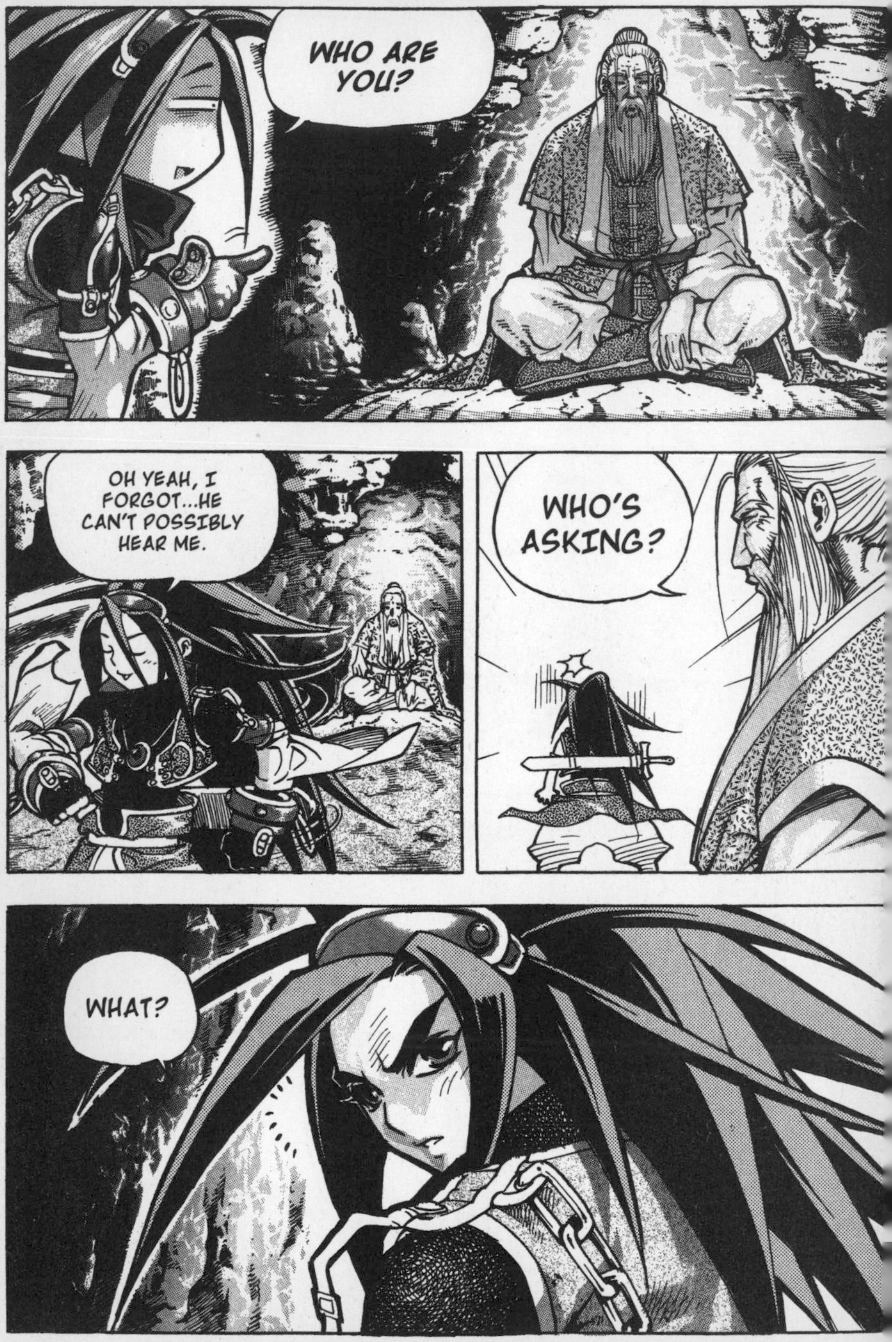
WHO ARE YOU?
OH YEAH, I FORGOT...HE CAN'T POSSIBLY HEAR ME.
WHO'S ASKING?
WHAT?

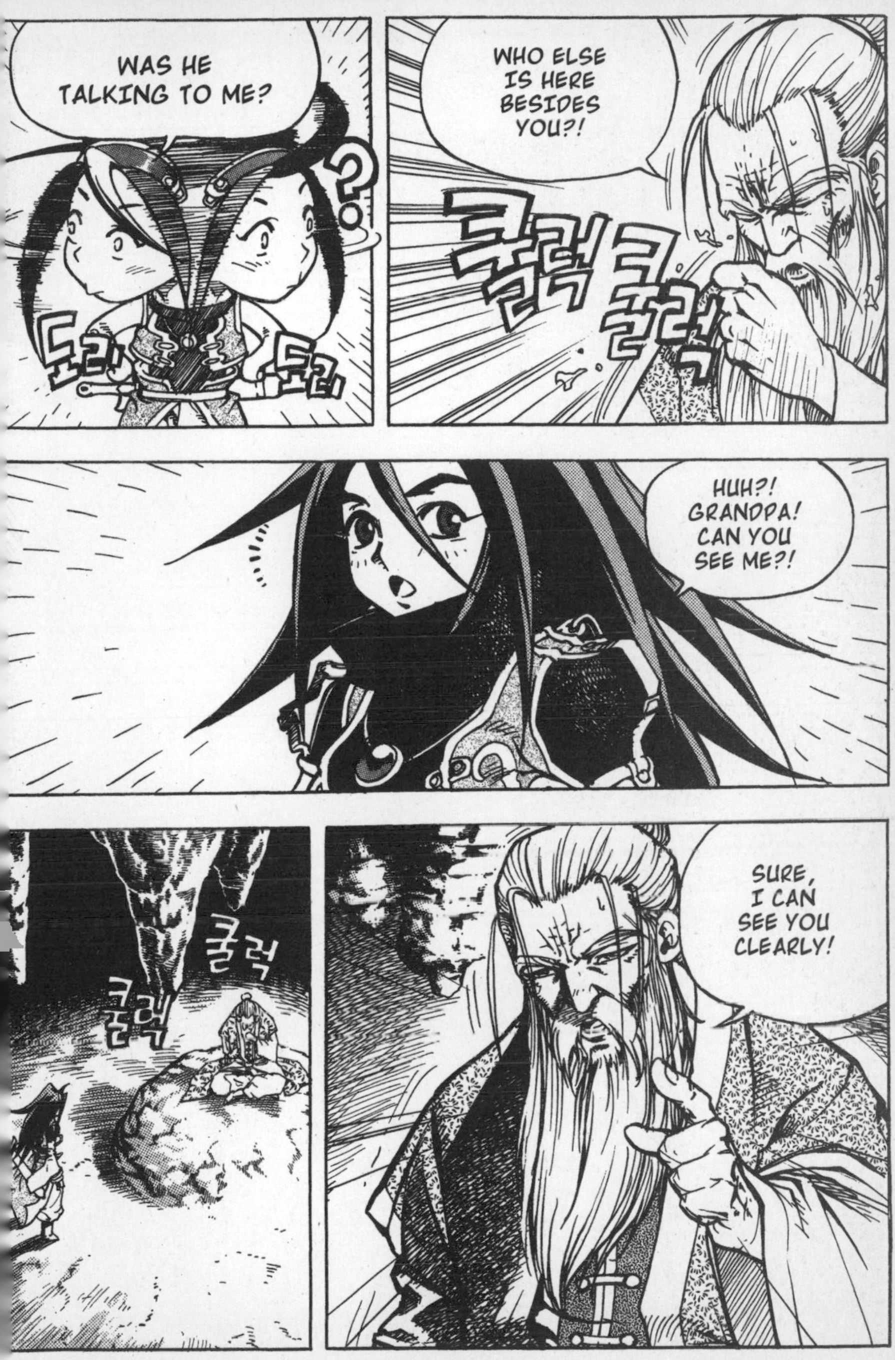
WAS HE TALKING TO ME?
WHO ELSE IS HERE BESIDES YOU?!
쿨럭 쿨럭
HUH?! GRANDPA! CAN YOU SEE ME?!
쿨럭
쿨럭
SURE, I CAN SEE YOU CLEARLY!

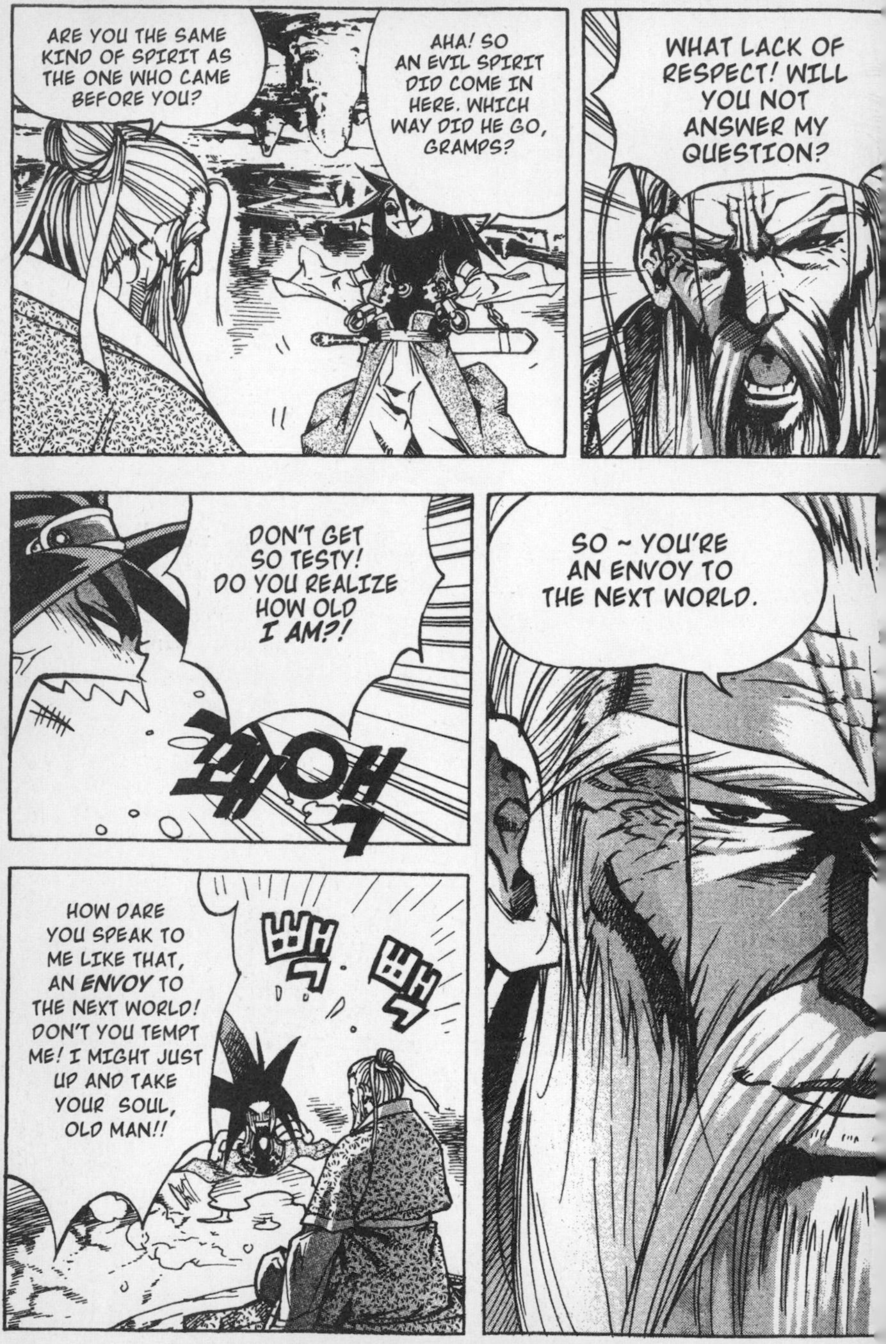
ARE YOU THE SAME KIND OF SPIRIT AS THE ONE WHO CAME BEFORE YOU?
AHA! SO AN EVIL SPIRIT DID COME IN HERE. WHICH WAY DID HE GO, GRAMPS?
WHAT LACK OF RESPECT! WILL YOU NOT ANSWER MY QUESTION?
DON'T GET SO TESTY! DO YOU REALIZE HOW OLD *I AM?!*
HOW DARE YOU SPEAK TO ME LIKE THAT, AN *ENVOY* TO THE NEXT WORLD! DON'T YOU TEMPT ME! I MIGHT JUST UP AND TAKE YOUR SOUL, OLD MAN!!
빽
빽
SO ~ YOU'RE AN ENVOY TO THE NEXT WORLD.

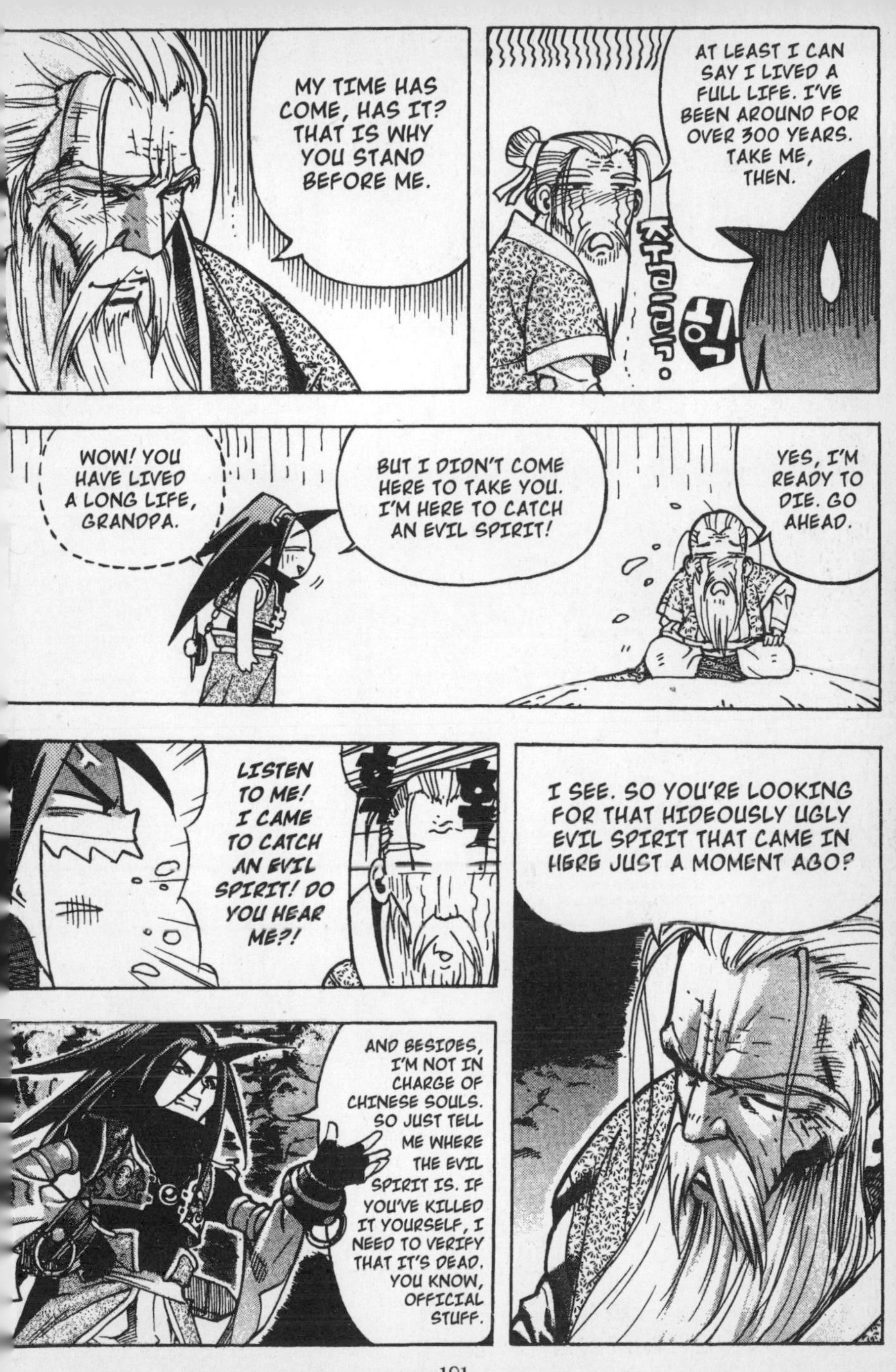
MY TIME HAS COME, HAS IT? THAT IS WHY YOU STAND BEFORE ME.
AT LEAST I CAN SAY I LIVED A FULL LIFE. I'VE BEEN AROUND FOR OVER 300 YEARS. TAKE ME, THEN.
WOW! YOU HAVE LIVED A LONG LIFE, GRANDPA.
BUT I DIDN'T COME HERE TO TAKE YOU. I'M HERE TO CATCH AN EVIL SPIRIT!
YES, I'M READY TO DIE. GO AHEAD.
LISTEN TO ME! I CAME TO CATCH AN EVIL SPIRIT! DO YOU HEAR ME?!
I SEE. SO YOU'RE LOOKING FOR THAT HIDEOUSLY UGLY EVIL SPIRIT THAT CAME IN HERE JUST A MOMENT AGO?
AND BESIDES, I'M NOT IN CHARGE OF CHINESE SOULS. SO JUST TELL ME WHERE THE EVIL SPIRIT IS. IF YOU'VE KILLED IT YOURSELF, I NEED TO VERIFY THAT IT'S DEAD. YOU KNOW, OFFICIAL STUFF.

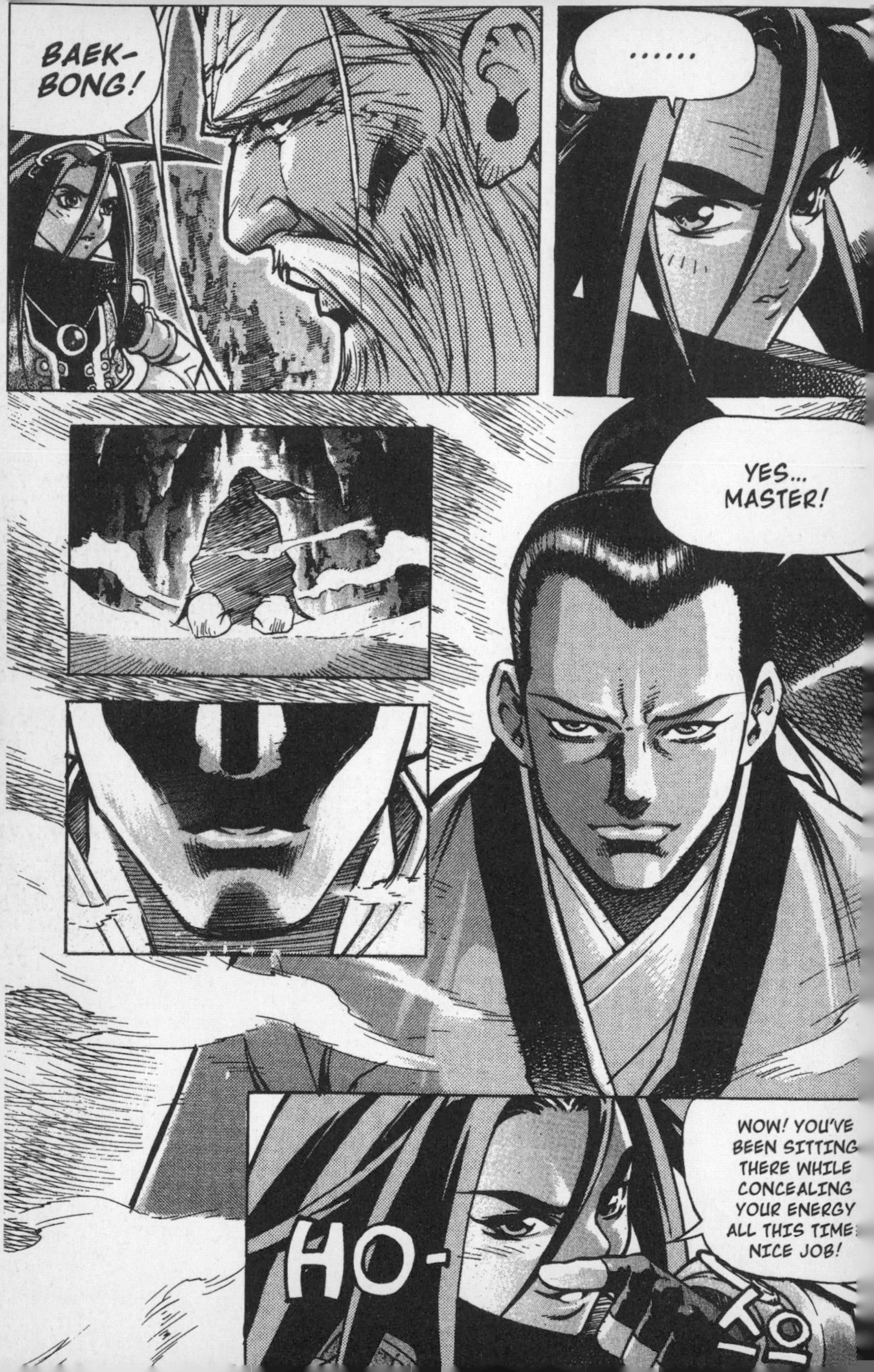
BAEK-
BONG!
......
YES...
MASTER!
WOW! YOU'VE
BEEN SITTING
THERE WHILE
CONCEALING
YOUR ENERGY
ALL THIS TIME
NICE JOB!
HO-
HO!

WHAT HAPPENED TO THAT BEAST WHO ENTERED HERE EARLIER?

I HAVE TAKEN CARE OF HIM!

DEAD ALREADY? AWESOME. YOU SAVED ME SOME TROUBLE. I'LL BE ON MY WAY NOW. ON BREAK. UNION RULES AND SUCH.

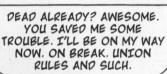

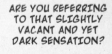

WAIT JUST ONE MOMENT~

BAEK-BONG, THERE IS A DIFFERENT ENERGY IN HERE NOW. CAN YOU SENSE IT?

ARE YOU REFERRING TO THAT SLIGHTLY VACANT AND YET DARK SENSATION?

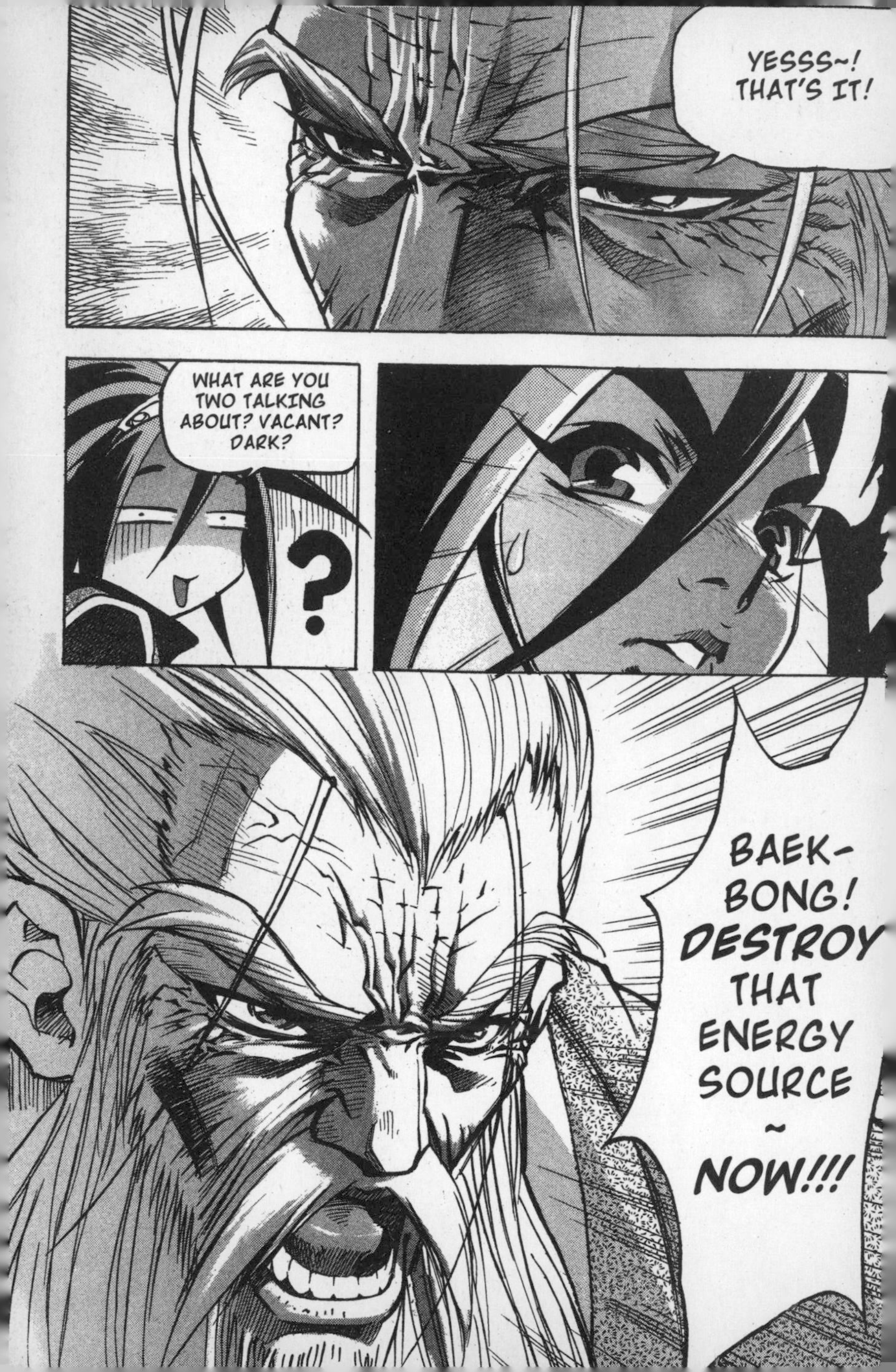
YESSS~! THAT'S IT!
WHAT ARE YOU TWO TALKING ABOUT? VACANT? DARK?
?
BAEK-BONG! DESTROY THAT ENERGY SOURCE ~ NOW!!!

IN THE NEXT VOLUME OF

KING OF HELL

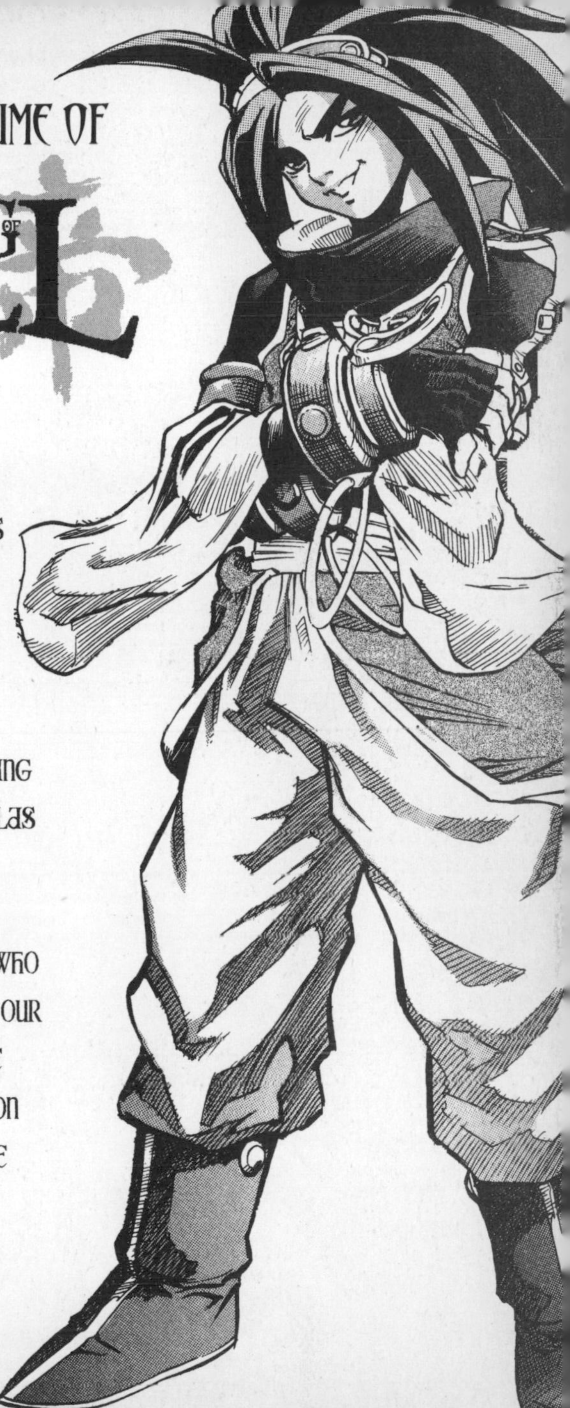

WHO IS THE MYSTERIOUS 300 YEAR-OLD MAN AND WHAT KIND OF THREAT DOES HE POSE FOR MAJEH? WHO IS RESPONSIBLE FOR CREATING THE RIFT BETWEEN WORLDS AND WHY ARE MORE APPEARING? AND WHO IS THE BEAUTIFUL WOMAN WHO PROFESSES A LOVE FOR OUR FAVORITE ENVOY TO THE NEXT WORLD? A DECISION SHE MAKES WILL CHANGE MAJEH'S LIFE FOREVER!

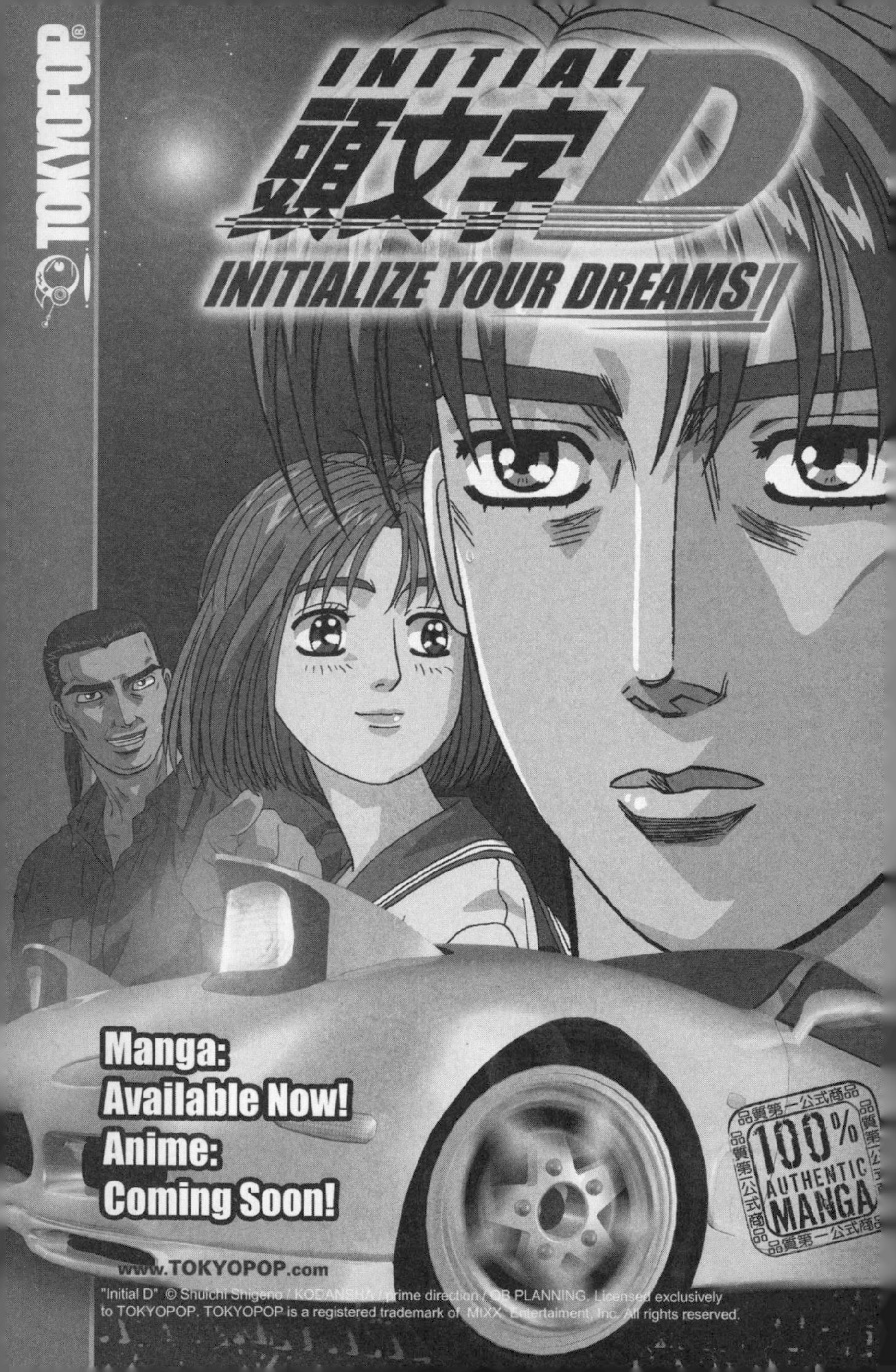
TOKYOPOP
INITIAL
頭文字D
INITIALIZE YOUR DREAMS!!
Manga:
Available Now!
Anime:
Coming Soon!
品質第一公式商品
100% AUTHENTIC MANGA
www.TOKYOPOP.com
"Initial D" © Shuichi Shigeno / KODANSHA / prime direction / OB PLANNING. Licensed exclusively to TOKYOPOP. TOKYOPOP is a registered trademark of Mixx Entertainment, Inc. All rights reserved.

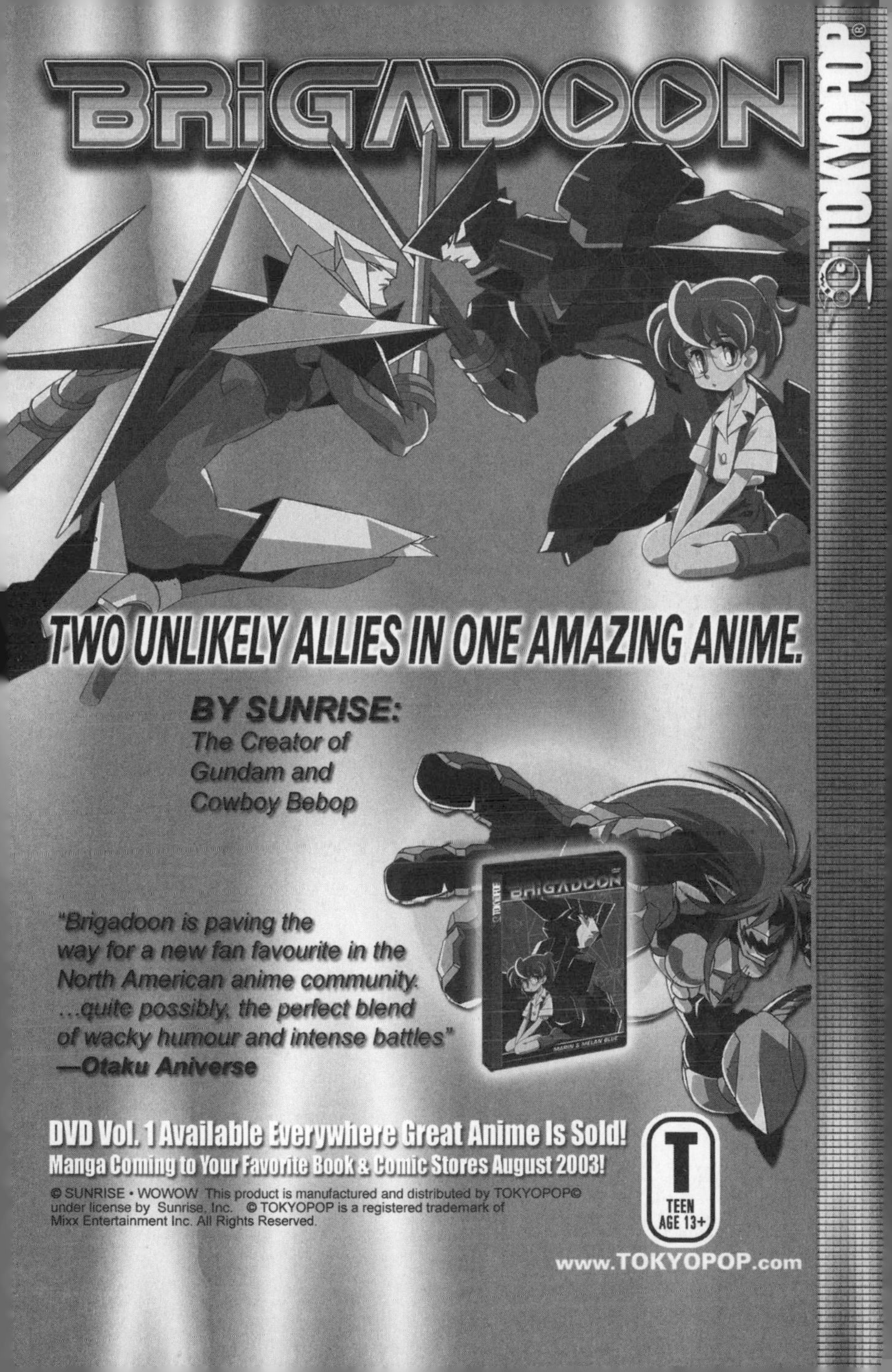

BRIGADOON
TOKYOPOP
TWO UNLIKELY ALLIES IN ONE AMAZING ANIME.
BY SUNRISE:
The Creator of Gundam and Cowboy Bebop
BRIGADOON
"Brigadoon is paving the way for a new fan favourite in the North American anime community. ...quite possibly, the perfect blend of wacky humour and intense battles"
—Otaku Aniverse
DVD Vol. 1 Available Everywhere Great Anime Is Sold!
Manga Coming to Your Favorite Book & Comic Stores August 2003!
T
TEEN AGE 13+
© SUNRISE • WOWOW This product is manufactured and distributed by TOKYOPOP© under license by Sunrise, Inc. © TOKYOPOP is a registered trademark of Mixx Entertainment Inc. All Rights Reserved.
www.TOKYOPOP.com

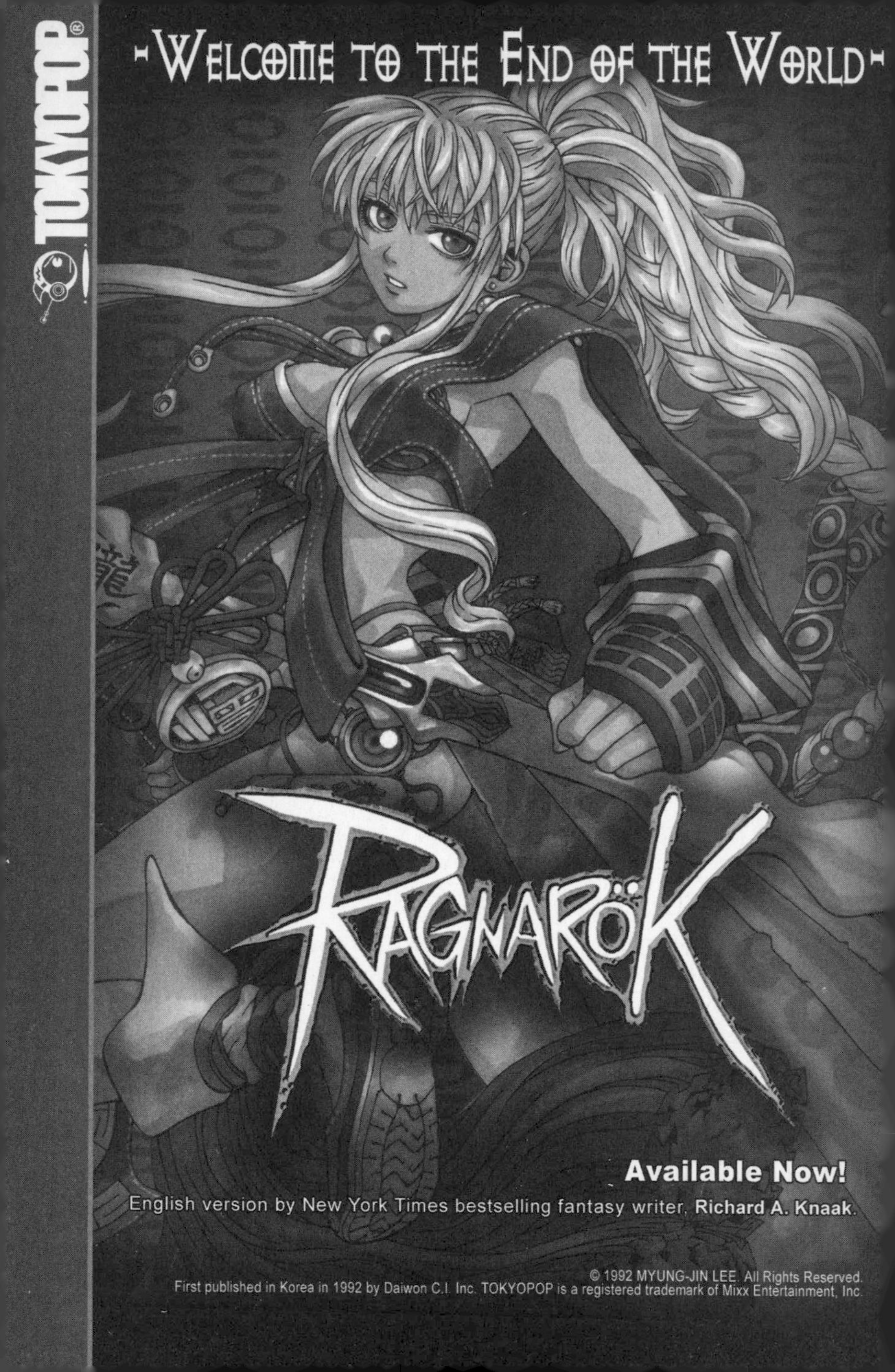
TOKYOPOP
-Welcome to the End of the World-
RAGNARÖK
Available Now!
English version by New York Times bestselling fantasy writer, Richard A. Knaak.
© 1992 MYUNG-JIN LEE. All Rights Reserved.
First published in Korea in 1992 by Daiwon C.I. Inc. TOKYOPOP is a registered trademark of Mixx Entertainment, Inc.